The Greatest Menace

A volume in the series
Culture, Politics, and the Cold War
Edited by Christian G. Appy

The
GREATEST
MENACE

Organized Crime
in COLD WAR AMERICA

Lee BERNSTEIN

University of Massachusetts Press
Amherst and Boston

LC 2002024571
ISBN 1-55849-345-X

Designed by Milenda Nan Ok Lee
Set in Adobe Minion and Schmutz Clogged
Printed and bound by Maple-Vail Manufacturing Group

Library of Congress Cataloging-in-Publication Data

Bernstein, Lee, 1967–
    The greatest menace : organized crime in cold war America / Lee Bernstein.
        p. cm. — (Culture, politics, and the cold war)
    Includes bibliographical references and index.
    ISBN 1-55849-345-X (cloth: alk. paper)
        1. Organized crime—United States—History. 2. United States—Social
    conditions—1945– 3. Cold War. I. Title. II. Series.

    HV6446 .B47 2002
    364.1'06'0973—dc21

                                                                            2002024571

British Library Cataloguing in Publication data are available.

The greatest menace is that the public will come to accept organized crime as something inevitable, as a necessary part of our social system.

—*Adlai Stevenson*

Everybody has some larceny in his soul.

—*Vincent Teresa*

CONTENTS

ACKNOWLEDGMENTS

I am particularly grateful to those who gave their time and intellect to critiquing all or part of this book: Lisa Albrecht, Eric Drown, Susan Green, Julie Greene, Jennifer Guglielmo, Randel Hansen, Leola Johnson, Anja Kirchmann, Josephine Lee, Lary May, Todd Micheney, Karen Murphy, Lara Nielsen, Caitlin Patterson, Riv-Ellen Prell, David Roediger, Lee Quinby, Martha Reis, Randy Rodriguez, Elaine Slott, Shirley Thompson, Steve Waksman, and Norman Yentman. I am also indebted to Betty Agee, Colleen Hennen, Gratia Lee, Jeannie Lusby, and Anna Vayr for advice and institutional support.

Audiences at the American Italian Historical Association, American Studies Association, Canadian Association of American Studies, the Economics Institute, Immigration History Research Center, the Conference on Race, Ethnicity, and Migration, New England American Studies Association, and the University of Minnesota Program in American Studies provided encouragement and feedback. At the University of Colorado, Brendan Malloy's careful and insightful research assistance helped keep the book moving forward. Christie Donner of the Rocky Mountain Peace and Justice Center helped me struggle with new ways to think about crime and punishment. Also, I am fortunate to have met Joy James. In addition to helping put criminal justice and incarceration at the forefront of contemporary scholarship, she never failed to offer insight and encouragement to others. My brother Matthew Bernstein provided guidance on current immigration law and policy. My approach to the intersection of crime, culture, and politics owes much to the model provided by Chris Wilson. I had the great fortune to be his research assistant and often felt his influence while working on this book.

Nan Alamilla Boyd provided feedback, support, and pre-release access to her own manuscript. In doing so, she helped me clarify my argument. Support from the Immigration History Research Center at the University of Minnesota deserves special mention. Its assistant director, Joel Wurl, and staff, particularly Lyda Morehouse, Halyna Myroniuk, and Tiimo Ryppa, provided a scholarly context for archival research. At the National Archives, Fred Romanski and Chris Wilhelm made my research trip invaluable. Tony Radosti of the Metropolitan Crime Commission of New Orleans, as well as Margaret Jones and Richard Cook of the Kansas City Crime Commission, provided access to records, clippings files, and minutes of board meetings. At the University of Massachusetts Press, Clark Dougan and Carol Betsch helped with publication details and patiently kept me on task, and Amanda Heller's editing produced a stronger book.

Ruth Jacobson, Elaine Slott, and Ronnie Slott introduced me to their memories and photographs of Meyer Lansky, Lucky Luciano, and Moe Polakoff. Ben Hunt insisted that I appreciate the difference between constructions of criminality and the prison walls they help to create. My friends Brad Conlin, Dave Fratto, Matthew Goldie, Paula Massood, Sam Morgan, Adam Newton, Scott Springer, and Shoki Goodarzi were always willing to talk about my somewhat unhealthy interest in organized crime and provide places to stay during my travels to archives and libraries. Weekly meetings with Ernesto Acevedo-Muñoz greatly aided my professional adjustment. Our discussions of contemporary Mafia depictions helped me understand the evolving roles of gangsters in U.S. culture. He deserves a special commendation for sitting through all of *Mickey Blue Eyes*.

Several grants aided my completion of this project. The University of Minnesota's first Ph.D. recipient in American studies, Joseph J. Kwiat, endowed a fellowship to enable doctoral candidates to attend the annual American Studies Association meeting. I was honored to receive the fellowship now named in his memory. Financial support from the University of Minnesota Graduate School included its Doctoral Dissertation Fellowship, Supplemental Research Grant, and Doctoral Dissertation Special Grant. The University of Colorado, along with the Humanities Department and College of Humanities and Arts at San José State University, supported the final stages of my writing with research and travel funding. A course release resulted from the extraordinary generosity of my colleague Scot Guenter.

Harriet Bernstein's daring and excellence provided all the direction I ever needed. Leonard and Nancy Bernstein, as well as my brothers Nate, Gabe, and Matt, showed patience and support throughout the writing of this book. Carol

Miller offered generous criticism while ensuring steady progress. She is my model for a humane scholarly life. Rudy Vecoli's influence on my thinking about immigration and the importance of ethnicity in American political and social life can be seen throughout this book. From the moment Chris Appy asked if a conference paper on Jack Lait and Lee Mortimer's *Confidential* series would be part of a longer work, his support and advice eased my navigation from graduate student to faculty member and the passage of this project from dissertation to book. The greatest support came from Lisa Gail Collins; she provided extensive feedback on virtually every page while teaching classes and working on her own book.

L. B.

The Greatest Menace

PROLOGUE

Vestal, New York, November 1957

Myth and reality collided in upstate New York in November 1957. Perhaps this was fated in a region where the names of small towns and cities are an atlas of ancient Rome, Africa, and Greece: Syracuse, Utica, Homer, Attica. The small town of Vestal is named for the virgins who tended the sacred fire in the temple dedicated to Vesta, the Roman goddess of the hearth.[1] Vestal, the town's founders probably hoped, would carry the same connotations of purity and virtue. The town's Parkway Motel, however, catered to the descendants of the vestal virgins' less virginal sisters.[2] On the afternoon of November 13, 1957, New York State Police officers Sergeant Edgar Croswell and Trooper Vincent Vasisko arrived at the motel on a routine call about a bad check. The motel, an anonymous little place along a stretch of Route 17 outside of Binghamton, was a great place to stay if you did not want your presence noticed. That's what brought Joseph Barbara Jr. there by coincidence on that same November day.

Officers Croswell and Vasisko observed Barbara, the twenty-one-year-old son of a well-known local character, reserving three rooms for two nights. His father, Joseph Barbara Sr., had owned the Canada Dry Bottling Company of Endicott, New York—a regional beer and soft drink distributorship—ever since the end of Prohibition made his previous occupation as a still operator in Scranton, Pennsylvania, obsolete.[3] In addition to his known past as a bootlegger, Barbara was a suspect in a series of murders in the early 1930s, although his only conviction was on a wartime charge of illegal acquisition of sugar.[4] Croswell and Vasisko, knowing the elder Barbara's reputation, took note of the son's activity. Croswell had been watching Joseph Barbara Sr. for nearly thirteen years. Just that week, Croswell had gotten a tip that Barbara had ordered two hundred pounds of steaks from Chicago.[5] The state police also knew that Barbara had from time to time had visitors with long arrest records for bootlegging, narcotics violations, and murder. So, when they found his son reserving three rooms at the Parkway, they decided to come back and see who showed up, and to keep an eye on the Barbara place in nearby Apalachin.

When the officers returned to the Parkway that evening, they observed three cars that looked out of place at the modest motel. Their suspicions were confirmed when they learned that the new Lincoln, Cadillac, and Pontiac were owned by James La Duca, Alfred Angelicola, and Patsy Turrigiano, respectively. (Turrigiano had three convictions for violation of alcohol laws during Prohibition.) When they came back after midnight for another look around, there was a second Cadillac, this one registered to the Buckeye Cigarette Service of Cleveland, a company owned by an ex-felon named John Scalish. In addition, Croswell was getting calls about a "meeting of George Rafts" out at Barbara's home, a reference to the actor famous for playing gangsters in a string of Hollywood films.[6]

Their interest piqued, the troopers remained at the Parkway until 2:30 A.M. but saw no activity. After some well-earned rest, they decided to drive by the hilltop estate of the Barbara family. The isolated home with a view of the Susquehanna River Valley stood on a high hill accessible only by a private road blocked by a chain. Barbara often used the secluded fifty-three-acre site for business meetings involving his soda distributorship—then the largest in upstate New York—and he had constructed several meeting rooms and a large parking lot on the grounds.[7] Since one of the cars at the Parkway was owned by a man from the nearby town of Endicott who'd been convicted for illegal operation of a still almost a decade earlier, Croswell brought along two agents of the Federal Alcohol and Tobacco Tax Unit.

When they reached the estate, the officers and revenue agents found over twenty-five expensive cars parked in the lot adjacent to the house and in a field. The four retreated to a nearby highway to discuss their plan of action. As they reviewed their options, a truck belonging to a local fish wholesaler emerged from the Barbara estate and sped past the officers. Within minutes, the truck passed them in the other direction as it doubled back to the Barbara home. During those few minutes, they figured, the fish wholesaler—a man with whom the troopers were already familiar—must have spotted them and called Barbara. As they returned to the estate, the officers saw about a dozen well-dressed men running from the house toward a grove of pine trees. Two cars then approached the officers. Croswell managed to stop one, a 1957 Chrysler Imperial, by blocking the road with his own car. Rather than rousting just a small group of local characters like Barbara, La Duca, and the fish wholesaler, the officers found themselves face-to-face with a crowd of well-known gangsters: Russell Bufalino, Vito Genovese, Joseph Ida, Dominick Oliveto, and Gerardo Carteno. They called in reinforcements to help track down those who'd fled on foot and set up roadblocks throughout the area. The twenty troopers who eventually participated in the search made easy work of the roundup. Sergeant Croswell gloated to a reporter: "Those city boys didn't have a chance. With their fancy shoes and their hats and coats snagging on tree branches, we could grab them easy. In fact we would have had a harder time getting them if it weren't for the fact they were such city slickers."[8] By 5 P.M. they had apprehended over fifty men in cars and another twelve walking through the woods and taken them to the state police substation in Vestal for questioning. Many of the men carried fat bankrolls, some with as much as $3,000 and none with less than $450.[9] Simone Scozzari, who'd traveled from California to attend the meeting, was holding $602 in cash and a $8,445.30 cashier's check. Despite Croswell's boasts, it is probable that as many as another fifty men had avoided capture, including Chicago gangster Sam "Mooney" Giancana and the former union official and extortionist Joseph "Socks" Lanza, longtime operator of Manhattan's Fulton Fish Market, who had booked a room at the Hotel Casey in Scranton, fifty miles south of Apalachin.[10]

The officers hoped to hold the group while trying to figure out if they had violated any laws or if any outstanding warrants existed for the conventioneers. What they found confirmed the worst fears of 1950s crime fighters: sixty-five Italian Americans with a combined total of 153 arrests and 74 convictions for homicide, narcotics, gambling, alcohol, and other violations. Federal authorities described the group as the "hierarchy of the Eastern Seaboard criminal world."[11] Among the leaders of criminal organizations present at the Apalachin meeting were Joseph Bonanno, Carlo Gambino, Joseph Profaci, Frank DeSimone, and Vito Genovese, as well as the future head of the Gambino crime organization, Paul Castellano. Fully half had been born in Italy, most of those in Sicily.[12] Although virtually all lived in New York, New Jersey, Pennsylvania, and Ohio, there were also visitors that day from California, Colorado, Illinois, and Missouri. One man who gave his name as Louis Santos turned out to be Santo Trafficante, then manager of Havana's Sans Souci nightclub and son of Tampa lottery operator Santos Trafficante.

The investigators discovered that all but nine had criminal records; some had completed lengthy prison terms. John Anthony DeMarco of the Cleveland suburb of Shaker Heights had a rap sheet that included arrests for murder, bombing, and blackmail. Several had been among the star witnesses at the U.S. Senate's sensational organized crime investigation earlier in the decade, where Senator Estes

Kefauver, chairman of the investigating committee, had described Apalachin attendee Joseph Profaci as "one of the top leaders of the Mafia." Because none of the men were wanted at the time, the troopers could not legally hold them on outstanding warrants. But if they could establish that the gathering itself constituted an illegal act or had been called to plan illegal acts, they would be able to hold them. When asked the purpose of the meeting, all the interviewees replied—according to testimony by the officers—that they had "found themselves to be at the Barbara home at the same time out of sheer coincidence. Most of them said they had come to the area on business and then just dropped in, unexpectedly, for a visit with their good friend. All denied that there was any advance planning to gather there; all denied knowing that the others would be present."[13] When state and federal authorities could find no legitimate reason to hold them, Sergeant Croswell, six feet tall and weighing two hundred pounds, resorted to intimidation. "We gave them a rough time in the station house," he proudly told a reporter, "but we couldn't even make them commit disorderly conduct there."[14]

What Troopers Vasisko and Croswell had uncovered was indeed a convention of the leaders of powerful criminal organizations that many simply called "the Mafia." They usually met once every five years, but after the murder of the feared New York gangster Albert Anastasia in October 1957, they decided to hold their second meeting in as many years. Anastasia, leader of the notorious "Murder Inc." since the execution of Louis "Lepke" Buchalter in 1944, had been murdered in a struggle for power within his own organization.[15] The timing of the meeting and later admissions by attendees point to an agenda topped by a discussion of the consequences of Anastasia's murder and the transfer of power to Carlo Gambino. In addition, subsequent investigations suggested that there was substantial internal concern over the pressure brought by the Federal Bureau of Narcotics. At the conference it would be decided whether to defy the bureau or to forgo the drug trade entirely.[16] The 1956 meeting had also taken place in Apalachin. Although the attendees had to drive past the state trooper substation in order to reach the Barbara home, that meeting had occurred without any police interference. Depending on which version of events people believed, Croswell was either a brave, untouchable police officer who slept at the trooper station after his marriage failed or a corrupt cop upset when Barbara rebuffed his demands for higher bribes. Barbara later claimed that he had long been paying off the local police (including Sergeant Croswell), but that their demands had grown so unreasonable that he decided to stop bribing them.[17]

There were few short-term consequences or rewards in the wake of the Apalachin gathering. From the perspective of law enforcement, the most promising outcome was a Justice Department investigation lasting over a year, which produced twenty-seven indictments of conspiracy to obstruct justice resulting from the participants' refusal to answer questions about the "true nature of their meeting." On May 21, 1959, in a coordinated sweep, narcotics agents in New York, California, Arizona, Texas, Florida, Ohio, New Jersey, Pennsylvania, and Massachusetts arrested Apalachin attendees as co-conspirators. Milton R. Wessel, head of Attorney General William P. Rogers's Special Group to Prosecute Organized Crime, secured long prison sentences against twenty participants in January 1960, but the U.S. Court of Appeals overturned these convictions by unanimous decision in November of that year.[18] Croswell's career got a significant boost from his role in the Apalachin investigation: he was appointed chief investigator for the New York State Organized Crime Task Force, established in response to the Apalachin revelations. Barbara, like many others present at his house, merely lost his license to carry a gun. The unwanted notoriety led him to sell his estate to a pair of enterprising area residents who hoped to turn the grounds into a tourist attraction and restaurant, though their plan failed when the town refused to change its zoning laws.[19] Even some not present at Apalachin faced questions about the meeting. An Italian appellate court questioned the exiled Charles "Lucky" Luciano for two hours, though Luciano claimed that "until I read all that trash in the papers, I never even heard of Apalachin. I still don't know where it is—and don't care. I'm clean, I even pay my income tax. They got nothing on me and never will have."[20]

Despite its limited short-term consequences, the Apalachin meeting left its imprint on U.S. crime-fighting agencies, state and federal legislative bodies, and the popular representation of organized crime. Clearly, the police had come across proof of the existence of the Mafia which had eluded Senator Kefauver and his committee and which J. Edgar Hoover's Federal Bureau of Investigation had long rejected. Prior to the Apalachin meeting, official FBI policy flatly denied that ethnic-specific organized crime existed. In a dramatic turnaround, by 1960 Hoover would declare in the *F.B.I. Law Enforcement Bulletin* not only that the Mafia was real but also that "the lawless legion infiltrates through every loophole, its booty flowing into underworld coffers whether it be nickels and dimes from a juke box in a bar in the smallest town or from a multi-million-dollar stranglehold on large metropolitan centers obtained through the domination of a few dishonest labor officials."[21]

The timing of the Apalachin bust could not have been better for the Federal Bureau of Narcotics (FBN), the only federal police agency that aggressively investigated Italian American organized crime. While Joe Barbara Jr. was making motel reservations, FBN narcotics agent Joseph Amato was testifying before the Senate Rackets Committee: "We believe there does exist a society, loosely organized, for the specific purpose of smuggling narcotics and committing other crimes. It has its core in Italy and it is nationwide. In fact, international." Now there was reason for more than a "belief." The myth of the Mafia took dramatic shape in the woods of upstate New York. Police agencies started calling the gathering "the Commission." Gangsters later acknowledged the importance of this exposure, but chose a more colorful name, "the Big Barbecue at Apalachin." Joseph Bonanno, who was arrested in Apalachin, later wrote that "those privileged enough to attend such a national meeting anticipated it with the same glee as do Republicans or Democrats when they meet every four years for their national conventions."[22]

Most disturbing to police agencies and legislative investigations was the presence of seemingly legitimate businesspeople at Apalachin. As he looked around the police station, Sergeant Croswell would have seen John C. Montana, one of Buffalo's leading citizens. The owner of the largest taxi operation in western New York, Montana had no police record, and his résumé included membership on the Buffalo City Council and attendance at the 1937 New York State constitutional convention, where he'd been a delegate. He had recently been named Buffalo's Man of the Year by the Erie Club, the social organization of the Buffalo Police Department.[23] The press took special note of James La Duca, a well-known labor official in Buffalo. In addition to being secretary-treasurer of the local hotel and restaurant workers union, La Duca was secretary and treasurer of the Magaddino Memorial Chapel, a funeral home in Niagara Falls owned by a family allegedly involved in criminal activities. When the New York State Committee on Government Operations issued its report on the gathering, it noted that "Mafia members use 'front people' who are completely trusted, as the means to own and operate various legitimate interests."[24]

Police agencies were coming to realize that postwar organized criminals had corporate faces. The *New York Times* reported that "some of the most important crime syndicate leaders today are men of outstanding public reputation with no criminal records." Rather than scar-faced, gun-toting Little Caesars, these were businessmen who adhered to the widely accepted "techniques of modern high-pressure public relations."[25] For example, behind the scrim of the seemingly legitimate Pueblo-based Colorado Cheese Company sat James Colletti, an associate of Joseph Bonanno, who allegedly used the company to distribute heroin. Others used businesses such as restaurants, olive oil importing, fuel distribution, produce markets, and real estate to obscure their catering to the illegal but ever popular demand for narcotics, prostitutes, and gambling.

Some similarities to the old image of the Sicilian Mafia suggested to police investigators that not everything had changed. Many of the men arrested at Apalachin were related by blood or marriage: four pairs of brothers, two sets of cousins, and a smattering of uncles, nephews, and in-laws. Brooklyn resident Joseph Profaci and Long Island resident Joseph Magliocco were second cousins and brothers-in-law. Buffalo resident John Montana's nephew Charles was married to one of Stephen Magaddino's daughters. Another Magaddino daughter was married to James La Duca. The Bureau of Narcotics, as well as popular opinion, now seemed to have concrete proof that the Mafia was indeed a "blood brotherhood" of immigrants from Sicily. Those not directly related by blood had other close ties. Many of those from the Apalachin region were members of the Society Concordia Castellammare Del Golfo of Endicott, New York. Joseph Barbara, Joseph Bonanno, Emanuel Zicari, Patsy Turrigiano, Ignatius Cannone, and the Magaddino family, among others, were all from the small Sicilian town of Castellammare Del Golfo.

Just as the cities of the ancient world lent their names to the cities and towns of upstate New York, Castellammare became a mythic connection between the old world and the new for those who tell the stories of the pantheon of American gangsters. In 1930 a series of murders in the American underworld became popularly known as the Castellammarese War. Prior to and during Prohibition, a faction of Italian-born criminals associated with Salvatore Maranzano traced their origin to the Sicilian town. This contingent included future prominent gangsters such as Joseph "Joe Bananas" Bonanno and Joseph Profaci of Brooklyn, Stefano Magaddino of Buffalo, and Joseph Aiello of Chicago. According to police and underworld sources, it was the Castellammarese who carried out the murder of Italian-born Giuseppe "Joe the Boss" Masseria at Scarpato's Restaurant in the Brooklyn beach neighborhood of Coney Island.

For historians, crime fighters, and gangsters alike, this murder marked the transition of Italian American crime from immigrant-based gangs of bootleggers and extortionists to a modern, corporate, organized underworld. Vincent Teresa, the Boston gangster who became a government informant, referred to this older generation as "greaseballs"—old-fashioned hoods more comfortable with bank robbery, theft, and extortion than with the stock swindles that made him a fortune in the late 1960s and early 1970s.[26] In reference to their outmoded handlebar whiskers, others dubbed them "Mustache Petes." After the murder of Masseria, Maranzano would appoint himself the "Capo di tutti Capi," or "Boss of All Bosses." He subsequently established the structure of New York's "five families." The first five bosses of these families, according to Mafia witness Joseph Valachi, were Tom Gagliano, Joseph Profaci, Joseph Bonanno, Vincent Mangano, and Charles "Lucky" Luciano. Three of the five "underbosses"—Thomas Lucchese, Albert Anastasia, and Vito Genovese—would themselves become bosses on the death, promotion, or deportation of their superiors.[27]

Although this organizational structure remained in place for several decades, the violence that led to its establishment did not cease. In addition to his criminal activities, Maranzano ran a Manhattan real estate company. According to Valachi, who was at the time one of Maranzano's (obviously ineffective) bodyguards, "some men pretending to be detectives walked into Mr. Maranzano's outer office and lined up everyone who was there against the wall. Then two of the fake detectives went inside, where they shot him and cut his throat."[28] Maranzano's 1931 murder coincided with the slayings of forty of his associates around the country. This final battle of the Castellammarese War established the new "capo," Lucky Luciano, the man who orchestrated the killings. Luciano's underboss, Vito Genovese, then took control of the old Luciano family.

After Maranzano—and later Luciano—masterminded the corporatization of organized crime, the younger generation of gangsters sought to establish themselves more firmly in the Anglo-American mainstream. Aided by the swindles, vice, and racketeering that powered their economic upward mobility, gangsters joined law-abiding second-generation Americans in moving to the suburbs during the postwar period. A member of the Buffalo-based Magaddino organization, Apalachin host Joe Barbara himself had moved from Scranton, Pennsylvania, to the rural hills of upstate New York. Luciano's underboss Vito Genovese left New York for the Jersey shore community of Atlantic Highlands. Detroit's Joseph Zerilli moved to exclusive Grosse Pointe. Gangsters with less money than these three settled in working- and middle-class suburbs in places like Queens, Staten Island, and northern New Jersey. Joe Valachi moved with his family to Yonkers, where he became a homeowner and sent his son to a private high school. Although his notoriety and colorful personality prevented him from becoming just another man in a gray flannel suit, Genovese made a concerted effort to endear himself to his Atlantic Highlands neighbors. He advised colleagues who followed him to the suburbs to "give to the Boy Scouts and all the charities. Try to make it to church. Don't fool around with the local girls."[29] Despite Genovese's advice, the violence continued throughout the 1950s. In fact, prominent on the 1957 Apalachin meeting's agenda was a discussion of the murder of Albert Anastasia, reputedly ordered by Genovese.

Because of the New York State Police raid, the survivors of the Castellammarese War did not get very far into their agenda. Instead, they became embroiled in various crime-fighting and political initiatives. In response to the Apalachin revelations, the attorney general established a Special Group to Prosecute Organized Crime, and New York State established its task force—efforts state and federal officials had declined to make when first recommended several years earlier by Senator Kefauver. By 1959, the Justice Department had convened four federal grand juries in a nationwide effort to proceed against "the country's 100 top racketeers."[30] With the Apalachin meeting, America received conclusive proof that a nationwide network of organized criminals existed. That they saw this reality through the lens of old gangster movie conventions also reveals that it would be difficult to separate this reality from older myths of ethnicity and criminality. Cold War–era Americans still perceived ethnic gangsters in terms established in Prohibition-era America, but the changes in criminal practices and in the larger society provided a window into new social and political contexts. No longer a despised immigrant group, Italian Americans occupied a position of relative privilege in the wake of World War II. Similarly, the virulent xenophobia of the World War I generation, while not relegated to the dustbin of history, had been grafted onto the new alien menace of communism.

In a speech to the assembled conventioneers at the annual meeting of the American Legion in 1957, J. Edgar Hoover gave shape to these dual anxieties:

> Eleven years ago our country had just emerged victorious from a devastating world conflict. As we then turned our attention to the problems confronting our Nation, we observed the rapidly growing, menacing two-headed monster of subversion and lawlessness. We recall that during the year 1946, 1,685,203 major crimes were reported by local, county, and state law enforcement agencies in this country. . . . Look at your watch as it ticks off 12 seconds. In that span a major crime has been committed somewhere in the United States. Last year a shocking total of 2,563,150 major crimes was reported by the Nation's police. The number is increasing this year. Actual Communist Party membership has declined. Thus, with an estimated population increase during the last years of some thirty million people, it would appear that we are losing the fight on crime and winning the battle against subversion. I assure you, nothing could be further from the truth. To give up the war on crime or to ease up in the battle against subversion will bring national disaster.

To Hoover, communism and lawlessness had become a "menacing two-headed monster." He insisted that national unity depended on taking action against what Virgil Peterson, operating director of the Chicago Crime Commission, called "barbarians in our midst."[31] As early as 1950, Illinois governor Adlai Stevenson, addressing a gathering of criminologists, told his audience that organized crime posed a challenge to U.S. society not because of the potential for violence or higher prices for the goods and services criminals controlled. Rather, "the greatest menace is that the public will come to accept organized crime as something inevitable, as a necessary part of our social system."[32] Stevenson convincingly raised the idea of an active electorate as the only antidote to political corruption and social decay.

In doing so, he reframed the issue of organized crime. To Virgil Peterson, there was no menace greater than the "barbarians" and "two-headed monsters" of crime-busting hyperbole. He—and those he influenced—clung to the previous generation's dichotomy between "honest citizens" and ethnic urban predators often stereotypically associated with organized crime. By pointing to the "honest citizens" themselves, Stevenson showed that the menace could not simply be contained and deported. In contrast to the vigilance committees and G-men of the Progressive and Prohibition eras, Stevenson saw organized crime in uniquely Cold War terms, embodied in his goal of arousing a diverse citizenry through a common fear of an outside enemy. Democratic politicians such as Kefauver, Stevenson, and later John McClellan and Robert F. Kennedy would thus marshal and transform the power of pre–World War II xenophobia by adapting the interpretive framework of anticommunism. The old menace of organized crime would prove compatible with, and would reinforce, the anticommunist worldview. In its attacks on immigration and unions, the postwar anti-crime campaign often echoed and amplified the tactics of anticommunist Cold Warriors. The crime busters also served the interests of law enforcement agendas—including regulation of drug use, gambling, and vice—not included in the ideological war of McCarthy-era politics.

The historian Ellen Schrecker insightfully reminds us that the anticommunist movement sought to convince the public that communism was "so bad and dangerous that it had to be driven out of American life."[33] Anticommunists used metaphors of disease (a "political cancer"), fanaticism, and even apocalypse to discredit party adherents and frighten the less-informed segments of the citizenry.[34] True, there were communists who, like others on the left and right, offered radical critiques of American culture and politics, though their threat was certainly overstated. Even if they did pose a danger to U.S. political, cultural, and economic life, some used that threat to discredit and harm others they saw as posing even reformist challenges. Many law-abiding liberals—especially if members of ethnic, racial, or sexual minorities—found themselves unable to move freely across borders, socialize in public places, or send newsletters through the mail.[35] Some political and government careers were damaged, while others received a boost from the scapegoating of radicals, progressives, and bohemians. Of course there were real communists. There were real spies. But Cold War anticommunists used their threat as a political opportunity to energize the far right. In doing so, they eroded the ability of Democrats to champion the social, cultural, and economic programs of the New Deal and World War II eras. Many liberals turned instead to defending the consumer society, bourgeois values, and capitalist hegemony that were increasingly becoming identified as "the American Way."

Whereas anticommunists had numerous critics who were suspicious of their tactics while sharing their sentiments, crime fighters faced little opposition. The American Civil Liberties Union (ACLU) gave Senator Kefauver a clean bill of health. Magazines and newspapers critical of Senator Joseph McCarthy's abuse of power failed to see the impending growth of police powers made possible by the fanning of anti-crime flames. *The Nation*, for example, shared many of the assumptions of the Kefauver Committee and, later, of the McClellan Committee, which investigated corruption in labor unions. Most tellingly, when the editors of the anti-McCarthy *New York Post* ran a critique of the senator's tactics, they used Mafia parallels, calling him a "one man mob" and a "political Murder, Inc."[36]

Anticommunists focused their attention on targets such as the State Department and Hollywood, thus adding a new chapter to the xenophobic anti-radicalism of the 1919–20 red scare. The organized crime investigations and depictions had similar roots in the earlier generation's attacks on the foreign-born. Fears of organized crime, however, revealed changes in ethnic and labor politics that remain hidden in studies of anti-radical paranoia. As John Higham pointed out in his pathbreaking *Strangers in the Land*, nativism translated "broader cultural antipathies and ethnocentric judgments" into "a zeal to destroy the enemies of a distinctively American way of life." Higham astutely argued that the growth of anti-Semitism in the opening decades of the twentieth century was rooted more in the rising fortunes of many Jewish Americans than in their recent arrival.[37] By the 1950s, this pattern was applied to labor unions as well as to the growing white ethnic middle class. As the working class achieved substantial wage gains—and none enjoyed greater success than the mob-influenced Teamsters—feelings of nativism and paranoia magnified the revelation of illegal acts into widespread suspicion of unions more generally, a perception from which the labor movement has yet to recover.

Cold War anticommunists never did achieve the ideological hegemony they hoped for in their efforts to undercut the viability of an American left. Nevertheless, as Schrecker argues, the impact of McCarthyism can be most powerfully seen when we consider what a vibrant progressive movement could have accomplished had it not been put on the defensive by the far right.[38] Even as it exposed the political force of intimidation and insinuation, McCarthyism also revealed that the government was not an all-powerful, WASP-dominated corporate body that could easily impose its will on ideological dissenters. Those who sought to eliminate the influence of organized crime also met with resilient forces that resented their portrayal of immigrants and workers as mere dupes of unscrupulous leaders. Particularly in the second half of the 1950s and into the 1960s, ethnic and union activists vigorously, if not always successfully, formulated and popularized strategies for reading crime stories or watching television programs against the grain. Both the labor movement and Italian American advocacy organizations offered images of their members that closely mirrored mainstream, often conservative visions of white middle-class life to counteract media images of racketeers and ethnic gangsters in *On the Waterfront* and *The Untouchables*. Their resistance emerged from a simultaneous critique and embrace of dominant 1950s mores. In his 1959 speech accepting the Teamster presidency, Jimmy Hoffa felt the need to tell "all Americans" that Teamsters "are respected citizens who live next door to you."[39] Hoffa was responding to accusations that Teamsters were somehow "un-American." That he did so by reminding his listeners that the Teamsters subscribed to markers of middle-class success illustrates how resistance and consensus coexisted.

Media representations of the Mafia elicited complicated forms of reception, spurring some civic-minded individuals to join citizens' crime committees and others to join organizations fighting stereotypes of "unholy" labor leaders and sinister Italian Americans. Still others were drawn to the illicit pleasures and triumphant machismo depicted in Mafia narratives. Rather than merely describing and accepting what the dominant culture said about the Mafia, I intend to show how certain texts and accusations either reinforced or destabilized social, political, and economic inequalities in a dialogue between production, distribution, and reception. That is, writers, the medium of delivery, and consumers of popular culture all exerted an influence over the meanings and effects of a text. Popular texts often allow for and encourage readings that offer strong critiques of social and economic inequalities. In discussing the relationship between journalists, true crime writers, and federal investigative agencies, I show how the relationship between production, distribution, and reception often simply turned out to be a form of social control, with the media acting directly as an organ of the Federal Bureau of Narcotics or the New York City Anti-Crime Committee, among others.[40]

At times, it seemed that television was even more influential than anticommunism on the era's crime fighters. During the 1950s, it provided an intimate and entertaining medium for those seeking to shape public opinion and policy. Between 1950 and 1955, the number of television sets in American homes rose from 3.1 million to 32 million. According to Stephen Whitfield, ten thousand new television sets were purchased *every day* in 1955.[41] But television did not merely distribute the messages; it played an important role in shaping them to fit the narrative desires of networks, viewers, and advertisers. Like the evening news, the crime dramas asserted that "everything you are about to see is true."[42] From the Kefauver Committee and the evening news broadcasts to *The Untouchables* and *Dragnet,* the media depiction of crime asserted the moral dominance of a conforming middle class that could vicariously break—or uphold—the law simply by buying a television set and watching the broadcasts.

Organized crime in Cold War America, like the state police bust in Vestal, was a collision of myth and reality. If we understand myths as stories we tell and have faith in despite their extraordinary details, we can see that they convey to believers a sense of commonality. Myths are stories whose great significance derives from the function they serve. Despite its fantastic story line and the glimpse it affords into a shadowy underworld, much of the Apalachin event can be confirmed from government, gangster, and journalistic sources. Organized crime stories and hearings were not "mythic" in the sense that they were false. Rather, Mafia stories served specific political and cultural agendas, reaffirming certain beliefs and values while discrediting others. Mafia stories served to explain, as M. H. Abrams argued about ancient myths, "why the world is as it is and things happen as they do, as well as to establish the rationale for social customs and observances and the sanctions for the rules by which people conduct their lives."[43] Like cultural and religious myths, the Apalachin story influenced contemporary and subsequent understandings of organized crime.

Myths play a particularly strong role in constructing a sense of "peoplehood." The story of deliverance from Egypt for Jews and African American Christians, of the Resurrection for Christians, and of apparitions and miracles for Roman Catholics are more than stories, they shape how people think about themselves in relation to one another, their faith, and their place in a diverse world. Many Cold War intellectuals and scholars would have been comfortable with the argument that modern, mass-mediated myths such as organized crime narratives also helped construct a people. From American studies scholars such as Henry Nash Smith—who sought to understand the role of frontier fantasies in American cultural life—to the French structuralist Roland Barthes or proponents of the early British cultural studies movement, European and North American intellectuals have sought new ways of understanding the roles of myths and stories in the shaping of political, social, and economic practices. Writing in the mid-1950s, Barthes insightfully offered readers a way to understand this dynamic: "What the world supplies to myth is a historical reality, defined, even if this goes back quite a while, by the way in which men have produced or used it; and what myth gives in return is a *natural* image of this reality."[44]

Rather than being falsehoods in need of debunking, myths rely on historical facts such as the meeting at Apalachin of national and international criminals. In turn, myths provide a basis for understanding—one that would prove instrumental to reforming criminal, labor, and immigration policy in postwar America. Crime stories and investigations were formed out of complex, decades-long struggles that implicated and helped to reaffirm shifting notions of class, gender, race, and ethnicity which had firm roots in social and political history. But they also helped construct a sense of "peoplehood" in that the increased vigilance against "the greatest menace" could energize and Americanize a diverse polity. This process would have grave implications for the criminal justice system, and tremendous costs for those who were deported and incarcerated in its name.

ORGANIZED CRIME
AS AN AMERICAN WAY OF LIFE:
Mafia Stories and Ethnicity

So these two gangsters are sitting in the dining room—or was it standing at the urinal?—of an almost empty Italian restaurant in Coney Island—or was it Newark? Anyway, this gangster, a kid, like nineteen, dressed in a new suit sits across from an old gangster. You know, one of the Mustache Petes—watch chain, silk suit, big mustache, like he's still in Sicily. They've finished eating. It's late. The old gangster gets up to go to the bathroom. Oh, yeah. That's right. They were in the dining room, but then the old guy goes to the bathroom first. Less than a minute later, two other gangsters—barely old enough to shave—come into the restaurant. They glide past the bartender, who knows better than to look up from the sink as he washes glasses. They start running as they enter the men's room in the back of the dining room, fire five rounds into the old guy's back as he takes a leak, and glide out through the kitchen alley exit. A classic gangland hit.

The story, or one like it, appears frequently in the annals of Mafia history. Versions of it describe the 1931 murders of Giuseppe Masseria and Salvatore Maranzano, two Sicilian-born gangsters prominent in the New York underworld. Masseria was typical of the "Mustache Petes," gangsters who settled disputes, lent money, and extorted businesses in Italian American immigrant neighborhoods. The story of their murder describes more than their individual deaths. It also describes the transition from intraethnic paternalism to the more modern, interethnic, service-providing Mafia of the 1930s. Later the story would reappear with the 1935 murder of Dutch Schultz—a Jewish, Bronx-born gangster then running the numbers racket in Harlem—in the Palace Chop House in Newark, New Jersey. More recently, the story was updated with the 1985 murder of Paul Castellano outside Manhattan's Sparks steakhouse.[1] Each time the story appears, it tells about more than an individual murder. It reinforces assumptions about Mafia morality, describes changes in organized crime and larger cultural transitions. In particular, the murder of the "Mustache Petes" signified a shift from Old World feudalism to New World capitalism. Conversely, the media accounts of the murder of Paul Castellano marked the pinnacle of the mafioso as celebrity, personified by John Gotti and Sammy "The Bull" Gravano, two gangsters later implicated in the murder. They came to exemplify the larger culture of celebrity that replaces substance with flash, products with information, and talent with style.

These Mafia stories, like many others, occupy a space between myth and reality. The bullets, dead bodies, struggles for money and power, and corruption surely ripped flesh, tore apart families, and affected communities. In this sense it is unfair to characterize the Mafia as solely a myth, as some scholars and community activists insist. Nevertheless, these stories enter American culture, circulate among calls for tougher crime laws, restrictions on immigration, and oversight of labor unions. They become grist for the front pages of our newspapers, are fictionalized in print and on celluloid, and pass into our living rooms on *The Untouchables* and *The Sopranos*. In this sense the Mafia is the root of an American genre, mirroring the relationship of U.S. expansionism to a Zane Grey western, warfare to a submarine movie, high school to an *Archie* comic book, or intimate relationships to a romance novel.

Mafia narratives emerged in the late nineteenth century and have remained standard fare throughout American popular culture. There was not a moment in the twentieth century when they did not exist. Despite this continuity, Mafia stories have changed over time. Two factors explain the shifts. First, organized crime has also changed over time. From the community-based toughs of the turn of the century to the Prohibition-era bootleggers of the 1920s and the waste management consultants and stock fraud perpetrators of today, organized criminals continue to take advantage of community need and greed. The crimes change in relation to shifting laws and opportunities. Second, Mafia stories distill broad social and cultural characteristics into more basic elements such as entertainment, fear, and desire. They change over time because the broader social and cultural characteristics do not remain stable. Late nineteenth- and early twentieth-century Americans were attracted to Italian American gangsters, but fears of the "Black Hand" and of characters like Tony Camonte in *Scarface* ultimately underscored the incompatability of southern and eastern European immigrants with dominant notions of American character. Anti-crime measures often merged with explicit anti-Italian and anti-radical agendas, setting the stage for the 1919–20 deportations of immigrant radicals, the 1924 immigration reforms, and arguably the 1927 executions of Sacco and Vanzetti. In contrast, postwar Mafia stories like *On the Waterfront* provided commentary on the morality of McCarthyism and the dangers of corruption. The *Godfather* films, beginning in the 1970s, can most fruitfully be seen in relation to that era's ethnic revivals and distrust of politicians. More recent narratives such as *The Sopranos* and *Analyze This!* poke fun at the habits of baby boomers obsessed with status and self-help.

Furthermore, Mafia narratives change because the significance of their key elements—most notably crime and morality, immigration and ethnicity, class and labor, race and gender, family and religion—are socially and culturally contested. People disagree about the political and economic consequences of these differences. The impact of race, gender, ethnicity, and class on our social, economic, and political power often depends on the outcome of these battles. Even when we lose these battles, the meaning of these elements alters—if only by being reinforced. The economic and political power, racial and ethnic status, and social and cultural significance of Italian Americans and other white ethnics dramatically changed from the 1880s, the period of their first large-scale immigration, to the Cold War era. The shifting descriptions and meanings of the Mafia shaped and responded to the desire for upward mobility, the interest in ethnic self-definition, and the ambivalence of the larger society over the inclusion of the southern and eastern European working class in the mainstream.

Inventing Ethnic Criminals: The Frontier, the Boardroom, and the Ladder

The terms "gangster" and "Mafia" inevitably invoke ethnic connotations. Whereas in the past they specifically referred to Italian American organized crime, it is quite common now to read of the "Russian Mafia," the "Jewish Mafia," the "Jamaican Mafia," and so on. In its unmodified form, however, "the Mafia" continues to connote Italian American gangsters. Ethnicity often shapes our understandings of crime, and crime often shapes our understandings of ethnicity. Although many have noted that ethnicity is "invented"—formed by social, economic, and historical factors rather than being an unchanging set of biological or cultural characteristics—the category of crime is often understood as a matter of common sense. Certain acts, no matter where or by whom they are committed, constitute crimes. On the contrary, crime too is invented, although the cultural and political "invention" of criminality should not be confused with an argument that crime is a figment of our imagination. Rather, as Christopher Wilson, David Papke, David Ruth, and others have argued, our understandings of criminal violations and policing participate in and respond to cultural, social, and political contexts.[2] Whether we define an act as criminal or licit is often determined by the person committing the crime, the physical and social location of the act, and even by popular stereotypes of ethnicity and social mobility.

When inventing the ethnic gangster, we often rely on other American cultural myths to explain social behavior that we deem criminal. Often we do this with little recognition of the historical situation in which the crime was committed. Instead of placing the criminal act within a social, political, and journalistic moment, we fail to recognize that, as Papke notes, "crime is not a discrete and merely controllable social fact but rather those parts of social experience which assorted forces, formations and individuals 'label' criminal."[3] When we look back on the gangsters of the past, we frequently do so through the lens of our assumptions about ethnic difference and the class mobility many white ethnic groups experienced over the course of the twentieth century. Sometimes, we see them as mythic characters who affirm clichés about the American past. We see them, as Robert Rockaway did in his classic study of Jewish gangsters, as icons: "The gangster epitomizes the virtues of the frontiersman and the cowboy—the man with a gun, who confronts society and the conventions alone and does as he pleases. By so doing, he acts out the fantasies and suppressed desires of many Americans."[4] In other accounts, ethnic neighborhoods become the Wild West, with poor European immigrants obeying a code of justice that somehow originated at the O.K. Corral: "The self-contained immigrant colonies of early twentieth century America were in a real sense frontier settlements. As had been true on the frontiers of the westward expansion, the absence of established institutions and their sanctions provided an environment of 'lawlessness' where conflict and violence always seethed just below the surface."[5] In these examples, ethnic crime exists "on the frontier," just at the edge of the recognizable social world but still uniquely American. Like Frederick Jackson Turner's famous mythology of the frontier, ethnic ghettos are a transitional space, that middle ground between "savagery" and "civilization."[6] It is a lawless world, but one with a relationship to the ordered world.

If observers saw the early American Mafia as a version of Old West justice, this perception quickly gave way to parallels to the corporate industrial economy and large, centralized government. The shift to industrialization and the growth of U.S. political institutions occurred at the same time as the turn-of-the-century immigration. As immigrant neighborhoods became less mysterious to native-born commentators, they employed new frameworks that compared gangs to government and corporate bureaucracies. The world they saw seemed to be organized along lines paralleling the law-abiding world: the "nation" was broken up into combinations instead of states; its leaders were dons instead of governors or CEOs; the banking was done by Jewish loan sharks or bankrolls; its people were entertained by Chinese or Jewish prostitutes or in Chinese opium dens. Instead of a frontier settlement in between chaos and order, the spatial metaphor employed was that of the "underworld." This hidden world existed just below the surface, but it mirrored the surface economy and society. In a description of Meyer Lansky, a Polish Jewish immigrant who became notorious in the 1930s, one observer wrote: "The thing that sets Meyer Lansky apart from most men who have achieved the American Dream is his line of business. He chose to pursue his ambitions not in steel or oil, not in automobiles or banking, but in crime. In that field he is as much of a visionary and innovator as Andrew Carnegie, Henry Ford, and John D. Rockefeller were in theirs."[7]

When describing the crimes committed by gangsters, we often rely on preexisting notions of ethnicity. We merely apply concepts such as the frontier or the American Dream to urban criminal personalities. During the heyday of the 1970s ethnic revival, Nicholas Gage observed that "clearly, the underworld in the United States is as much a melting pot as any other aspect of our culture, and the opportunities for vice have attracted just as many ethnic groups as the opportunities for legitimate achievement."[8] As a means of envisioning how crime operated in the early part of the twentieth century, the construction of the underworld relies on building materials readily available to the American imagination. The ethnic underworld is invented by means of analogies to the "visible" world, whether to Billy the Kid, Andrew Carnegie, or the melting pot. In this way the ethnic gangster is invented, albeit with a basis in deeds actually committed by immigrant gangsters in the early 1900s.

Prior to the Cold War, ethnic criminals were constructed by many different groups that often had competing agendas. Because of their differing objectives, the gangsters they portrayed had qualities that revealed the unique motivations and biases of those doing the observing. The exposé method of analysis was perhaps the most prevalent. With origins in Progressive-era investigative journalism and realist fiction, these portrayals brought the reader into a hidden world of crime that had strict boundaries and stood in opposition to the legitimate world. The reporter acted as a tour guide into the seedy underbelly of the urban immigrant community for a white, middle- and upper-class audience, many of whom would have been reform-minded. Some versions of this model valorized the ethnic criminal, but constructed him or her as operating in a distinct world that was often unknown to the mainstream population. The second model was more sociological in orientation, focusing on a theory of ethnic succession that would later be most clearly articulated by Daniel Bell in the 1950s as "the queer ladders of social mobility." Beginning with the Irish and continuing on to current immigrants, Bell argued, each generation used crime as a means of entering the American mainstream community of consumption. The third argument—one put forward most coherently by middle-class ethnic advocacy groups—viewed ethnic crime as nothing more than a false stereotype employed by the media, politicians, and historians for specific (often xenophobic) reasons.

Tour Guides: Progressive-Era Reformers

In *How the Other Half Lives*, Jacob Riis acted as a tour guide for his middle-class readers into New York City's immigrant tenements: "Suppose we look into one? Be a little careful please! The hall is dark and you might stumble over the children pitching pennies back there. . . . [T]here where the hall turns and dives into utter darkness is a step, and another, another. A flight of stairs. You can feel your way, if you cannot see it."[9] Through his text, Riis's readers, or viewers of his "magic lantern" slide shows, could vicariously enter the world of the "other half" and simultaneously pass judgment on the parents who let their kids pitch pennies in the dark hallway. In was clear to Riis's late nineteenth-century readers that ethnicity was inextricably tied to the criminal acts and morally questionable behavior of the immigrant community. Riis's Italians were violent, his Chinese unscrupulous, and his Jews greedy. They did things for mysterious reasons and in shadowy locations. What is perhaps most striking about this passage is the darkness. We cannot see the immigrants' behavior. Riis implies that their way of life existed in the shadows of New York City, just down the street and around the corner from the neighborhoods of his audience.

Riis took his contemporaries into a world of crime, illicit sex, and juvenile delinquency, joining the tabloid reporters in arousing the interest of his readers. He piqued and held their interest with sex and violence while, as Robert Snyder argues, "warning of what to fear on a walk down a dark side street."[10] As a reformer firmly rooted in the Progressive era, Riis saw the cause of immigrant crime as a combination of "backward" native cultures unsuited to American modernity and the degraded environment created by poverty, overcrowding, and substandard housing. Immigrants, this thinking goes, have a propensity toward crime, and the overcrowding and exploitation in the urban slums exacerbated this predisposition.

In the shadows of Riis's urban underworld were ethnic gangs that, while closed to outsiders, were emblematic of the "legitimate" political and economic world. These ethnic connections threatened the perceived equality of opportunity in the public realm of business and politics and had to be exposed and eliminated. Italians relied on common ethnicity, rather than equal opportunity, to unfairly corner legitimate markets and to peddle drugs. These sensationalized connections were often the driving force behind the exposé model of ethnic crime. The overriding message here is that immigrants rely on favors and shady connections rather than the open market, valorized as "the American Way." Cultural differences and economic disadvantages did in fact shape immigrant crime, as Jenna Weissman Joselit points out in her study of Jewish gangsters. "Both arsonists and horse-poisoners," she writes, "relied on the insularity of the Jewish community for their respective success. Each created a silent network of individuals—some willingly silent, others reluctantly so—from which they derived their illicit income."[11] The immigrant community rallied around its criminals and thereby threatened the viability of an ordered society. Their criminal acts, like the motivations and beliefs even of law-abiding immigrants, remained mysterious and hidden. Part of this inscrutability was by design, part a result of the distorted perception of those doing the looking.

Although the ethnicity of the criminals made them mysterious and dangerous to outside observers, the mass media contexts for their sensational popularity often influenced the meaning of crime. Given the right kind of attention, as Lincoln Steffens revealed, an isolated act can become evidence of a crime wave. Steffens, a turn-of-the-century muckraker, described the connection between law and reporting: "I enjoy crime waves. I made one once, Jake Riis helped; many reporters joined in the uplift of the rising tide of crime; and T.R. [Theodore Roosevelt, then New York City's police chief] stopped it. I feel that I know something the wise men do not know about crime waves and so get a certain sense of happy superiority out of reading editorials, sermons, speeches, and learned theses on my specialty."[12] If the shadowy corners and secret societies into which Progressive-era journalists shone their lanterns seem suspiciously conspiratorial, it is only partly because the criminals intended it to be this way. The "shadows and darkness" that were revealed provided a convenient (and profitable) lens through which to view crime in general.

Similarly, Progressive-era social organizations documented crime in poor neighborhoods in an effort to improve living conditions and help European immigrants assimilate into the white middle class. Organizations such as the Jewish Kehillah and the Society to Aid Jewish Prisoners also regularly entered the immigrant neighborhoods as an act of both surveillance and social work.[13] As institutions seeking to influence the larger society's perception of immigrants, they brought a social and political vision to their documenting of organized crime.[14] Rather than tying crime to ethnicity, these social reformers and bourgeois ethnics attributed crime to the neighborhoods in an effort to distance themselves from criminality, enhance their reputation, and counter the stereotypes advanced by journalists like Riis. According to this assimilationist view, criminals display an understanding of the American capitalist system but are excluded from it by virtue of their ethnic difference. Each generation of immigrants thus produces a large number of criminals because of these obstacles to upward mobility. Criminals merely apply the principles of entrepreneurship, or so this thinking goes, to illicit markets. If they were brought into the mainstream—whether by ethnic groups, civil organizations, social organizations, or the criminal justice system— the problem would ebb.

Crooked Ladders: Theories of Ethnic Succession

In his 1953 essay "Crime as an American Way of Life," Daniel Bell argued that "crime has a 'functional' role in the society, and the urban rackets—the illicit activity organized for continuing profit rather than individual illegal acts—is one of the queer ladders of social mobility in American life."[15] Bell's thesis appeared to shake the myth of the American Dream. Rather than America's being a land where anyone who worked hard enough could make an honest buck, Bell argued that opportunities for immigrants were not equal to those of WASPs; immigrants had to rely on an alternative mode of ascent in order to get rich. Once the money was made, the goal shifted to the "search for an entrée—for oneself and one's ethnic group—into the ruling circles of the big city."[16] The next new ethnic group then filled the shoes of the "legitimized" ethnic group, fulfilling the model of ethnic succession. "There was a distinct ethnic sequence in the modes of obtaining illicit wealth," Bell proposed, beginning with the Irish, followed by the Jews and the Italians. Later historians and sociologists accepted his thesis almost wholesale, adding rungs to his ladder for Caribbean, Latino, and Asian immigrants.[17]

The idea that crime is tied to the "morals and manners of a society" contrasts the belief that criminals are deviant or outside the social system. Instead, criminals are seen as participating in a social act. The gangsters whom Bell described were participating in an alternative service economy. Even thieves and pickpockets in some cases were social actors who supported the morals and manners of society. While most people would quibble with this means of acquiring wealth, few would argue that the goal was itself "un-American." In their desire for social mobility and increased wealth, ethnic criminals could be seen as entrepreneurs searching for ways to realize the dream of economic advancement in a class system constructed to exploit their labor. As Ellen Andrews Knodt says in "The American Criminal: The Quintessential Self-Made Man?" the accumulation of wealth is the primary American marker of success, regardless of the means by which it was achieved. By putting Al Capone and Arnold Rothstein in the same category as Cornelius Vanderbilt and John D. Rockefeller, Knodt argues, public praise for gangsters was not unlike that received by "robber barons." The only thing separating Capone from Vanderbilt was ethnicity. Because of their ethnicity, immigrants like Capone were "caught between the cultural ideal of success and the reality of a social structure which places obstacles to its realization." The barriers to the "cultural ideal" of economic advancement made crime a "normal response," Knodt writes. "It is not surprising, therefore, that various immigrant and minority groups have constituted a hierarchy of crime, each new group succeeding the previous one as the older one was allowed to move more into the mainstream of society and achieve success through accepted means."[18]

The ethnic succession model thus locates the social roots of crime in the "values of this society" but essentially ignores the values of the immigrant community. Gangsters, however, surely tell us something about the communities from which they emerge. The communities and kinship structures built by the immigrants, as Jenna Joselit writes, "anchored the activities of its more deviant members."[19] While economic desires present in the society at large spurred immigrants to commit criminal acts, local and ethnic factors determined the specific nature of their criminality. For example, a Jewish shoplifter named Stiff Rivka recalled that she was always unusually productive during the Jewish High Holidays. Rivka valued monetary gain, but the Lower East Side influenced the type and timing of her crimes.[20] In their influential study *A Family Business: Kinship and Social Control in Organized Crime*, Francis Ianni and Elizabeth Reuss-Ianni explored the Mafia in Italy, the circumstances of immigration, and the formation of Italian American organized crime. They found that "Italian-American criminal families [were] a form of social organization patterned by tradition and responsive to culture."[21] Like other immigrant social structures, the Mafia provided its members with an organization that preserved aspects of Italian culture while helping them acculturate to new values. Organized crime was part of a larger immigrant social system created out of the familiar and new elements of immigrants' social milieu.

The So-Called Mafia: Ethnic Pride and Stereotypes

Even though European immigrants did commit real crimes and organized themselves along ethnic lines, in the context of the media, gangsters were not so much people as frames through which others could view criminal acts. That is, gangster stories tell us something about the people and cultures that see them, as well as something about the criminals and immigrant communities themselves. Robert Lacey describes the fascination with ethnic criminals as "America's film script view of itself."[22] Portrayals of the lives of ethnic criminals were riddled with narratives taken from fictions such as cinema, novels, and sensationalized news stories. Real immigrant gangsters were portrayed in terms of the drama and exaggeration that make films interesting and entertaining. Some see the treatment of ethnic criminals by the press, politicians, or police as wholly racist or xenophobic, others as part of a general suspicion of the city, still others as expressing a fear of the disintegration of "Victorian virtue" and (in the case of prostitution) a larger backlash against non-domesticated, non–Anglo-American women.

This argument was taken to an extreme by Dwight Smith, who maintained that the Mafia itself was a figment of overactive and xenophobic imaginations. The public, Smith argued, had been brainwashed by false stereotypes of immigrant gangsters. "My concern here," he writes in *The Mafia Mystique*, "is with the extent to which the public has been conditioned by mental pictures that now congregate around the term 'Mafia.' . . . Our unfortunate predicament is that imagery has tended to overwhelm fact and to blur our vision of the real world."[23] Despite this overstatement, Smith insightfully argues that from the earliest mention of the Mafia in the American press (in New Orleans in 1890) to the overzealous prosecution of Italian American criminals, the "Mafia mystique" has shaped mainstream perceptions of Italian Americans, leading to limitations on civil rights, unwarranted accusations, and general stereotypes that are applied to all Italian Americans. Thus, in addition to being an inaccurate representation of crime, the "film script" view of America contributes to the overall understanding of an entire ethnic group. Just as ethnicity influences the types of crimes committed, the invention of the gangster influences our understanding of ethnicity.

Smith was right to argue that media fabrication plays a role in popular understandings of organized crime. The circulation of stories often makes them seem true; the repetition breeds authority, regardless of authenticity. One sensationalized discussion of Meyer Lansky reported that he had "achieved the directorship of a network of enterprises as big as General Motors. His personal fortune is estimated to be somewhere between $100 million and $300 million."[24] But, like Lincoln Steffens's "crime wave," Lansky's "hidden fortune" was a journalistic conceit; a reporter for the *Miami Herald* arbitrarily chose the figure in 1967. The circulation of the myth in newspaper account after newspaper account eventually erased its initial fabrication. Limited knowledge of Lansky's illegitimate businesses coupled with a constantly repeated story helped construct his public persona.

Just as Meyer Lansky was constantly described in terms of his Jewishness, ethnicity became the yardstick by which historians and sociologists measured organized crime throughout the twentieth century. How we understand crime is dependent on the ethnicity of the person committing the crime, while ethnicity is often informed by how we define criminal behavior. Much of the hysteria surrounding ethnic crime, and the fact that it is usually tied to an organized, "underground" social structure, begins to sound paranoid, xenophobic, and conspiratorial. What do we make of the constant repetition of the stereotypes? Egal Feldman argues that the Progressive-era focus on prostitution was an effort to cleanse the cities mounted by people who dreamed of a pure America in both the moral sense and the racial sense. Reformers blamed a national decline in "morality and virtue" on immigration. It was argued that immigrants, more than any other portion of the population, profited from prostitution and the concomitant "loosening" of morals and profaning of women.[25] Feldman reveals a view of ethnic crime that subsumes the judgment of criminality into a more general disgust for immigrants and the supposed deterioration of moral propriety.

Inner-city conditions, personified by immigrant criminals and prostitutes, offered a convenient explanation for the perceived loss of purity in the society at large. Behind the construction of the ethnic criminal, according to Feldman, lurks the "impression, at times, that vice followed immigration as night does day."[26]

Crime, in this formulation, threatened the population at large, regardless of whether they were direct victims (or customers) of ethnic criminals. Fear of crime prompted political debates on the effectiveness of U.S. immigration policy. Immigrants not involved in the "vice industry" fell victim to the ethnic stereotypes circulating throughout the culture. Simply put, being an immigrant became a criminal act. Some writers view this phenomenon as part of a more general fear of cities as hotbeds of radicalism, full of plotting outsiders intent on disrupting the American Way. According to John Brazil, "Hysteria over criminal and ethnic conspiracies joined fears of bankers' plots, trusts, and political radicalism that swept the country at the turn of the century. In the short run this speculation promoted talk of restriction of immigration; in the long run it was to obscure the interpretation of organized crime for decades."[27]

Ethnic crime was thus seen as part of a larger pattern of immigration, urbanization, and industrialization that was tearing America away from its past.[28] The stereotypes that circulated in the press derived from the belief that traditional morality was in a state of decline. That women immigrants and their children were working outside the home upset many in the urban elite. "In the 19th century," writes Robert Snyder, "when most Americans saw women as the caretakers of morality, crime reporters spilled much ink over prostitution."[29] The cultural historian Elliot Gorn lists the virtues supposedly under siege by ethnic criminals: "Piety, hard work, sobriety, steady habits, frugality; a strict division of sexual roles into home, nurturance and moral elevation for women; work, productivity and patriarchal authority for men; above all, tight control of bodily desire and the checking of all forms of lust—these were the central virtues. It was, of course, a bourgeois culture, a culture that at once facilitated, sanctified and set moral limits on the process of acquiring property, building businesses and consolidating fortunes."[30] These values were class based, but also ethnoculturally based. The appropriateness of patriarchy, class hierarchy, and Protestant restraint were put into question by ethnic crime, even while the acquisition of property remained the dominant goal.

Whether in the progressive, sociological, or mythic models, it is clear that there are limits to what we can know about crime. We will probably never learn Stiff Rivka's whole story. She, like the other criminals in this study, will always be perceived through the lens of moral judgments and public fascination. As Snyder writes, "Under closer examination, crime news turns out to be concerned with far more than episodes of lawbreaking. . . . as such, it has defined America's ethnic and racial minorities, from the immigrant Irish of the 19th century to the African Americans of the 20th. And it has often defined them through stereotypes. . . . The result has been a skewed and pathological picture."[31] The distortion of crime begins at the moment of reportage. Historians sometimes add layers to this distortion rather than going back to the archives to uncover the interests involved in the surveillance and reporting. Toni Morrison's view of the reporting of ante-bellum African American crime in the white press is applicable here. She writes in *Beloved*:

> There was no way in hell a black face could appear in a newspaper if the story was about something anybody wanted to hear. A whip of fear broke through the heart chambers as soon as you saw a Negro's face in a paper, since the face was not there because the person had a healthy baby, or outran a street mob. Nor was it there because the person had been killed, or maimed or caught or burned or jailed or whipped or evicted or stomped or raped or cheated, since that could hardly qualify as news in a newspaper.[32]

Morrison forces us to acknowledge that the reporting of crime, and the writing of history based on those articles, also accepts the unstated position of the reader as the frame of reference. Organized crime did and does exist, but its representation and policing are laden with ideological and political assumptions. Crime functions as a social act by both criminals *and* their surveyors.[33]

Crime Stories and Cultural Citizenship

The dominant political and popular culture of the 1950s perceived organized crime as a conspiratorial threat to national security as serious as that posed by communism. This view had sources and consequences far beyond the criminal justice system, shaping understandings of citizen responsibility and helping people comprehend the shifting meanings of race, ethnicity, and class. The crass foundation of this view of crime was a belief that permeated the early Cold War period: political and cultural dissent could not be tolerated. Attention to organized criminals focused on political and cultural differences—nation of birth, political views, sexual nonconformity—as often as on the crimes themselves. Stamping out undesirable behavior called for defining desirable and undesirable qualities of the populace. In what follows I analyze this exclusionary notion of citizenship and difference.

Iris Marion Young has argued that a "notion of egalitarian politics of difference," rather than a desire to "transcend difference," is what characterizes an improved public sphere. She argues for a sense of difference that "comes to mean not otherness, exclusive opposition, but specificity, variation, heterogeneity."[34] Mary Louise Pratt posits the recognition of a "polyglot" citizenry as one alternative—"not . . . simply a polity whose citizens speak more than one language, but a polity that is, and sees itself as, multiply constituted, as *consisting of* heterogeneity at the level of the individual and the collectivity."[35] By tying organized crime to citizen action, postwar crime fighters explicitly sought to create a collective national community that looked instead with suspicion on dissent and difference. To reveal this larger consequence of organized crime during this period, I examine how broader assumptions about ethnicity, class, race, gender, and national unity shaped prevailing notions of crime and criminals, and vice versa. This book marks my engagement in a form of cultural analysis that seeks to document and understand how national communities create dominant and marginalized insiders through persistent attention to fearsome outsiders.[36]

In tying the construction of outsiders to the fear of crime, politicians, news and entertainment outlets, and others both relied on and determined notions of what it meant to belong to a "national community." The simple act of reading the newspaper allowed some citizens to participate in actions of exclusion, abetting a national project of achieving order and unity by locking some people up and keeping others out. [37] Paradoxically, in creating and reflecting an inclusive sense of appropriate behavior for law-abiding citizens, crime news created exclusions, and thus a source of contestation. The pervasive view that crime was the product of deviance supported assertions that the native-born white middle class was inherently honest, and these views presupposed a definition of citizenship that privileged the role of the white bourgeoisie. It followed that all potential threats came from beyond this group, or from, as Robert F. Kennedy referred to the Teamsters Union, "enemies within." During the 1950s, Richard Hofstadter aptly dubbed these beliefs "the paranoid style in American politics." More recent scholars have analyzed the multiple uses and outcomes of Cold War paranoia: Michael Rogin described "the politics of demonology," Virginia Carmichael "the Cold War perfecting myth." Elaine Tyler May and Alan Nadel used the anticommunist policy of "containment" as a metaphor for the culture of the period more generally.[38] But for too long the focus on anticommunism alone has characterized our understanding of Cold War political culture.

A historian of the American newspaper industry wrote, "We know a time, an era and a place by the crimes that fascinate it,"[39] a media-centered version of Dosteyevsky's famous aphorism that we can measure the humanity of our society by entering its prisons. How we describe the crimes that surround us shapes and reflects our social practices, particularly inequalities based on race, class, and ethnicity. That this is so within the context of ambivalent moral tales in which the outlaw is both desired and reviled suggests that these social practices are themselves in a constant state of flux.

CAPONE'S OLD TOWN:

Housing Desegregation and the Middle-Class Ideal in Cicero, Illinois

Cicero, Illinois, was Al Capone's town. During Prohibition, first Anton's Hotel and later the Hawthorne Inn headquartered Capone's gambling, alcohol, and prostitution interests. Cicero was well situated to serve as Chicago's vice district: it was surrounded on three sides by the city of Chicago, but Chicago law enforcement had no jurisdiction. Perhaps more important, particularly given that a contingent of Chicago police officers had ignored this lack of jurisdiction when they murdered Capone's brother Frank in Cicero on election day 1924, Cicero's police and politicians proved willing to overlook the vice in exchange for bribes and campaign contributions. Chicago residents consumed most of the illicit goods and services, but Cicero's white working class had its own Jazz Age. The town's biggest employers, Western Electric, Hotpoint, and Thor, built telephones and appliances and paid high wages to workers. Later, World War II kept Cicero's racially integrated factories humming, although African American workers commuted to Cicero from Chicago, despite Cicero's affordable housing, because of the racists the city was said to harbor.[1]

In 1951 gambling and prostitution establishments still lined Cicero's Cermak Boulevard. That year, the all-white city of sixty thousand residents became national news when Harvey and Johnetta Clark and their two children—an African

American family then living in a one-room apartment in what was described as a "firetrap building on the South side of Chicago"—attempted to move into a four-room unit in the DeRose Apartments at 6139 West Nineteenth Street in Cicero. The owner had recently sold the property to an African American realty company after her attempt to raise the rents in the rent-controlled building failed. Cicero police officers greeted the Clarks' initial attempt to move into the apartment by beating Harvey Clark, a Chicago bus driver, who, like his wife, was a graduate of Fisk University. Intimidated but not defeated, the Clarks obtained a federal court order with the help of the Chicago NAACP's Legal Committee and made a second attempt to move into the apartment. On Tuesday, July 10, this time under court-ordered police protection, the Clarks moved their furniture into a third-floor apartment in the twenty-unit building. Nine white families moved out of the building the next day, and the police detained the Clarks in violation of the court order. That night, Wednesday, vandals entered and destroyed the apartment, throwing many of the Clarks' possessions out the window. Amid talk of lynching, the Clarks fled to a friend's home in Chicago. On Thursday, the last ten families living in the building moved out just before a group of whites set fire to the building while the police watched.

The police were actively involved in all these events, warning white tenants of the violence to come and detaining the Clarks until the end of the working day so that the arsonists could fit their efforts to maintain Cicero's strict racial segregation into their busy schedules. *Time* magazine reported that "the crowd was good-natured, as if going to a game, and the cops acted like ushers politely handling the overflow at a football stadium." More to the point, Harvey Clark recalled that police chief Erwin Konovsky told him, "I'll put a bullet through your head if you ever come back." In response to the actions and inaction of the Cicero police, Governor Adlai Stevenson mobilized five companies of the Illinois National Guard. They attacked rioters with bayonets and rifle butts and arrested groups of young people who entered the building. It was the first time since a 1933 mine war in southern Illinois that state troops were used to control a civil disturbance.[2]

Like the miners, the residents of Cicero were primarily eastern and southern Europeans by birth or descent: Czechs, Italians, Irish, Poles, Lithuanians, Slovaks. Estimates of the number of rioters ranged from four thousand to eight thousand. Most observers agreed that this was the worst mob violence the area had seen in years. Although young people were the most violent and visible participants, reporters noted the presence of "housewives in cotton dresses" or "a father holding his child on his shoulder to give him a better view."[3]

The violence continued through the night, as young people pushed past guards to enter the apartment building at midnight on the second night of rioting. On Friday the thirteenth, Illinois declared a state of martial law covering the thirty square blocks around the building. State authorities arrested for unlawful assembly anyone who did not keep moving. Over the next several days, the troops surrounded the building with barbed wire and arrested 117 people.

"A Not Unnatural Reaction": Interpreting the Riot

The Clarks never did move to Cicero, instead accepting an invitation from the city of Norwalk, Connecticut, including a scholarship for piano lessons for daughter Michelle.⁴ In setting aside money for her piano lessons, Norwalk's donors were responding to press accounts, which rarely failed to mention that rioters had tossed the Clarks' piano out the third-story window. By neatly encapsulating the larger pattern of racial violence that characterized the postwar years, the Cicero riots served to symbolize for the press the national struggle over housing desegregation. The scale and severity of the attacks on the Clark apartment alone would have raised Cicero's visibility for the national media. When these factors were compounded by the particular characteristics of the town's white ethnic working class and Cicero's part in the operations of Chicago's most famous gangsters, the riot became a sensational example of the larger social and cultural questions the nation faced.

Other examples in postwar Chicago, while similarly indicative of the individual and collective horrors of the battle over desegregation, did not receive the media attention or engender the offers prompted by the events in Cicero. Immediately after the war, the Chicago Housing Authority built a housing project near the South Side airport for two hundred veterans and their families. After word spread that four or five African American families would be moving in, fifty white squatters took over every remaining apartment. The Chicago police evicted them, but when two African American families arrived, several days of rioting ensued, marking the first postwar outbreak of violence in the city over desegregation. In August 1947, when seven African American families moved into a public housing project in Fernwood, on the outskirts of Chicago, African American passengers were taken off buses and streetcars and beaten by a crowd of white men and boys. Local newspapers and national magazines expressed surprise that many of the 118 people arrested were from "good families." Two years later, white neighbors broke every window in the Johnson home in Chicago and threw firebombs through the broken glass: the Johnsons were thought to be the "first Negro family to live south of 71st Street." On Peoria Street in 1949, the visit of a black family to a Jewish family was enough to incite both anti-Semitic and racist violence.⁵

Any one of these events could have served to highlight the role of violence in maintaining racial segregation during the postwar period. They received ample press coverage, particularly in Chicago, but the local and national media outlets saw something far more menacing in the Cicero riots than in these earlier outbreaks. Comments from public officials and civic leaders, along with editorials in the national and local press, were not only expected, they were required. When Chicago's leading Catholic dignitary, Samuel Cardinal Stritch, met invitations to speak out against the rioting with silence, many took it as tacit support for the Cicero rioters.

Some commentators in the press condemned the rioting by criticizing the victims. Others shared Stritch's unwillingness to criticize opponents of desegregation. This coverage rarely mentioned the Clarks or the rioters, instead focusing on "outside organizations"—the NAACP, or, in typical Cold War fashion, the Soviet Union—for instigating the crisis. The *Chicago Tribune* did not view the riot as racist, instead arguing that it was a "not unnatural reaction from a public maddened against rent controls."[6] Camille DeRose, owner of the building, agreed, charging that the riots "arose from the growing form of communism implicit in *rent control*."[7] Clifton Utley, Chicago's most popular TV commentator, was disturbed by the riots, but not because of the outrageous denial of the Clarks' wish to live in Cicero. Utley feared the propaganda value of the violence to Asian and European communists: "If the citizens of Cicero had gotten together and tried to think up ways of helping communism and Soviet propaganda, they could scarcely have evolved a more effective course."[8] To virtually all commentators, the Cicero riots signaled a cultural and political crisis, but most sought to deny the riot's consistency with the daily practice of segregation. In keeping with these denials, a Cook County grand jury blamed the people most directly associated with the Clarks' move to Cicero for the riots: the former owner of the property to which the Clarks sought to move, a former attorney for the owner, a rental agency for the property, and George Leighton, NAACP attorney for the Clarks.[9]

When a special federal grand jury was convened at the request of the NAACP, it wisely reversed the earlier Cook County decisions, throwing out the indictments against Leighton and the others associated with the Clarks. The jury returned indictments against Henry J. Sandusky, president of Cicero's town council, along with the town attorney, town fire marshal, and four Cicero police officers, including Police Chief Konovsky, for "conspiracy to prevent any Negro inhabitants from occupying and owning property in Cicero."[10] Sandusky, the town attorney, and the fire marshal were acquitted just after Sandusky's reelection in June 1952, but the four police officers were found guilty of violating the Clarks' civil rights. Despite these efforts, Cicero would remain all white and would draw a new round of national media attention in 1966 when Martin Luther King, Jr., spent the summer bringing to light northern racism in Chicago.

What made the Cicero riots unique was not that some people defended the rioters. After all, many in the mainstream media during the early 1950s found fault with people who insisted on equal access to housing, jobs, schools, and public facilities. What distinguished these riots was Cicero itself: the press looked on in amazement at the spectacle of a town shaped by a white ethnic working class willing to live with the legacy of Al Capone but unwilling to live with a decent, well-educated, patriotic African American working-class family. *Time* marveled that a town like Cicero could riot over the Clarks. Clearly, a family consisting of parents who were university graduates, one of whom had fought heroically in World War II, would be assets to any town, particularly Cicero: "Grimy Cicero, Ill., which huddles close to Chicago's west boundary has never had a reputation for being exclusive. During the roaring twenties, the Torrio-Capone mob roared through Cicero's streets in armored cars, ruled its wide-open gambling joints, honky-tonks and whorehouses." The usual cry that the presence of African Americans lowered property values or resulted in higher crime rates could not apply to Capone's Cicero. If anything, *Time* seemed to argue, the Clarks would lift the town's reputation. This town had nothing to protect.[11]

Outside the Chicago area, Cicero's ethnic character and its connections to organized crime made the riot seem especially odious. To the *Baltimore Afro-American*, the rioters were "8,000 frenzied, blood-thirsty descendants of immigrants from the Mediterranean area of Europe." Their status as loyal Americans was far more questionable than that of Harvey Clark, "an Air Force veteran of World War II." *Life* magazine's 5 million readers were treated to a two-page spread headlined "New Disgrace for Cicero: In Capone's Old Town a Mob Pillages a Negro's Home." In photographs recalling images of the crowds at post–World War I lynchings, *Life* depicted mobs of elated Italians and eastern Europeans with slicked-back hair, wearing leather jackets, waving fists, and giving the readers of *Life* the Italian American equivalent of the finger. These images contrasted sharply with those of the neatly dressed Clark family. In photos, eight-year-old Michele is crying. The traditional domesticity of the Clark family legitimized their claims for civil rights to *Life*'s readers, while the so-called mobsters (in one shot a "young hoodlum curses a guardsman as he lifts shirt to show wound") presented clear evidence of their undesirability.[12]

But when a *New York Times* editorial expressed the hope that African Americans would "not hold responsible for this hurt those multiplied thousands throughout the country who look on such events as outrageous and intolerable," it revealed the converse danger of blaming Cicero for the problem of racism in the United States. Because of the town's reputation as a "hangout of gangsters," the editorial continued, "we were not too surprised when it appeared, also, as the point at which ugly and irrational behavior made itself manifest." Racism, according to the *Times*, was thus limited to violent outbursts by people like the primitives of Cicero. Virgil Peterson, head of the privately funded Chicago Crime Commission, used a similar explanation in defending the rights of African Americans to live in previously segregated neighborhoods:

For over thirty years, the home owners and other residents of Cicero had tolerated the presence of the infamous Capone gang. There was little genuine public indignation over commonplace alliances between officials and gangsters. At least, the public was never aroused to an extent where officials found it necessary to rid the village of Capone gunmen. Then in the summer of 1951, a young Negro family moved into Cicero. The moral as well as the legal right of Negroes to live in the village could not be questioned. Immediately, however, the people of Cicero rose up in arms. The building in which the Negro family was living was virtually wrecked, and the family had to flee for safety.[13]

Rather than condemning the racist violence, Peterson marveled at the level of corruption that Ciceronians had tolerated. Although his support for desegregation was commendable, his demonization of the working-class immigrants of Cicero posed no threat to the continuing segregation in wealthier suburbs also experiencing racist upheaval in the early 1950s. Just nine months before the Clarks tried to move to Cicero, local whites had attempted to burn the Oak Park home of Dr. Percy Lavon Julian, an African American chemist, professor, and civil rights philanthropist. Just one month before the Cicero riots, a bomb was thrown into Julian's front yard in a second attempt to scare him out of town. Peterson and the *New York Times* might have pointed out that the very case that affirmed the Clarks' right to live in Cicero concerned one of Chicago's most prominent middle-class African American families. The 1940 case of *Hansberry v. Lee*, involving the parents of playwright Lorraine Hansberry, resulted in the U.S. Supreme Court overturning an Illinois Supreme Court decision that allowed whites to deny housing to African Americans.[14] Ultimately, Peterson's politics, like those of the *New York Times*, encouraged readers to blame ethnic Ciceronians for the entire problem of segregation.

Some observers insisted that the racism of the Cicero rioters could be taken as representative of the wider social ills that characterized racial segregation, economic inequality, and the shifting meaning of white ethnic identities. NAACP general secretary Walter White asked, "What evil thing had transformed such people into beasts, as savage as those from whom they had fled, in their denial of a place to live to a veteran who had given almost four years of his life to preserve that freedom they found here?" Their shared history of oppression should have made white ethnic Ciceronians and African Americans potential allies in the fight for civil rights. How strange, White mused, that the same people who cheered for Afro-Cuban White Sox player Minnie Minoso in the afternoon rioted against the Clarks in the evening. What was the relationship between their ethnic loyalties and the psychological investment in whiteness that led to their actions? A transformation had led to this riot, but not one simply attributable to the continued influence of the Prohibition era. Rather, as *Commonweal* magazine argued, the Cicero riot represented a broad-based failure of churches, schools, and civil society. Robert St. John, a well-known newspaper correspondent and former resident of Cicero, pointed out that the immigrants of Cicero may have consumed illegal beer during Prohibition, but they had "no desire for the companionship of strange young women or even for gambling. When establishments were opened for such purposes in Cicero, a vast majority of the customers came from Chicago." It was the corruption that wealthier Chicagoans brought which had caused the "moral disintegration" that led to the riot of 1951, not the inherent inferiority of Bohemians and Italians. Cicero, as these observers noted, was affected by a larger pattern of ethnic and class change. Its racism justified attention not because it was unusual but because it might hold the key to understanding American racism and segregation in general.[15]

These views, however, were in the minority. The overvisibility of Cicero's rioting depended on the invisibility of the continuing segregation in wealthier communities. Most condemnations of the Cicero rioting actually served to maintain the racial and economic status quo. The riots confirmed for people across the political, economic, and racial spectrum that gangsters and hoodlums had to be singled out—often by ethnic heritage—and held up for special contempt for subverting an essentially righteous American culture. The Clarks could be lionized as innocent victims—clearly a major step forward for a popular and political culture that rarely questioned legal segregation. But the violence was not an aberration that could be dismissed as the work of a foreign-born menace. Nevertheless, from Greensboro, North Carolina, in the 1940s and 1950s to the Boston busing crisis of the 1960s and 1970s, privileged whites continued to blame ethnic working-class whites for the intransigence of racism in the United States.[16]

When Walter White wondered "What evil thing transformed such people into beasts?" he was asking how the oppressed of Europe could so quickly come to identify with the most violent aspects and actions of white supremacy. An equally valid reading of White's question would look at the transformation of the working-class ethnics of Cicero into something less than human in the eyes of the larger culture. Organized crime was similarly used as a convenient, if misleading, explanation for the continuing inequality of certain ethnic groups. This is not to say that the Ciceronians—or organized criminals—were unwitting scapegoats or that their actions were the figment of other people's overactive imaginations. The racism and violence of Cicero, like the whorehouses and gambling dens of Cermak Boulevard, were problems that required attention. Organized crime, however, was a real, if overemphasized, aspect of postwar culture. Between 1915 and 1940, the percentage of the foreign born within the total white population of the United States fell from 22.7 to 9.7 percent. In 1941, Courtlandt Van Vechten argued that the statistics on the criminality of the foreign born belied the assumption that immigrants were prone to crime. Van Vechten examined Census Bureau figures as well as those of the National Resources Committee and found that they showed "a commitment rate of 11 [prisoners] per 10,000 for native-born white males over 15 and only 5 per 10,000 for foreign-born white males over 15. The native rate is two and a fifth times as great as the foreign rate." Similarly, data from the state of New Jersey resembled the national pattern when it reported that the percentage of "foreign-born (white)" prisoners fell from 42.7 to 6.3 percent between 1910 and 1950.[17] Despite these disproportionately low figures, immigrants occupied a position of over-visibility in the press and in public policy debates.

The real threat of organized crime lay not in the sensationalized portrayals of vice-riddled underworlds but in the easy explanations it provided for the social and economic rifts that gave rise to violence, racism, labor unrest, and other problems. By focusing on a small cabal of foreign-born criminals, federal, state, and local law enforcement agencies, along with criminologists, the mass media, citizens' crime committees, chambers of commerce, and others, thwarted calls for ambitious solutions to these problems.[18]

Crime and the Middle-Class Ideal

The Cicero rioting displayed competing definitions of criminality that centered on the middle class itself, like the "enemies within" that Robert Kennedy would describe at the end of the decade. The greatest menace could be found even in those suburbs that had become virtual synonyms for the "American way of life." Turning a rather mundane story into a national crisis, the *Christian Science Monitor* warned its readers in 1955 of an "epidemic" of shoplifting "by young middle class wives and mothers, most of them college graduates with average family incomes of $8,000 a year."[19] The story clearly aimed to demonstrate that the virus of crime had infected even the central symbol of domestic containment. No longer confined to the urban underworld, criminality now posed a threat even to the idealized suburban middle class. Americans have long linked crime with the foreign born, an association that persists in contemporary politics and culture. In fact, the word "illegal" is now a persistent prefix for the word "immigrant." But this pattern should not obscure the historical and political particularities of immigrant crime during the 1950s. Consider how the image of Al Capone changed from his 1920s heyday to his depiction in postwar popular culture. His early public persona paints Capone as a twisted version of the American success story, an underworld equivalent of the Horatio Alger hero. The media focused on his charitable acts as much as his violence. Even his machine guns were turned harmlessly into "Chicago typewriters." Hollywood stand-ins like *Scarface*'s Tony Camonte (1932) and *Public Enemy*'s Tom Powers (1931) embodied the rise of working-class ethnic outsiders as a perverse reflection of urban success. As Powers (James Cagney) makes his way up the ladder of the criminal underworld, he enters the circle of the city's elite, albeit as a provider of illicit alcohol. Camonte (Paul Muni) rises to power under similar circumstances—amid *Scarface*'s police chases, shoot-outs, and moral indignation—as an American dreamer who refuses to emulate the working-class drudgery of his immigrant mother.

By the 1950s, with its ambivalence over the increasing corporatization of American life, Capone could no longer be seen as personifying the myth of the "Self-Made Man"—the subtitle of a 1930 Capone biography. Frank "The Enforcer" Nitti and Jake "Greasy Thumb" Guzik, the fictionalized public enemies of *The Untouchables*, served to draw parallels between gangsters and corrupt (or allegedly corrupt) politicians, union officials, and corporate executives. Unlike the "self-made men" of the Prohibition era, these were the "organization men" so celebrated and vilified at the time. These postwar gangsters were in fact the ultimate organization men. Racketeering, drug smuggling, prostitution, gambling, and the other crimes targeted by police and investigative agencies were transformed from the work of "mobs" to "organized" crime. Among the most visible targets of suspicion were Frank Costello, Johnny Dio, Tony Provenzano, Jimmy Hoffa, Tommy D'Alesandro Jr., William O'Dwyer, and countless others. Costello owned a lucrative real estate company, D'Alesandro was the mayor of Baltimore, Hoffa the president of the largest labor union in the country, O'Dwyer the U.S. ambassador to Mexico. Their mainstream success placed them in contrast to earlier incarnations of the type who provided illicit luxuries to the urban elite while paying politicians and police to look the other way.[20]

Critics both inside and outside the universities offered broad damnations of the corporatization of American life. Many observers saw the decline from "rugged individuals" to bureaucratic drones as threatening traditional (albeit stereotypical) masculine roles. These "white-collar" men, wrote C. Wright Mills, "are cogs in a business machinery that has routinized greed and made aggression an impersonal principle of organization." Others, including David Riesman and William H. Whyte, also documented the trend and offered warnings to men who worked in large organizations. Riesman, who derisively called white-collar workers "other-directed," thought it unfortunate that conformity was seen as virtuous by the culture at large: "Modern popular culture stresses the dangers of aloneness and, by contrast, the virtues of group mindedness." Similarly, the sociologist E. Franklin Frazier argued that middle-class African Americans were wrong to try to make themselves over "in the image of the white man." In this attempt at conformity, "the black bourgeoisie exhibits most strikingly the inferiority complex of those who would escape their racial identification." Robert Lindner went so far as to call the conformist male "a psychopath," and the criminologist Edwin Sutherland pointed to the newly dubbed "white-collar crime" as evidence that privileging economic gain regardless of the means of obtaining it inherently tainted the middle-class ideal. Within this context, gangsters were no aberration. The quest for status via conformity to a white middle-class male standard was evidence of a sick—even criminal—society.[21]

Debates over the value of conformity raised even larger questions about the continued presence of class, racial, ethnic, and gender cleavages. At best, conformity masked rather than eliminated inequalities arising from the nation's diversity. As David Colburn and George Pozzetta argue, the assertion of conformity "blurred the reality of an America that still retained deep racial and ethnic fault lines and of social movements that sought much more than individual access."[22] Some, however, believed that conformity would provide the means to end exploitation and oppression. The conservative critic Norman Podhoretz blamed individual "non-conformists" for their own oppression: "There was great beauty, profound significance in a man's struggle to achieve freedom *through* submission to conditions. . . . The trick, then, was to stop carping at life like a petulant adolescent and to get down to the business of adult living as quickly as possible [and strike the] perfect attitude of the civilized adult: poised, sober, judicious, prudent." Liberal defenders of conformity, including Daniel Bell, Edward Shils, and Seymour Martin Lipset, among others, celebrated a society able to absorb all comers into a consensual middle class.[23] Always the exception, C. Wright Mills argued in *The Power Elite* that a docile, conforming middle class clearly benefited a ruling class interested in a stable workforce and continuous profits. But most of those searching for someone to blame for the decade's conformity looked to outsiders. Some even thought that conformity represented the influence of communism on an idealized "Americanism." As a *Look* magazine article argued in 1958, the new conformist male had "forgotten how to say the word 'I.' He had lost his individuality. In the free and democratic United States of America, he had been subtly rooked of a heritage that Communist countries deny by force." Others, as Barbara Ehrenreich points out, blamed an all-powerful "matriarchy" for forcing men into emasculating jobs so that women could control the economy.[24]

The focus on crime and criminals complemented and altered this criticism of conformity. For example, reading about or viewing sensationalized acts of violence could provide an outlet for vicarious rebellion without threatening the mortgage payment. This function might explain the continued presence of Mickey Spillane's Mike Hammer novels on best-seller lists. Organized crime, however, occupied a unique place in the conformity debates. Criticizing the conformity of a criminal gang could highlight misgivings about one's own compromises. It was more comfortable to ignore larger patterns of housing segregation while depicting Cicero's working-class rioters as "dupes" or "puppets of the powerful forces of organized crime, political corruption, and the greed of real estate manipulators."[25] So long

as wider suspicions of "organization men" were projected onto organized criminals, anxieties about conformity in general threatened few psychological or material consequences.

Organized criminals, corrupt labor union leaders, and even the rioters of Cicero
were portrayed as consummate "organization men" who put the interests of the
group above any ambitions for personal power. Following this reasoning, some
scholars interpreted the criminal activities of gangsters as no different from white-
collar occupations. That they had entered organized crime not from the ranks of
the corporate bureaucracy but from working-class immigrant neighborhoods like
Cicero or from the rank-and-file labor movement presented a complex challenge
to the traditional dominance of middle- and upper-class WASPs. As in the Prohibition era, the presence of organized crime said as much about the demand for
illicit goods and services among otherwise law-abiding citizens as about the criminals themselves. In addition, the organizations providing the goods and services
often accepted the increasing corporatization of U.S. life and adapted mainstream
practices and hierarchies to the contingencies of an underground economy. Thus
in most cases it would have been disingenuous to criticize either the product
offered or the corporate means of production and distribution. To rationalize this
contradiction, critics of organized crime and racketeering focused not on what the
gangsters were doing but on "the element" doing it. The mass media joined government bodies not only in condemning certain behaviors but also in associating
those behaviors with particular ethnic and class positions, specifically white
working-class ethnic men.

Their calls for public action put into sharp focus the place of organized crime
in the debates over the desirability of conformity. Public officials and commentators supported conformity in general but asked their listeners, readers, and con-
stituents to consider the meaning of conformity for groups making their way into
the mainstream. During a speech before the associates of the FBI National Academy, FBI director J. Edgar Hoover derided the attention given Benjamin "Bugsy"
Siegel and "his criminal scum" just after Siegel's 1947 murder: "The glamour that
surrounded his life in all its vile implications was shockingly disgusting. Siegel was
a symbol. He fronted for more sinister and despicable characters—the 'untouchables' who hire mercenaries to do their dirty work. I have no doubt of law enforcement's ability to cope with such characters, but I know that law enforcement
is shocked by public indifference. Its fullest measure of protection cannot be given
until every citizen not only recognizes his duty but has the courage to discharge
his duty."[26] The representation of gangsters as "sinister and despicable characters"
was also a call to action. Gangsters were not merely a potential threat to lives and
wallets; unlike common thieves, they demanded vigilance from all citizens. Calling

Bugsy Siegel a "symbol" revealed that he stood in for larger problems of crime and justice.

Symbols, however, could conceal the actions of the criminal justice system at the same time that they revealed changing conceptions of citizenship. The symbolism of Siegel and other white ethnic gangsters did not result in higher conviction rates for white ethnic criminals. Outside the glare of publicity, police officers and prosecutors turned their attention to African Americans. In Michigan, where African Americans constituted 7 percent of the general population in 1950, 40 percent of the prison population was African American. Nationally, African American men accounted for 25 percent of all arrests in 1952 but approximately 5.5 percent of the U.S. population. Prominent scholars began to recognize that the definition of what constituted a crime had clear ties to a racial caste system. Gunnar Myrdal showed that African Americans routinely received longer sentences than whites convicted of the same crimes, were more often denied parole, and were rarely represented on police forces. Another observer noted that "inspection of southern crime statistics shows relatively few offenses booked under 'violation of segregation laws,' but the writer is convinced, from years of observation and from illustrative cases obtained from Negro acquaintances, that in the South such cases considerably swell the number of Negro offenses booked under 'creating a disturbance on a public vehicle,' 'resisting arrest,' 'assault,' 'felonious assault,' 'manslaughter,' and 'murder.' "[27]

Thus, while the mass media and politicians turned white ethnic criminals into symbols, it was African Americans who bore the brunt of increased surveillance and incarceration. To say that organized crime is best understood on the level of symbolism is not to say that Bugsy Siegel, Al Capone, and Lucky Luciano were not real. Rather, it is to say that their significance transcended the actual crimes they committed and shaped how Americans saw—and did not see—crime.

3

"CRUISING THE URBAN INFERNO":
Professional and Popular Views
of Organized Crime

"I do have an affection for the bad boys," revealed Croswell Bowen in his 1954 true crime book *They Went Wrong*. The bad boys he wrote of included "two murderers, a reformed convict, a thief, a violent policeman, and an American fascist." To right what he called their "weird ways," Bowen proposed channeling boys into gangs "with constructive purposes." He used his own "gang," Yale's exclusive Society of Skull and Bones, as a model, although he didn't make clear how street gangs with equally colorful names like the Amboy Dukes, the High Hats, or the Spanish Campians would go about getting the money to acquire what has been described as a tomblike structure with a gymnasium and a baronial dining hall, a summer camp in the Thousand Islands, and senior members including presidents, governors, and publishers. While the details of his amateur criminology needed fleshing out, Bowen did clarify one thing: although he came from a privileged background, he was deeply attracted to and identified with criminals.[1]

During the 1950s, as at other times, observers differentiated crimes by type and seriousness. White-collar crimes, violent crimes, property crimes, organized crimes: scholars applied a wide variety of assumptions and methods to studying them all. Some pointed to biological predisposition, others to poverty and environment, still others to a culture that valorized greed, and some to the Cold War itself, claiming that people who anticipated nuclear disaster could not be expected to act responsibly. Despite this dissension, most agreed that crime was a more serious problem than ever before, particularly in cities. Contrary to widespread fears that crime was considerably worse than at any other time in U.S. history, however, national rates of crime and incarceration rose only slowly throughout the 1950s. According to the Uniform Crime Reports, 1,686,690 major crimes were reported in 1948. There were fluctuations over the intervening years, but by 1959 the figure had dropped to 1,630,430. Politicians and commentators nevertheless claimed an upsurge in crime which local, state, and federal authorities were un-equipped to handle. Indeed, during the first six months of 1952, New York City newspapers reported what looked like a crime wave: 331 murders, 507 rapes, 4,630 stickups, 4,017 felonious assaults, 22,005 burglaries, 13,649 cases of grand larceny (over $100), 6,151 stolen cars, 1,792 narcotics complaints, and 2,222 other felonies.[2]

Criminologists who sought to understand the acts behind the figures most often employed socio-structural explanations. In doing so, they went far in dismantling older biological, or positivist, explanations that looked to the human body for the causes of crime. Despite the scholarly change of faith, popular "true crime" texts like Bowen's had a greater impact on social policy because of their ability to incorporate new critiques while retaining the old positivist assumptions about criminal causation. At the same time that readers could shake their fists in anger, they could also share Croswell Bowen's affection for bad boys by joining him and other popular writers on a tour of the voluptuous extremes of vice that existed far from their living rooms or commuter trains.

In this chapter I look closely at the rejection of positivist distinctions by crim-inologists and at the reassertion of dualistic notions of honesty and dishonesty within popular culture and the criminal justice system during the 1950s. As crim-inologists sought complex explanations for the social, political, and economic in-equalities that shaped both criminal behavior and the perspectives of the society at large, many popular crime writers and crime fighters, often in direct opposition to these scholars and professionals, pointed to moral or physical failings that demanded immediate and harsh penalties. The bad boys had their own specific social origins, but to the writers of tawdry exposés of urban depravity they served as the antithesis of the bureaucratized white middle-class male of the postwar years. Through reading books, comics, and newspapers and watching television, true crime consumers could denounce the illicit pleasures of gambling, boozing, and fraternizing with criminals while indulging an ongoing fascination with such behavior. This contradiction served to normalize certain practices (Ivy League male rituals or heterosexual marriage, for example) while pathologizing others (male gang rituals or sexual promiscuity). And it dramatized moral and legal conflicts while allowing people to avoid any discussion of the conditions that actually led to crime. At the same time that the public enjoyed watching and reading about criminal deviance, they were assured that it was the deviance of poor people—particularly the foreign born and African Americans—from cultural standards of appropriate behavior that created crime.

Gazing on Other People's Reality

The nineteenth-century Italian criminologist Cesare Lombroso theorized that crime was evidence of "an atavism, or the survival of 'primitive' traits in individuals, particularly those of the female and nonwhite races." Twentieth-century criminologists, inheritors of this tradition, struggled with the role of the body in determining the propensity to crime and the type of crime committed. Some, like Earnest Hooton and William Sheldon, conducted broad surveys of criminals and concluded that the only way to understand behavior was to evaluate body type, psychiatric type, and temperament. Clarence Jeffery better represented the field's movement away from Lombrosian criminology when he called for studies describing "the conditions under which behavior comes to be defined as criminal, and how legal norms intersect and are integrated with the norms of other institutional structures."[3] This focus on the body—called "constitutional" criminology by those in the field—persisted in spite of the critiques, though these "critical" positions represented the culmination of more than fifty years of struggle against Lombroso's dominance.

During the 1940s and 1950s, some criminologists argued that criminal behavior could be correlated directly with physical characteristics. Hooton, the infamous Harvard criminologist, epitomized for many the failings of the biological position. In his 1940 manifesto, *Crime and the Man*, Hooton argued that "tall, thin men tend to murder and to rob; tall, heavy men to kill and to commit forgery and fraud; undersize, thin men to steal and burglarize; short, heavy men to assault, to rape, and to commit other sex crimes, whereas men of mediocre body build tend to break the law without obvious discrimination or preference." His ideas did not necessarily imply racial or regional differences. Each ethnic and racial group, after all, contains a wide variety of body shapes. But Hooton took pains to make clear in his dismissal of social forces as "the universal alibi" explaining why "New Americans" were predisposed to criminality: "It is not inequality of opportunity, but inferior capacity for grasping environmental opportunity which stigmatizes the anti-social New American."[4]

Hooton's rejection of social factors ultimately brought about his fall from grace within criminological circles, even among those who subscribed to some constitutional criminological principles. Replacing the biological determinists in the field of constitutional criminology, psychologists gained adherents both within the growing criminal justice system and in universities throughout the postwar period. In his overview of "psychological criminology" at the Second International Congress of Criminology at the Sorbonne in 1950, Walter Bromberg argued that the growth and acceptance of psychiatric approaches to crime had occurred during and immediately after World War II, when military psychiatrists came across Allied soldiers who had committed crimes under the extraordinary pressure of battle as well as "war criminals" among opposition forces. Others considered the origin of the psychological paradigm an outcome of World War I. In any case, researchers increasingly accepted "the wider social meaning of aggression . . . as a personal and mass experience, both directly or displaced symbolically in neurotic illnesses."[5]

By the early 1950s, clinical psychiatrists were a mainstay in the courts of major urban centers, including New York, Chicago, Baltimore, Detroit, Cleveland, and Pittsburgh. They provided opinions on the mental health of the accused and sometimes made recommendations for "disposition, probation, supervision, and psychiatric treatment." Each case before the New York City criminal court received the attention of a psychiatrist. In addition, staff from private and university clinics in other locations participated in evaluating the accused and recommending treatment. Yet considerable disagreement persisted over how psychological profiling might shape new responses to crime and punishment. In 1952 the chair of the recently founded Association for Psychiatric Treatment of Offenders, Melitta Schmideberg, affirmed traditional methods of penology, while other researchers recommended lobotomy for sexual predators, hypnotherapy for psychopaths, and psychoanalysis for all criminals, although most in this young field urged further research in all these areas.[6]

The shift from biology to psychology occurred within a climate of growing hostility toward all constitutional criminology. This critique found an articulate spokesperson in Edwin Sutherland, the most prominent American criminologist of the first half of the twentieth century. Sutherland, in a series of scathing critiques of positivist criminology, insisted that crime was a social construct. Criminals conformed to a set of expectations, albeit ones outlawed by those in power. By pointing to body or psychological type as the determining factor in criminality, Sutherland argued, constitutional criminologists ignored the fact that laws differ from location to location. Sutherland wondered how Hooton "reach[ed] the conclusion that eyes of one color are superior to eyes of another color, or that one stature is superior to another." These decisions reflected social and aesthetic values, not inherent inferiority or superiority. Echoing Lombroso's atavisms and stigmata, Hooton and Sheldon associated certain physical appearances with primitivism and childishness, but without explaining why they favored some characteristics and denounced others. Using descriptions and solutions better suited to the barnyard than the criminal justice system, Sheldon used the terms "thoroughbredness" and "mongrel" to refer to superior and inferior body types, concluding with a call for selective breeding to fight crime. According to Sutherland, criminologists ought to scrutinize and reject these class- and race-biased assumptions in order to reach more accurate conclusions and solutions to the problem of crime and punishment. He saw definitions of crime and the acts they described as embedded in a social process that sanctioned some behavior while outlawing other behavior. Rather than looking to the body of the offender, he urged, criminologists must look to laws and community norms.[7]

Instead of being viewed as physical or psychological deviants, criminals were increasingly being seen as able students of illicit lessons. Like all students, criminals learned their behavior under specific social conditions. Thus, some theorists maintained, criminal behavior did not deviate from a set of socially accepted practices. To the contrary, it conformed to a set of practices that sanctioned the breaking of laws. This concept of socialization was an important addition to the field of criminological thinking, which had been dominated in the United States by scholars busy chronicling the bumps, body shapes, atavisms, and racial characteristics that supposedly predicted a propensity to crime. Sutherland's death in 1950 did not diminish the impact of his ideas on criminologists. Many academic articles and popular textbooks for the new professionals accepted his theory of "differential association" and applied revised versions of his thesis that "a person becomes delinquent because of an excess of definitions favorable to violation of law over definitions unfavorable to violation of law. When persons become criminal they do so because of contacts with criminal patterns and also because of isolation from anti-criminal patterns."[8] Throughout most of his life, Sutherland posited that criminals conform to a countercultural value system in a process identical to that which makes other people conform to the dominant values. His last major work, *White Collar Crime*, powerfully extended this argument to business practices. He concluded that "white collar crime has its genesis in the same general process as other criminal behavior, namely differential association."[9] Like muggers and drug dealers, thieves in white collars learn their behavior from one another in conformity to an unscrupulous value system.

Sutherland's group theories of crime not only transformed how many people thought about criminals but also blurred the line between illegal and legal business practices. Sutherland's fieldwork led to the conclusion that, rather than being aberrations in an otherwise honest industry, "many types of violations of law are industry-wide in the sense that practically all firms in the industry violate the law." He quoted a used-car salesman who summarized his experience and that of his peers: "They said they would starve if they were rigidly honest." Similarly, advertisers readily acknowledged the steady stream of false advertisements issued by department stores. Instead of governmental outrage toward white-collar criminals, Sutherland found "fraternization between the two forces," as in the Federal Trade Commission's lack of oversight of existing truth-in-advertising laws.[10] Of course, information about unscrupulous used-car salesmen or misleading advertisements were far from revelations; locating this behavior within the realm of differential association, however, represented the culmination of an important critique of Western criminology. Positivists saw crime as a problem of psychopathic personalities or physical inferiority, and sociologists blamed poverty or social disorganization. Sutherland, by contrast, urged scholars to ask why the legal system sanctioned corporate theft while criminalizing petty theft.

Although Sutherland argued that "crimes of business are organized crimes," he did not apply his theory to what most people understood as organized crime: the "mobs" that provided prostitution, alcohol, drugs, gambling, and violence for a fee. He focused exclusively on the use of illegal means to sell legal products and services. Others, however, extended his ideas to organizations that used legal means to sell illegal products and services. Using Sutherland's methods, Alfred R. Lindesmith argued that "the underworld serves to meet demands for goods and services which are defined as illegitimate, but for which there is nevertheless a strong demand from respectable people. Prostitution, gambling, and liquor during prohibition are examples. It is, therefore, a mistake to regard the underworld as a separate or detached organization; it is rather an integral part of our total culture. It is implicit in our economic, political, legal, and social organization." Some still saw crime—particularly predatory crime—as evidence of individual or collective pathology. But even violent crimes were increasingly defined as corporate; a means to make money, a product to be marketed, complete with employees and customers—and victims. In terms of both what it tolerated and what it criminalized, society was "organized for crime." Sutherland's and Lindesmith's ideas later came to dominate criminological circles, but during the 1950s they marked a radical departure from the conventional assumptions of criminology and the justice system.[11]

The view of crime as business and business as crime posed a substantial threat to resilient notions of crime as the product of pathology, particularly among the working class, people of color and immigrants. One criminologist saw in this shift a potential for changing the way society understood and fought crime: "The significance of white collar crime for criminological theory can be simply stated: it is logically forcing a revision of many theories of causation." To those who followed Sutherland, the most widely accepted measure of crime, the FBI's Uniform Crime Reports, could no longer be trusted, as it focused only on criminals arrested by police departments, neglecting offenders caught by government agencies that regulated white-collar crime. Sutherland's departure from conventional wisdom undermined reports of "crime waves" and questioned the assumption that crimes committed by poor people were more significant than those of the professional class. He wrote: "The average loss per burglary is less than one hundred dollars, a burglary which yields as much as fifty thousand dollars is exceedingly rare, and a million dollar burglary is practically unknown. On the other hand, there may be several million dollar embezzlements reported in one year. Embezzlements, however, are peccadilloes compared with the large-scale crimes committed by corporations, investment trusts, and public utility holding companies; reports of fifty million dollar losses from such criminal behavior are by no means uncommon."[12] The old sources, methods, and conclusions were unreliable indicators of the causes and costs of crime.

During the 1950s, research on juvenile delinquency, which had earlier been blamed on the innate inferiority of certain races and classes, joined in the shift away from positivism. Studies of juvenile delinquents made reference to class origins in order to explain criminal tendencies, downplaying racial and ethnic differences. For example, Davis and Havighurst found "that middle class families tend to rear their children more rigidly than do lower-class families and that differences in socio-economic status are more important in rearing than those of race," and that "middle-class Negro mothers tend to approximate the tightness of control of white middle-class mothers as opposed to the permissiveness of the lower socio-economic group mothers in both races." Poverty rather than race became the naturalized marker of potential criminality.[13]

Others agreed with the New York Labor Youth League, a communist front organization, which blamed juvenile delinquency on the potential for nuclear war: "The eager-eyed, fresh-faced, gentle-spoken child of a generation ago has changed (if, indeed, he was not always an idealization). But so has the world around him and the home in which he lives. Thousands of pupils are less capable of being interested in what they are doing in school. And just as the boys know they face some Army service, all the children are at least dimly aware that their adults have now perfected weapons that can blow every school in the world to bits." Despite arguments about class difference and the potential for a nuclear holocaust, Puerto Rican migrants to New York and African Americans in many cities remained the focus of some criminologists. But other groundbreaking studies, most notably Albert Cohen's *Delinquent Boys: The Culture of the Gang*, argued that delinquency was a form of masculine protest in a world increasingly devoid of masculine proving grounds—the same argument C. Wright Mills had made about white-collar fathers. To still others, the causes of working-class crime came down to absent fathers and dominant mothers, a situation that created a "compulsive reaction-formation" resulting in deviant masculinities.[14]

These arguments constituted an important critique of positivism but could still easily be seen as providing the basis for xenophobic, racist, and misogynist theories about the causes of crime. In fact, these so-called "conflict models" of criminal etiology can be viewed as the forerunners of "culture of poverty" arguments that blame the poor for their own poverty. But at the time this was something new. Nineteenth- and early twentieth-century criminology had focused on the supposedly innate biological inferiority of African Americans and immigrants. The conflict theorists hoped to convince global policy makers that any propensity to crime among these groups resulted from social conditions such as poverty, over-crowding, and cultural dislocation.

Regardless of the intent of conflict theorists, the idea of "group factors" as causes of crime was ultimately co-opted by policy makers and crime fighters hoping to loosen deportation protections and tighten immigration restrictions. Despite this sustained criticism of positivist methodologies and conclusions, the rise of the sociological model did not erase the blame placed on particular groups of people for the problem of crime; the basic premise that the source of criminal behavior lay in the body was not rejected outright. As one criminologist argued, "Heredity determines what the organism can do while environment determines what it does do."[15]

A Landscape of "Voluptuous Extremes"

In a 1956 speech, FBI director J. Edgar Hoover remarked that "textbooks are filled with theories on crime causation . . . but the real cause can be stated in simple terms: crimes are committed by those who lack a sense of moral responsibility. For the most part, they commit crime knowingly and with deliberate intent." Hoover's reliance on morality kept him free to leave unquestioned the social and economic inequality that most criminologists saw as primary etiologic factors. Instead, he focused on personal and parental moral weakness, much as he explained the other "twin enemy of freedom," communism: "Let us never forget that strength and good character, like charity, begin at home. So long as the American home is nurtured by the spirit of our Father in Heaven and is a center of learning and living, America will remain secure."[16] In contrast to the wide acceptance of Sutherland's ideas in university settings, political and popular treatment of organized criminals resisted the shift away from theories of innate inferiority. By focusing on the explanatory power of foreign origin and working-class roots, crime fighters and popular writers could retain the prejudices of racial determinism while mining modern criminal cartels for new material.

On the whole, popular crime stories were critical of the criminal justice system and university criminologists, particularly when it came to issues of penology. Where criminal psychologists advocated tests of sanity, newspapers greeted such suggestions with suspicion. Where sociologists urged the criminal justice system to take into account structural issues such as poverty and alternative peer groups, the mass media saw only wrong choices by wicked people. Where penologists urged rehabilitation, parole, and indeterminate sentencing, the media celebrated long, fixed, and harsh prison sentences. Even news stories that avoided sensationalism described the what and the who while avoiding the question of why.[17] And sensationalism was not easy to avoid. As one criminologist acknowledged, "Even with the most idealistic leadership, no paper can exist without either a subsidy or readers and advertisers."[18] News outlets that sought to cover current events objectively, such as the *New York Times* and the *Christian Science Monitor*, could not ignore the appeal of crime stories, long a staple of the derisively named "yellow journalism" People disliked crime, but they certainly liked reading, listening to, and watching crime stories.

Crime stories appeared in newspapers as features, gossip columns, serialized book excerpts, and hard news items. They were a staple of TV talk shows and series; Desilu Productions' popular series *The Untouchables*, based on the exploits of Eliot Ness and Al Capone in Prohibition-era Chicago, was one well-known example, as was the radio-turned-television drama *Dragnet*. "True crime" was featured in comic books, magazines, and popular nonfiction. Perhaps best known is Bernarr Macfaddan's *True Detective*. Founded in 1924, *True Detective* had a circulation of over 450,000 by 1953. Lev Gleason's seven comic book titles included the popular *Crime Does Not Pay* and *Crime and Punishment*. Gleason reported a total circulation of 2,354,027 in 1953. The Best Detective Group included *Crime, Best True Fact Detective, True Crime Cases,* and *True Cases of Women in Crime*, with a circulation of over 1 million issues. Hillman's *Real Clue Crime Stories* presented the "inside truth about crime!!" in each issue. Marvel Comics' "Blue Unit," which included both science fiction and true crime titles, had a circulation of 4.8 million. Furthermore, nonfiction works such as *Murder, Inc., The Luciano Story, The Big Bankroll: The Life and Times of Arnold Rothstein, Underworld U.S.A.,* and Nathan Leopold's *Life Plus 99 Years* topped best-seller charts throughout the decade, and some appeared in serialized form in *Reader's Digest*. But Jack Lait and Lee Mortimer's *Confidential* series topped them all in circulation and sensationalism. Impressively, J. Edgar Hoover's anticommunist screed *Masters of Deceit* was the fourth-biggest-selling nonfiction book of 1958, selling well over 2 million copies in hardback and paperback combined. Even Hoover's sales, however, were dwarfed by Lait and Mortimer's series, which reached over 4 million by 1963.[19]

Lait and Mortimer transformed many of the contentious issues of the day—racial and gender stratification, communism, and immigration, to name a few—into a mass conspiratorial vision of the impending downfall of Anglo-Saxon dominance over American political, social, and economic life. Both men worked at William Randolph Hearst's *New York Mirror*, Jack Lait as the infamous McCarthyite editor of the newspaper, Mortimer as the entertainment editor. In their eyes, criminals joined communists, gays and lesbians, African American men and women, all women, and the foreign born in an underworld conspiracy that threatened the righteousness of U.S. institutions. At the same time, however, Lait and Mortimer saw all but communists as objects of attraction, free from the moral restraints of bourgeois sexuality and propriety. These authors combined outrage about and fascination with vice districts, often providing phone numbers, prices, and locations for the houses of prostitution, gambling halls, and drug dealers they condemned. Despite their ambivalence, Lait and Mortimer joined the wider field of crime writers in creating a binary between the innocent and the guilty in an attempt to present their readers with a vision of community activism that purged all dissent and difference. They described all their targets as predators in league with an international cartel of organized criminals. Their publications called for the participation of readers in passing judgment not only on crime but also on American ideological, racial, and sexual diversity.[20]

The *Confidential* series portrayed American culture and capitalism as innocent and normative while pathologizing dissenters, as Virginia Carmichael has written of Cold War rhetoric in a pervasive "explanatory narrative that achieved the status of perfecting myth." Their solution to the problem of crime did not resemble that of the criminologists who sought to resolve issues of social and economic inequality. This "perfecting myth" called for demonizing the threat of communist infiltration in mass media and political contexts. In addition to targeting communists and "fellow travelers," Cold Warriors tarred a wide variety of behavioral "imperfections" with the "politics of demonization."[21] But true crime texts reveal a more complicated pattern than is usually acknowledged by students of anticommunism. The avalanche of texts that glorified both the forces of law and order and organized crime suggests that while the good guys won in the end, the life of an outlaw held substantial attraction. In *Chicago Confidential* (1950), Lait and Mortimer provided directions to sources of forbidden pleasure even while denouncing their presence. They scorned the goings-on at Orchestra Hall, where "every concert will find a blonde bobbed head snuggled on a manly black shoulder," but also reported that "at the Flamingo, on West Madison Street, our waitress said, 'Do you wants Toots to come out?' Toots was a talented red-headed grinder who had just finished her number." They let their readers know that they could find marijuana growing wild along the city's drainage canal system and on a "35-acre trace at Lemont."[22] While Lait and Mortimer envisioned a Cold War America that would purge all dissent, vice, and deviance, the cities they described revealed a truth far more interesting than any consensus.

In their efforts to eliminate vice, the authors relied on racist assumptions about the moral integrity of white people and the criminality of racial and ethnic minorities. Many popular books and magazines in the early 1950s represented white people as honest (though corruptible) and people of color and the foreign born as corrupt (though redeemable). To criminologists, deviance was more than a product of individual pathology; it was a socio-structural phenomenon that revealed power relations dividing along racial, ethnic, and class lines. In contrast, true crime literature consistently framed criminals as physical and ideological outsiders while relying on assumptions about the inherent morality of whites. For example, *Chicago Confidential* defines Nordic immigrants as "indistinguishable" from native-born whites and therefore irrelevant to a book on crime. In one passage we discover that determining what makes some aspects of city life "confidential" and others commonplace depends largely on racist assumptions: "Numerically, Swedes and other Scandinavians make up one of the largest segments of Chicago's population. They are important in every field of endeavor, have added immeasurably to the city's wealth and well-being. Their girls are entrancing. But they do not belong in a book of this nature, because they have provided little local color. The sections in which they live are indistinguishable from other neighborhoods. They are remarkably minor in crime, vice and gambling, and not important in politics."[23] So much for Chicago's Swedes. Lait and Mortimer wanted to capture the "voluptuous extremes" of 1950s Chicago, not the ordinary (that is, white, northern European, well-off) lives of Scandinavian Americans. Consequently, because they blended into Chicago's power structure, Swedish immigrants and their descendants did not figure prominently in *Confidential*. They became, in effect, the category that remained unmarked throughout the book: normal white folks. Their indistinguishable characteristics, however, made possible the distinguishing mark of pathology with which the rest of the work is obsessed.

Lait and Mortimer balance the self-exposure of their editorial process with claims of journalistic neutrality. In their chapter on "Bronzeville," Chicago's African American neighborhood, Lait and Mortimer defend their methods and conclusions:

> It is not the purpose here to impugn or condone. But those who knew these neighborhoods twenty years ago are appalled at the change. Filth and overcrowding, a general spirit of roughhouse, a superfluity of saloons and pool-halls and dance-halls, garbage in the streets and in the alleys, and the unmistakable odor of marijuana, are surface indications of the terrific transformation. When you venture beyond these you find dingy dens, depraved homosexual exhibitionism, lumber-camp licentiousness, drunkenness, dope and every sinister sign of virtually uncontrolled abandon.[24]

By denying that they were in fact making a judgment ("it is not the purpose here to impugn or condone"), Lait and Mortimer operated as if their gaze were neutral. This rhetorical process depended on determinations, as this passage indicates, of good and bad behavior. It is instructive to contrast Lait and Mortimer's assumptions with those of their contemporary, Bronzeville's own Gwendolyn Brooks. Brooks was well aware that the racial geography of Chicago coincided with the vice districts. She did not, however, portray the neighborhood's vice in such a way that judging behavior was also a judgment of naturalized pathology. In "The Sundays of Satin-Legs Smith," Brooks writes:

> People are so in need, in need of help.
> People want so much that they do not know. Below the tinkling trade of little coins

The gold impulse not possible to throw
Or spend. Promise piled over and betrayed.[25]

Rather than finding pathology, Brooks frankly acknowledges her protagonist's attraction to material goods that are otherwise out of reach. She does not ascribe this attraction to individual or racial pathology, however, but blames it on historical and social "promise piled over and betrayed." To Brooks, Bronzeville is a community of comfortable tastes, sights, sounds, and secrets, not "dingy dens, depraved homosexual exhibitionism, lumber-camp licentiousness."

The danger that Lait and Mortimer observed reveals their desires and fears, their vision of propriety. Seeking to justify their judgments and deflect the accusations of racism they must have feared, they include descriptions of African Americans who conform to their vision of appropriate behavior, "the many thousands of respectable Negroes who not only take no part in such places and practices, but who have only a vague idea of their existence. We cannot stop with every paragraph to make such observations. This book is not intended to be all-inclusive and there is nothing 'confidential' about the fact that a majority of Americans are decent, or reasonably so, and we proceed with that premise."[26] Lait and Mortimer imagine the difference between decency and indecency as simultaneously fixed and permeable, depending on the ability of African Americans to conform to their own standards of heterosexuality, sobriety, and respectability. Thus, in their litany of pathologies, and their concession that "a majority of Americans are decent, or reasonably so," they drew the boundary between abnormal and normal while arguing that it was possible to transcend that boundary.

If the African American working class could transcend licentiousness via economic advancement, the white middle class could, by contrast, transgress, with the help of Lait and Mortimer, into the secret places in the heart of urban America. In order to counteract the explanation that social inequalities led to crime, the authors asked the readers of their Washington Confidential (1951) to "cup your ear and we'll let you into a little secret about these 'slums.'" In this most explicitly political book in the series, they took their readers into their confidence and revealed that the poor section of Washington was a fabrication of the "Reds and Pinks," and that Eleanor Roosevelt was one of the chief propagandists who exploited this "blot" on Washington: "This particular slum, always photographed, always on every sight-seeing itinerary, is only a couple of blocks long and is surrounded on all sides by presentable Negro homes. But this slum is permitted to remain behind the Capitol only so the lefties will have something to breast-beat over." Readers were privy to a secret: poverty was not nearly so bad as those arguing for economic justice would have them think. Furthermore, they could rest assured that their own standard of living had no bearing on what little poverty did exist. Those few examples of substandard housing could be chalked up to the pathological behavior of the residents: "Under Negro occupancy, some of the best dwellings in Washington, once residences of ambassadors, cabinet officers and the hated capitalists, now look like the slums the Fair Dealers decry."[27]

Speaking confidentially, Lait and Mortimer offered their readers a way of understanding crime and poverty that reinforced their hopes for a smaller government that worked in conjunction with a rigid hierarchy delineated along lines of class, race, and gender. By emphasizing what came to be seen in the 1980s and 1990s as a "culture of poverty" rather than innate biological inferiority, Lait and Mortimer accepted arguments that inferior habits and attitudes unique to subcultural groups contributed to increased criminality. Others echoed these views. One study went so far as to argue that African Americans' "lack of self-respect, lack of self-confidence, a distaste for hard work, a habit of dependence upon white friends, lack of regard for the property of others, a feeling that 'the white folks owe us a living,' a distrust of the white man's law, and a tendency to 'let tomorrow take care of itself' " produced "the incidence of social conditions which are associated with crime."[28]

Poor neighborhoods were small and self-generating in Lait and Mortimer's cultural geography, but their greatest danger lay in their role as a vice district where middle-class white men might temporarily transgress expectations of fidelity, sobriety, and frugality. Perhaps ingenuously facilitating this process, Lait and Mortimer provide prices (and locations) for the services of African American prostitutes—broken down by darkness of skin—as well as the location of gun and drug dealers, though the chroniclers of vice assumed "that most of our readers have an idea of the effects of habit-forming drugs." Their descriptions of "reefer parties with their dark, crowded rooms where the mixed sexes reach orgiastic stimulation" may have been more than voyeuristically attractive to some readers, who were urged to honor segregation for their own protection: "Before the Negro avalanche," their name for the great migration of southern African Americans, "whites and Negroes did business together. But that is past. Now it is dangerous and sometimes lethal for a white stranger to enter the section after dark and few venture there alone by the light of day. Rent-collectors usually demand police escort. Even respectable Negroes tremble if they are well-dressed or display valuables. Muggers draw no color lines. White women are unsafe there-abouts at all times, even if escorted." Readers hoping to "cruise the urban inferno" were invited, aroused, yet admonished by the text. The authors warned readers of the possibility of a mugging and told of white female minors lured by jazz musicians brandishing marijuana into having "unnatural sex relations."[29] While describing the pleasures of vice districts in detail, they warned that white people could be corrupted and victimized by vice, while African American migrants seemed inevitably to corrupt "decent" neighborhoods.

This argument was not a simple return to biological determinism. By asserting that the "majority of Americans were decent" and that "even respectable Negroes" were afraid of crime, Lait and Mortimer created gradations of normality and abnormality alongside largely rhetorical absolutes. Just as white people were corruptible, racial and ethnic minorities and the working class were redeemable. The figure of a well-dressed African American woman walking through a dangerous neighborhood and the recollection of that neighborhood before the "avalanche" served as evidence that it was possible for outsiders to elude the category of deviance reserved for them. So, while "normal" was clearly constructed as white, male, middle-class, heterosexual, and Nordic, the door to admission was held half open. Racial and ethnic distinctions thus functioned deceptively in Lait and Mortimer's true crime literature. They were not recognized as obstacles to material wealth, nor as inevitable routes to pathological behavior. Instead, the authors avowed that distribution of rank was a matter of individual merit rather than social hierarchy. In other words, they presented inequality as the result of fair competition rather than the natural outcome of biology. The reader was asked to recognize which side of the "voluptuous extremes" he or she was on, but at the same time was taken into the author's confidence and allowed to experience the thrill of the pathology.

Unofficial Reality behind the Facade of Bourgeois Life

Race and ethnicity served as markers of suspicion to readers and writers of this era's true crime literature. A reliance on obvious and visible markers of difference, however, could never tell the whole story. Like Cold War anticommunists, true crime writers made sure to tell their readers that appearances deceive. Seemingly legitimate businesspeople could be wrapped up with organized crime. Seemingly upright entertainers could be communists. Seemingly "normal" Americans could be suspicious outsiders, maintaining loyalty to a secret ethnic criminal organization. During the 1950s, the idea of a "front" pervaded anticommunist rhetoric in well-known arenas such as the House Un-American Activities Committee and popular fare like *The Manchurian Candidate*. What you see, perceptive viewers would learn, is not what you get. Beneath the surface of politics, entertainment, and business lurked alliances between communists and mafiosi that gained strength through secrecy. To some, an underground criminal organization posed a greater threat than communism or even the Soviet Union. Ed Reid, a reporter for the *Brooklyn Eagle*, assured his readers that corruption thrived on invisibility: "The treasury of the Mafia is apparently bottomless and the organization represents a greater threat to the United States than the Communist Party. We know in which direction to face where the communist threat is concerned. The Mafia is all around us and we are just beginning to get some idea of the extent of its machinations. A liaison of Mafiosi and Communists would result in complete chaos. Such an alliance is not beyond the powers of imagination." By linking two feared organizations with which his readers would have had little direct contact, Reid relied on dread of the unknown. To many purveyors of popular renderings of the Mafia, organized crime, like the Communist Party, relied on loyalty to a secret, foreign hierarchy; like the Communist Party, it relied on the appearances of legitimacy to spread its influence silently; and, like the Communist Party, it had the potential to compromise our freedom. In *U.S.A. Confidential* (1952), Lait and Mortimer defined the Mafia as a "secret blood-brotherhood with a strong centralized government and a disciplined membership."[30] But this blood-brothership operated using the same tools of political organizing as the Communist Party.

According to the *Confidential* series, a loosely related front organization known as "the Cartel" provided "many of the brains of the organization, such as mouthpieces, accountants and auditors, advisors and management front-men, such as chain hotel owners, distillers, bankers, etc. Virginia Hill, the message center, is a full stock-holder." This "stunt" of utilizing fronts like Hill, the former girlfriend of slain gangster Bugsy Siegel, Lait and Mortimer pointed out, was "also utilized by the Reds." The fronts "are prominent and respected Italians of whom the public hasn't the slightest suspicion, and they include leading bankers, contractors, politicians, judges and foreign-language newspaper publishers." J. Edgar Hoover similarly described communist "fellow travelers" and "fronts" as the link between legitimate and subversive political forces: "The value of fellow travelers and sympathizers lies in their alleged noncommunist affiliation. They are more valuable outside: as financial contributors, vocal mouthpieces, or contacts between Party officials and noncommunists." To Hoover, communist "fronts" posed a grave danger to U.S. society. Either by starting new organizations or infiltrating older organizations with party members, communists could deceive "do-gooders" who had no intention of joining the party. "In this way," Hoover wrote in *Masters of Deceit*, "the Party is able to influence thousands of non-communists, collect large sums of money, and reach the minds, pens, and tongues of many high-ranking and distinguished individuals." Because Communists knew that "they are not welcome," they simply found unsuspecting people to do their dirty work.[31]

Lait and Mortimer linked communists and the Mafia by claiming that the Mafia used prestigious Italian Americans, including entertainers, civic organizations, and fraternal clubs, as fronts for criminal enterprises. In addition, the appearance of personal legitimacy provided mafiosi a way to hide criminal activity. They named Frank Costello and Frank Sinatra as examples of these two kinds of "fronts."

Costello was born in southern Italy in the 1890s and emigrated to New York's East Harlem with his parents as a young boy. By the 1950s he was well known as the owner of slot machines and casinos in New York, New Orleans, and other locales. In the 1940s, Costello's ownership of slot machines in New York made him a target of Mayor Fiorello La Guardia's widely publicized campaign to rid the city of illegal gambling. In *New York Confidential*, Lait and Mortimer identified Costello as the New York manipulator for Lucky Luciano, "the mightiest of the syndicate personnel." In *U.S.A. Confidential* he was promoted to president of "Unione Siciliano of U.S.A.," the front organization for the international Mafia. But Costello's outward appearance, journalists warned, could never belie the fact that his wealth was accumulated from honest people's nickels and dimes dropped in slot machines. Upon his incarceration on a contempt of Congress charge, the *New York Post* declared: "Frank Costello's ruthless pursuit of riches and respectability which won him the shadowy throne of the underworld ends today in the stony grayness of a federal penitentiary. The Hell's Kitchen Machiavelli, whose dark powers became fearful legend, will be locked in a cell for only the second time in a career pockmarked with crime." The *Post* contrasted Costello's ill-gained economic and political power with the rewards of conventional propriety. No matter how much wealth he accumulated, Costello would never be able to lose his accent: "It was true his money had bought him judges and corrupted justice and plummeted him from small-time hoodlumism to silk-lined luxury. But it couldn't buy him what he wanted most—the kind of social acceptance a successful businessman takes for granted at the golf club."[32]

Costello exemplified the model of criminal behavior described in 1953 by Daniel Bell as an "American way of life." Bell hypothesized that ethnic criminals like Costello merely applied the principles of entrepreneurship to illicit markets. Once gangsters made their money, the goal shifted, according to Bell, to the "search for an entree—for oneself and one's ethnic group—into the ruling circles of the big city." Bell's "ladder" was reflected in the *Post*'s portrayal of crime as a quest for respectability, though this pursuit was depicted as a ruse: "Through it all he tried to conform to the social norm. He hired a press agent and a psychiatrist, lounged at Hot Springs, played a little golf, wore silk next to his skin and custom tailored suits. But it needled his pride because he was kept off the racetrack as 'an undesirable.'" His studious attempts to blend in, the *Post* writers argued, provided only a veneer of respectability over the true villain within. Rather than focusing on the norms that excluded him, the *Post* focused on Costello's awkward attempts to mimic those norms. In contrast to Bell's hope that the United States could absorb all comers—even former thieves—into a universalized, post-ideological middle class stood Lait and Mortimer's contention that "a thief is always a thief. These modern pirates could not go straight. As soon as they dip their sticky hands into something legitimate, it goes crooked."[33]

If Frank Costello exemplified for Lait and Mortimer and other crime writers the attempt by criminals to hide their true nature behind a mask of expensive clothes, speech lessons, and club memberships, Frank Sinatra more closely exemplified the anticommunist concept of the "front." Sinatra, who had once punched Mortimer in a Hollywood nightclub, never shed his image of having mob ties. Mafia-controlled nightclubs and unions made possible his early success, and many writers claimed that he paid off the favor throughout his career. Sinatra, like many other entertainers who gained fame and wealth, started out in a working-class immigrant enclave. At the turn of the century, according to Mortimer, "all Italians had to pay tribute, a tithe of their earnings, from the dollar-a-week of the corner bootblack to the five thousand a night of Enrico Caruso. Failure to pay meant the Black Hand letter, and continued failure, death. Now the Mafia is smoother. It 'owns' acts on a ten-per cent business deal. Frank Sinatra was discovered by Willie Moretti and is the pet of the Fischettis. He gave a gold cigarette case to Charlie Luciano, inscribed 'To my friend.'" Mortimer based his description of Sinatra's ties to New Jersey gangster Willie Moretti on the Federal Bureau of Narcotics' Sinatra file. Mortimer secured a place on the list of "friendly writers" privy to FBN surveillance information when Commissioner Harry Anslinger became confident that he would not contradict the bureau's approach to narcotics control. According to the FBN, Mortimer reported, "the crooner had been adopted by underworld big shots for the specific purpose of making his sponsors seem respectable, thereby furthering their business enterprises, which included, among others, the wholesale distribution of narcotics." This backhanded reference to the use of communist fronts was thus a double slur. The FBN report went on to state, wrote Mortimer, "that Frankie was by no means a rare case. Many well-known entertainment figures had been 'captured,' either with or without their knowledge, by the underworld, the Communists, or both. The Communists and the gangsters both have the same motive, acquiring respectability by association with prestige names. Frankie's contacts with both groups are numerous."[34]

Those who promoted the idea of "fronts" relied on ignorance to spur fear and suspicion. By linking communism and the Mafia, they found that each hated organization could be used to discredit the other. The Mafia was bad because it subverted U.S. organizations, just like the communists; the communists were bad because they subverted U.S. organizations, just like the Mafia. Just as Hoover could discredit as communist fronts "thousands of bleeding hearts, pseudo-liberals, sympathizers and dupes," Lait and Mortimer could question the loyalty and patriotism of people from poor Italian American neighborhoods. Frank Sinatra did not seem an isolated example to them. The authors described in similar terms virtually every Italian American in the public eye. Congressman Vito Marcantonio, for example, "was on intimate terms with Mafia hoodlums, accepted campaign contributions from them, associated with and fronted for their racketeers in New York and Washington, and welcomed them into his American Labor Party." Baltimore mayor Thomas D'Alesandro Jr. became the "Siciliano protector" of "madames, gambling dens, and dope-peddlers." Italian American politicians—

particularly leftist Italian American politicians—were fronts for or actual members of the Mafia. Ultimately, the entire political and corporate elite increasingly seemed to serve as a mere front for the Mafia. The nation "could be beholden to, not to say slaves of, swarthy, sinister men, many of them ex-convicts, who traffic in bodies of women, making and supplying dope-fiends, dealing in extortion, smuggling, bootlegging, hijacking, bribing and murdering in the principal cities and states of the union; and these hyenas were a controlling influence in nominations and elections; that they owned vast commercial and industrial enterprises, labor unions, even some newspapers, and that their pirate hands gripped the steering wheels of enormous financial fleets."[35]

Lait and Mortimer used the concept of Mafia fronts to discredit in particular those who advocated government-run anti-poverty programs. It was Marcantonio's radical political agenda as much as his Italian American origins that made him a target of Lait and Mortimer's vitriol. It was not just radicals they despised; liberals such as D'Alesandro also came under attack, along with government programs that aided the poor. Just as political conservatives intimated that the depression-era WPA proved communist infiltration of the U.S. government, Lait and Mortimer derided it as a "national shakedown" by racketeers and ward heelers, an outlet for the "contracting and concrete business" dominated by the underworld. As for Truman's anti-poverty Fair Deal, Lait and Mortimer wrote that in Mafia-controlled Kansas City, "nothing moves there, including Harry [Truman], without an OK" from the mob. If Lait and Mortimer were to be believed, the course of the country was being "hatched over 'dago red' wine" in Italian American neighborhoods in Kansas City, Chicago, New York, and Baltimore. "Black Hand threats, appeal to blood relationship and national pride," spread "through the pages of powerful Italian language newspapers," were but the latest manifestation of the "bossism" that had permeated immigrant neighborhoods in an earlier era.[36]

The authors admitted that their research technique amounted to little more than getting "information from cab drivers and those $5-an-hour chauffeurs. We take a person with vast knowledge and small imagination, we overtip atrociously, we give them our books and they think they're big shots." Not surprisingly, their books continually received scathing reviews and were the subject of numerous lawsuits. The *Chicago Tribune* reviewer thought that *Chicago Confidential* would make a good "party pastime: a game called 'Check the Inaccuracies.' Par is eight to the page." According to a *New York Times* reviewer, the book had "all the verisimilitude of a three dollar bill." The *New Republic* argued that Lait and Mortimer "have contributed more to the spread of Fascist ideas than any other writers in our history," comparing *U.S.A. Confidential* to the anti-Semitic writings in Gerald L. K. Smith's monthly *The Cross and the Flag*. Similarly, one reviewer of *Washington Confidential* remarked, "How the Nazis would have loved this book as proof of the decadence of democracy! The Kremlin will like it not less," drawing particular attention to the pattern of "race hatred" against Italian Americans, Jewish Americans, and African Americans.[37]

As sales increased, lawsuits began to stream in from politicians, businesspeople, labor unions, and others criticized by the authors. One bar sued a Washington, D.C., bookstore for selling *Washington Confidential*, which described it as a hangout for prostitutes. Maine's Republican senator Margaret Chase Smith sued for $1 million after *U.S.A. Confidential* called her "a lesson in why women should not be in politics." Dave Beck, executive vice president (and later the indicted and ousted president) of the Teamsters Union, sued the authors for $300,000 for calling him a front for "Italians in New York, Chicago, and Detroit" who controlled gambling and prostitution in Seattle through the Teamsters. The Neiman Marcus department store of Dallas and fifty-four of its employees sued for $7.4 million after the authors advised potential johns that "some Neiman models are call girls" but that the salesgirls charged much less. In San Francisco, Lait and Mortimer claimed, Sally Stanford could provide the "best [girls] for sale." She also sued the authors. Despite at least twelve lawsuits against the first four books in the series, only the Neiman Marcus suit resulted in a substantial payment, public retraction, or apology.[38]

By challenging the book on the level of fact, the lawsuits and bad reviews only contributed to the dangerous attraction of the *Confidential* series. Despite, or perhaps because of, these scathing denunciations, the books sold extraordinarily well. *U.S.A. Confidential* went to number two on the *New York Times* best-seller list the same week it garnered its sixth lawsuit. In the first three weeks after its release, one Washington, D.C., bookstore reported selling eight thousand copies of *Washington Confidential*. Nationwide, among nonfiction books in 1951, it was outsold only by *Look Younger, Live Longer* and *Betty Crocker's Cook Book*. The authors appeared on Walter Winchell's and Kate Smith's television shows and turned out new installments filled with racist, xenophobic, misogynist, anticommunist, homophobic rants and Mafia stereotypes every year for more than a decade. Both the xenophobic *Around the World Confidential* (1956) and the misogynist *Women Confidential* (1960) sold well, but neither eclipsed the *Chicago, New York, Washington*, or *U.S.A.* volumes. The series topped 4 million copies in hardback and paperback before 1963. Even more remarkable, these sales were achieved without the support of the major book clubs. In short, to the vast majority of readers, the factual limitations were beside the point.[39]

Rather than considering it as nonfiction, it is better to compare the *Confidential* series to comic books. Like Superman's Metropolis, Lait and Mortimer's cities were "in the grip of fiends," according to George Legman's study *Love and Death*.[40] The paranoia of these books provided a conduit for hostility unavailable in other approaches to crime. Criminologists asked readers and policy makers to examine root causes, to alleviate inequality and poverty, to treat illnesses. Lait and Mortimer, as the *New Republic* pointed out, justified lynch law. They participated enthusiastically in the Cold War process Michael Rogin has called a "politics of demonology"; they associated all the evils of society with tags such as "communism", "the Mafia," or "immigrants." Despite protests, their beliefs that criminals threatened not only property and person but also the purity of capitalist values and a vague notion of freedom circulated widely throughout the 1950s. When such beliefs were attached to particular groups of people—immigrants, gays and lesbians, people of color—as they often were, pathology was constructed by the dominant culture as endemic to that group. Sander Gilman argues that this is also true of ideologies and concepts that are perceived as a threat to a given social order: "Difference is that which threatens order and control; it is the polar opposite to our group."[41] Thus, by locating threats within "the Mafia" and "communism" dominant media and political forces during the 1950s were able to define their own practices and beliefs as safe and normal.

True crime literature contributed to the cultural work necessary to reaffirm the simplistic notions of guilt and innocence that some criminologists questioned. Many readers found watching the bad boys pleasurable, but this pleasure would not lead to the social dissolution that deputy attorney general William P. Rogers feared when he warned that comic book crime would provide "blueprints" for amateur extortionists. On the contrary, true crime writers saw that the line between honesty and dishonesty had been blurred and sought its reinscription. As Marshall McCluhan observed: "To put the matter simply, we no longer have a rational basis for defining virtue or vice. And the slogan 'Crime Does Not Pay' is the expression of moral bankruptcy in more senses than one. It implies that if crime could pay, then the dividing line between virtue and vice would disappear." The cultural work of true crime was to reestablish this line with as little uncertainty as possible.[42] The texts indeed provided, in some cases, intricate details about how to rob a bank or run a "protection racket" or where to buy drugs or sex. But by the end of each text, the definitions of virtue and vice were clearer than ever. By first illustrating the possibility of release from social codes that respected property, sobriety, and heterosexual monogamy but then reasserting the idea of justice as the containment of transgressive acts, these texts placed limitations on the terms of the "norm" which excluded some segments of their audience and ultimately achieved widespread acceptance of the perspective of the police and prosecutors.

Paradoxically, Lait and Mortimer's *Confidential* series allowed readers vicariously to transgress and then reaffirm the dividing line between legal and illegal behavior. That line, according to the authors, corresponded with the lines that maintained urban housing segregation and that marked the supposedly permanent differences between immigrants and the native born. A paradox exists in their seemingly contradictory belief that Italian Americans and African Americans could still assimilate into the middle-class mainstream. How could these people enter the middle class if their differences denoted inborn pathology? Lait and Mortimer maintained that discrimination was based on individual merit rather than racial or national origin. Yet they urged readers to be wary of even those who looked and acted "normal," as they could be fronts for the nefarious groups from which they had emerged. Furthermore, their often titillating descriptions of illicit pleasures acknowledged that even middle-class white men could and often did transgress.

So long as people could move both up and down the "crooked ladder" of respectability, then the promise of America would remain intact.[43] If attraction to the "bad boys" drew writers and readers to true crime, they could walk away with a confirmed sense that ethnic and racial differences correlated with social pathology. At a time when criminologists were urging the justice system to jettison this simplistic link, Lait and Mortimer spoke in a voice that resonated more deeply with Cold War sensibilities and echoed the loudest political voices of the era. Aping those who asked Americans to protect their freedom by eliminating ideological challenges to capitalism, Lait and Mortimer achieved a far wider and more influential reach than more thoughtful writers who linked criminal behavior to the social problems of postwar America.

"AN ALL-STAR TELEVISION REVUE":

TV, the Mafia, and the
Kefauver Crime Committee

New York City's federal courts were busy in March 1951. On March 13, David Greenglass presented key testimony in the celebrated spy case that resulted in the execution of his sister and brother-in-law, Ethel and Julius Rosenberg. Within days of Greenglass's stunning testimony, the federal prosecutor revealed that he was considering asking for the death penalty. The "ceremonial slaughter" that came to pass has dwarfed the testimony occurring in another courtroom.[1] In our historical and cultural memory, the Rosenberg trial and executions remain landmark moments of the Cold War. They attracted widespread interest while occurring, but competed for public attention with the hearings of Senator Estes Kefauver's organized crime committee, then being televised to greater renown.

The scandalous Rosenberg trial was no match for the Kefauver Committee's New York hearings. On that same day, March 13, gravelly voiced Frank Costello became, in the words of *New York Times* TV critic Jack Gould, "television's first headless star." Honoring his request that his image not be broadcast, the cameramen focused on the gangster's fidgeting hands. Each day, viewers tuned in their television sets from morning till evening. These hearings transfixed viewers around the nation. Previously unknown outside his native Tennessee, Estes Kefauver, the committee chair, became a celebrity, even appearing on the CBS game show *What's My Line?*, whose panelists easily guessed his identity. There seemed no limit to the hopes people had—and not just for the Kefauver inquiry. Discussions of the broadcast hearings revealed utopian dreams of how television would transform the nation. In "an open letter to the television industry," one TV critic wrote that "the event has revived in some measure the ancient, original form of Athenian democracy, in which all citizens of Athens participated directly in public affairs." Verbatim transcripts of testimony filled the daily papers, relegating the Rosenbergs to a few column inches, often on inside pages. People cheered for New Hampshire senator Charles Tobey's fire and brimstone and witness Virginia Hill's vampy comebacks, while the Rosenberg trial was greeted with far less fanfare in the mainstream media.[2]

The Octopus and the Tennessee Mountain Man

Senator Estes Kefauver's Special Committee to Investigate Organized Crime in Interstate Commerce took its place in the overlapping and often indistinguishable areas of popular culture and Senate politics. Estimates of the exact size of its television audience vary. Kefauver put the figure at 30 million viewers for the New York proceedings, a number (as many writers have observed) larger than the audience for the 1951 World Series. A more conservative estimate of 17 million was still a huge audience at a time when fewer than 8 million television sets were in use in the United States. According to the early ratings service Videodex, 69.7 percent of New York City's television sets were tuned to the hearings. Clearly, the Kefauver Committee proceedings were by far the most widely followed Senate hearings of the decade, reaching a larger audience than even the Army-McCarthy hearings of 1954.[3] Kefauver's trumping of the World Series is ironic in view of the fact that local stations in many cities refused to show the Army-McCarthy hearings because they would preempt early season baseball games and game shows. Sixty percent of U.S. viewers received coverage of the McCarthy hearings, though mostly only late evening summaries.

In addition, the "Kefauver Show" received amplified coverage from popular magazines such as *Newsweek*, *Collier's*, and *Time*, which devoted articles and special issues to the intersection of crime, ethnicity, television, and immigration policy during the hearings. Because of its broad exposure on television and in the popular magazines, some contemporary observers hoped that the Kefauver Committee would promote wider civic understanding of the issues involved and popularize the need for new anti-crime legislation. When people saw the dimensions of the problem for themselves, these observers believed, they would recognize that they had a personal stake in the legislative outcome. A *New York Times* reporter expressed his optimism that television would educate the audience and inspire action:

Last week's all-star television revue . . . marked an epoch for television and gang-sterdom alike. . . . What television has done is to provide the implementation for the goal of Senator Kefauver's committee. Once the set has been tuned in to the pro-ceedings in the Federal Building it has taken extraordinary will power to turn the receiver off. Whether sitting at home, in an office or at a bar, the viewer becomes a participant to see with his own eyes, to hear with his own ears, and to form his own opinion at first-hand. The power to elicit this public participation is a priceless asset at a time when democracy is facing one of its severest tests.

Occurring just as television's extraordinary influence on U.S. culture and politics was beginning, this broadcast, in the eyes of this analyst, provided an opportunity for an increased level of citizen participation in the practice of democracy: "The last week has demonstrated with awesome vividness what television can do to enlighten, to educate and to drive home a lesson."[4] But what lesson did the viewers get? What was the evidence on which they formed their opinions? Since the Ke-fauver Committee entered U.S. culture as a TV program, on what terms did it enter, and how might it have been influenced by its role as entertainment? Ulti-mately, the Kefauver Committee built on the notoriety of familiar figures such as Lucky Luciano and created strong associative links with the mass popularity of sensational crime stories in U.S. popular culture. The central participants in the television broadcasts were real politicians, law enforcement officials, and gangsters, each of whom entered the hearing room with a particular agenda and ambitions. Kefauver and his committee became something more than an investigative body convened to draft and garner support for anti-crime legislation. Their influence, like that of Lait and Mortimer's *Confidential* series, entered a larger context of popular representation. The crimes and criminals on which the Kefauver Com-mittee focused and the distribution of their images in the mass media allowed the public to learn about the social and economic costs of organized crime by causing them to reconsider previously held notions about the innate pathology of Italian American criminals within the context of concerns about conformity, commu-nism, and "fronts." In this way, the Kefauver Committee presaged the future power of television to hold public attention and shape opinion.

There were many direct connections between the committee and the mass me-dia: politicians often become celebrities and behave like journalists during hear-ings, and TV viewers get to enter the proceedings via daily broadcasts. Kefauver wrote that "had it not been for the press of America, there would never have been an investigation because it is the press which has been exposing and asking for prosecution and the cleaning up of criminal conditions for a long, long time." In addition to giving featured interviews in numerous publications, Kefauver acted as a journalist himself, writing several articles for the *Saturday Evening Post*. His

media appearances were not limited to coverage of the committee. He provided
the introduction for Humphrey Bogart's 1951 film *The Enforcer*, which fictionalized
the sensational "Murder, Inc." trial of the previous decade, and delivered an introduction and epilogue for *Captive City*, a 1952 film about a crusading small-
town newspaper editor who goes to Washington to testify before the Kefauver
Committee after he discovers that his city is controlled by a crime syndicate. When
New York television audiences turned off their sets, they could go out and catch
The Enforcer on a double bill with Edward G. Robinson's *Operation X* at the
Yorktown or Beacon theaters while the Kefauver hearings were in town.[5]

Hollywood movies, the human interest story in the *Saturday Evening Post*, and
the Senate inquiry engaged in a project of presenting and defining ethnic criminals, but for different reasons. Hollywood sought ticket sales, the *Post* sought to
increase circulation, and Kefauver sought legislation as well as name recognition
to advance future political campaigns. Despite these different interests, their images and narratives entered 1950s culture simultaneously. Film, television, the print
media, and politicians relied on one another. Their subject matter, clichés, and
insights mirrored one another: fictional representations in the mass media used
Kefauver as supporting evidence, and Kefauver used fictional representations for
dramatic effect. The public experienced the Kefauver Committee, true crime literature, popular fictional representations, and law enforcement as overlapping and
reinforcing visions of criminality and legality.[6]

When discussing organized crime, the committee relied on the familiar characters of television drama to familiarize the audience with the secret workings of
gangster operations. And like those TV dramas, the hearings had a sponsor. The
sponsor of the New York hearings, *Time* magazine, bought full-page ads in New
York newspapers advertising the hearings like any other crime show: superimposed
on a hand holding a pair of dice, the copy in one ad reminded readers to tune
in to "Channel Seven WJZ-TV today and every day. The Editors of *Time* present
in the public interest every day—all day though Wednesday, March 21. CRIME IN
NEW YORK. Eyewitness viewings of the Senate Committee Hearings at Foley
Square." The Young and Rubicam advertising agency quickly joined in what
seemed to be an infectious spirit of public interest. Their full-page ad following
the hearings posed a question to New Yorkers: "With staggering impact, the tel-
ecasts of the Kefauver investigation have brought a shocked awakening to millions
of Americans. How can we stop what's going on? *Is there anything we can do about
it?*"[7] In the merging of public affairs and popular entertainment, advertisers could
act in what they saw as the public interest while helping to popularize a new
medium that would generate profits for years to come. They learned that Kefauver's dramatic moral debate about good and evil ensured a wide audience.

In the early days of television, advertisers used what now appear to be crude
sales techniques: Sergeant Joe Friday of *Dragnet* extolling the virtues of Chester-

field cigarettes before nabbing a Los Angeles shoplifter, for example. Like the producers of *Dragnet*, Kefauver helped push sponsors' products while questioning witnesses or describing his goals and methods to the readers of his articles. He did not sell particular consumer items (although he did endorse films and television programs). Nor did he hawk the products of Time-Life or its advertisers from the dais in the hearing rooms. Rather, he was selling a political agenda. The committee sought to promote and popularize anti-crime legislation. Throughout the hearings, Kefauver drew on media images and popular theories that depicted crime as the pathological behavior of poor people too lazy or ignorant to work their way up the economic ladder honestly. In this he relied on information collected by other government agencies. He selectively packaged testimony and viewpoints provided by local district attorneys and Federal Bureau of Narcotics agents, and his reliance on these sources created a predictable outcome.

Commissioner of narcotics Harry Anslinger saw the committee hearings as an opportunity to publicize the extensive investigations of his bureau and to influence the national agenda on the treatment of those who distributed or used illegal drugs. In March 1950, shortly after the Senate authorized the committee, Anslinger offered his full cooperation; he was one of the first witnesses the committee called. In addition, narcotics agents helped locate witnesses who were ducking subpoenas. The Federal Bureau of Narcotics assigned agents George White and Charles Siragusa to work directly for the committee.[8] In an effort to advance bureau policy, Anslinger argued that the committee should advocate for "new legislation requiring mandatory imprisonment of 2 years, 5 years and 10 years for first, second and subsequent offenders, respectively. Also, deportation should be made mandatory." He hoped that the FBN would grow in the wake of the Kefauver Committee's highly publicized campaign against organized crime. In a letter to Assistant Secretary of the Treasury E. H. Foley Jr., his immediate superior, Anslinger spelled out his goals: "The Bureau of Narcotics should be brought to prewar strength immediately if the resurging narcotic traffic is not to create new underworld leaders of the type of 'Legs' Diamond, 'Lucky' Luciano, 'Waxey' Gordon and 'Lepke' Buchalter."[9] The FBN advised the Kefauver Committee to investigate and call as witnesses some of the most infamous gangsters of the 1940s and 1950s. In particular, Harry Anslinger recommended that Kefauver subpoena Joe Adonis, Carlos Marcello, "Dandy" Phil Kastel, Sam Vitale, Meyer Lansky, Charles Fischetti, Harold "Happy" Meltzer, Carlo Gambino, and the man who would prove the most dramatic witness of the investigation, Frank Costello. The bureau also recommended that the committee investigate Lucky Luciano, but, when the gangster volunteered to testify in person, strongly advised Kefauver to resist any attempt by Luciano—living in exile in Italy since his postwar deportation—to enter the country.

The committee relied on and expanded Anslinger's belief that the Mafia had been the primary conduit for illicit narcotics in the United States since the end of World War II. To this the committee added labor racketeering and gambling, among other criminal activities. The FBN became much more than a resource for the Kefauver Committee. Bureau agents provided committee members with lines of questioning and flowcharts to help them identify relationships between interstate Mafia organizations and international smuggling operations. Perhaps most important, by the inception of the committee in 1950, the FBN had already established a way of thinking about the Mafia that attracted Kefauver's interest along with that of a public drawn to the secretive world of organized crime.

The testimony of Anslinger and his agents provided the committee's earliest image of the national and international dimensions of organized crime. Anslinger's appearance before the committee, although in closed session, also supplied the public with tidbits of the kind of testimony they could expect in the months to come. His long-cultivated relationships with friendly reporters ensured that the testimony would enter the public record in ways that would complement his own information and interpretations. After Anslinger's initial appearance before the committee in August 1950, Drew Pearson reported that the commissioner "definitely puts the finger on the Mafia, or 'Black Hand' society, as the 'brains' behind organized crime in the country. Anslinger reported key bosses of organized crime are usually Sicilians. He named such notorious figures as Frankie Costello, Joe Adonis and Phil Kastel; and Joe Accardo and Charlie and Rocco Fischetti of Chicago. The top dog in the Mafia, running the underworld from Rome, allegedly is Lucky Luciano, former vice lord of New York City."[10] Pearson is perhaps the most overlooked Cold War columnist. Although his current name recognition may lag behind that of Walter Winchell and Joseph Alsop, during the 1940s and 1950s his syndicated commentary, "Washington Merry-Go-Round," appeared in seven hundred daily newspapers and on two hundred radio stations. Aware of the role of publicity in inciting political action, Pearson used his column to publicize the "Friendship Train," the "Letters to Italy" campaigns, and the "tide of toys" for European children, along with the Kefauver Committee's anti-Mafia campaign.[11]

Anslinger's testimony was even more sensational than Pearson intimated. In his appearance before the committee, Anslinger described an organized crime empire of "intercountry and intercontinent" scale. "No study of interstate criminal activity in this country would be complete without some reference to the so-called Mafia," Anslinger said. Because of its long history, foreign origin, and ethnic exclusivity, the Mafia presented policing agencies with a particularly difficult challenge:

> The Mafia perfected principles admirably suited to the successful perpetuation of a criminal clique. One is absolute self-sufficiency, no resorting to the law for justice or vengeance; another is extreme secrecy; another, drastic retaliation—almost always murder—for any substantial violation of the gang code. Besides the alliance in crime,

there are usually the bonds of blood or intermarriage and of common locality of origin to weld the organization into cohesive resistance to penetration by law enforcement instrumentalities. Consider this, and you will conclude that the Mafia is a vicious, fearsome thing which should be ruthlessly exterminated.

The combination of oaths of silence and common blood made the Mafia a special kind of criminal problem, Anslinger concluded. "Here is a nation-wide organization of outlaws in a sort of oath bound, blood-tied brotherhood dedicated to complete defiance of the law."[12]

In separate testimony reminiscent of Senator Joseph McCarthy's famous speech in Wheeling, West Virginia, earlier that year, Commissioner Anslinger produced a "secret document" that describes "a vicious, sinister combine, interlaced and intertwined, sprawled across the nation. Its members are engaged in gambling, narcotics, white slavery, counterfeiting, extortion, murder, and other rackets. The tentacles of those in Florida, New York, California, and elsewhere reach across the country. There are approximately 800 names here, 50 of whom are indicated as major criminals. About 300 are in our files as known narcotic violators." The document, later leaked to Jack Lait and Lee Mortimer and printed as an appendix to their best-selling *Washington Confidential*, revealed that the Mafia was a self-sufficient organization that never turned to governmental agencies to resolve in tragang disputes.[13] The octopus-like organization of Anslinger's description became a favorite metaphor for Kefauver, inspiring *Time* magazine to feature on its cover Kefauver's smiling face superimposed on a cartoon drawing of an octopus holding guns, drug paraphernalia, cards, and other tools of the crime trade in its numerous tentacles.

Other connections to Cold War anticommunism were more direct. In describing the Mafia as a "government within a government," the committee used rhetoric that both defined insiders and excluded outsiders, much like the anticommunist crusade taking place at the same time in that other New York City courtroom. As Kefauver wrote in the United Nations publication *U.N. World*: "It is true that crime plays no favorites among nations. The thug and his more suave superior are not native phenomena to the United States. Their habitat is not confined to Britain, France, Japan, or China. They are everywhere. With rare exceptions they have no patriotic concept of country. They are interested only in themselves, and national borders are of no more concern to them than county lines." Kefauver argued that criminal conspiracies endangered not only individual citizens but national sovereignty as well. His committee was shedding light on the "shadowy, international criminal organization known as the Mafia, so fantastic that most Americans find it hard to believe it really exists." Even to place a small wager or drop a nickel into a slot machine at the local drugstore, Kefauver warned, was to finance an international conspiracy that threatened American democracy and all nations. Senator Edward Martin of Pennsylvania told the audience of his biweekly radio address that "like sovereign nations," the gangsters "divide up the country into exclusive territories," raking in profits that are "second in size only to the annual tax receipts of the Federal Government."[14]

The subtle references to a secret government created clear parallels to anticommunist rhetoric. Often these parallels were explicit. In his comments before the Kefauver Committee, Spruille Braden, head of the privately funded New York City Anti-Crime Committee, spelled out these links: "Joe Stalin, if he had planned it that way, could not find a speedier and surer way to defeat the democracies than by subsidizing these gangsters and foul politicians. Actually, as I have seen in other countries how closely the gangsters and Communists work together, I sometimes wonder if the Soviet is not, at least in some measure, inciting these vermin to defile our system of law and order." Braden argued that gangsters like Joe Adonis, Frank Costello, "and the rest of this scum are among the Kremlin's best allies." In a reference to the trial occurring elsewhere in the Foley Square courthouse where he was making his comments, Braden described the threat posed by gangsters who bribe and corrupt public officials as worse than the alleged theft of nuclear secrets that would result in the Rosenberg executions: "Perhaps, in a sense, they are even more dangerous than the spies convicted of stealing our atomic and military secrets. After all, by ingenuity and hard work we can compensate for and replace these thefts, but the loss of morality in government will cause us to lose our self-respect and the respect of other peoples. From such a catastrophe no nation has ever recovered."[15]

The investigation into the threat of an internal communist conspiracy did not go unchallenged. The Rosenbergs had their defenders, and the Hollywood Ten refused to answer the questions of the House Un-American Activities Committee. Like this resistance to McCarthyism, those facing subpoenas and accusations from the Kefauver Committee resisted the authority of the committee along with its characterization of the threat posed by the Mafia. When he read Drew Pearson's column about Anslinger's testimony, Philip Kastel, one of the people named by Anslinger, wrote directly to the commissioner. Kastel, a New Yorker who had moved to New Orleans to oversee Frank Costello's growing gambling investments, sought to clear his name: "For your information I am not of Italian origin, or of Italian extraction, or Sicilian. I am not a member of what is described as the 'Mafia,' or so called 'Black Hand' society, nor have I ever been a member of said society, nor have I been or ever belonged to a society or organization similar, or remotely related thereto. It is inconceivable to me that a man placed in such a trustworthy position and being able to so expertly gather facts, as you are, could actually have made such a statement, or caused such a statement to be published." Anslinger did not deny any of the statements in Pearson's article. He wrote back: "Our files reflect considerable information regarding your activities. If you wish, you may send us a written statement in detail of your activities since 1920, year by year in chronological order."[16] The publicity angered Kastel, but it also shows how accusations would generate swift rebuttal. This would be a lesson for Kefauver and later crime busters—most notably Robert F. Kennedy, whose racketeering investigations targeted Jimmy Hoffa and the Teamsters. These rebuttals, however, did not usually reach the public with the same force and consistency as responses that supported the information put out by the mainstream media and government investigative bodies, though their existence and articulation were crucial to the contemporary fascination with gangsters. It was nevertheless virtually impossible for those whose names appeared in print as a result of leaked closed-door testimony to clear their names.[17]

The gangsters would get their chance to appear before the committee—whether they liked it or not. But before they got the chance, a series of witnesses from the FBN appeared. Their testimony achieved wide distribution in the popular print media. On September 28 and 29, 1950, Kansas City agent Claude Follmer presented baseball diamond–shaped diagrams to illustrate for the senators and the viewing public the inner workings of a nationwide crime syndicate. Despite his having presented this information in an earlier closed session, the committee eagerly publicized these theories before the assembled reporters.[18] Human interest biographies of the agents and gangsters appeared in the press, familiarizing the public with the witnesses they would see on their television screens.

Professional organizations, most notably the American Bar Association, trumpeted the need for legislation to combat the evils detailed by the bureau's agents. In response to the Kefauver Committee, the Bar Association formed a Commission on Organized Crime specifically to deal with the complicity of lawyers in protecting gangsters. The committee's chief counsel, Rudolph Halley, who served on this commission, sketched a picture of the Mafia for the ABA just as Anslinger had in the early days of Kefauver's investigation: "A great many of the mobsters . . . belong to an organization [that is] composed at least primarily of Sicilians and is known as 'Mafia.' This is a carry over of the old Sicilian Black Hand and has extremely strong power in the underworld because of its ruthless methods of stamping down opposition and its reputation for certain retribution against those who oppose it." After the close of the hearings, Kefauver continued to focus on a sinister underworld defined by its subversion of traditional forms of social relationships, writing in *Crime in America*: "The Mafia today is actually a secret international government-within-a-government. It has an international head in Italy—believed by United States authorities to be Charles (Lucky) Luciano."[19]

The crimes committed by these gangsters provided sensational copy, but the publicity had the consequence of mobilizing many Italian Americans and some Jews to protest the insinuation that ethnic origin played a central role in causing criminality. Ethnic advocacy organizations leveraged their political influence to place significant pressure on the FBN and ultimately on the Kefauver Committee. In closed-door testimony (again leaked to columnist Drew Pearson), Anslinger provided a document alleging that Jewish Americans served as primary providers of capital to the Mafia. Phil Kastel was only the latest in a long line of Jewish criminals to come to the public's attention. Jewish gangsters had indeed worked alongside Italian American gangsters since the Prohibition era. Jake "Greasy Thumb" Guzik, Dutch Schultz, Lepke Buchalter, Bugsy Siegel, and Meyer Lansky were virtually household names, and the belief that Jews provided the capital for the Mafia was pervasive. Leo Katcher's 1959 biography of Arnold Rothstein, the man credited with fixing the 1919 World Series, bore the title *The Big Bankroll*.[20] To Jewish organizations, whether these Jewish Americans had provided start-up funds for Mafia ventures was beside the point. The accusations clearly gained their currency from old anti-Semitic saws about Jewish economic exploitation which had fueled Russian pogroms and Nazi atrocities. The Concord, New Hampshire, chapter of the Anti-Defamation League contacted committee member Charles Tobey to denounce Anslinger's accusations angrily. Senator Tobey, in turn, wrote a characteristic expression of outrage to Anslinger. Pressure continued to mount on the commissioner when New York senator Herbert Lehman wrote to the secretary of the treasury, the senior-most official to whom Anslinger reported. In the wake of these protests, Anslinger denied having made any reference to people of the Jewish faith.[21] Nevertheless, ethnic advocacy organizations continued to protest the stereotypes being used to make organized crime seem especially sinister, fearing that the publicizing of crimes committed by Italian and Jewish Americans would tarnish the reputations of law-abiding members of these groups.

Despite protests from advocacy organizations and the powerful evidence relating economic class and the influence of criminal role models with the propensity to crime, the long-standing popular link between ethnic origin and criminality remained as strong as ever. Like others before and after, the Kefauver Committee turned to simplistic and nativist explanations for the causes of crime. The committee members' viewpoints on immigrant criminals, in fact, merely softened the harsh rhetoric of others such as Anslinger and the journalists who covered organized crime for the Hearst newspaper chain. In their best-selling *Chicago Confidential*, the right-wing reporters Jack Lait and Lee Mortimer argued that "racketeering has been the contribution of our immigrant hordes." They granted that these immigrants had brains, albeit sly ones. But they came in hordes, roved in packs, and lived like animals.[22]

Contrary to these ugly stereotypes, instead of gun-toting gangsters out of *Little Caesar*, the television audience for the Kefauver Committee hearings were more likely to see conservatively dressed businessmen who lived in affluent suburbs. Rather than dealing in murder like their Prohibition predecessors, these gangsters dealt in "money and information." Kefauver charged this new generation of gangsters with using ill-gotten gains to enter the ranks of the mainstream: "Gambling profits are the principal support of big-time racketeering and gangsterism. These profits provide the financial resources whereby ordinary criminals are converted into big-time racketeers, political bosses, pseudo businessmen, and alleged philanthropists." This was not a transformation he celebrated. As they entered the political and business mainstream, these mobsters endangered the clear-cut distinctions between good and evil which gave the Kefauver hearings such widespread entertainment value.[23]

Even as the gangsters relied on blood oaths and ethnic loyalties, they had grown wealthy along with the service industry of the postwar years. As they left behind the tommy guns and speakeasies of the Prohibition era, gangsters looked increasingly like their more legitimate neighbors. Once they started sending their children to private schools and colleges, some feared that the villainous infiltration of mainstream America would be completely camouflaged and impossible to fight. Without the immigrant or working-class accents, these new mobsters would blur the distinguishable differences between criminals and "decent" Americans. *Time* alerted its readers to this threat, reporting that the gangster "lives comfortably but not fabulously in a respectable neighborhood, contributes to charity, hobnobs with café society, is a friend to politicians, sends his children to summer camp and the big kids to college." Rather than the "mob bosses" of a previous era or the "dons" of later decades, *Time* called the leaders of organized crime "high level executives." Just as Senator McCarthy's paranoid anticommunist accusations of well-bred radicals in the State Department overturned earlier images of bomb-throwing, bearded anarchists, the Kefauver hearings emphasized the new invisibility of organized crime. Mobsters looked like business executives, lived in the same neighborhood, contributed to political campaigns, and acted like good citizens—all with the goal of sinking their tentacles into "legitimate enterprises."[24] Their appearance and tastes did not immediately connote difference and inferiority. Indeed, the gangster's affinity for mainstream and elite practices was what seemed most frightening to the Kefauver Committee and its many viewers.

Not even the crimes they committed made these gangster-businessmen indistinguishable from other Americans. The gambling enterprises in which they engaged, for example, did not necessarily make them outcasts; Kefauver himself was known to play cards, and FBI director J. Edgar Hoover frequented racetracks. Unwilling to risk charges of hypocrisy, Kefauver did not damn the act of gambling. Only its scale and motivation made the practice illegitimate. As a "past-time," it presented no problem, but as a "business" gambling became dangerous. "I don't think you can legislate to fully prevent [gambling]," Kefauver told an interviewer. "Individual people will probably always bet and wager with one another. Our aim has been to try to take the organized element out of it, and not subject the people to operations in which that element is involved." A *Collier's* writer reminded his readers that the biblical character Solomon gambled, and that the Irish Hospital Sweepstakes put gambling receipts to good use; but "the numbers racket has been a particularly unsavory form of gambling because of the character of its sponsors and protectors." By singling out the rackets, Kefauver made sure that only the gambling controlled by "unsavory characters" would be targeted for condemnation. Accordingly, *Time* magazine reported that Kefauver "likes a quiet game of stud poker himself. . . . But it would be nice if Estes Kefauver could arrange to have it run by a nicer set of fellows."[25]

If Kefauver felt that Americans should fear gangsters because they looked and acted like average businesspeople, the reverse was also true: if businesspeople looked like gangsters, what did this say about the sanctioned activities of the men in gray flannel? Did their practices and ethics also resemble the gangsters'? Monopolistic practices and acquisitive ethics had resulted in great concentrations of wealth throughout the United States. At a time when only about 8 million television sets were in use, many Americans resorted to watching the Kefauver hearings through the windows of appliance stores, and in the New York area, this meant going to Korvettes. Korvettes typified the pattern whereby local operations such as McDonald's or Holiday Inn would balloon into regional or national chains during the 1950s. Eugene Ferkauf, the Jewish son of a luggage store owner, opened twenty-five Korvettes appliance superstores in the New York area, achieving profits that dwarfed the income of the entire immigrant neighborhood from which he had come. Even old industrial giants like General Motors were becoming multinational behemoths. The growth of a handful of corporations suddenly seemed to transform local, national, and international economic landscapes.[26] Many welcomed this economic expansion and centralization after decades of depression and war. But it also recalled the concentration of wealth typified by the gaudy fortunes of Andrew Carnegie, J. P. Morgan, and John D. Rockefeller. Kefauver evoked the efforts of late nineteenth-century trustbusters when he described his committee's work as within the tradition of fighting monopolies:

> The American people have always feared great concentrations of power. It is perfectly obvious that if concentration of economic power is dangerous in perfectly legitimate business activity, it is more than dangerous in the hands of criminal elements. It is essential that at the outset the Committee ascertain how much of the country's wealth is in the hands of organized criminals whether directly or indirectly. One racketeer in Chicago is reported to have as much as $150,000,000 in Washington secreted in bank vaults.[27]

The centralization of money and power in ever-larger corporations rather than small businesses and farms seemed to threaten the democratic values typified by the yeoman farmer and small businessperson. Kefauver positioned himself as the champion of these ideals in his crusade against organized crime. The preadolescent fans of television's Davy Crockett would have recognized *Time* magazine's description of Kefauver: "Last week homely, rawboned Estes Kefauver, always eager to please, was trudging through California, doggedly intent on the trail of Big Crime. His gait was steady and a little flat-footed. His air was mildly astonished, as befitted a wary Tennessee mountain man inspecting the sinful sight of the big cities."[28] Kefauver had tapped this populist image during his earlier Senate campaigns when he stumped through Tennessee in a raccoon cap. The image would again be put into service during his two presidential campaigns, when a biography characterized Kefauver as "this modern Davy Crockett."[29] It was as a "Tennessee mountain man" that Kefauver—a Yale-trained lawyer from a prominent family, a U.S. senator in a suit and horn-rimmed glasses—wished to enter America's living rooms, the spokesman for an ideal that was incorruptible, tough, and pure. It was an image that appealed to masses of viewers, who shared Kefauver's skepticism about the growing concentration of wealth in America.

A Splendid Nightmare

Without question, the committee fascinated virtually all Americans who had access to a television set. This fascination did not necessarily imply that all viewers shared Kefauver's loathing of the gangsters. Many—perhaps most—of the viewers surely agreed that the criminal conspiracy had to be stamped out and the traditional moral order imposed. The moral outrage and frontier masculinity that Kefauver presented as a purifying force met with enthusiastic support from his committee's dedicated audience. William Howard Moore estimates that 95 percent of those who wrote letters to committee members supported their efforts. These letters, along with the overwhelmingly positive treatment Kefauver received in the mass media, "suggest that very few citizens could not identify with someone on the Committee." *Time* magazine, according to a Kefauver biography, received 115,000 letters, virtually all favorable. A public opinion poll of people enrolled in political parties (thus ruling out those who were not naturalized citizens) found that fully 94 percent "had a favorable reaction" to the Kefauver Committee.[30] Clearly, nearly all viewers were rooting for the Tennessee mountain man in his battle with the Mafia octopus.

Nevertheless, the hearings had a side effect unexplained by this seemingly universal support for the crime busters. Much to the chagrin of Senator Kefauver, a lot of people identified with or were attracted to the witnesses. In part this had much to do with the composition of the new middle class, many of whom came from the same working-class backgrounds or immigrant origins as the gangsters they saw on television. According to the 1950 census, there were 10,033,385 foreign-born Americans out of a total adult population of 96,818,969. More than one in ten Americans had been born outside the United States, 718,086 of them in Italy.[31] Factoring in their children and grandchildren would surely multiply the number of Americans who considered foreign origin a source of strength and positive identification rather than an indicator of criminality. To be sure, many immigrants saw the gangsters as a cause for embarrassment and outrage, but this alone was not enough to make them identify instead with the members of the committee. Rather than threatening outsiders, the criminals marching across the TV screen were as familiar as neighbors.

According to the estimates of polls, 5 per cent of Americans openly disagreed with the committee. Even those Americans who did not could still take pleasure in the stories of illicit adventures related by the investigators and personified in the public mind by the witnesses. By taking Harry Anslinger's advice and calling as witnesses only the best known of American gangsters, Kefauver provided an entertaining look into the secret lives and tax returns of characters the public had been reading about in newspaper columns and true crime stories for many years. These were not just gangsters but celebrities, and the easily digestible narrative that contributed to the popularity of the hearings allowed many viewers to perceive the proceedings as a performance. Kefauver promoted this perception in a shrewd ploy to gain popular support for the legislative goals of the committee; but in enlisting the conventions of popular entertainment, he risked trivializing the very danger he sought to reveal.

Early on, critics and general viewers alike were aware that the hearings were a show as much as an investigation. In a biography of committee counsel Rudolph Halley, *Collier's* magazine pointed out his familial connection to a member of the entertainment profession:

> To his roles of cross-examiner and sleuth, Halley also added that of producer. It was he who staged the hearings, selected the witnesses and directed the order of their appearance. Halley is a nephew of the late playwright Sam Shipman who wrote "East is West," "Friendly Enemies" and other Broadway hits. To Anita Loos, author of "Gentlemen Prefer Blondes," Halley's New York show was such a smash hit that she wired: "You're a greater dramatist, Rudy, than your uncle ever was." As dramatist, Halley made what may be the crime committee's greatest contribution. Through television he brought the gangster right into the living room.

The popularity of the hearings ensured that gangsters would continue arriving in living rooms long after the committee disbanded. For example, *A Nation's Nightmare,* a CBS radio documentary series inspired by the Kefauver Committee, focused each week on a different transgression: one week gambling, the next waterfront crime, and so on. The program explicitly portrayed criminals as irredeemable and featured Kefauver-friendly guests such as Virgil Peterson of the

Chicago Crime Commission and Morris Ploscowe of the American Bar Association's Commission on Organized Crime. Listeners learned that they were paying excessive prices for goods and services so unsavory characters could profit from the exploitation of hardworking Americans. Universal outrage should have been expected. But when reviewed in *Newsweek*'s radio and television section, even this standard anti-crime format became the "splendid nightmare," a half-hour of pleasurable revelations to relieve the everyday monotony of listeners' lives.[32]

Coverage of the the "Kefauver Show" was as likely to be found in the entertainment pages as in the news pages of papers and magazines. In keeping with the genre conventions employed by the committee and later used in fictional treatments of the hearings, the mass media eagerly capitalized on the entertainment value of mobsters. In their reviews of the "performances," the entertainment columnists overwhelmingly preferred the criminals to the investigators: their dramatic appeal was unquestionable. The *New York Times*'s Jack Gould explicitly described the hearings in terms of their entertainment value: "It has been an almost incredible cast of characters that have made their entrance on the screen. The poker-faced Erickson, the saucily arrogant Adonis, the shy Costello and the jocose Virginia Hill might have been hired from Hollywood's Central Casting Bureau."[33] Reporters gladly promoted the committee's pretension to moral superiority. In writing about the hearings as entertainment, however, they betrayed their pleasure in the committee's amoral foils.

Initially seen as a supplement to the hard news coverage of the hearings, the entertainment stories soon moved to page one. The hearings as show business became the story as much as the witnesses' revelations about the inner workings of the crime syndicate. This was most clearly true in the case of Bugsy Siegel's onetime girlfriend, Virginia Hill. Although she played only a minor role in the committee's conspiracy theory, her sass and sex appeal made her a favorite of reporters. Hill had been a regular in gossip columns since the late 1930s. All the best-known columnists wrote about her: Westbrook Pegler, Hedda Hopper, Walter Winchell, Ed Sullivan, and *Daily Variety*'s Florabel Muir. Her notoriety expanded after the murder of her boyfriend, Bugsy Siegel, on June 19, 1947. Hill was in Paris when the mobster and Vegas casino developer was shot in her Beverly Hills home, but her tearful interview in the *Los Angeles Times* fascinated readers.[34]

Public discussion of Hill did not center on the same xenophobic stereotypes that shaped perceptions of Italian American and Jewish American gangsters. Her gender and class, as well as her southern roots, were prominently featured in the drooling discussions of the camera friendly Hill. According to *U.S.A. Confidential*, Hill was an "Alabama whistle-stop kid who had never worn shoes until she was sixteen." Although they clearly subjected her to derision, Lait and Mortimer found her particularly emblematic of 1950s American culture. In tongue-in-cheek homage they called for replacing the Statue of Liberty: "So we suggest, respectfully, even tenderly, that the aged bimbo step down—and in her place we erect a statue of Virginia Hill, holding high a jimmy instead of a torch." Lait and Mortimer replace the icon to immigration with Hill, who would symbolically extinguish the beacon by wielding a burglar's crow-bar. More disturbing to Lait and Mortimer, Hill symbolized a common theme of theirs, the emasculation of men. According to their logic, the frustration men experienced at the hands of castrating women like Virginia Hill drove them to crime: "America has become a matriarchy. Women own it and run it. There are more of them and more of them vote. They have come into their own—also to our own. Instead of less crime there is more. Instead of less corruption there is more. . . . Doting mothers raise soft sons, plump for laws so they can't work in their youth and don't have to in their manhood. America is becoming a land of manicured hermaphrodites, going the way of Rome." Lait and Mortimer blamed women for everything that had gone wrong since passage of the Nineteenth Amendment. Mortimer must have felt that he was doing his part to save men from a pernicious force when he suggested that the committee call Hill as a witness and explore her sources of income.[35]

Hill's appearance before the Kefauver Committee may have originated with the efforts of this right-wing columnist, but virtually all commentators expressed the widespread sexual objectification of women in their coverage of her appearance. Not far from Mortimer's put-down of Hill as "high class hooker" was the description by a *New York Times* reporter who defined the witness in explicitly sexualized terms. Emanuel Perlmutter, who wrote entertainment and news stories about the hearings, seems to have found Hill quite desirable: "It was hard to believe that the witness possessed even minor physical imperfections. Smooth-browed, blue-eyed, with a classic profile framed by luxuriant, chestnut-colored hair, she was easily the most photogenic witness to occupy the stand since the hearings started." He spoke of her in items evoking a Hollywood screen goddess's illicit sexual desirability: "She registered emotion as naturally as a first-rate movie star. She was laconic, indignant, sarcastic, haughty, hurt or amused as the nature of her answers warranted. Throughout her subjection to persistent questioning by Mr. Halley and the blinding glare of the floodlights in the hearing room she maintained her hauteur and look of impeccable grooming."[36] Some found that her physical aggressiveness enhanced her sex appeal: on the way out of the hearings, she slapped one reporter, Marjorie Farnsworth of the *New York Journal-American*, and kicked Lee Mortimer, to applause and cheers from the crowd.

Hill could not use her popularity, however, as protection from prosecution. As Mortimer had urged, Halley's questions focused on Hill's tax returns. Halley found that Hill spent lavishly and openly. "We knew she had spent $11,000—almost $2,000 a week—on a six-week vacation" in a year when she reported a $16,000 income to the IRS. "We had every voucher she signed and every phone call she made while at Sun Valley, [Idaho]." A tax lien was put on her Spokane, Washington, home later in 1951 after the IRS discovered that Hill had spent almost $250,000 between 1942 and 1947 while reporting a total income of $130,000. Hill's husband, a native of Austria who had been detained in the United States during World War II, left in June 1951 after the Immigration and Naturalization Service threatened to deport him. The IRS auctioned her possessions and house in August, and Hill fled the country in September, eventually settling in Vienna with her husband and son. Tragically, Hill took an overdose of sleeping pills at age forty-nine on March 24, 1966, in Koppl, near Salzburg.[37]

Media infatuation could not save Frank Costello either. Born Francesco Castiglia in the Italian region of Calabria, Costello emigrated to the United States with his family at age four, moving into the same East Harlem neighborhood that produced New York mayor Fiorello La Guardia and Congressman Vito Marcantonio. But Costello took a different path to prominence. After an early arrest for illegal possession of a gun, he became a rumrunner in the 1920s. During the 1930s and 1940s, he derived his income from substantial investments in illegal gambling enterprises. Through payoffs to local law officers and politicians, Costello was able to run the Beverly Club casino outside New Orleans without interference throughout the immediate postwar years. He also illegally leased slot machines to fraternal organizations in the New York area, a prime target of his former neighbor Fiorello La Guardia's anti-vice campaign in the 1930s. By 1951, Costello was living in a Central Park West penthouse paid for with income from (according to Kefauver's investigation) legitimate nightclub, real estate, liquor, and oil investments.[38] Costello quickly emerged as the most dramatic witness of the hearings, eclipsing even his friend, former New York City mayor William O'Dwyer, who took leave from his post as ambassador to Mexico to testify before the committee. For contemporary viewers and historians alike, Costello came to "symbolize the underworld the committee was seeking to investigate."[39] Costello's drama, however, could not be attributed to startling revelations. Instead, it was his persistent resistance and ultimate refusal to testify at all that riveted viewers.

After his first day of testimony, reporters knew they had discovered a major new TV star. "Television acquired yesterday its first beheaded star—the bashful Frank Costello," wrote Jack Gould in the New York Times. "In what, for video, was an unprecedented program, the cameras were trained hour after hour on the hands, arms and chest of the principal player at the Senate committee's crime inquiry, yet during the testimony there was not even a glimpse of his face. He was the man in the cathode mask." Costello's lawyer, George Wolf, objected to having Costello televised "on the ground that Mr. Costello doesn't care to submit himself as a spectacle. And on the further ground that it will prevent proper conference with his attorney in receiving proper advice from his attorney during the course of the testimony." Senator Herbert O'Conor (serving as chair in the absence of Kefauver) ordered that "the defendant not be televised." The television networks, choosing to interpret this as ban on showing the witness's face, merely shifted the camera to Costello's hands. Costello answered the committee's questions throughout the day, but his nervousness and resistance did not earn him the same rave reviews Hill had garnered. As one critic remarked, "Costello's testimony was often spiced with passages of low-grade literacy, ample in the uses of double negatives and the substitution of the letter 'd' for 'th.' "[40]

After two days of testimony, Costello became convinced that the presence of the television cameras would endanger his health and disorient him, leading to inadvertently perjured testimony. On March 15, after numerous protests to the committee, Costello stood up and left. His lawyer justified this action, saying:

> During the entire proceedings, powerful, blinding Klieg lights were on all the time, motion picture cameras were grinding and hordes of photographers have been roaming the room, as they are at this moment, standing directly in front of the witness, as they are at this moment, and darting about. With the intolerable conditions that existed, it became apparent that the witness was unable to testify properly, that the witness could not properly concentrate on the subject matter of the questioning and that, as a result, his answers were incoherent, unintelligible and at times inconsistent and seemingly contradictory.[41]

The committee threatened to charge Costello with contempt if he failed to reappear. Several days later he testified again but, in a repetition of his earlier performance, left in the middle of being questioned. His performance before the Kefauver Committee won him a band of unlikely supporters—civil libertarians and judges—who eventually achieved a reversal of his contempt of Congress charge and a halt to deportation proceedings.

"This Warm and Glowing Box"

If television served to turn a political hearing into an entertaining program, it is also true that the hearings transformed what had been primarily a commercial and entertainment medium into a political tool. A hearing previously accessible to most people only through the description and analysis provided by print reporters, radio broadcasts, or brief newsreels could now be watched in its entirety by anyone with access to a bar, an appliance store, or a friend with a television set. The Kefauver hearings helped define television during a critical moment of its development; some hoped that it would come to serve loftier democratic ends than simply providing the updated vaudeville routines, quiz shows, and baseball games then dominating the airwaves. Some even hoped that television viewing would become an act of citizenship comparable to voting or serving on a jury. The Horace Mann School in the Bronx canceled classes during the hearings so students could take in the national civics lesson. Similarly, a criminology professor at Rutgers University canceled his regular lecture and had his students watch the hearings, claiming that the lesson was "one that could never be equaled in classrooms." Another observer of the hearings remarked: "Through the medium of the camera's perceptive eye the individual has had a liberal education in government and morality. Television's qualities of intimacy and immediacy have made the experience so personal that the TV viewer actually is closer to the scene than the spectator in the courtroom."[42]

The new relationship between criminal investigation, legislative politics, and television seemed to promise a transformation in the meaning of citizenship. The *New York Times* expressed great hopes that viewers would become a more active electorate: "Television brings this show to the people, and there is an eager, widespread interest in it. The shady figures come out of the shadow, even when they are faceless, as Frank Costello chose yesterday to be. We could not help wishing as we saw this drama unfold, in the first two days of hearings, that the public of this great city would show the same interest at election time, when such interest could be effective." The hearings, argued the British journal *The Spectator*, would extend the promise of participatory government: "This warm and glowing box has been revealed to be the new instrument of democracy."[43] Senator Ed Martin revealed his hope that the impact of the criminal investigation would extend to other aspects of citizenship: "Looking back to the election of 1948, when we were electing a President of the United States, a new House of Representatives, and one-third of the United States Senate, the record shows that 49 percent of the eligible voters in the Nation did not go to the polls. Only through the ballot box can we rebuild confidence in our form of government and erect a structure of morality that will bar the racketeer and the chiseler."[44] Raising public awareness about organized crime would be the first step toward creating a reinvigorated electorate.

Costello's contempt of and for the committee unleashed a fierce debate about this new influence on American public life. All agreed that television would transform the political process by reaching an ever wider audience, but what impact this would have sparked the sharpest disagreements. Trial lawyers and civil libertarians were particularly wary of the "warm and glowing box." Did the viewers have a right to see the Kefauver Committee proceedings? If not, how should officials weigh the public's desire to view sensational testimony against the rights of suspects and witnesses? Costello and his attorney pitted Costello's legally binding rights as an individual against a perceived right of the television audience to observe the proceedings. While the American Civil Liberties Union praised Senator Kefauver's treatment of witnesses, criticism from other sectors quickly mounted. Future Supreme Court justice Abe Fortas argued that televising congressional inquiries impeded the role of the judiciary and threatened the constitutional separation of powers. If the Kefauver Committee could stage a hearing before a vast television audience, Fortas reasoned, the evidence in any criminal trial that ensued would already be known to the jury and would have to be disallowed.[45] Legal scholar Alan Barth suggested, within his larger critique of government investigations, that this hearing would have been better handled behind the closed doors of a grand jury room. The positions these legal critics laid out provoked the prominent columnist Walter Lippmann to call for an immediate stop to the broadcast of any hearings that might lead to a criminal trial. Although Kefauver disagreed with what he characterized as an extreme position, he was willing to discuss such a moratorium, as evidenced by his introduction of Lippmann's column into the *Congressional Record* and his support for Wisconsin senator Alexander Wiley's resolution to study the impact of television on the political process.[46]

Congressional investigations like Kefauver's have the explicit task of collecting and disseminating information so that members of Congress can make educated decisions about necessary legislation. Television merely extended the audience for this informing function. Ultimately, however, television did more than simply go beyond educating members of Congress. When Virginia Hill played to the cameras with her sarcastic double entendres, she was using her star billing and charisma to shift public attention away from the senators' probe into her unexplained income. In contrast, by literally framing Costello's hands as they fidgeted and played with papers, the television cameras highlighted his discomfort and implied that he was hiding something. Television, many learned, did not just disseminate information. In skilled hands, it had the power to channel information toward a particular conclusion. Providing data to Congress was a primary objective of Senate inquiries like the Kefauver Committee; but the broadcast effectively changed the process from one of informing to performing for an audience. When Frank Costello stood up and walked out during his testimony, blaming the lights and the cameras' effect on his health, he foreshadowed the conflict that would accompany this extension of television's reach. A former counsel to the Federal Communications Commission, Telford Taylor, wondered if televising hearings would "exploit and aggravate the sensational features which all too frequently disfigure Congressional investigations." Taylor feared what the entertainment reporters celebrated, namely, that "a venal committee and an uninhibited advertiser might prostitute the investigative process and concoct a 'show' to the political advantage of the one and the financial benefit of the other." A commercialized medium would pervert democratic principles and basic rights even while it served to provide access to the political process in ways never before available. But even Taylor's pointed criticism was expressed as a modest wish for some oversight. He suggested that private foundations underwrite the cost of televising future proceedings and that the government construct special hearing rooms to minimize the intrusiveness of cameras, like the glass booths already in use at the United Nations. "Under proper safeguards," Taylor concluded, "the televising of public hearings should be a highly beneficial thing, both in principle and in fact. The citizen's opportunity for direct contact with governmental proceedings has been greatly enhanced. If the opportunity is intelligently exploited, our democracy will be strongly reinforced."[47]

When the Kefauver Committee moved from investigating to prosecuting witnesses for contempt of Congress or other charges, members of the judicial branch explicitly countered what they perceived as the legislative branch's excesses. Some legal scholars and judges maintained that televised investigations denied witnesses their right to due process. To them, the Kefauver Committee had abused its power. In fact, federal courts dismissed or reversed on appeal most of the committee's cases, often citing abuse of power and the pressure of television. For example, Charles E. Nelson, a Washington, D.C., bookie who appeared as a witness before the committee had turned over files that recorded detailed information about his lotteries and numbers operations. The committee turned the files over to the U.S. attorney for the District of Columbia, who used them to convict Nelson and others. U.S. Circuit Court judge David Bazelon, who wrote the opinion overturning the conviction, told an interviewer that "Nelson's freedom of choice had been dissolved in a brooding omnipresence of compulsion. The committee threatened prosecution for contempt if he refused to answer, for perjury if he lied, and for gambling activities if he told the truth."[48] Most of the contempt cases against uncooperative witnesses met similar fates. Of the forty-five citations, federal judges upheld only three convictions.

Allen Klots, a former special assistant to Secretary of State Henry Stimson, sought a complete ban on television hearings, arguing that everyone "becomes self-conscious and easily confused" on the witness stand. Agreeing with Costello's attorney, Klots raised the specter of the nation's communist enemies: "When we add the heat and glare of klieg lights, cameras, microphones, and all the other paraphernalia that usually go with television and radio broadcasting, the experience becomes for most people a species of torture. Indeed it is much too close to the familiar methods that totalitarian rulers use to elicit 'facts.' " Yet Klots's call to protect the rights of people "convicted before the bar of public opinion" was virtually drowned out by those heralding an "exciting extension of democracy." Some hoped that "this development of 'electronic journalism' " would extend to all proceedings of Congress, state legislatures, White House press conferences, and trials. Frank McNaughton, a journalist who provided commentary for the televised hearings, answered his own question "Would a TV Congress Improve Democracy?" not only with an enthusiastic yes but also with the prediction that "television ultimately will break through" congressional roadblocks. Similarly, *Newsweek* urged that "as many Congressional hearings as possible [be] televised." *The Spectator* remarked that "television has pointed the way to what may amount to a fresh court of appeal; where the ultimate verdicts will depend on the instinct, the perceptiveness and perhaps the prejudices not of twelve jurymen but of millions." The jury system would be transformed by television's new role as the conduit for citizen participation. The only negative consequence, according to the *Christian Century*, might be "the effect on the young if criminals and their hangers-on manage to 'stage an act' with such effect that the cameras glamorize them." Recalling the "public glorification" of Prohibition-era gangsters, Senator Martin warned that public indifference posed a graver threat than mass media glitz.[49]

Ultimately, however, it was the glitz that became the lasting contribution of the Kefauver Committee. Walter Lippmann predicted that "long after only the oldest reporters can still remember who Frank Costello was, or even Virginia Hill, Senator Kefauver's name may remain connected, like Lord Sandwich's and a quick lunch, with the grandeur and the miseries of conducting public affairs in front of the television audience."[50] The immediate outcome of the investigation proved Lippmann essentially correct. In 1950 Estes Kefauver was the junior senator from Tennessee with little recognition outside his native state. Just two years later he made his first run for the Democratic presidential nomination, announcing his decision even before Truman decided not to run. Despite winning the popular vote in the primaries, he lost the nomination to Adlai Stevenson.

His sudden popularity cannot be attributed to any great legislative legacy. Estes Kefauver and his committee won few short-term political victories. Of the 221 crime-related proposals the senators submitted for legislation, only a handful passed. The Boggs Act was the most important law to grow out of the Kefauver investigation. Sponsored by Louisiana representative Hale Boggs in the House and Kefauver in the Senate, it was one of the earliest "mandatory minimum" sentencing laws. The Boggs Act represented a major victory for Harry Anslinger and the Federal Bureau of Narcotics. It gave life to Anslinger's strong belief that drug dealing and drug use should be punished with lengthy incarceration. The bill called for a two-to five-year sentence for a first offense, five to ten for a second offense, and ten to twenty for a third offense. If drugs were sold to a minor, the act mandated a sentence of twenty years to life. In addition, the act mandated that those convicted of a third drug offense be barred from receiving a suspended sentence. Neither the Boggs Act nor the Kefauver Committee would have any major impact on organized crime. Some illegal casinos were closed down even as Las Vegas was growing from a small desert town to become a gangster-controlled gambling mecca. Kefauver's greatest hope—the establishment of a permanent Federal Crime Commission—would have to wait.

Despite the lack of a legislative legacy, the Kefauver Committee left a cultural legacy that would catapult the senator and others involved with the committee into the popular limelight. Kefauver accepted a special public affairs Emmy Award from the Academy of Television Arts and Sciences while stumping in New Hampshire in 1952. His book *Crime in America* remained on the *New York Times* bestseller list for twelve weeks, rising as high as number four. Four years later, Kefauver beat John F. Kennedy in a floor vote at the Democratic convention to win the vice presidential nomination. Other members of his committee capitalized on their political celebrity as well. Senator Herbert O'Conor appeared twenty-eight times on the CBS television series *Crime Syndicated*. Committee counsel Rudolph Halley appeared eighteen times on the same show and was soon elected president of the New York City Council, the second most powerful elected office in New York City.[51]

Both the hopes and the criticism surrounding the interrelationship of television and participatory democracy raised important questions that hinged on definitions of crime and criminal justice. Television and the Kefauver Committee formed an alliance from which each would benefit. Television, as *The Spectator* celebrated, did become a "new instrument of democracy," but not quite the sacred tool implied by the metaphor of klieg lights illuminating the sin that lurked in the shadows of polyglot cities. The committee's reliance on celebrity gangsters, sensational revelations, and the conventions of Cold War anticommunism made its hearings one of the most widely watched broadcasts of early television. But this reliance raised questions in the minds of both the subjects of investigation and professionals within the criminal justice system about the power of television to influence public opinion.

Many people blamed public apathy for the infiltration of organized crime into local communities and electoral politics. Television's power to entertain, educate, and stir the emotions of viewers seemed to mark the end of this apathy even as it raised new concerns about the rights of the accused. The connection between television, politics, and crime raised an even larger question in the minds of many: Would this aroused populace get off their couches and do something about the crime and corruption threatening their pocketbooks, their values, and their country?

"THE PROPER ACT OF CITIZENSHIP:"

Local Crime Committees and the

Response to Organized Crime

Virgil Peterson, operating director of the Chicago Crime Commission, was one of the many who blamed public apathy for the kinds of "sordid conditions" Senator Kefauver uncovered in his hearings. An apathetic citizenry, Peterson warned, would protect corrupt officials, ignore criminal enterprises, and prevent respectable public officials from doing their jobs.[1] In 1951 the Chicago Crime Commission sponsored a conference that led to the formation of the National Association of Citizens' Crime Commissions (NACCC). The following year, Peterson was elected its first president.[2] Members of crime commissions already at work in Philadelphia, Baltimore, Kansas City, Jacksonville, Miami, Tampa, St. Louis, Washington, Burbank, New York, and Chicago were in attendance. A representative from the Detroit Economic Club pledged to form an anti-crime committee in that city, and the Cleveland and Dallas crime committees soon joined. In his acceptance speech before the gathered members of the press, Peterson condemned "the failure of many people to understand the insidious influence of gangsters on government at all levels. People get excited over the dangers of communism, but the danger [of crime] is more insidious on some local levels."[3]

To be "insistent in the performance of the proper act of citizenship": this was the goal of the Kansas City Crime Commission, founded in 1950, according to its constitution. This concept of citizenship enlisted all Americans in the war on crime. Cold War anticommunism, and especially the era's fascination with and fear of nuclear annihilation, provided a parallel, redefining the responsibilities of citizenship and reinforcing warnings about the dangers of apathy. As J. Edgar Hoover wrote in his *Masters of Deceit*: "Citizenship carries with it not only *rights* but *obligations*. One of those is to do *our* part to preserve, protect, and defend the United States against all enemies, whether domestic or foreign. . . . Therefore, those individuals who place information they have regarding the communist conspiracy into the proper hands are making a contribution of great value to the security of their country."[4] It was not enough simply to be anticommunist oneself. Citizens were asked to take active measures, such as informing on neighbors and co-workers or joining in Civil Defense drills, in order to prevent the backsliding and apathy that would give the nation's enemies an entrée into American's communities. By symbolically deputizing the general public, Hoover took steps to popularize political activism toward his ends. Similarly, the citizens' crime committees of the decade, many of which had grown out of anti-crime efforts in the 1920s, sought to transform the state-sponsored activity of law enforcement into popular police actions.

Private Associations of Public-Spirited Citizens

Kefauver Committee member Senator Lester Hunt, in response to the overwhelming number of newspaper stories, constituent letters, and local crime commissions, asserted: "This committee has served as a powerful searchlight, exposing widespread national and local crime conditions to public gaze. Its activities have had a tremendous effect upon the whole field of law enforcement. Everywhere throughout the country citizens, made suddenly aware of the character and ramifications of organized crime, have risen up to demand greater vigilance in stamping out crime and corruption." Awareness of the problem, however, did not automatically provide a conduit for action. Watching television would not be enough to expel corrupt politicians and businesspeople. In order to reveal the "dark world between crime and politics," the article continued, public opinion would have to be directed toward "a permanently established private association of public-spirited citizens." Like Hunt's powerful searchlight, citizens' crime committees would "provide both knowledge and guidance," according to the Kefauver Committee.[5] By revealing the evil and guiding the good, local crime-fighting committees tied definitions of citizenship directly to the act of unmasking and eliminating criminals.

The Metropolitan Crime Commission of New Orleans (MCC) made explicit the religious overtones of Senator Hunt's reference to darkness and light. In the epigraph to the report that led to its founding in 1954, the MCC quoted from the Gospel according to John: "And this is the condemnation, that light is come into the world, and men loved darkness rather than light, because their deeds were evil. For every one that doeth evil hateth the light, neither cometh to the light, lest his deeds should be reproved."[6] Although several predated the Kefauver Committee, citizens' crime commissions such as the MCC shaped the definition of both criminality and citizenship, noting that the possibility of redemption from crime existed in their cities, but that immediate and harsh action by engaged citizens would be necessary to bring it about. The consecration of citizenship and damnation of corruption became interdependent concepts: if you were a criminal, you were not a citizen; and if you were a citizen, you fought against crime.

To be sure, other citizens' organizations sought more compassionate approaches to fighting crime. Some lobbied for prison reform and the rights of prisoners, earning important victories in several states. In addition, the mass media occasionally used their influence to advocate on behalf of prison reform, as in the case of a 1952 *Saturday Evening Post* article on Louisiana's state prison system. After the *Post* described the system as "America's worst," Louisiana reporters and radio commentators successfully lobbied for a new prison. In addition, some religious groups offered alternatives to incarceration and inclusive visions of the civic polity. The Pennsylvania Prison Society, the Louisville Council of Churches' Committee on Institutions, the South Dakota Council of Churches, and the Sioux Falls Ministerial Association all issued explicitly religious calls for social justice. Whether broadly criticizing the practice of incarceration or documenting overcrowded prisons and routine use of torture, they were fulfilling what they saw as the obligations of religious piety. Despite the efforts of the church-based social justice movement, notions of Christian piety among politicians and mainstream publications more often involved retributive forms of punishment. On the whole, prisoner advocates enjoyed neither the political access nor the wide public support achieved by the citizens' crime committees. Advocating for progressive reform was a political liability, while calling for authoritarian approaches to criminal justice proved to be a political advantage.[7]

Citizens' crime commissions differed from one another in size, scope, and relation to traditional law enforcement agencies. They ranged in size from the venerable Chicago Crime Commission with twenty-five full time employees to several commissions with only an operating director and a stenographer on the payroll. Many investigators and staff members were former employees of a wide variety of government agencies, including the Federal Bureau of Investigation, the intelligence divisions of the armed services, local police forces, and prosecutors' offices. Citizens' crime committees acknowledged the role of government in law enforcement, but most were private bureaus that did not answer to a broad voting constituency.[8]

Citizens' committees had an interest in reform but rarely called for sweeping political or economic changes. Citizen activism did not involve changing the relationship of the poor to the rich or the dominant to the dispossessed. Many commissions sought to detach "citizenship from its modern roots in institutional reform, in the welfare state and community struggles, and rearticulate [it within] the more Victorian concepts of charity, philanthropy and self-help," as Stuart Hall and David Held subsequently argued about Britain under Margaret Thatcher. Reflecting this philosophy, some citizens' crime committees advocated nongovernmental approaches to fighting crime, to the exclusion of traditional government-based police agencies. Spruille Braden, whose résumé included ambassadorial postings to several Latin American countries and an appointment as assistant secretary of state for American republic affairs, asserted in 1955 that his New York City Anti-Crime Committee would expand the obligation of citizenship to include fighting crime. As he assured the board of directors of the NYCACC, the solution to organized crime resided in the consumer and citizen rather than increased police powers: "Your Committee, on principle, is opposed to the expansion of government. In particular it deprecated the creation by the Federal, State, or local governments of super-agencies to combat organized crime."[9]

Other commissions maintained close ties to governmental crime-fighting organizations and supported strong and visible policing, but recognized that those who did not work directly for these agencies could also contribute to vigilance campaigns. In Missouri, for example, the Kansas City Crime Commission grew out of a grand jury investigation and had close ties to the police force. From early in its history, the KCCC has offered rewards for information leading to convictions.[10] Similarly, municipal court judge Nochem S. Winnet initiated the Citizens Crime Commission of Philadelphia in 1951 for the purpose of recommending changes in that city's criminal justice system. Not all commissions were so closely tied to the police and courts. The Baltimore, Chicago, and St. Louis crime commissions all emerged from local chambers of commerce. Some were explicitly hostile to the police force. The Metropolitan Crime Commission of New Orleans, while originally part of the mayor's office, quickly became independent from and antagonistic toward the notoriously corrupt New Orleans Police Department. Most crime committees nurtured relationships with the mass media instead of the police; the New York City Anti-Crime Committee, which grew out of a Kings County (Brooklyn) grand jury recommendation, was particularly notable for its strong ties to the mass media, including the New York Times. The Chicago Crime Commission saw itself as a watchdog agency of the court system, keeping tabs on criminal cases from arrest through parole and advocating for long prison sentences.[11] Whether complementary or critical, all independent crime commissions held that adequate crime fighting required citizenship participation beyond jury duty.

Despite these differences, crime commissions invariably included members of the city's economic elite and cultivated close relationships with local newspapers, ensuring that they would be taken seriously and would reach a wide audience. Through their power, prestige, and publicity, the commissions played a key role in shaping and maintaining civic attention to crime in many cities. The 1953 membership list of the KCCC board of directors reflected the national trend, reading like a Who's Who of Kansas City's corporate leaders: presidents of the Gas Service Company, Kansas City Life Insurance, Allen Chevrolet (the employees of the KCCC were mandated to drive Chevies), the superintendent of the local Standard Oil refinery, the executive manager of the Chamber of Commerce of Kansas City, the executive vice president of Trans-World Airlines (TWA), the president of Kansas City Southern Railway, the presidents of the Federal Reserve Bank of Kansas City and Kansas City Power and Light, among others. Similarly, the New York City Anti-Crime Committee included the chairman of IBM, two former ambassadors, and several bank presidents. In general, members of the boards of directors were male, though Martha Franklin of the Kansas City Women's Chamber of Commerce did serve on the KCCC board during the 1950s.[12]

Committees in Miami, New York, Gary, St. Louis, and other cities joined in this movement in the years immediately preceding the Kefauver hearings, providing a national structure that influenced Kefauver's call for a federal investigation of crime. The Kefauver Committee returned the favor by publicizing the efforts of local commissions around the country. The Crime Commission of Greater Miami (CCGM), formed in 1948 by the Dade County Bar Association, earned public recognition for providing Kefauver with records of its investigations. In 1950 the director of the California Crime Commission, along with Edmund Brown, the state's new attorney general, took the podium with the Kefauver Committee at press conferences.[13] Committees in smaller communities such as Burbank, California; Tampa, Florida; Reading, Pennsylvania; and Phenix City, Alabama, joined the national movement in the years immediately following the hearings. The Kefauver Committee provided the legitimacy and visibility necessary for the crime committees to influence crime-fighting agendas. Their era of greatest influence spanned the first half of the 1950s. Many folded before the 1960s, though several—including those in Chicago, Kansas City, and New Orleans—still exist.

These influential citizens' groups operated on the assumption that local and national crime was controlled by small but dangerous criminal organizations. The Kansas City Crime Commission, for example, concluded that "approximately twenty individuals are responsible for most of the organized criminal activities [in that area] in the past five years." In 1950 the Jackson County grand jury that supplied the KCCC's first members expressed the hope that the twenty-six indictments it was returning would wipe out organized crime in the city. By identifying such an absurdly small group of people—most of them foreign born—as responsible for the recent upsurges in crime, the KCCC could imply that the vast majority of Kansas City's population were honest citizens. This policy of containment led to a reliance on deportation as a primary goal for fighting crime. As in the red scare of 1919–20, by associating unwanted behavior and ideologies with those who were not native-born Americans, the KCCC insinuated that everything would be fine if they could just get rid of the immigrants. The commission sought the deportation of Italian-born Charles V. Carrollo as early as 1950. The Immigration and Naturalization Service began proceedings against him in 1951, deporting him to his native Sicily in 1954. The KCCC then quickly began pressuring federal immigration authorities to deport others they considered undesirables.[14]

Combating this small band of criminals drew attention to a supposed international conspiracy of Italians and Italian Americans. Although this idea was not wholly false, by focusing on Italian American gangsters, crime commissions could sometimes achieve partisan goals while ignoring other culprits. When Charles Binaggio, head of Kansas City's First District Democratic Club and an investor in illegal gambling casinos, was shot dead along with Charles Gargotta in April 1950, local and national newspapers ran a photograph of the bloody corpses sprawled beneath a portrait of President Truman at the club. To Kansas City Republicans, Truman had long been a symbol of that city's Democratic machine. In this way, crime coverage could simultaneously pin the blame on a handful of foreign-born gangsters and smear the powerful Kansas City Democrats. The presence of New York City resident Frank Costello at Binaggio's wake added fuel to suspicions of a national syndicate that controlled illegal activity. The additional presence of powerful Democratic leaders increased speculation in St. Louis and Kansas City newspapers about the reach of the Mafia's tentacles in the state. As one observer noted, "Here was an ugly picture of the unholy alliance between crime and politics paraded before the entire American public." As a result of this coverage, the Democrat-controlled Kefauver Committee added Kansas City to its tour, drawing on KCCC member and former federal grand jury investigator Max Goldschein for evidence of a criminal conspiracy dominated by the slain political leader. The prominence of Goldschein in Kefauver's Kansas City campaign was in keeping with the paradox of ethnicity and ideology in postwar America. After Italian *carabinieri* killed Salvatore Giuliano, a Sicilian bandit-hero, in July 1950, the Kansas City press and the KCCC increasingly trumpeted the international ramifications of local crime. Yet at the same time, they pointed to "ethnic" victims and investigators to affirm the non-ideological nature of their anticrime agenda. The following February, the *Kansas City Star* reported Kefauver's finding that Missouri had "narrowly escaped falling into [the] control" of a gambling syndicate headed by Lucky Luciano. The city's "unholy alliance" was thus dominated by a dark power that would require a national crusade. Expelling local residents and blaming crime on conspiracies based in Sicily protected the perception that citizens were inherently moral while deflecting criticism that an anti-Mafia campaign was also anti-Italian.[15]

Elsewhere, this deflection explicitly raised questions about the suitability of some immigrants for American citizenship. Making use of the perception of citizens as insiders who needed to be kept informed of the siege mounted by ethnic outsiders, the Kefauver Committee mocked the people appearing before them. Republican senator Charles Tobey of New Hampshire made it clear that as far as he was concerned, witnesses had few of the rights otherwise applicable to all citizens when he questioned Moses Polakoff, attorney for Charles Luciano and Meyer Lansky:

> *Senator Tobey*: How did you become counsel for such a dirty rat as [Luciano]?
>
> *Mr. Polakoff*: May I ask who you are, sir?
>
> *Senator Tobey:* My name is Senator Tobey. That isn't germane to this hearing but just a question of human interest. There are some men beyond the pale. He is one of them.
>
> *Mr. Polakoff*: I don't want to get into any controversy with you about that subject at the present time, but under our Constitution every person is entitled to his day in court whether he is innocent or not. When the day comes that a person becomes beyond the pale of justice, that means our liberty is gone. Minorities and undesirables and persons with bad reputations are more entitled to the protection of the law than are the so-called honorable people. I don't have to apologize to you . . .
>
> *Senator Tobey:* I didn't ask you to.
>
> *Mr. Polakoff*: Or anyone else for whom I represent.
>
> *Senator Tobey:* I look upon you in amazement.
>
> *Mr. Polakoff*: I look upon you in amazement, a Senator of the United States, for making such a statement.
>
> *Senator Tobey:* Let me say something to you. If I were counsel and that dirty rat came in, I would say, "You are entitled to representation but you can't get it from me. I will have no fellowship with you. Get out of my office and find your representation somewhere else."[16]

In this remarkable exchange, Senator Tobey drew a distinction between legal citizenship and social "fellowship" and insisted on clear moral boundaries that would exclude the "dirty rats" as ineligible for the latter. To Polakoff, extending constitutional protection to those who committed undesirable acts ensures that those who obey the law will have them when they need them.

The contextual specificity of "the public" was clear in the testimony of others who "had fellowship" with criminals though not engaging in illegal practices themselves. Like Moses Polakoff, James Adducci, a member of the Illinois House of Representatives from Chicago's immigrant-heavy West Side, challenged the righteous indignation of the committee members. In his testimony before them, Adducci pointed out that his accusers were blurring important legal issues. When

Committee Counsel Rudolph Halley raised suspicions that Adducci knew criminals, he replied: "I come from a very funny district. I have every element there is
in the world, I guess, in my district. I have the pimp, the jack roller, the safeblower,
the dope fiend. . . . Skid Row is in the heart of my district, where all those so-
called hoboes come in and congregate." Because he represented some dishonorable
people, the committee questioned Adducci's honor. Adducci demonstrated toler-
ance, pointing out that those who in one district are "so-called hoboes" are a
constituency worthy of representation in another. These attempts to break down
the sharp distinctions between lawlessness and righteousness did not go far. For
example, *Time* magazine grounded its defense of the committee in the moral
absolutes its members drew between the righteousness of the investigators and the
dishonorableness of the witnesses: "At Kefauver's right sat judicial-mannered Herbert O'Conor, Wyoming's Lester Hunt and New Hampshire's pious old Charles
E. Tobey, no lawyer, who glared with Yankee outrage at uneasy officials and sullen
thugs, burst out at intervals to denounce the sinners, once with such eloquence
that he moved himself to tears." In contrasting the pious senators with "sleek and
handsomely sullen hoods," a "burly bookmaker," and Italian Americans with
"raspy voices," *Time* was able to acknowledge the legal inaccuracies of Tobey's
points (he is "no lawyer") while supporting him on the grounds that he "denounced the sinners."[17]

Time's sympathetic treatment of Tobey's "Yankee outrage" and his denunciation
of sinners marked Jewish Moe Polakoff and his immigrant clients as evil outsiders.
Tobey saw Luciano and Lansky as "beyond the pale" and assumed that this gave
him license to make unsubstantiated charges before a television audience. Honest
Americans would "know what to do" once the television and newsreel lights joined
forces with a Christian redeemer in illuminating organized crime. By appealing
to his religious convictions, the senator found a way to define citizenship that
emphasized piety over legality.

Such thinking did not originate with Senator Tobey and the other members of
the Kefauver Committee. Even before the KCCC's board of directors drafted their
constitution "insisting on the proper act of citizenship," a motion was introduced
at an organizational meeting to invite Virgil Peterson, director of the Chicago
Crime Commission (CCC), and Austin Wyman, chairman of the board, to speak
to the Kansas City commission. Peterson served as a quasi-ambassador for the
citizens' crime commission movement. He flew from city to city, advising the
American Municipal Association on how to fight organized crime. The CCC was
at the forefront of the national movement, having been founded in 1918, during
the post–World War I crime scare. Peterson was a popular speaker and writer
whose *Barbarians in Our Midst*, with a glowing introduction by Senator Kefauver,
became a national best-seller in 1954.

The Chicago Crime Commission's ambitious publications included a journal,

Criminal Justice, as well as annual reports, numerous pamphlets, and press releases on specific issues. Its staff included former FBI agents and police investigators, and it enjoyed substantial financial support from Chicago's richest residents. The commission's court observers provided information on each case heard in Cook County and recorded "detailed statistical data relating to the performance on the part of law enforcement agencies, prosecutors, and the courts." The CCC sought increased professionalization of the Chicago Police Department while urging citizen involvement in the criminal justice system. In particular, Peterson urged political leaders to remove themselves from influencing the department's hiring, administration, and promotions. Next to increased professionalization, the most important objective of the Commission was to "drive rackets and racketeers out of Chicago." Peterson linked these goals to the duties of citizenship: "Law and order are the very pillars upon which society rests. Those charged with enforcing law and administering justice must be energized to the full performance of their duty or our social structure deteriorates. A crime commission that is independent and fearless, adequately financed, and equipped with a trained staff can make it possible for the average citizen to be equipped with facts that will assist him in making democracy work."[18] Peterson's goal, like that of the national movement he helped to establish, was never limited to lowering crime rates. He sought to strengthen democracy by creating an informed and active public, suspicious of judges, politicians, and political appointees.

Peterson defined the problem of organized crime in less conspiratorial terms than many of his contemporaries. In contrast to Federal Bureau of Narcotics head Harry Anslinger's and Kefauver's vision of the mob as a tight-knit hierarchical organization based on blood ties, Peterson more accurately argued that gangsters were part of a loosely allied band who cooperated with one another only occasionally. In addition, Peterson imported ideas of social anomie from the criminology conferences he frequented. "In newly settled and somewhat primitive communities gambling as well as prostitution has operated with little restraint," he wrote. "As society becomes more stable and as the population assumes a degree of permanency, invariably steps have been taken by the residents to place restriction on gambling and vice."[19] Peterson saw hope for criminals; perhaps revealing the influence of the Chicago school of sociology, Peterson believed that as migrants and immigrants adapted, they would develop internal restraint and earn their place in the larger community. But in the short term, the instability of newcomers demanded increased policing by established residents. Furthermore, Peterson's characterization of criminals as "barbarians" owes much to theories of racial and ethnic hierarchy reminiscent of Cesare Lombroso.

In *Barbarians in Our Midst,* Peterson drew a firm line between that "restrained" citizenry and "primitive" outsiders. The book explicitly linked crime rates to the introduction of newcomers to U.S. cities. As a result of the large number of war-related jobs, Chicago's population had increased by about 6 percent during the 1940s to 3.6 million. Peterson warned that this unstable population of over 200,000 newcomers provided new recruits for the city's criminal dynasties, dating from the Prohibition era. Focusing on the Al Capone–Frank Nitti gang of Chicago, the Binnagio gang of Kansas City, and the Costello–Adonis gang of New York, Peterson stated explicitly that urban crime was the work of Italian American gangsters who possessed "the ideals and frequently employed the methods of ancient barbaric tribes."[20] The infiltration of the political system by these barbarians demanded swift and strong action. Citizens' crime committees, Peterson claimed, would purify democratic principles. As citizens fought the "barbarians," their stake in democracy would increase, along with their sacred political status. If people only "realized that frequently the actual political rulers of cities and states are underworld bosses who possess the instincts, traditions and methods of barbarians," they would demand a "housecleaning." Should the politicians refuse or prove unable to do the job, "the respectable citizens of the locality [would] hold them accountable at the next election."[21]

Hue and Cry

The rhetoric and practice of fighting crime addressed cultural issues beyond reducing illegality. Crime fighters consistently referred to the perceived apathy of the increasingly prosperous Anglo-American middle class as a greater menace than that posed by lawbreakers. They believed that renewed participation in public life and a willingness to sacrifice for the benefit of the community would restore hope and honesty. These appeals to an honest citizenry defined what the anthropologist Renato Rosaldo calls "cultural citizenship," which he differentiates from legal definitions of citizenship. Cultural citizenship "refers to the right to be different and to belong, in a democratic, participatory sense. In this context, the term 'citizenship' broadly encompasses a sense of belonging, as in full citizenship versus second-class citizenship, and more narrowly includes legal definitions, where one either is or is not a citizen."[22] Rosaldo argues that people can lack legal citizenship status yet maintain influence and ties within a community. For example, people who reside in the United States illegally can and do participate in civic debates and shape local, regional, national, and international agendas. From street festivals to cooperative child care, people express and reinforce membership in civic bodies in ways not recognized by the legal definition of citizenship.

Conversely, people can have legal citizenship yet lack the prestige and power to transform that status into political legitimacy. Some people who—because of economic, racial, gender, or sexual status—remain disenfranchised because of persistent inequality find both overt and covert ways to transform or resist social, political, cultural, and economic experiences. In Walter Benn Michaels's ironic construction, "Wops and kikes can participate in American elections, but being able to participate in American elections doesn't make them American."[23] Culture, not legal status alone, determines what defines an American. Citizenship depends on how people understand that category within their daily experience. We articulate the meaning of citizenship when we associate "Americanism" with certain people and behavior. We similarly articulate the meaning of citizenship when we disassociate "Americanism" from other people or behavior regardless of their legal status. Like political citizenship, cultural citizenship is something that can be lost or gained, stolen or conferred.

Whereas legal citizenship is defined and debated in courts and legislative chambers, cultural citizenship is defined and debated throughout society—in streets and schools, homes and fraternal lodges, in workplaces and parks. The mass media are perhaps the most visible and powerful sites for defining, reinforcing, and transforming cultural citizenship. Because of their unique power to report and shape public agendas simultaneously, the mass media were a primary front for virtually all citizens' committees in their war on crime. Working with the press instead of government officials signaled a belief on the part of these committees that even honest officials were ill equipped to confront the problem of crime. For example, rather than work with the federal government, Virgil Peterson distanced the National Association of Citizens' Crime Commissions from Kefauver's call for a National Crime Commission financed by Senate appropriation. The NACCC announced that combating citizen apathy via media campaigns would instead be its primary goal and strategy. The first annual meeting of the organization took place in New York City and followed the lead of the New York City Anti-Crime Committee's focus on "informing and arousing public opinion" rather than on the oversight of the criminal justice system practiced by the Chicago Crime Commission. According to Spruille Braden, chair of the NYCACC, the national association planned to work with the media to "expose those fellows in the show window, giving public opinion a chance to operate."[24]

More than any other organization, the NYCACC focused its efforts on mass media campaigns. The organization cultivated relationships with local and New York–based national media outlets, even placing the wife of the publisher of the *New York Times* on its board. The NYCACC's first investigation looked at corruption on the New York waterfront, already in the public eye because of a Pulitzer Prize–winning series of articles in the *New York Sun* and thus a sure publicity generator. The major New York and New Jersey newspapers, as well as *Fortune, Business Week, Harper's, Reader's Digest, Collier's,* and a CBS documentary, quickly made the NYCACC a leader in the crime commission movement. Its later efforts focused on corruption in the perishable foods, garment trucking, and building industries. During the garment trucking campaign, the NYCACC cooperated with NBC in producing a documentary about a "Mr. X" who controlled the ladies' garment industry. From food to clothing and shelter, Braden argued, "the gangsters have begun an intensive campaign to control every facet of our lives."[25]

By focusing their energies on the media rather than directly pressuring the police and courts to arrest and prosecute criminals, the NYCACC could go after people who had not broken the law but who were contributing to "atrophying morality." Many of the "most heinous rackets," Braden explained, "are kept within the strict letter of the law, making indictment, prosecution, and conviction almost impossible." In fighting such undesirables, the police were limited by constitutional restrictions, laws, and public expectations. The NYCACC faced no such limitations. "Fortunately," said Braden, "the 'hue and cry' techniques" developed by the New York committee "afford the one means by which 'legal rackets' can be countered. That is, by placing the malefactors in a show window with the spotlight of public opinion continuously playing on them." The "hue and cry" method explicitly rejected the expansion of police practices, preferring "the Old Anglo Saxon common law process of pursuing a criminal with horn and voice." And the "horn and voice of today are the press, radio, and television."[26] Because laws did not exist to stop undesirables from moving into positions of power, the NYCACC provided this service during the four years of its existence.

Despite working separately from government-based crime fighters, the NYCACC and NACCC did not often criticize them. They were distinct from—but not necessarily antagonistic toward—professional law enforcement workers. Other crime committees went further, making investigation and exposure of wrongdoing by public officials their primary activities. Some committees were moved to operate outside the criminal justice system because they viewed local police departments as either indifferent to crime or themselves riddled with corruption. A few, including the Metropolitan Crime Commission of New Orleans and the Russell Betterment Association of Phenix City, Alabama, antagonized politicians, police, and district attorneys by focusing almost entirely on the corrupt criminal justice systems in their regions.

This strategy was both practical and theoretical. Fighting crime in New Orleans meant fighting systemic corruption in a police department. Eliminating organized gambling in Phenix City meant confronting the Russell County deputy sheriff and the circuit solicitor, both of whom were later implicated in a bribery and murder scandal. While perhaps a primarily practical approach, focusing on corrupt officials enabled the crime committees to articulate a definition of community engagement and cultural citizenship distinct from that governing elected and appointed officials. In taking these actions, groups such as the MCC and the RBA suggested that their government officials were not representative of the morality or values of the citizenry. Whereas some, like the New York and the Chicago committees, merely argued that government agencies were ill equipped to combat corruption and organized crime, the MCC and the RBA identified their crime fighters as the primary source of corruption and organized crime in their communities. In New Orleans, the MCC's antagonistic relationship with the police department necessitated that it work closely with the media—in this case the *New Orleans Times-Picayune*—to publicize the scope and nature of police corruption. More than simply public relations, the media campaign of the MCC represented a primary strategy for fighting crime.

Aaron Kohn, a former FBI agent fresh from an investigation of corruption in the Chicago Police Department, headed the effort to clean up New Orleans. The Chicago City Council had hired Kohn to head the Emergency Crime Commission after Republican committeeman Charles Gross was murdered in 1952. Kohn concluded in his final report that the commission "will serve its purpose only if it helps to create understanding of some of the major symptoms of the Chicago problems, so that citizens may find incentive to take constructive action through public servants, not 'political bosses.' " Kohn's distinction between public servants and political bosses suggested that elected officials could not be trusted to clean up corruption since some were themselves the source of corruption. In his report, Kohn called for the resignation of police commissioner Timothy O'Connor and the firing of Chicago police captain Redmond P. Gibbons for failing to perform the duties of their office. Kohn urged that the Police Department, in addition to cooperating with the Chicago Crime Commission and the Citizens of Greater Chicago, enlist "the assistance of the press, radio and TV stations to publicize the identities and efforts of extraordinarily cooperative citizens."[27] His sensational report on crime and his plan for making a recharged citizenry the solution to it brought Kohn national exposure as someone willing to confront corrupt politicians and police officials.

This publicity led the city of New Orleans to bring in Kohn to head a similar investigation. The Special Citizens Investigating Committee was predated by the Special Citizens' Committee for the Vieux Carré, founded in response to the "Mickey Finn" murder of a tourist in the French Quarter on New Year's Eve 1950. The national media coverage of this crime threatened tourism to the city, a major source of revenue. The New Orleans Commission Council (or City Council) formed the Special Citizens Investigating Committee in response to the Kefauver hearings and a series of newspaper articles describing systemic police corruption. As executive director and chief investigator of the committee, Kohn quickly ran into roadblocks put in place by the New Orleans Police Department and the Commission Council that had hired him. In his report Kohn described an organized system of graft throughout the New Orleans Police Department, paid by operators of illegal lotteries and other gambling concerns. Kohn argued that local law enforcement agencies could not combat vice because the gangsters had already corrupted them. The City Commission suppressed the final report for several months, releasing it only after a sympathetic commissioner leaked it to the press.[28]

The suppression of the report made it clear that Kohn had touched a nerve in the upper reaches of New Orleans politics. The police sued the Special Committee and arrested Kohn for refusing to reveal his sources. After a bitter lawsuit resulted in a court injunction against the committee, Kohn was drafted by a citizens' group to found and serve as director of the Metropolitan Crime Commission of New Orleans. According to Kohn, the job of citizens' crime committees was to expose official corruption with the cooperation of the media, a conclusion he arrived at after discovering the unwillingness of government officials to police themselves. The MCC located the problem of crime in an alliance between corrupt police, politicians, and criminals. By providing leads to the *New Orleans Times-Picayune*, Kohn helped establish a cooperative relationship with the local media, which contrasted with the police department's hostility toward Kohn and the MCC.[29]

Its antagonistic relationship with the police was not the only factor that distinguished the MCC from the larger crime committee movement. Unlike Virgil Peterson, Kohn was highly critical not only of political corruption but also of the standard police practice of arresting African Americans not under suspicion for any crime, simply in order to fulfill the chief of detective's desire for large numbers of arrests. "Frequently," he reported, "when a Bureau car 'needs' pinches for their monthly record and even though assigned elsewhere, they often raid the Negro belt."[30] Kohn also argued that betting should be made legal in order to eliminate illegal profits. The MCC's attention to systemic racism and calls for legalized gambling placed Kohn in sharp contrast to Peterson, Kefauver, and Braden. Although he did write a letter in support of Peterson's national commission, because of Kohn's unique stands and controversial tactics, his organization chose not to join the national organization.[31] Like the other crime committees, however, the MCC made a broad call for citizen participation as the solution to corruption and organized crime. But unlike most other committees, it did not extend this participation to cooperating with law enforcement officials. The MCC's criticism of the police eventually led to Kohn's arrest. Elsewhere, anti-vice efforts that exposed political and police complicity had even more serious consequences.

Phenix City, Alabama, lies just across the Chattahoochee River from Fort Benning, Georgia, the army's biggest infantry training center during the 1940s and early 1950s. The army trainees helped support a strip of bars, pawnshops, gambling halls, and brothels. In 1951 ten Phenix City residents founded a countywide citizens' crime committee, the Russell Betterment Association, in response to the inability or unwillingness of the local police and political establishment to clean up the city. One of their first initiatives was an unsuccessful attempt to impeach the local sheriff. As a result, the home of Hugh Bentley, one of the founders of the RBA and a local sporting goods and appliance store owner, was bombed.[32]

The RBA was outraged at what its members described as gangster control of their county. In 1954 one of the RBA's founders, former state senator Albert L.

Patterson, won the Democratic nomination for attorney general of Alabama in a bitterly fought primary in which both candidates hurled accusations of "gangster ties." In Alabama at the time, the Democratic nomination was enough to make Patterson the state's next attorney general. Although he did close down vice in this "Sodom on the Chattahoochee," it was not in the way he might have preferred. On April 18, 1954, Patterson was murdered outside the law office he shared with his son John. Later that year, the Russell County deputy sheriff and the circuit solicitor for Phenix City, both of whom had grown wealthy on graft, were indicted for the murder. Governor Gordon Persons had by then declared martial law in Russell County and stripped the county sheriff, the Phenix City police chief, and all his officers of badges, weapons, and squad cars. The state's National Guard and Highway Patrol assumed police duties in the region, and Fort Benning's soldiers were barred from the city during the crisis. The Phenix City Ministerial Alliance invited the Reverend Billy Graham to conduct "a sin-killing, old-time revival reaching into every soul." By November, town officials had regained control of local affairs; they razed the strip of honky-tonks amid plans for a "modern shopping center."[33]

Phenix City and the Russell Betterment Association quickly became a national cause célèbre. Editorials advised that "the nation should take a long look at the Alabama assassination, for it bears directly on a national problem. This is the problem of the moral strain to which boys drafted for service are subjected." With "carnivals of liquor, gambling, and prostitution" hugging the border of an army training center, no parent could ignore the problems of this small town. After Patterson's death, his son and law partner, John Patterson, ran unopposed for attorney general, vowing to "get the gangs that killed my father." In 1955 the National Municipal League, along with *Look* magazine, credited the Russell Betterment Association and the local Junior Chamber of Commerce with exposing corruption and installing new officials, and proclaimed Phenix City an "All American City." *Life* magazine argued that the Allied Artists film *The Phenix City Story* was "one of the finest little crime shockers of the year." The film, shot on location in Alabama, featured the efforts of John Patterson (portrayed by Richard Kiley) to restore honor to Phenix City.[34]

Most crime committees did not antagonize local police. Some cooperated with the police, as did the New York City Anti-Crime Committee. The chair of the New York organization expressed hope that his organization would complement the "after the fact" investigations of official agencies and "keep tabs on racket activities before they came within the ken of official investigations" so that "unofficial investigators would win public support for official agencies and grand juries." The mass media publicized and celebrated the efforts of citizens' crime committees. Media campaigns emphasized non-governmental solutions, which appealed to the fiscal conservatism of several leaders of the movement, particularly

Virgil Peterson and Spruille Braden. But for the most part these campaigns resulted from the committees' realization that some towns and cities were run as actual criminal enterprises structured for maximum profit by corrupt police and politicians. In turning to the media as a conduit for and shaper of citizen action, the committees ultimately asserted the belief that citizens must remain vigilant and active. They could not trust their elected officials to solve the problem of crime in their communities, nor could they allow citizenship to be defined only in relation to formal state agencies. Not only would this approach be ineffective in solving crime, but also, some citizens' committees argued, it would give license to elected criminals to reap maximum profits from their illegal enterprises.[35]

"Freedom Is a Frightening Thing"

Ineffective or corrupt law enforcement was not simply the result of professional and moral failure on the part of those entrusted to fight crime. Organized crime and official corruption proved to the citizens' crime committees that communities had failed to live up to the obligations of a united citizenry. What had been a "shadow government" operating in the dark corners of immigrant America seemed to be taking over entire municipalities, major cities, even U.S. Army bases during a time of war. It was able to do so, according to crime committees, because the citizenry had grown apathetic in the years since World War II.

In December 1949, the American Municipal Association held its annual convention in Cleveland. According to Peterson, who addressed the closing session, "considerable time" was devoted to "discussing methods of combating syndicated crime," the theme of that year's convention. Illinois governor Adlai Stevenson told the gathering, "The greatest menace is that the public will come to accept organized crime as something inevitable, as a necessary part of our social system." Stevenson saw lax law enforcement as evidence that "a large segment of the population does not want effective law enforcement, at least not badly enough to labor for good government as diligently as those who want bad government labor for it." This lack of collective will provided gamblers, narcotics dealers, and racketeers with the opportunity to create "a state within a state, an inner enemy, a totalitarian underworld."[36] That is, the menace of organized crime bored away at the democratic principles at the core of U.S. political culture. Crime was the ghostly doppelganger of business, government, entertainment, and family, which threatened to take government away from "the people." Stevenson believed that strengthening traditional control over those institutions would result in stamping out the problem.

The notion of the corruptibility of a broad range of Americans proved particularly disturbing during the 1950s. The presence of a foreign-born menace, while itself distressing to crime fighters and journalists, could be addressed with tightened immigration laws and xenophobic sentencing guidelines. Scapegoating the foreign-born for the larger problem of crime also served as a salve; if Italian Americans and other immigrants could be held responsible, crime fighters could continue believing in the innate purity of Anglo-American citizens. In many cases, this was the overly simplistic framework many commentators chose to believe in. If criminal behavior pointed to the presence of "un-American" people, then the solution lay in a strong assertion of exclusionary Americanism. When Estes Kefauver pointed to the presence of international organized crime in American culture and politics, he did more than call for new regulations and laws to control the spread of illicit activities. He was asking for a reaffirmation of an older principle of Anglo-American citizenship, one that emphasized rural values and simple pleasures. Some blamed the ebbing of this vision of cultural citizenship on the turn-of-the century wave of immigration from eastern and southern Europe, personified by the witnesses before Kevauver's committee. The frontier vision contrasted with the vision of diamond-studded tie clips and expensive suits and the urban pleasures of sex, drugs, and high-stakes gambling which the gangsters sought to control. Decency, honor, and citizenship were thus circumscribed through staged displays of immigrants in many of the crime investigations of the 1950s.

In this way these investigations articulated a vision of citizenship that updated older racialized and nativist notions of "Americanism" within the context of Cold War anticommunism. Just as citizenship could be disassociated from legal status, criminality could be disassociated from violation of any given law. Some people could safely break some laws, as when "law-abiding citizens" placed bets or engaged in games of chance. Only the most naive police officer did not know about the gaming tables in local Elks' Clubs. Betting at a racetrack's pari-mutuel window was legal, but phoning in a bet to a bookie was not. Playing roulette at a church or synagogue social gathering was legal, but not in the back room of a barbershop or bar. Few crime committees called for the criminalization of all gambling. In addition, the prominent criminologists who were focusing on white-collar crime never appeared before the Kefauver Committee, and other crime committees rarely addressed this problem.[37]

By ignoring lawbreaking among native-born whites, crime committees, elected officials, and the popular press utilized a rhetorical strategy that created the concept of the inherently "good" American. Benedict Anderson described this act of inventing a community as inscribing a "unique sacredness" applicable to members. His model is particularly cogent in this case. American citizens were virtuous people who had been "suckered" by sleazy outsiders who held individual gain above community solidarity. That "America's boys" were fighting the Korean War to "preserve the blessings of Democracy," as one observer of the hearings noted, only increased the patriotic fervor of the Kefauver Committee.[38]

This "uniquely sacred" citizenry was invented in different ways for different purposes. *Collier's*, for instance, appealed to this sense of community to create an audience for its advertisers. Its rhetoric was similar to the senators', though used in a commercial context. Whatever their motives, when addressing "the public," "the people," or "American citizens," politicians and media outlets imagined as a unified whole what in actuality was a diversity of experiences and investments in the status quo. In doing so, they transformed a polyglot group—lawbreakers and law-abiders, native born and foreign born, whites and people of color—into an orthodox entity.[39]

This process of containment was the obverse face of the fear that crime and corruption would ultimately infiltrate and take over cherished government institutions. National best sellers such as *In Every War But One* and *Tomorrow!* tapped into a widespread anxiety that public apathy would lead to failure of the collective will and even to nuclear annihilation. *In Every War But One* noted that in Korea, an alarming number of captured U.S. troops were cooperating with the enemy by disseminating communist propaganda and providing military intelligence. *Tomorrow!*, Philip Wylie's novel about a heroic civil defense initiative, illustrated the interconnections between crime, citizen apathy, and nuclear fear like few other Cold War novels. In a subplot, a bored middle manager at a midwestern bank falls deep in debt to gangsters. Although the Baileys are an "average" family, their lack of community spirit results in their moral disintegration:

> The Baileys, in sum, were not intentionally evil people. Like many, they were engaged in striving toward that place in life where their hypocrisies, small dishonesties, speculations and shady deals would become "*unnecessary.*" To them, as to millions of other American families, not only "keeping up" but "getting ahead" have priority over conscience; honor is a luxury they conceive of as desirable, even ideal, but possible only to those lucky few who somehow have run all the gantlets, crossed all the goals, and bought all the nationally advertised essentials, including airplane trips abroad, summer homes, large annuities and permanent vaults.[40]

The solution to these hypocrisies and dishonesties coincided with Wylie's prescription for the communist nuclear threat: an active citizenry connected by way of community-based civil defense. The Baileys live next door to Henry Conner, a Civil Defense warden:

> Henry sat with some thirty men and women, block wardens, section heads, neighbors, old friends, most of them his own age, many of them people with whom he'd gone through grammar and high school in Green Prairie. . . . Most of the men were employed in good positions, like Henry Conner [an accountant for a large hardware store]; most of the women were housewives. But Ed Pratt, sitting in a kitchen chair

with his hat still on the back of his head and a toothpick in his teeth, was a house painter. Joe Dennison, his broad backside propped on the window sill and his blue shirt open, owned and ran a bulldozer, contracting privately for its use. . . . Civil Defense had been an interesting way to learn unknown things concerning a city, how it is put together, and what makes it run; it had been at the same time that humanly more valuable thing: an opportunity to demonstrate private skills and special knowledge.[41]

For Wylie, as for Adlai Stevenson, only an active citizenry could save America from nuclear annihilation. His images of such a citizenry emphasized constructive small-town values, personified by the hardware store employee, the housewife, the painter, and the construction worker—not the self-interested banker next door.

In response to the generalized fear that citizens were opening the door to the destruction of their own communities and civic institutions through their inaction, some crime committees began to work with or within state and local governments in the hope of enforcing their vision of citizenship. No longer simply a matter of rooting out a few gangsters, their crime-fighting agenda shifted to one of reclaiming beloved institutions and values. In Minnesota, for example, George Mac-Kinnon, who called for the creation of a Minnesota Crime Commission during his failed 1956 race for governor, warned the Minneapolis Rotarians that Frank Costello had reportedly called for "the ultimate infiltration of numerous legitimate business enterprises." When entering legitimate businesses, MacKinnon charged, Costello and his kind "bring with them their disrespect for law and ethical business standards. They continue to use racketeering methods and illegal practices. There comes a day when they become so strong and strategically located in so many different ventures, and so secure economically, that they control the community at its key points." When two local gangsters, Isidore "Kid Cann" Blumenfeld and Tommy Banks, became the largest stockholders in the Twin Cities Rapid Transit Company, MacKinnon's fears seemed to be coming true. Although MacKinnon lost the election, the state financed the Commission to Study Juvenile Delinquency, Crime, and Corrections and formed Minnesota's first Department of Corrections.[42]

In contrast to those who thought that citizens merely needed to be "shown the light," the Commission to Study Juvenile Delinquency, Crime, and Corrections focused on the potential corruptibility of all people, citing as an example a fifteen-year-old study conducted by *Reader's Digest* in which products with minor problems were sent out for repair: "63 percent of garage men, 64 percent of radio repairmen, and 49 percent of the watch repairmen lied, inserted unnecessary work and charged for work not done, for new parts not needed, and parts not installed." Similarly, the California Crime Commission feared that the problems imported by foreigners had spread beyond the immigrant enclaves, and that narcotics and "the abortion racket" threatened to make criminals out of everyone. In Washington, Warren Olney III, deputy attorney general in charge of the criminal division, reported that " 'bennies,' 'goof balls,' 'pep pills,' and 'thrill pills' were being dispensed illegally to truck drivers all over the country."[43] Citizens' crime committees wanted to reshape the meaning of citizenship, but they also wanted to maintain existing power structures out of a fear that the barbarians were already succeeding in sacking civilization. As J. Edgar Hoover warned, "Freedom, divorced from authority and discipline, is a frightening thing and is the first step toward total moral degeneration."[44] In the face of a beast this fierce, it did not matter that good people could recognize danger when they saw it. Local police forces were simply unequipped to deal with the savvy—albeit barbaric—gangs. *Collier's* reported that "the modern mobs are so tough, so well heeled, so respectable, and so influential that Uncle Sam may have to step in and help local officials cut them down. But before this is done, the underworld links to the upperworld, the scope and pattern of its operations all over America must be bared. Given the truth, Americans will know what to do—even about the mobsters."[45] Dealing with the sinister alien conspiracy that was endangering American political and corporate systems required drastic measures: deportation and tightened immigration restrictions.

Deportation and the Protection of Citizenship

Mobsters were outsiders and citizens were honest. In order to maintain this distinction, the Immigration and Naturalization Service and the Justice Department would have to show that mobsters had lied in order to become naturalized (as they tried to do with Frank Costello and Meyer Lansky), and Congress would have to tighten immigration statutes to further regulate America's borders. The Kefauver Committee recommended that "the immigration laws should be amended to facilitate deportation of criminal and other undesirable aliens. . . . Some of the criminals who occupy key positions in criminal gangs and syndicates are alien-born. Some came into this country illegally. Some have never been naturalized. Others obtained naturalization certificates by concealing their criminal activities." In a later recommendation, the committee went further, asking Congress to punish those who "smuggle, conceal, or harbor aliens."[46]

In mentioning the practice of deportation in the Cold War context, one brings immediately to mind the use of deportation to muzzle or exclude foreign-born leftists. The U.S. government denied visas, confiscated passports, and deported radicals throughout this period. In this sense, deportation served the interests of the broader anticommunist movement, as it had during the Palmer raids of 1919–20. Once again the U.S. government was using immigration policy to control dissent in the hope of securing an ideological consensus.

Those with some knowledge of Chicano history, labor history, or the history of the Border Patrol might also be reminded of the militarized and racist "Operation Wetback" of 1954, known as "Operation Terror" by leftists of the time. This large-scale deportation targeted Mexican-born agricultural and industrial workers in the West and Southwest. Its scale is reflected in the fact that, whereas in 1949 the INS apprehended about 310,000 people, in 1954, largely as a result of "Operation Wetback," this number exceeded 1 million, before dropping back to 256,000 the next year. According to the Labor Department, 1,700 so-called illegal aliens were apprehended per day at the peak of this operation.[47] There were even cases of native-born Mexican Americans who were stripped of their citizenship and deported during this period.[48] In terms of numbers and long-range impact, "Operation Wetback" was among the most significant events in U.S. immigration history. The largest number of deportations were for entering the United States without a permit or for overstaying temporary work or tourist permits. This was the stated motive of "Operation Wetback." One relief organization estimated that fully 87 percent of its cases were targeted for deportation for this reason.[49] In addition, some deportations resulted from specific criminal associations or actions before or after legal immigration. The deportation of radicals was made possible under the Internal Security Act and the 1952 McCarran-Walter Act, leading one person indicted under the Internal Security Act to dub "McCarranism our Mc-Carthyism."[50] Many judges, journalists, and activists objected to this use of deportation on primarily free speech grounds. But beyond a small handful of immigration lawyers and judges of rare courage, criminal deportation raised few eyebrows.[51]

The use of criminal deportation dates to a 1910 law which "decreed that aliens identified with prostitution in the United States should be deported."[52] The use of deportation against contract laborers dates to 1888, and against radicals to a 1917 law calling for the expulsion of anarchists, who had been deemed excludable at time of entry in 1903.[53] Beginning in 1917, people could be deported if the reason for their exclusion had not been discovered at time of entry. These reasons ranged from obtaining a visa by fraud or misrepresentation of facts (including marriage status or place of birth) in order to obtain non-quota status, to concealing previous crimes or creating a false identity in order to cover up earlier deportation.[54] Deportation was later expanded to include paroled federal prisoners.[55]

Criminal deportation centered in particular on what were called "crimes of moral turpitude," a Victorian concept that first appeared in an 1891 act.[56] What did "moral turpitude" mean? Early in the twentieth century, U.S. Appeals Court judge Learned Hand defined crimes of moral turpitude as those that violated "commonly accepted mores."[57] A search for more specific definitions leads to contradictory answers ranging from petty larceny to murder. The Immigration and Nationality Act of 1952 (the McCarran-Walter Act) created a specific provision for violators of narcotics laws, including non-convicted drug addicts. It is important to add that judges routinely issued "suspensions of deportation," but this was not always quite the blessing it seemed, since these suspensions could be denied or lifted for such "moral" lapses as adultery or excessive drinking.[58] Ultimately, few people were deported either for concealing previous crimes or for committing crimes of "moral turpitude" after immigration.

Rather than wait for new legislation, Attorney General J. P. McGranery hoped to "restore the dignity of citizenship" by stripping foreign-born racketeers and criminals of their U.S. citizenship. In 1952 McGranery compiled a list of "unsavory characters" who would become targets of Justice Department deportation cases. He promised to "rid the country of naturalized Communists," but leaked only the names of foreign-born criminals. The film star Charlie Chaplin made the list for "grave moral charges," including speaking with "contemptible regard for the high state of womanhood." The Justice Department also instigated denaturalization proceedings against Frank Costello, Al Capone associates Nicholas Circella and Anthony Volpe, Philadelphia numbers operator Hyman Chaim Stromberg, and Cleveland's Alfred Polizzi, who had a string of gambling and Prohibition violations dating to 1920. The very existence of the list, however, proved the undoing of some of McGranery's cases. The Supreme Court agreed with gangster Joe Acardi's lawyer, who argued that the appearance of his client's name on the list had prejudiced the Board of Immigration Appeals against him. The Department of Justice brought denaturalization actions against many who appeared before the Kefauver Committee. After Kefauver witness Joe Adonis served two and a half years in the New Jersey state prison in Trenton, his deportation was ordered in 1953. Albert Anastasia lost his citizenship the next year after the Justice Department proved that he had lied about his police record when he applied for naturalization decades earlier.[59]

As denaturalization and deportation became primary tools for fighting organized crime, the idea that the foreign-born were infecting the public with the disease of crime provided an impetus not only for anti-crime deportations but also for anti-immigrant measures more generally. Despite a drastic reduction in emigration from southern and eastern Europe in the decades after World War I, the 1950s saw a resurgence of nativism. A Pennsylvania organization, the Neighborhood Prayer Band, justified draconian anti-crime measures by pointing to the foreign origin of the criminals featured in Kefauver's crime hearings. In a letter to Kefauver they wrote: "Let's clean house thoroughly. Send every foreigner back where he belongs, or put these degrading murderers behind bars where they can't pollute our growing boys and girls." Many viewers of the hearings believed that the Italian surnames of the witnesses identified the source of the problem and that immigration quotas should be adjusted accordingly.[60]

The debate over immigration quotas eventually resulted in the McCarran-Walter Act, with its generous quotas for northern and western Europeans and few slots for the rest of the world. Nevertheless, new voices were beginning to be heard in the conversation about the meaning of American citizenship. The McCarran-Walter Act attracted wider opposition than previous immigration restriction acts, and was passed over President Truman's veto. Civil rights groups, immigration lawyers, judges, elected officials, and media outlets joined in the debate over immigration quotas, which had remained stable since 1924. As second- and third-generation descendants of southern and eastern European immigrants became divided along class lines, access to political and media outlets increased. Along with this new prestige came the ability to reshape local and national agendas from within the political and economic center. Some in the traditional Anglo-American elite welcomed these changes as signs of progress and democracy; others saw them as dangerous harbingers of the imminent corrosion of Americanism. In seeking to—as they saw it—protect America from immoral forces, some turned to the xenophobic wing of the anti-radical and anticommunist movements. Others explicitly or implicitly linked political corruption, labor racketeering, drug trafficking, gambling, extortion, and other such crimes to the class mobility of white ethnics.[61]

The contrast between citizenship and criminality could be used equally by those who were comfortable with a large federal bureaucracy (often Democrats) and those who sought to shrink the role of the federal government (often Republicans). In seeking to increase the powers of the bureaucracy, the Kefauver Committee came into conflict with many citizens' crime committees distrustful of government. The answer Kefauver came up with was to depend on a powerful federal Justice Department, Internal Revenue Service, and Immigration Service to combat ethnic organized crime while admitting that "the crisis of law enforcement which has been uncovered by the committee is basically a State and local crisis."[62] Despite their ideological differences, the Kefauver Committee relied on citizens' crime committees and the mass media where it could not legislate: on the level of state and local government.

There would be other Senate inquiries to catapult politicians into celebrity status. Later in the 1950s the McClellan Committee brought Robert F. Kennedy into the public eye in a standoff with Teamster president Jimmy Hoffa. Like Senator Kefauver, Kennedy drew on the national network of local crime committees in striving for wide public acceptance of his views. In 1955 Spruille Braden, chairman of the New York Anti-Crime Committee, reported on the latest infiltration of the octopus, foreshadowing the next great organized crime investigation: "In a recent city-wide trucking strike in New York, the accepted spokesman of the trucking union in this community was replaced by order of James R.

Hoffa. . . . Hoffa put in as spokesman a man who has been a life-long associate of the worst gangsters in this city [and] is a friend and associate of several major figures in the ranks of gangsterdom."[63] The specific targets of investigation might change, but one thing remained constant: those whose questionable contacts brought them before future congressional inquiries were, and would remain, "beyond the pale."

THE MAN IN THE PIN-STRIPED SUIT:

Lucky Luciano and the
Federal Bureau of Narcotics

What did it take to join the ranks of public-spirited citizens in 1950s America? The icon of the middle-class white male—the man in the gray flannel suit—provided an ironic answer. Tom Rath, the protagonist of the novel, and subsequently the film, whose title has become something of a period cliché, commutes every day between his Manhattan job and his family in the Connecticut suburbs. In the film version, a friend on the train tells Tom (Gregory Peck) about an opening in public relations at "United Broadcasting." Tom says he knows nothing about p.r., but his companion replies: "Who does? You got a clean shirt, you bathe every day, that's all there is to it." Tom eventually takes the job, and the story quickly became a lesson in responsibility to family and the virtues of honesty and integrity. As Betsy Rath (Jennifer Jones) says to her husband, "For a decent man, there's never any peace of mind without honesty." It is Tom Rath's honesty rather than his ambition that makes him the hero.[1]

A clean shirt did not necessarily connote decency. To be a decent man, honest and loyal to his family, Tom has to keep his work ethic and his ambition in check. Far from connoting decency, one influential criminologist of the time argued, white collars were increasingly the uniform of criminals. Edwin H. Sutherland reminded readers of Thorstein Veblen's 1899 insight: "The ideal pecuniary man is like the ideal delinquent in his unscrupulous conversion of goods and persons to his own ends, and in callous disregard of the feelings and wishes of others and of the remoter effects of his actions, but he is unlike him in possessing a keener sense of status and in working more far-sightedly to a remoter end." Sutherland went further: his 1949 study *White Collar Crime* showed that the criminality of corporations was characterized by a high rate of recidivism as well as secrecy and conspiracy. Most important, Sutherland overturned the widely held assumption that crime rates were higher among the mass of the population with low incomes and lower among the few with high incomes.[2] You could no longer tell a criminal by the way he or she looked, dressed, or smelled, Sutherland argued. Criminality had infiltrated and co-opted American corporate life itself.

The changing fears of crime during the late 1940s and early 1950s reflected the same Cold War anxieties that manifested themselves in attacks on domestic and foreign communists. Both McCarthyites and anti-crime crusaders drew representational power from the perceived threat that communists and criminals alike posed to a perpetually unstable corporate, ethnic/racial, and gender hierarchy. In some of the most prominent cases of red-baiting, Senator Joseph McCarthy, among others, argued that it was the people who appeared most stable—the bureaucrat, the housewife—who posed the greatest danger to freedom, loosely defined. McCarthy, in his infamous speech to the Women's Republican Club of Wheeling, West Virginia, urged his listeners to be wary of people who seemed most safe. He reserved special venom for Secretary of State Dean Acheson, describing him as a "pompous diplomat in striped pants, with a phony British accent," who "proclaimed to the American people that Christ on the Mount endorsed communism, high treason, and betrayal of sacred trust." Those who seemed most blessed with intelligence, good manners, and grace, those "who have had all the benefits that the wealthiest nation on earth has had to offer—the finest homes, the finest college education, and the finest jobs in Government we can give, . . . the bright young men who are born with the silver spoons in their mouths are the ones who have been the worst." The clichés of normalcy—the gray flannel suit, and the heterosexual nuclear family—were used to intimidate and silence critics of capitalism. Cold War anticommunism's greatest horror culminated in the execution of a middle-class husband and wife—the parents of two young boys—who, according to the judge who sentenced Ethel and Julius Rosenberg to death, "placed their devotion to their cause above their own personal safety and were conscious that they were sacrificing their own children, should their misdeeds be detected." By arguing that outward conformity in behavior and family relationships could mask ulterior motives, Cold Warriors sought to suppress those who did not conform to their ideological mandates.[3]

Like fifties anticommunists, fifties crime busters also drew attention to people who seemed to conform in appearance and values in order to make the problem of crime seem especially menacing. Organized crime became the most prominent symbol of criminality. The danger posed by the Mafia, like that posed by the Communist Party, resided precisely in its adherence to corporate appearances, methods, and language. The means employed by organized criminals resembled those of legitimate corporations; in dress and style, gangsters were no different from corporate executives. Your neighbor in the suburbs might just as easily work for the Mafia as in p.r. for United Broadcasting: the gray flannel suit could just as easily be a cover as a uniform of middle-class conformity. The Italian American deportee Charles "Lucky" Luciano clearly embodied this danger in the early postwar years. He seemed to break with the methods and appearance of the Italian American mobsters of the Prohibition era. Embraced by the media and vilified by crime-fighting agencies as the head of a multinational vice industry, Luciano was the focus of newspaper stories, popular nonfiction, Senate inquiries, and constant attention from the Federal Bureau of Narcotics.

The record of public attention to Lucky Luciano smacks of the anti-Italian prejudice in place since media outlets, social reformers, and police agencies first shouted "Mafia" in the late nineteenth century. Nevertheless, this was not merely-another instance of the scapegoating of Italian Americans for the failures of the criminal justice system. World War II and the immediate postwar years represented a watershed for Italian Americans. Like other white ethnics, many Italian Americans had by now gained entry into the middle class. Italian American men appeared prominently not just in gray flannel but also in baseball uniforms, judges' robes, and stylish suits, crooning behind microphones. Although well-known Italian Americans such as Joe DiMaggio, Frank Sinatra, and Judge Ferdinand Pecora sometimes faced accusations of mob ties, because of their success, talent, and mainstream acceptance, Italian Americans were increasingly being embraced as "ideal pecuniary men," despite the "ideal delinquency" of some.

These competing visions of Italian Americans played out in the representation and pursuit of Lucky Luciano. Perhaps even more than Luciano, Charles Siragusa exemplified the shift taking place in perceptions of Italian Americans. As the Federal Bureau of Narcotics' chief European agent, Siragusa achieved professional advancement by donning a pinstripe suit and going undercover. Coincidentally, as young children these two New Yorkers had lived for a short time within blocks of each other in the Italian section of lower Manhattan.[4] Their paths would converge in postwar Italy. Although Italian Americans remained a largely working-class population in the 1940s and 1950s, there were many success stories, and these led some observers to perceive a fracturing of Italian America along class lines. The increasing class mobility of southern and eastern Europeans in general and Italian Americans in particular during the postwar years was fraught with questions about assimilation and accommodation. Cold War politics provided a way for Italian Americans to embrace Americanism symbolically by actively denouncing communism both within Italian American communities and in the pivotal

1948 Italian election, which pitted communists against anticommunists.⁵ Italian Americans seized the opportunity to declare the superiority of American-style democracy and to proclaim their loyalty to the American mainstream.

The pursuit of Luciano by Siragusa performed a symbolic function. If Luciano represented the "old" Italian Americans, whose persistent foreignness was taken as a sign of their inevitable criminality, Siragusa represented the "new" Italian Americans, who were achieving inclusion in the American middle class. (Of course, it was Siragusa's ethnicity that enabled him to pass as an underworld gangster in the service of U.S. espionage. For this he would earn the Exceptional Civilian Service Medal, awarded for "outstanding courage in the face of danger while performing assigned duties.") In contrast to Luciano, who turned to crime in order to amass riches, Siragusa lived, according to a *Saturday Evening Post* feature, "simply and happily—when he has time—with his wife and two sons in a bare modern Rome apartment." Siragusa's Italian American version of *Father Knows Best* served in the mass media as a foil for Luciano's pathologies: as a child Luciano was a dutiful but misunderstood son, doted on by a simple mother but rejected by a tyrannical father. As an adult, when not incarcerated, he lived in hotels and dated showgirls of questionable morals.⁶

This contrast between Siragusa and Luciano reveals the give-and-take that featured in the ongoing debate over assimilation and ethnic identity. On the one hand, it was important that Siragusa be seen as embracing middle-class mores while denouncing a fellow ethnic who had committed numerous high-profile crimes. On the other hand, it was equally important that he be seen to do so as an Italian American. This process was one of imposing uniformity while celebrating difference. The effect of lionizing Siragusa and demonizing Luciano was to reinforce an ideological consensus across demographic lines. In the case of Luciano, this process had an importance beyond the role it played for the shifting ethnic and class identities of Italian Americans. In particular, the FBN targeted Luciano as a pathological drug kingpin to advance its drug enforcement agenda and discredit other possible solutions to the problem of illegal drug use. By focusing on a conspiratorial vision of foreign manipulation while silencing the medical and rehabilitative models advocated by many within the medical and social work community, commissioner of narcotics Harry J. Anslinger could shape public perception of drug smuggling and drug use. Lucky Luciano and Charles Siragusa thus served Anslinger's goal of placing the resurgent drug problem within a criminal justice framework at a time when rival agendas were arising to challenge his power.

From this perspective, the celebrated investigations of crime and communism appear to have been more than crass purges of dissent. Instead of trying to eliminate the differences within America's borders, politicians and the mass media exploited them as a means to an end. In defining his theory of the "normalization" process as practiced within prisons, Michel Foucault wrote: "In a sense, the power of normalization imposes homogeneity; but it individualizes by making it possible to measure gaps, to determine levels, to fix specialties and to render the differences useful by fitting them on to another. It is easy to understand how the power of the norm functions within a system of formal equality, since within a homogeneity that is the rule, the norm introduces, as a useful imperative and as a result of measurement, all the shading of individual differences." Numerous studies have followed Foucault's lead to show how difference has historically been employed to rank people along lines of gender, race, class, ethnicity, sexual orientation, and so on. Siragusa's difference made him useful, and in this we see how the attempt to build a postwar consensus relied on the contrast between "good" differences and "bad" differences. Just as Luciano served as the epitome of bad behavior in his role as "the sharpest hood of them all," Siragusa served as the perfect foil because he "rendered differences useful" by conforming to the middle-class ideal of the 1950s.[7]

The Making of a Vice Overlord

Lucky Luciano's contemporaries viewed his exploits with the mix of outrage and attraction typical of popular reactions to representations of sexuality, crime, and drug use. Frequently denounced as a violent and corrupting influence in American culture and politics, Luciano was also regularly featured in gossip columns and personality features in local and national media outlets both before and after his deportation. Perhaps most tellingly, although he was usually described as the "president" of the "Unione Siciliano," some saw him as a viable candidate for the Congressional Medal of Honor.

Born Salvatore Lucania in 1896 in the Sicilian village of Lercara Friddi, he moved with his family to New York's Lower East Side in 1906. Luciano's family knew many people like themselves who had wanted to make the trip but initially could not emigrate because of the cost. They would remain poor. According to his memoir: "We had a calendar that come from the steamship company in Palermo, which was where you got on the boat. My old man used to get a new one every year and hang it up on the wall, and my mother used to cross herself every time she walked past it. Sometimes we even went without enough to eat, because every cent my old man could lay his hands on would go into a big bottle he kept under his bed."[8]

Charles Siragusa was born in the United States to Italian immigrants in 1913 and spent his first two years in the overcrowded Lower East Side, Luciano's neighborhood. Siragusa's family also deferred some needs in order to facilitate future gratification. His Sicilian-born father sold Prudential insurance policies to the immigrants from many lands who peopled the neighborhood. Siragusa moved away at an early age, retaining few firsthand memories of the notorious criminals who lived among the low-wage workers. Nevertheless, the gangsters with whom he briefly shared the most crowded neighborhood in the United States left an impression on family lore. "The night I was born the Mafia hoods killed a man down the street. They blew his brains out, upsetting the midwife who delivered me," Siragusa recalled. He would retell with great animosity a family legend about a grandfather killed in Sicily by the island's notorious Mafia. After his retirement from the FBN in the 1960s, Siragusa acknowledged that these stories had shaped his career path: "I made a vow to fight the Mafia when I was a grown man. My chance arrived when I was offered a job with the Federal Bureau of Narcotics."[9]

Both families had hopes of upward mobility. The Siragusas moved to the (then) suburban Bronx, but the father returned to Little Italy each day to sell policies and collect payments from his customers. Their savings soon allowed the family to enter the lower-middle class. While the Lucanias saved money in a bottle under the bed, the Siragusas became homeowners and "sealed the transaction by taking out a thirty-year first mortgage and then a twenty-year second mortgage."[10] The two boys also had contrasting visions of how to achieve upward mobility. Whereas Luciano graduated from delivery boy and small-time drug dealer to illegal liquor distributor, Siragusa graduated from a special program for academically talented children in the New York City public school system and went on to New York University.

Siragusa parlayed his scholastic success as well as his Italian heritage into jobs with the Immigration and Naturalization Service and the wartime espionage service, then into a successful career with the Federal Bureau of Narcotics. "At first I was based in the United States," he recalled, "posing as a hoodlum in my pin-stripe suit with the wide lapels and the fancy shoes. Because of my Sicilian ancestry and face, I was able to infiltrate successfully into Mafia-controlled gangs and to finger, time and time again, the drug pusher, the peddler, the small-time dope overlord."[11] Siragusa's Sicilian heritage made him useful as an agent, allowing him to gather evidence otherwise unavailable to the FBN. In order to fulfill his childhood vow, Siragusa would need to join the ranks of the enemy, a strategy he continued to use as he rose through the FBN hierarchy.

During the Prohibition years, Luciano's primary source of income was the illegal sale of alcohol. His earnings financed his own undercover operations in a world of wealth closed to most Italian Americans at the time. His success was legendary, marked by an expensive wardrobe and a suite at New York's exclusive Waldorf-Astoria under the name "Charles Ross." Toward the end of his life, Luciano recalled that "around 1925, I had a take of at least twelve million dollars from booze alone for the year." He was well aware of the limited options available to an ambitious Italian immigrant with only a few years of elementary school education: "In them days when an honest department store clerk was drawin' down maybe twenty-five dollars a week at most, my guys was gettin' paid by us two hundred a week plus what they was makin' on their own."[12]

After the repeal of Prohibition, Luciano and his associates operated illegal gambling clubs, supplemented by the hijacking and reselling of legal merchandise. In 1936 he became the target of a young special prosecutor for the City of New York with grand political ambitions, Thomas Dewey. After the highly publicized extradition of Luciano from Hot Springs, Arkansas, Dewey won convictions of the gangster and his co-defendants on sixty-two counts of compulsory prostitution and extortion on testimony from prostitutes and "bookers" that Luciano was running a citywide ring of sex workers. In his closing statement Dewey summarized his perception of the importance of the case by demanding "a conviction . . . in the name of the safety of the people of this city" (words he would later come to eat after Dewey, now governor, agreed to commute Luciano's sentence). Luciano received an unprecedented prison term of thirty to fifty years. Despite his protests that he was innocent of Dewey's charges, Luciano was never able to shake the reputation of a "white slaver," gained in the 1936 trial.[13]

Luciano's years in prison coincided with World War II and Dewey's election as governor of New York. In a bizarre coincidence, both Siragusa and Luciano played important roles in U.S. military intelligence. After obtaining a job with the OSS, Siragusa spent the war years in Italy gathering information and tracking down foreign spies, while Luciano became the central figure in the navy's "Operation Underworld," one of the stranger stories of World War II. "Operation Underworld" began in response to an unexplained fire aboard the French luxury liner *Normandie* in New York Harbor in 1942. Amid anxiety over lax security on the waterfront, the U.S. Navy perceived the presence of Italian-born dockworkers as a potential threat. Naval intelligence turned to an unlikely patriot, Lucky Luciano, for advice and assistance in securing the waterfront. Luciano's participation aided him in achieving two goals: he wanted to be transferred from upstate New York's Dannemora Prison to Great Meadows, closer to friends and family in New York City; and he wanted a reduction in his sentence. On May 8, 1945, V-E Day, attorney Moses Polakoff requested executive clemency for his client based on Luciano's unusually long sentence and his war service. Dewey commuted his sentence after an in-depth review by the New York State Parole Board, stipulating that Luciano return to Italy.

It was unclear exactly how much help Luciano provided to "Operation Underworld." According to stories that circulated just after the war, Luciano secured the New York docks through his emissary Joseph "Socks" Lanza and later put Italian American deportees living in Sicily at the "disposal of the Allies." "Did the High Command need Sicilian saboteurs for destroying a strategic bridge, for blocking a harbor or dynamiting a tunnel?" asked a writer for *UN World*. "Lucky's men were on the spot and would do the job with pleasure. Nor did they ask compensation. All they wanted was that Mr. Luciano's sentence should be commuted."[14]

Contradicting official OSS information, which consistently denied any involvement with criminals, the naval intelligence officer who directed "Operation Underworld," Lieutenant Commander Charles Haffenden, disclosed Luciano's involvement in the covert operations to an interviewer in 1947. In an attempt to limit the damage inflicted on his presidential aspirations by the conflicting stories, Governor Dewey called for an investigation into the rumors of secret meetings between Luciano and naval intelligence officers. New York State's commissioner of investigations, William B. Herlands, conducted the investigation into "Operation Underworld" in 1954. He received word from the director of naval intelligence, Rear Admiral Carl F. Espe, that "contacts were made with Luciano . . . and that his influence on other criminal sources resulted in their cooperation with Naval intelligence which was considered useful to the Navy." At Espe's request, this news did not reach the public until after both Luciano and Dewey were dead. Although it might have vindicated Dewey, Espe thought it would "do the Navy no good."[15] When made public, the findings of the Herlands Commission revealed that Luciano, along with Meyer Lansky, Joseph Lanza, Joe Adonis, and other mobsters, had assisted the navy by helping to maintain the "free and uninterrupted flow of supplies out of this port of New York to the war theater, and to England, and there was to be no interruptions or stoppage of any kind. There was [sic] various levels of investigations. . . . One group would learn of anticipated labor trouble at a dock that would have to be stopped or prevented."[16]

The parole board had based its recommendations on a letter Lieutenant Commander Haffenden had written to Charles Breitel, Dewey's legal counselor, confirming Luciano's involvement in "Operation Underworld." Partisan questions about the commutation arose almost immediately. The pro-Dewey New York Daily Mirror featured what Newsweek columnist John Lardner called "the Luciano war legend," while the New York Post, then owned by the prominent Democrat Dorothy Schiff, routinely insinuated that Dewey had accepted bribes as a condition of the commutation.[17] Dewey's political opponents claimed that he had been paid off by Luciano and later constructed the Haffenden story as a cover.[18] In any case, Dewey had agreed with the parole board that Luciano's wartime assistance justified the commutation of his sentence, provided Luciano returned permanently to his native Italy. He would be sent back to prison if he tried to reenter the United States.

Deporting foreign-born people as a stipulation of parole or commutation was common; Dewey signed seven other such commutations on the same day as Luciano's. In spite of the regularity with which similar deportations occurred, Luciano's release, deportation, and subsequent activities served as a keystone of postwar crime fighting. His deportation ultimately made it possible for him to be portrayed as the foreign manipulator of an international smuggling operation based in Italy.

For a brief time after his deportation, Luciano fell into obscurity. After some media attention to his going-away party aboard the *S.S. Laura Keene*, he had an unremarkable first year of exile. In 1947, however, Lucania turned up in the chic Havana suburb of Miramar—and in Walter Winchell's syndicated column. He had legally entered Cuba using his given name, Salvatore Luciana, and his Italian passport. On the heels of Winchell's report, articles in *True, Newsweek, Time,* countless major newspapers, and two popular nonfiction books (Michael Stern's *No Innocence Abroad,* and Sid Feder and Joachim Joesten's *The Luciano Story*) catapulted Luciano simultaneously into the media limelight and the drug enforcement searchlight.[19]

The U.S. government reacted swiftly to the discovery that Luciano was in Cuba. In response, the Bureau of Narcotics prevented the shipment of all medicinal narcotics to Cuba pending his deportation. Because Luciano also had visas for Bolivia, Venezuela, and Colombia, FBN chief Harry Anslinger threatened the governments of those countries with similar action should they admit Luciano. Anslinger justified this action by recalling Luciano's youthful arrest for heroin possession and, according to *Newsweek,* rumors that he had "dabbled in smuggling dope into the United States before." Officials "feared that any narcotics sent to Cuba for medicinal purposes might fall into his clutches." Alfredo Pequeño, Cuba's interior minister, promptly arrested Luciano on February 22, 1947 and returned the newly dubbed "Unlucky" Luciano to Genoa aboard the Turkish ship *Bakir* on April 12. After a showcase trial on prostitution charges and an uneventful deportation, Luciano was suddenly "the most important drug smuggler in the world."[20]

Harry Anslinger was by that time obsessed with Lucky Luciano—obsessed enough, in fact, to write an unpublished biography of the underworld figure called "The Boss." He believed that Luciano was the primary exporter of heroin and other narcotics into the United States. In interviews Anslinger rarely failed to point to Luciano as the greatest force in U.S. drug smuggling. *True* magazine was one of the first popular magazines to feature his theory:

> Sight has been lost of the fact that Lucky, from his new headquarters in the Albergo Turistico in Naples, is as grave a menace to the American people as he was when he operated out of a tower suite in the Waldorf-Astoria. Take it from Commissioner Harry Anslinger, head of the United States Treasury Department's Bureau of Narcotics, Lucky is the largest single figure in the traffic in this contraband in America today. The reason he directs all dope shipments from Italy to the United States has nothing to do with nostalgia. It is based on the fact that it is the country that pays the highest price for illicit drugs.

Anslinger's disdain for Luciano quickly became mutual. In a telling choice of words, Luciano complained that "when the Russians land on the moon, the first man they meet will be Anslinger, searching for narcotics." In one of his famous malapropisms, Luciano conveniently mispronounced the commissioner's name "Asslinger."[21]

Shortly after Luciano's return to Italy from Cuba, his name began to emerge in virtually every major drug seizure by U.S. Customs officers and the Bureau of Narcotics. When Port of New York patrol officers seized $1.1 million worth of pure heroin in 1947 from a French freighter, the largest haul in U.S. history to that time, customs investigators immediately suspected Luciano's involvement. In a 1948 seizure of $640,000 worth of heroin, Herman Lipski, the chief of the Customs Enforcement Division, noted that "it was the belief here that Charles (Lucky) Luciano, deported underworld leader, was involved in the smuggling attempt." By the time customs agents discovered $1 million worth of opium and heroin (as well as twenty-two two-ounce bottles of illegally shipped Chanel No. 5) aboard the French ship *Bastia* in 1949, it was clear to numerous police agencies that Luciano had to be stopped. Italian police officials arrested Luciano in July 1949 after Vincent Trupia, an Italian American from New York, was arrested in Rome in possession of $500,000 worth of cocaine. According to Giusseppe Dosi, head of Italy's International Police Section, Roman police detained Luciano in response to a Federal Bureau of Narcotics request. He was released the following week, but Italian authorities barred him from Rome for the remainder of his life.[22]

Despite repeated attempts, neither American nor Italian drug enforcement officials ever obtained conclusive proof that Luciano was running an international smuggling operation. They based their pursuit of him on the contention that an increase in drug smuggling had "been coincidental with Luciano's deportation from the United States to Italy" and that "Luciano was receiving large monthly amounts of money from the United States." Luciano did in fact live quite regally off large payments from U.S. gangsters. The contention that drug smuggling increased after Luciano's deportation requires some examination, however. It is virtually impossible to calculate what quantity of drugs evades detection and finds its way into the veins, nostrils, and lungs of consumers. Arrest figures do support the FBN contention that in comparison to the war years, the late 1940s saw a dramatic upsurge in drug smuggling and use. Total arrests for smuggling rose from 3,180 in 1948 to 5,273 only one year later. But even Bureau of Narcotics data do not support the conclusion that this resulted from a new consolidation of the drug market. In fact, the total amount of illegal narcotics seized had actually gone down—a trend that continued in 1950. More people were being arrested for bringing in smaller quantities of illegal narcotics, a decline some in the Bureau of Narcotics tried to attribute to Luciano's supposed tactical shift of "trying numerous small shipments, instead of risking large supplies on single ventures." Arrest and consumption rates in the 1950s were consistent with prewar figures. Any apparent postwar increase was a result of the fact that the lack of available merchant ships and the stepped-up military patrols had created an unusually low rate of drug use during the war. The drug-smuggling vessel *Bastia*, for example, was a former Liberty Ship. Finally, although heroin and opium originating in the Middle East and Asia did often move through southern France and Italy, the Bureau of Narcotics acknowledged that the two most popular illegal drugs—cocaine and marijuana—came principally from Peru and Mexico, respectively.[23]

Nevertheless, Lucky Luciano became the most visible figure in representations of illegal drug smuggling. When a major heroin ring was broken up in San Francisco in 1952, the Federal Bureau of Narcotics argued that "Luciano was behind it" and was "controlling all drug smuggling from Italy." In another case, the FBN joined forces with the Royal Canadian Mounted Police to stop a group of Montreal restaurateurs from smuggling heroin. The chief of the Mounties' Criminal Investigation Department, James R. Lemieux, told one reporter that "the syndicate 'definitely' was linked with an international narcotics cartel headed by deported vice overlord Charles (Lucky) Luciano." Even if Luciano went unnamed by police investigators, the press routinely associated drug sales in their cities with Luciano. Whenever investigations resulted in the arrest of large-scale smugglers, the press reported their relationship to Luciano.[24]

In addition, prosecutors urged drug dealers to name Luciano as their source in exchange for lighter sentences. When they refused they felt the consequences. In 1956 two heroin dealers, Ralph "Sunny Cheeks" Zanfardino and George Palmieri, were arrested with $400,000 worth of heroin and received sentences of six to twelve years and seven and a half to fifteen years, respectively. The prosecutor felt justified in asking for these unusually long sentences for the two, "who as first offenders might have been given a two-year minimum sentence," because "their lack of cooperation had thwarted attempts of federal authorities to track down the suspected chief of an international dope syndicate," a clear reference to Luciano. Many factors, most notably the Boggs Act of 1951, made possible these draconian (by 1950s standards) sentences. Prior to 1951, the maximum penalty for these crimes would have been ten years in prison, and as first offenders, Palmieri and Zanfardino would likely have received far shorter sentences. In addition, the association of the heroin with one of its points of origin, communist China, made their crime particularly vulnerable to aggressive prosecution.[25] By the time Zanfardino and Palmieri came to trial, the pieces were in place. As Italian Americans selling relatively large quantities of heroin, they fit into a framework of crime, pathology, and demonization already developed around Lucky Luciano.

Just as Luciano had gained prominence during the 1950s, by 1957 Charles Siragusa was a crime-fighting celebrity on a par with Al Capone's nemesis Eliot Ness. Ness would soon pen his own "as-told-to" autobiography and be reinvented in the highly rated TV program based on his Prohibition-era exploits. The *Saturday Evening Post* featured several stories on Siragusa as Ness's crime-busting successor. Ness and Capone personified the polarization between the native-born "good" and a foreign-born "evil" in their many incarnations throughout the twentieth century. Similarly, Siragusa provided the perfect Cold War foil to Luciano, using his Italian heritage as a strategic tool in his efforts to arrest mobsters. As the *Saturday Evening Post* proclaimed: "Charles Siragusa is of Sicilian origin himself; one of his uncles was murdered by the Maffia on the lower East Side of New York for refusing to kick back part of his working pay. With memories like that, Siragusa knew what he was talking about when he talked about the Maffia, and he knew what he was up against now—not a string of cheap dope peddlers but some of the most tightly organized criminals in the world," including Luciano, referred to in the article as "the big one."[26]

It was not only the popular press that drew on Siragusa's Italian heritage as evidence of his unique qualifications for fighting drug smugglers. Harry Anslinger sent Siragusa first to Little Italy and later to Italy for just this reason. Two other agents, Garland Williams and George White, had preceded Siragusa as FBN representatives in Europe, but Siragusa received much of the credit, both from the bureau and from the media, for slowing the heroin traffic. According to Anslinger, Siragusa first rose to prominence in Trieste, headquarters of an Italian smuggling operation, where he "easily assumed the character of a deported Italian mobster looking for a connection to supply his boys back in New York. He pitched into this task with his customary verve and, knowing Italian and its dialects, played the role with ease, securing 10 kilos of heroin and bringing in more than twenty persons." Anslinger added, "This case, as we knew almost any of them might have, involved Lucky Luciano."[27]

If the drug problem in the United States originated in Italy, its solution lay in using as government agents those Italian Americans who accepted the dominant middle-class ideology of the period. Like naval intelligence during World War II, the Federal Bureau of Narcotics needed "native informants" to gather information and make arrests. In doing so, the FBN revealed the subtle change in perceptions which had taken place with regard to Italian American ethnicity and crime. Like the larger U.S. culture, the bureau was defining the terms under which the children and grandchildren of European immigrants could assimilate into the American mainstream, and both Luciano and Siragusa played important roles in this process.

A New-Style Frame-Up

Although crime-fighting agencies were right to pursue drug smugglers, the larger campaign drew on Cold War fears of foreign infiltration to shape public perceptions of the dangers and attractions of illicit drug use. Luciano attributed the charges against him to "an old-style frame-up" and complained that they were "spoiling my reputation."[28] The basis of the claims made by narcotics and customs agents were weak, and Luciano's indignation over a spoiled reputation seemed a bit late and disingenuous, but targeting Luciano was actually a new-style frame-up. Central to this frame-up was not a smoking gun with Luciano's fingerprints or a packet of heroin stashed in the unsuspecting deportee's luggage. Rather, this frame-up centered on public relations. Recalling Tom Rath, the "man in the gray flannel suit," who entered postwar corporate culture as a public relations man, FBN agents relied on the tools of public relations, issuing press releases, cultivating relationships with friendly writers, and closing off relationships that seemed to work against their interests.

Why did they frame Lucky and how did they do it? Luciano's mystique predated the 1950s inquiries into organized crime, but he already occupied a place in the Cold War perspective on organized crime not only for what he revealed about commonplace assumptions concerning Italian Americans but also for what he concealed. The Federal Bureau of Narcotics did not frame Luciano out of a personal vendetta, as Luciano feared. Anslinger was driven by the desire to steer public perceptions toward the belief that drug use was a criminal act and away from the increasingly popular view that it represented a medical or psychological disorder. Treat the addict, many social workers, lawyers, judges, and doctors argued, and drug smugglers will no longer have a constituency. Anslinger influenced the focus of U.S. drug policy long after his retirement by arguing, to the contrary, that discrete cartels of foreign origin were solely responsible for the postwar influx of narcotics.[29]

According to his published writings, private memos, and professional correspondence, Anslinger was reluctant to authorize any public portrayal of drug addicts. Before the media attention to the Beats, positive portrayals of drug use were rare, but Anslinger believed that even negative portrayals would result in an upsurge in drug use. Not only would such publicity show the curious how to use drugs, but it might also make prosecutors, judges, and juries feel sympathy for the plight of "sick" drug abusers. In fact, as he hypothesized in a directive to his district supervisors about the upturn in drug use, "much of it is due perhaps to irresponsible and uninformed propaganda to which the courts and prosecutors are systematically subjected." From this perspective, all portrayals of drug use—whether positive or negative—constituted propaganda that would result in shorter sentences and more drug addicts. The district supervisors agreed that short sentences derived from understandings of drug use that contrasted with the bureau's criminal paradigm. The Seattle supervisor expressed his concern that a local judge "is particularly lenient with colored violators and some time ago when sentencing one of our defendants, as near as I can recall, said: 'I realize that colored people do not have the same opportunities for maintaining a standard of living as white people have.' "[30]

Anyone who presented views that contradicted bureau policy felt the power of Anslinger's enmity. The bureau actively discredited anyone who sought to treat drug addiction as a sickness rather than as evidence of a global conspiracy. During the 1940s Anslinger had cautiously cooperated with Dr. Arthur La Roe, head of the privately funded American Narcotic Defense Association (ANDA), but the two quickly parted ways once La Roe began offering medical explanations of drug use to the press. The FBN and Anslinger also discredited the New Jersey Narcotic Defense League (NJNDL). At the time, New Jersey had one of the most draconian drug laws in the nation: any person caught using drugs for non-medical purposes could receive a one-year jail sentence. The state's U.S. attorney, William F. Tompkins, recommended life commitment to the state hospital for anyone committed a third time to an institution for treatment of addiction. In protest of these punitive approaches, NJNDL head Abe S. Berliner advised that the state should treat drug addicts as "sick people not as criminals." When Eleanor Roosevelt awarded him the league's "Fellowship Medallion," Anslinger noted his skepticism in Berliner's growing file. When, in the early 1950s, Berliner spoke out against a tough state drug law, FBN agents in New Jersey called him a "crackpot" and a "publicity hound." Anslinger soon went beyond this petty name-calling. In a clear abuse of his position, he requested that the New Jersey State Police conduct an investigation of Berliner. Despite the failure of the police to find evidence to support his contention, Anslinger told presidential aides and New Jersey politicians that the NJNDL was a "collection racket" for Berliner's insurance business.[31]

Anslinger also punished government officials who deviated from his views. Municipalities with growing drug problems often put together task forces to examine the situation and recommend programs to counteract the trend. Local FBN supervisors usually took part in these task forces and reported back to Anslinger. In Detroit, the Mayor's Committee for the Rehabilitation of Narcotic Addicts, formed in 1951, was one such task force. The committee members thought it prudent to begin a narcotics education program in the local schools. One officer from the Detroit Police Department's Narcotics Bureau suggested screening a Canadian film, *Narcotic Addict*, as part of this program. This alarmed Anslinger, who quoted the policy of the UN Commission on Narcotic Drugs in his response: "The [UN] Economic and Social Council . . . considers it advisable to re-state the policy adopted by the Opium Advisory Committee on Opium and other Dangerous Drugs of the League of Nations, namely, that propaganda in schools and other forms of direct propaganda can be employed only in certain countries where drug addiction has assumed widespread proportions (China, Iran, India, and Thailand); and that in other countries where it is of a more sporadic character (European countries and countries on the North American continent), such measures would be definitely dangerous." Anslinger had served as the U.S. representative to the UN commission and helped shape the policy. When the police officer contacted the Canadian film distributor anyway, Anslinger's assistant commissioner referred to him as a "chump." The officer was eventually "relieved from the narcotic detail," and the Mayor's Committee did not show the film. In a similarly vindictive maneuver, when the state of Missouri loosened its harsh penalties for drug possession in 1958, Anslinger cut the number of agents serving the state from seven to three.[32]

Despite its power to withhold access to resources, the Federal Bureau of Narcotics could not preempt all depictions of drug use. *Look* magazine published a photo-essay advocating what the FBN derisively called the "British" solution of treating addictions rather than locking up criminals. The title of the article indicated that *Look* saw the paradigms as polarized: "The Dope Addict: Criminal or Patient." The photo-essay featured "Donn," a twenty-two-year-old trying to kick a heroin habit. "Sociologists urge that the addict is ill and his care is a problem for doctors. Penologists insist that the addict is a criminal and the only way to solve the narcotic problem is to make the laws more severe," read the commentary, which posed a slight criticism of Anslinger's position in this debate: "For 40 years, penologists have had their way; but the dope problem remains unsolved." Anslinger could not explicitly censor *Look*, as he had the Detroit Mayor's Committee, but he could and did go after "Donn." The Federal Bureau of Narcotics tracked down the San Francisco Police Department and FBI records of Donn Whiton Areya. Finding that his age was twenty-five, not twenty-two as claimed in the article, FBN agents derided the article for its "bleeding heart tone" and strongly suggested that the inaccuracy was a deliberate distortion.[33]

In addition to discrediting writers, publications, government officials, and community activists who dared suggest a medical approach to narcotics use, the bureau cultivated relationships with accommodating editors and freelance writers. Among the people referred to as "friendly writers" were Frederic Sondern, editor of *Reader's Digest*; Lee Mortimer, syndicated columnist for the *New York Mirror* and co-author of the best-selling *Confidential* series; Michael Stern, writer for *True*; and Joachim Joesten, co-author of *The Luciano Story*. In his true crime exposé of the Mafia, *Brotherhood of Evil*, Sondern made clear his admiration for Anslinger in a chapter titled "The Remarkable Mr. Anslinger." In a foreword, Anslinger returned the favor by praising the book as "compulsory reading for every law enforcement officer in the United States." He also recommended the book in his correspondence with friends and professional colleagues. *Life* magazine cooperated with the FBN from the 1930s onward. The editors regularly sent stories to the bureau for final approval, a privilege Anslinger received in exchange for exclusive information about FBN cases.[34]

Sometimes "friendly writers" did not follow all of Anslinger's suggestions. When they rebelled, he cut them off. For example, he directed agents to "ignore all further communications from Mr. Felix B. Streyckmans, Managing Editor of the *Kiwanis* Magazine," after publication of an article by Margaret Krieg advocating educational programs against drug use in schools. The bureau had agreed to co-operate with Krieg, but she did not incorporate all of their recommendations. Among other ignored suggestions, Anslinger wanted Streyckmans to call teenagers who used drugs "young hoodlums."[35]

Other writers served as direct conduits for the bureau's public relations. Rather than bothering to write an article only to have the bureau edit it, one author, Sam Pryor, simply asked Anslinger if the department could "draw up a short story for me on this subject? I think it will be a fine opportunity to give the legislation you have in mind a good boost." Pryor was no freelance writer but executive vice president and assistant to the president of Pan American Airways and president of the Boys' Clubs of America, and so his name on an article would have carried substantial clout. The department did provide the article, which appeared under the byline Samuel F. Pryor in *St. Joseph Magazine*, though it was actually written by Carl DeBaggio, an FBN employee.[36]

In contrast to its cooperation with journalists, the FBN worked to prevent the motion picture industry from showing drug use in any form. The bureau had contributed to the Motion Picture Association of America's code, which added provisions on the portrayal of narcotics in 1958, although it dated back to the days of the Hays Office of the 1930s. Although the original code included the clearly stated provision that "crime shall never be presented in such a way as to throw sympathy with the crime as against law and justice, or to inspire others with a desire for imitation," the revised code specified how this ban would be applied to narcotics:

> Drug addiction or the illicit traffic in addiction-producing drugs shall not be shown if the portrayal;
>
> (a) Tends in any manner to encourage, stimulate or justify the use of such drugs; or
> (b) Stresses, visually or by dialogue, their temporarily attractive effects; or
> (c) Suggests that the drug habit may be quickly or easily broken; or
> (d) Shows details of drug procurement or of the taking of drugs in any manner; or
> (e) Emphasizes the profits of the drug traffic; or
> (f) Involves children who are shown knowingly to use or traffic in drugs.

The film industry enforced these provisions by self-censorship and by submitting story outlines to the Bureau of Narcotics. The code did allow some portrayals of drug use, but in practice, the MPAA and the FBN rejected even films that showed the deleterious effects of narcotics use. Many filmmakers expressed concern that the invisibility of drug use would lead to an increased problem, but Anslinger did not budge. For example, Samuel Goldwyn planned to produce a film about drug use similar to *The Lost Weekend*, a 1945 movie that detailed the self-destructive behavior of an alcoholic. Anslinger's refusal to cooperate sank the project, for only bureau cooperation would guarantee the level of authenticity Goldwyn sought. Anslinger also routinely denied Hollywood's requests for access to bureau personnel and intelligence, advising his California district supervisor that "the Motion Picture code prohibits the showing of the narcotic traffic in any form."[37]

Despite efforts by the MPAA and the FBN, filmmakers outside the Hollywood mainstream did produce and screen films about drug use. When this occurred, force replaced coercion, as bureau agents worked with local police using public indecency ordinances to close them down. Described by one agent as "a dramatization of the life of a female narcotic addict, enacted and produced by a cheap cast at a low cost," *Marihuana* had been a favorite film in urban vice districts around the country for decades; bureau agents had been monitoring showings at theaters across the country since the 1930s. When local ordinances allowed, the bureau worked with local police forces to stop screenings. Typical was a 1952 incident involving a double feature at Miami's State Theater of *Marihuana* and *Escort Girl*. Hoping to capitalize on the viewing public's illicit desires, the theater advertised the films as a "Shocking Exposé of America's Narcotic and Vice Menace—Uncensored Lowdown on Call Girl and Reefer Rackets." Bureau surveillance photos homed in on a poster showing a man injecting a woman with a hypodermic needle. FBN agents in Miami working with the local police closed the show. The police seized the print and arrested Paul Baron, manager-owner of the theater, for "displaying obscene and lewd literature and obstructing traffic by use of a sound apparatus." Although Baron received only a suspended sentence on the traffic ordinance, the bureau had achieved its primary goal of censoring titillating portrayals of drug use.[38]

In this climate the "friendly writers" were left to define the problem along bureau lines. Articles by Mortimer and Stern highlighted the role of Italian American deportees, particularly Lucky Luciano, in international drug smuggling. The *Saturday Evening Post* incorporated Anslinger's approval and suggestions in its feature on Siragusa. When the story was initially proposed in 1954, the *Post* refused to comply with FBN requests for final approval, and the article did not go forward. In 1956, however, the *Post* again proposed the article. In addition to the provision that the bureau edit the article "after it was written and before it was published," the FBN demanded apologies for an earlier article on "dope clinics" and one by former assistant U.S. attorney D. Lawrence Kolb to which Anslinger had objected. The *Post* agreed to these conditions, turning editorial approval over to Anslinger.

The magazine sent a writer and a photographer to Rome to stage the photographs and write an article that would, in Anslinger's words, "glamorize Charlie Chan, alias Sherlock Holmes, alias Charlie," his pet names for Siragusa, revealing an attraction to crime movies that focused on intuitive and scientific detection.[39]

Anslinger wanted Siragusa to serve as the poster boy for his agency's efforts to stop the flow of drugs originating in Italy. In particular, he was sensitive to emerging charges that the Federal Bureau of Narcotics was unjustifiably targeting Italian Americans for the drug traffic problem. Generoso Pope Jr., publisher of the Italian American daily *Il Progresso* and the *New York Examiner*, argued that the Mafia was a myth created by the "reds" to throw U.S. crime fighters off the track, while the Sons of Italy argued that the Mafia was nothing more than a fictitious stereotype that betrayed an underlying anti Italian prejudice. Anslinger intended the *Post* story to highlight Siragusa's Italian heritage in order to counter these charges. Anslinger's arguments that Jewish Americans were bankrolling the Mafia earned similar rebukes from the Anti-Defamation League of B'nai B'rith and Senator Herbert Lehman of New York, prompting Anslinger's reversal on this point. In a similar strategy in 1952, recently retired bureau agent Gon Sam Muc wrote a two-part series in the *Post* detailing his experiences with San Francisco's Chinatown drug dealers. Gon also appeared in Lee Mortimer's books and columns as a hero of efforts to end the drug traffic. In a move that further emphasizes the ethnic and racial context of the bureau's public relations, Anslinger denied permission to Anglo-American agents who received similar offers from the press.[40]

To one critic it seemed that Anlinger "does not want to win the discussion as much as he wants to eliminate it." His carefully orchestrated campaign to control drug coverage helped him achieve his policy objectives, and the Federal Bureau of Narcotics grew, if not always with the speed or to the size he would have liked. The Narcotic Control Act of 1956 increased penalties for violations of existing narcotic and marijuana laws and provided funds for a training school for state and local officers.[41] This legislation was a turning point for the bureau's concerted effort to disseminate its methods and viewpoints around the nation. Yet Anslinger's campaign to bolster support for his views and for expanding the Federal Bureau of Narcotics illuminates larger questions about the significance and costs of that era's insistence on ideological conformity.

"He Is Definitely Not Normal"

Mr. Hopkins, Tom Rath's boss and mentor in *The Man in the Gray Flannel Suit*, exemplifies the difference between the kind of man who builds a company and the bureaucrat who lives off it. Hopkins represents the entrepreneur who would sacrifice his personal life for the greater glory of the corporate machine. After realizing how Hopkins has destroyed his family in building the company, however,

Rath decides that he is ultimately a nine-to-fiver. In the end, Hopkins confesses that if he had it to do over again, he too would join the anonymous ranks. In a reversal of the heroic narrative of success, blending in becomes virtuous.

Anslinger's obsession with Luciano was motivated by the specific organizational and ideological concerns of the Federal Bureau of Narcotics, but questions of what broader social issues it reflected and why it took hold of him with such force remain. The observations of the sociologists C. Wright Mills and David Riesman offer a possible answer. Mills and Riesman were among the most prominent critics of the emerging middle-class norm, characterized by whiteness, the heterosexual nuclear family, suburban living, corporate work for men, housework for women, and consumption for all.

This age of strict role assignments was rife with anxiety over what to do about the multitudes who did not conform, whether they were corporate leaders like Mr. Hopkins or gangsters like Luciano. Riesman speculated that such noncon-formists "may be unable to adapt because they lack the proper receiving equipment for the radar signals that increasingly direct attitudes and behavior in the phase of incipient population decline. They may refuse to adapt because of moral disapproval of what the signals convey. Or they may be discouraged by the fact that the signals, though inviting enough, do not seem meant for them." Did Lucky Luciano, along with other ethnics of European origin as well as African Americans, fail to adapt because they despised middle-class mores or because they were excluded from them by prejudice? Was nonconformity a result of job discrimination or of physical and cultural inferiority? Popular analyses of Luciano suggested that multiple explanations could be applied, depending on the context. In one popular true crime book, Luciano was simultaneously a "sleek beetle-browed mobster" whose crimes were a mark of his Sicilian heritage and the head of a "far-flung narcotics organization already submerging the United States," who had chosen to break the law for personal profit.[42]

Underlying the views that Luciano was an atavistic throwback and a cunning manipulator of global economies was a critique of the increased corporatization within the mass mediated culture described by Riesman, Mills, and Marshall McLuhan, among others. Critics both inside and outside the universities offered damning appraisals of this development. Mills saw the "white-collar" men as "cogs in a business machinery that has routinized greed and made aggression an impersonal principle of organization." The new bureaucracy presented a danger that could potentially destroy democracy. The presence of a variety of "enemies within" called into question the rightness of the changes taking place. These trends, Riesman warned, marked the end of individual freedoms: "The enormous potentialities for diversity in nature's bounty and men's capacity to differentiate their experience can become valued by the individual himself, so that he will not be tempted and coerced into adjustment or, failing adjustment, into anomie. The idea that men are created free and equal is both true and misleading: men are created different; they lose their social freedom and their individual autonomy in seeking to become like each other."[43] White-collar crime was not the only problem of an increasingly corporate culture. All white collars—criminal and otherwise—threatened social freedoms and the central tenets of masculine individualism.

By pointing to the evils of Luciano's criminal enterprises, both those who critiqued conformity and those who embraced it could render Luciano's difference useful. To social critics, Luciano's organization revealed the dangers of all organizations. Luciano was seen as corporatizing the consumption of both sex and drugs, compounding the more general bureaucratic threat to masculine individualism. As Judge Morris Ploscowe wrote in his popular 1951 book *Sex and the Law*:

> The Luciano mob decided it would take over the business of booking women for houses of prostitution as well as the business of prostitution itself. It forced some of the bookers out of the business. Others were put to work for the new combination on a salary basis. Many of the houses were also taken over by the mob, whose aim was to establish a monopoly in commercialized prostitution in New York City. Luciano himself said to a group of associates, "We are going to put every madam in New York on a salary, and then the whole city will be working for us, and [like true monopolists] we will raise the prices: Two-dollar houses will become four-dollar houses, four-dollar houses six-dollar houses, and so forth.

Although Ploscowe was resurrecting Luciano's 1930s vice convictions to advance his moral crusade to limit sex to marriage, it was the medium of degeneracy—organized crime—that came under his particular scrutiny. Ploscowe's focus on Luciano's involvement in vice crimes and drug smuggling did not upset his misogynist notions of male and female sexuality, just as 1950s dictates about appropriate sexual behavior did not protect women from male sexual aggression. In fact, Ploscowe did not see the rape of prostitutes as rape. Prostitution in any form may have threatened the ideal of monogamous heterosexual marriage, but it was the higher prices and greater profits brought about by monopolization of the sex industry that disturbed Ploscowe more.[44]

Luciano represented a contradiction. Responses to organized crime revealed a more general fear of the loss of social freedom within bureaucratic organizations, but his nonconformity raised other concerns. Those outraged by drug use saw its connection to all forms of nonconformity as threatening. Charles Siragusa was not only out to get the Mafia; he was also battling nonconformity. He asked readers of his memoir to "consider the person who becomes dependent on heroin. In a great majority of cases he is definitely not normal. . . . He may be contemptuous of his fellow men or a guy who thinks it is fashionable to be a nonconformist. Nonconformity in his case means shooting heroin into his veins." Other commentators linked the nonconformity of drug use to sexual promiscuity and racial mixing. Jack Lait and Lee Mortimer argued in *Washington Confidential* (1952) that drug use by white women in jazz clubs owned by gay men led to their having sex with African American musicians. In extreme cases, some authors betrayed a fear that foreign-born dealers could harness and exploit the sexuality of native-born females by addicting women to drugs while simultaneously using narcotics to deprive "American" men of their sex drive. Lait and Mortimer presented the thesis that while drug use "decreases desire in the male, it stimulates sexuality in women addicts. White slavers use it to break down the resistance, seduce, and afterward to bind their victims to them." The vision of heightened sexual desire in women and male impotence powerfully linked sex and drugs with xenophobia and the threat of nonconformity.[45]

In defiance of federal drug enforcement policy, a joint committee of the American Bar Association and the American Medical Association advised the FBN to advocate for treating addicts rather than locking them up. That the FBN rejected this recommendation should not come as a surprise. Not only did it contradict long-standing bureau policy, but also the position that drug use was a medically treatable problem did not resonate with contemporary sensibilities and anxieties. Like McCarthy's targeting of the State Department and Alger Hiss, the FBN's focus on the Mafia and Luciano served larger ideological goals. But Luciano became the period's "ideal delinquent" because his image bridged the multiple paradigms of Cold War criminology, crime fighting, and media representation. This image ultimately outgrew the FBN, achieving currency through the growing movement to increase the size and power of international police agencies. The focus on Luciano, according to one journalist, forced "people all over the world to realize that sooner or later international criminal gangs must be opposed by an international organization of law."[46]

Drastic changes in international policing were occurring throughout the postwar years, and the specter of Luciano remained a useful public relations tool. To many people, Luciano highlighted the growing concern over the problem of international drug smuggling and drug use. The move to centralize and consolidate international narcotics control materialized on several fronts. First, there was a push for the United Nations to set up an international narcotics police to supplement its Commission on Narcotic Drugs. In addition, Interpol, which dated back to 1923, changed drastically during the late 1940s and early 1950s. After attaining official UN sanction in 1940, it underwent a rapid increase in the number of member nations and achieved status as an independent agency in 1956. Its growth cannot be singularly credited to Luciano, but his international reputation grew out of the same perception that local and national police agencies were ill equipped to deal with criminal practices that did not respect national borders.

International treaties and enforcement were a response to the increasing com-
plexity of global crime, but also to specific Cold War concerns. Virtually all Eastern
Bloc members dropped out of Interpol in the late 1940s, and the agency became
increasingly associated with Cold War political alliances, but it also reacted to
what was described as a residual danger of the "increasing interdependence of
countries."

> The development and improvement of means of transport has made the crossing of
> frontiers easier, and favoured international crime, whether the criminal has extended
> his nefarious activities to several countries or perhaps sought refuge in a part of the
> world far removed from the scenes of his crimes. The economic conditions resulting
> from the world wars, the movement of populations which followed them, and the
> ever increasing interdependence of countries have still more favoured a situation
> which is favourable to this form of crime and increased need for world-wide action.
> . . . It was the existence of the international criminal which brought about the birth
> of the International Police.[47]

Much of the work of Interpol relied on the input of the U.S. Treasury Department.
The Bureau of Narcotics, like the Bureau of Customs and the Secret Service, were
then housed within the Treasury Department. As chief European agent, Siragusa
served as an unofficial liaison to Interpol. Among Interpol's many high-profile
efforts was the creation of its version of the FBI's "Ten Most Wanted" list. Distributed to police agencies around the world, this "international black list" included Luciano until his death in 1962.[48]

Luciano's death also marked the end of Anslinger's directorship of the FBN.
Luciano collapsed on the afternoon of January 26 while picking up American
movie producer Martin Gosch at Capodichino Airport in Naples. Gosch had arrived to iron out the details for a planned film about Luciano. The two men were
being tailed at the time by a U.S. Bureau of Narcotics agent collecting evidence
to tie Lucky Luciano to an international heroin-smuggling ring recently uncovered
in New York City. According to deputy commissioner of narcotics Henry Gior-
dano, "We were ready to move against him with the Italian authorities."[49] Appro-
priately, Luciano's death was observed by representatives of the two institutions
that had watched him and shaped his image since his deportation in 1946: the
media and the Bureau of Narcotics.

Charles Siragusa returned to the United States in 1958 and continued his rise
within the Bureau of Narcotics, moving from field supervisor to assistant director.
When he later became head of the Illinois Crime Commission, Siragusa kept in
close contact with the bureau. Luciano's death and Anslinger's retirement in the
same year marked the end of one chapter in the history of the bureau, though its
framework for understanding the nation's drug addicts would survive. That same

year a Senate subcommittee looked into communist involvement in drug trafficking, with particular attention to "Red China" and Cuba. According to committee reports, the star witness, Charles Siragusa, testified that "cocaine came from Cuba and that the sudden influx of narcotics was 'definitely a Communist project' aimed at raising money, demoralizing Americans, and discrediting Cuban exiles in Miami. He added that the cocaine trafficking had been insignificant before the Fidel Castro regime came to power in 1959."[50] Drug traffic thus remained a malleable tool of U.S. policy makers, whether it was used to demonize political enemies or support allies. In the early 1970s the writer Alfred McCoy found evidence that Chinese Nationalists—not Communists, as the FBN alleged—were cultivating opium in order to finance guerrilla campaigns. In addition, McCoy argued, U.S. military and intelligence forces had encouraged opium and heroin use in Southeast Asia in the 1940s and 1950s to "hedge the growth of popular liberation movements.[51]

The focus on Lucky Luciano by the mass media and the Federal Bureau of Narcotics reveals how crime in the postwar era came to be situated within a larger ideological context. When commentators expressed fears that Luciano was smuggling drugs across national borders, they were fulfilling the policy goals of the Federal Bureau of Narcotics. But they were also illuminating underlying anxieties about 1950s conformity. Luciano had come to represent an international threat to an American nationalist myth built on controllable sexuality and "submission to conditions." One popular biography of Luciano noted: "Like chop suey, veal scaloppini, and the parakeet, crime has gone international. The mob that operated from rock-bound coast to sun-kissed shore, now skips oceans and Federal boundaries with the same unhampered ease that it formerly crossed state lines."[52] In contrast to Luciano, but also like Chinese American chop suey or Italian American veal scaloppini, Charles Siragusa symbolized an appropriation of the earlier immigrant generation's ethnicity. Luciano's threat to 1950s conformity stood him in sharp contrast not with native-born Anglo-Americans but with that other Italian American who could be incorporated into and even glorified within Cold War American culture. The FBN's concerted public relations campaign helped popularize and generalize the difference between the man in the gray flannel suit and the man in the pin-striped suit.

UNHOLY ALLIANCES:

The Senate Rackets Committee, the Teamsters, and Labor Politics

In a 1997 speech before a Detroit local of the International Brotherhood of Teamsters, Larry Brennan, head of the Michigan Teamsters, expressed his skepticism that continued government oversight could be explained by the union's latest scandal, the improper funding of Teamster president Ron Carey's reelection campaign. It was the Democratic Party—also at the center of the scandal—rather than the Teamsters, Brennan implied, that was to blame for any impropriety: "If there's ever a mob it's the Department of Justice, the Department of Labor and the I.R.B. [Independent Review Board]. I'll tell you this—the money that was paid to the Democratic Party was nothing but protection. If they ever let us get into the citadel in Washington, I wouldn't be surprised if we brought the whole Government down. Everybody understand—that's why they're investigating us, because they don't want that to happen." Noticing *New York Times* reporter Jeffrey Goldberg scribbling notes, he spoke directly to him: "You, newspaper reporter, you're under control by the Government, too. You're afraid to say what the truth is. I know exactly how you are. You'll only print what you think will make news." For Brennan, government and press allegations that Carey violated federal laws in his 1996 campaign were not evidence that the union had failed its membership and continued to be "mobbed up." Instead, it was the Democratic Party, soliciting "protection" like a blackmailer, that was corrupt. Without these strong-arm tactics,

Brennan implied, the union could transform politics to the benefit of its membership. At least one union member, Vern Alstatt, agreed with this last point: "I need somebody to protect my job and my pension," he said. "I don't care about that other stuff."[1]

Brennan's harangue reached back to Teamster president James R. Hoffa's real and symbolic trials in the late 1950s and early 1960s. Hoffa's actions and his siege mentality during the postwar years set the stage for the long and difficult relationship between the International Brotherhood of Teamsters and the federal government. It began in the 1950s with televised hearings into the corrupt practices of Hoffa and other Teamster leaders. Robert F. Kennedy, chief counsel for the Senate Committee on Government Operations, headed by Arkansas Democrat John McClellan, pursued the investigation with passion. After some jurisdictional wrangling, the Senate authorized a Select Committee on Improper Activities in the Labor or Management Field in January 1957. The committee—popularly known as the Senate Rackets Committee—was composed of members of McClellan's Government Operations Committee as well as the Labor Committee. Kennedy ultimately found that the Teamsters' leadership had garnered large personal profits while limiting the gains of union members by entering into illegal dealings with banks, employers, and mobsters. According to the Rackets Committee, in addition to overtly illegal contract negotiations that lowered the pay of Teamster members, the union's leadership had also sought personal enrichment from selective allocation of the many health, welfare, and real estate opportunities available through the union.

The consequences of this investigation were not limited to the conviction of union officials. It achieved greater significance from the chief investigator's use of the mass media to publicize his findings. Robert Kennedy learned the importance of media exposure from Clark Mollenhoff, a writer for *Look* magazine and the Cowles newspapers, who told Kennedy that a labor rackets investigation "could be bigger than the Kefauver crime investigations."[2] Ironically, this idea of a media-oriented "holy crusade" was co-opted by Hoffa, who used it to gain and solidify his position as general president of the Teamsters. His role as "the enemy within" ultimately turned him into a classic bandit: vilified by the state, protected and promoted as a hero by his followers.[3] Through his speeches and interviews, and, most forcefully, through the Teamsters' public relations apparatus, Jimmy Hoffa reversed and reformulated the signifying practices of the McClellan Committee and its chief counsel.

The larger significance cannot be explained solely by the media campaign Kennedy mounted. As I will show, the investigation, the Teamsters' defense, and the distancing tactics of the AFL-CIO illuminate a larger shift in the role of labor unions and the meanings of working-class identity in postwar America. The New Deal had brought the promotion of unionization efforts under the control of the

Wagner Act. World War II signaled a period of relative labor-management co-operation based on common goals, high wages, and federal subsidies. Workers in heavy industry made remarkable gains not only in wages but also in the effective use of political pressure to gain access to government and corporate decision makers. During the postwar years, workers understandably hoped to maintain or increase their power and quality of life. But because management could no longer rely on federal subsidies to sustain high wages and labor peace—and did not want to raise prices or cut profits—they often targeted wages and benefits to make up the difference. In the years immediately after the war, this meant an increase in labor-management conflict. For example, in late 1945 and 1946 there were 4,630 work stoppages affecting almost 5 million auto, steel, electrical, coal, and railroad workers.[4] Furthermore, business organizations such as the U.S. Chamber of Commerce and the American Management Association blamed unions and labor leaders for work stoppages, utilizing anticommunist and anti-crime rhetoric to discredit "labor bosses" with seemingly endless reservoirs of power and shallow pools of morality. Although their goals differed, anti-labor politicians, liberals, and the leadership of the AFL-CIO all saw the exposure of corruption within the labor movement as an opportunity to place the larger and more pressing issue of labor-management relations before the public.[5]

Of course, the Teamsters' leaders were not passive subjects for others to debate. In the way its officers defended themselves from corruption charges, the union influenced the labor movement as a whole, as well as U.S. labor policy and labor-management relations. On the one hand, its tactics and relationship to known criminals recalled an earlier time of labor wars and oppositional stances toward management and government. On the other hand, the Teamsters were proof that World War II and the postwar years marked in the words of Mike Davis, "a watershed of enormous importance in reforging blue-collar identity."[6] The events of those years allowed the white working class, in exchange for a repudiation of radical political and economic stances (and individuals), to embrace American patriotism. Indeed, the disproportionate number of working-class men with ties to the military demanded this embrace. Immediately following World War II, many workers used their status as veterans to argue for a more egalitarian nation.[7] The sight of striking workers in army uniforms, however, would give way to a new meaning of patriotism, as the American way increasingly became defined in terms that privileged the corporation. As Gary Gerstle argues, labor leaders of the 1930s used the language of "Americanism" to shape an independent political and economic movement that served working-class needs. The war years, while marking a period of substantive gains, also marked a loss of workers' ideological independence. The postwar period further limited the possible meanings of Americanism, with corporatist, traditionalist, and anticommunist values dominating virtually all sectors of U.S. society.[8]

While many labor leaders were seeing their political influence crumble in the face of the red-baiting tactics used to marginalize or silence critics of capitalism, the Teamsters sought to benefit from changes both within the working class and on the national political stage. Unlike the CIO, which in 1950 expelled two left-led affiliates that had organized office workers, the Teamsters realized that the future growth of the labor movement depended on organizing unskilled and white-collar workers.[9] By 1960, white-collar workers outnumbered industrial workers for the first time. In part because of its aggressive efforts to organize these workers, the total membership of the union increased from under 600,000 as recently as 1945 to almost 1.7 million in 1959, a growth of 175 percent. The influence of sheer size was compounded by the new political alignments of the late 1950s. As a Republican, Jimmy Hoffa found allies among some of the most anti-labor politicians of the day, including Barry Goldwater of Arizona and Karl Mundt of South Dakota. Hoffa's party allegiance did not save him from prosecution or a prison term, but his use of it within the Teamsters Union constituted a strategy for confronting class inequality that was well attuned to the Cold War assault on the left.

"These People Are Americans"

There had been earlier investigations into labor corruption in the thirties, forties, and fifties. The Senate Committee on Commerce investigated racketeering in 1933 and 1937, and in 1947 the House Committee on Expenditures in the Executive Department held hearings on racketeering in industrial relations, focusing on Philadelphia's Dock Street produce market. The 1950s brought House committees on government operations, as well as education and labor, into the mix. Most prominently, Senator Estes Kefauver revealed a link between organized crime and labor racketeering during his sensational investigation into organized crime in the early years of the decade. Although Kefauver's revelations resulted in the expulsion of the International Longshoremen's Association from the AFL-CIO, no significant labor legislation followed from his hearings. In contrast, the McClellan Committee's investigations would lead to new, restrictive legislation.[10]

Indications that this would be so emerged in the summer of 1957, when Jimmy Hoffa went on trial for bribery in federal court. The prosecution and defense raised issues well beyond the specific charges in question, turning the trial into a statement of positions that would dominate the multi-year confrontation between the federal government and the Teamsters. Although this was not the first arrest for Hoffa, then vice president of the Teamsters, it was the first trial in the wake of the McClellan Committee's investigation of the notoriously corrupt union. The previous February, Hoffa had accepted documents from Cye Cheasty, a lawyer and former Internal Revenue Service investigator, containing the names of four witnesses the committee planned to subpoena. Unbeknownst to Hoffa, Cheasty had told Robert Kennedy, chief counsel of the committee, that Hoffa had offered to pay him $2,000 a month if he could get a job on the committee and pass information to Hoffa. Instead, Kennedy hired Cheasty, provided him with documents, and had the FBI photograph Hoffa accepting these documents from Cheasty on a Washington, D.C., street corner. On March 13 Hoffa was arrested and charged with attempting to bribe a committee investigator. He was acquitted of all charges in July.[11]

Hoffa regarded his acquittal as exoneration. After all, he argued, Kennedy had entrapped him by getting Cheasty to pass him the documents. Kennedy disagreed. He felt that Hoffa had manipulated the racial and class loyalties of the jury, consisting of eight African Americans and four whites, when another Detroit native, boxer Joe Louis, showed up at the trial and shook hands with Hoffa as he entered the courtroom, leading committee member Barry Goldwater to comment that "Joe Louis makes a pretty good defense attorney." In addition, Kennedy criticized Hoffa's hiring of Martha Malone Jefferson, an African American lawyer from Los Angeles, who became a visible presence in the courtroom. The Hoffa team countered that the "Brown Bomber" was there only to court Jefferson, his future wife, not to bolster Hoffa. Kennedy nevertheless called Hoffa's methods "extreme" and an "insult to the court, to the judge, to the legal system, to the jury, and to the colored race."[12] The problem, according to Kennedy, was compounded by some of the jurors' previous brushes with the law: a few had convictions for drunkenness, another had a son in jail on narcotics charges, and "still another juror," Kennedy revealed, had "refused to take a lie detector test on the question of whether he was a homosexual." When Judge Matthews sequestered the jury after a series of pro-Hoffa editorials and advertisements appeared in the *Baltimore Afro-American*, Kennedy justified, in his words, "locking them up" not just because of the sensational press coverage but on the grounds that they were morally corrupt anyway. As for Joe Louis, his former career as a boxer was enough to suggest a connection to "the underworld."[13] The charges and evidence under consideration seemed incidental to Kennedy, who saw the acquittal as proof of Hoffa's corruption, not his innocence.

In the wake of his acquittal, a victorious Hoffa was called to answer questions before the McClellan Committee. The estimated 1.2 million television viewers saw a casual Jimmy Hoffa responding as if he believed he could weather the brief storm of the Senate committee as he had earlier inquiries, most recently into Teamster involvement in the Detroit jukebox racket.[14] Despite the flurry of damning charges brought by the committee, Hoffa was elected president of the Teamsters on October 4, 1957, at the Eden Roc Hotel in Miami Beach. In response, the Teamsters' parent federation, the AFL-CIO, suspended the Teamsters on October 24 and threatened to expel their largest affiliate permanently if Hoffa remained an officer of the union, a threat that was soon carried out. Hoffa quickly became the outcast of both labor and anti-labor forces. His speech before the Miami Beach conventioneers addressed the tarnished reputation of the union in the wake of the hearings. Hoffa told the crowd, and the larger audience who would read about the speech in media accounts:

> I want to say that a great injustice has been done to the individual members of the Teamsters Union. You are the people whose good name has been smeared. And I want to say this to the whole country: the 1,500,000 working American men and women that make up this International Brotherhood of Teamsters are your next door neighbors. They aren't gangsters. They aren't hoodlums. They are respected citizens who live next door to you; who go to the same churches and synagogues; whose children go to the same schools that your children go to; who serve the Red Cross and the Community Chest the same as you do. Our members belong to the same clubs and societies that you do. These people are Americans. I am proud to be one of these people.

In contrast to Kennedy's focus on the deviance of Hoffa and the jury that acquitted him, Hoffa focused on respectability, family, worship, and community, stressing the Teamsters' conformity to the postwar suburban ideal. The improved economic and social standing of the working class—brought about by such recently acquired gains as cost-of-living adjustments, improved health care and retirement benefits, paid vacations, and long-term contracts—allowed Hoffa to make this comparison.[15]

In their opening statements before the McClellan Committee on June 30, 1958, both Kennedy and Hoffa demonstrated that the investigation was about much more than corruption within the Teamsters Union. Indeed, what was being debated was the role of labor unions in postwar America. Kennedy proclaimed that the union corruption was evidence of a larger problem that could be solved only through legislative redress and citizen action. He was helped in publicizing this message by numerous media outlets. Typical of the mainstream coverage was John Bartlow Martin's seven-part series in the *Saturday Evening Post*, "The Struggle to Get Hoffa." Martin began by focusing on the two protagonists: "This is the story of a great congressional investigation and the man who led it, Bob Kennedy. It is a story of a great union and the man who led it, Jimmy Hoffa. It is the story of the collision of the two most powerful forces in American life." Whereas Kennedy's "pursuit of Jimmy Hoffa has become a holy crusade, the Teamsters Union has at times appeared more like a gigantic criminal conspiracy than a labor union." Although Martin insinuated here that these "powerful forces" made for a fair competition, elsewhere he resorted to hunting analogies to suggest that in this contest of wits, only one of the competitors stood for the values of a civilized society. In the first article of the series, "Kennedy Sets a Snare," he repeated several times that the hearings were Kennedy's "holy crusade" to get the "power hungry" Hoffa. *Look* magazine joined the chorus, even citing the size of the Teamsters as evidence of wrongdoing: "By consorting with gangsters, racketeers and hoodlums, [Hoffa] has placed in his grasp a strategic union that numbers 1.5 million members and has some $37 million in its treasury."[16]

Kennedy intended to make Hoffa "the symbol in the minds of members of Congress of what needed to be corrected." Hoffa's planned alliance with the International Longshoremen's Association (expelled from the AFL-CIO for corruption) and the Longshoremen's and Warehousemen's Union (expelled for communist sympathies) provided a particularly potent symbol for Kennedy: "The worst elements of the American labor movement are creating an unholy alliance that could dominate the United States within three to five years. . . . Many of the individual leaders of this planned alliance are not reasonable men; they are variously tainted by corruption, racketeering, and gangsterism and a few even by communism. Together they would constitute a subversive force of unequaled power in this country." By presenting Hoffa's alliance as virtually forged in the flames of hell, Kennedy showed acute awareness that the hearings' performative function would guide public opinion. He justified this strategy as the most effective way of educating legislators and the viewing public: "It was our job to present the facts so that members of Congress could see clearly the areas in which legislation was necessary."[17]

This symbolic agenda soon exceeded the specific legislative agenda, implicating larger assumptions about the meaning of class inequality and the role of the labor movement in postwar America. By comparing Teamster officials to the already familiar gangsters of the matinee screen, television dramas, and the Kefauver investigation, Kennedy and the McClellan Committee's members raised the eyebrows of people throughout the labor movement who saw the charges Hoffa faced as an indictment of their efforts on behalf of working people. The Teamsters, argued Kennedy, "have the look of Capone's men. They are sleek, often bilious and fat, or lean and cold and hard. They have the smooth faces and cruel eyes of gangsters; they wear the same rich clothes, the diamond ring, the jeweled watch, the strong, sickly-sweet-smelling perfume." And like the Prohibition-era gangsters they resembled, these union officials were "the dregs of society."[18]

During the hearings, which ran from June 30 through July 3, the committee put off questioning Teamster officials, focusing solely on organized crime figures. These hearings provided dramatic testimony for the television audience but had little direct connection to the specific charges of corruption within the Teamsters Union. However, by locating this testimony within the context of a debate over working-class identity in Cold War politics, they become the crucial element of the McClellan Committee hearings. They began with the introduction into the record a list of 137 Italian Americans who were either present or associated with those present at the meeting at the home of Joseph Barbara in Apalachin the previous November.[19]

Martin Pera, an agent of the Federal Bureau of Narcotics, provided a framework that guided the committee's subsequent questioning of the Apalachin witnesses, among others. Pera displayed a detailed organizational chart of mob figures and responded to Senator McClellan's inquiries regarding the secret workings of organized crime families. "The intermarriages are significant," he told the committee, "in that often times you wonder whether these people want to marry each other. Yet the marriages take place. Let's say two people of a prominent status within the Mafia if they have children, you will find that their sons and daughters get married. They don't marry on unequal terms too often. . . . In other words, a leader within the organization would not have his child marry to someone who is a nobody within the organization."[20] What appeared to be conformity to middle-class values was merely a front for strengthening criminal loyalties.

Next, Kennedy paraded a Who's Who of organized crime figures before the television audience, including Joe Profaci, Vito Genovese, Thomas Lucchese, and a beleaguered John Montana, a prominent Buffalo businessman who had been present at Barbara's. Senator Irving Ives, the vice chair of the committee, who was from the region of upstate New York that included Apalachin, followed the line of questioning suggested by Pera in his questioning of John Scalish, an attendee at the Apalachin conclave:

> *Senator Ives:* I want to ask the witness if he is married?
> *Mr. Scalish:* Yes.
> *Senator Ives:* What was your wife's maiden name?
> *Mr. Scalish:* I decline to answer that on the grounds that it might tend to incriminate me.
> *Senator Ives:* My Lord, is it that, bad? Are you ashamed of your wife? That is pretty serious, to make that kind of statement. I asked you, are you ashamed of your wife?
> *Mr. Scalish:* I decline to answer the question on the grounds it might tend to incriminate me.[21]

The senators repeated this pattern of questioning with other witnesses, also asking the witnesses about their country of origin, revealing that assumptions about organized crime had changed little since the Kefauver hearings seven years earlier. Witnesses Joe Profaci and Vito Genovese were facing imminent deportation as a result of denaturalization proceedings initiated by the Department of Justice. Profaci was born in Palermo, Sicily, in 1897, but had lived in the United States since the 1920s. His two arrests and one conviction prior to emigrating had served as the basis of the denaturalization case against him. By responding "no" to the standard immigration question regarding criminal background, Profaci had made possible his naturalization, but by lying he had in the same breath laid himself open to the possibility of a future deportation. Attorney General William Rogers had provided this information to the committee. Efforts to deport Profaci and Genovese predated the hearings, but any incriminating statements the two made might help the Justice Department make its case. Not surprisingly, Genovese and Profaci declined to answer the committee's questions.

Profaci joined John Scalish and other attendees of the Apalachin conclave in a chorus of "I decline to answer on the grounds that it may incriminate me" in response to virtually every question asked of him. This mantra did not go unnoticed by participants or observers. Senator McClellan lectured Scalish: "If you can't state that you have been in some legitimate business, some enterprise that wouldn't tend to incriminate you, there is no way, and I don't care what law you have or constitution or anything else, there is no way to keep the human mind from drawing inferences." The members asked numerous loaded questions in expectation that the witness would "take the Fifth." McClellan asked James La Duca, a union official from Buffalo who attended the infamous conclave, "Do you regard yourself as a common hoodlum?" "Are you a member of the Mafia?" and "Is there one single thing, one single activity, in which you are now engaged, or in which you have ever been engaged, about which you can tell the truth under oath without running the risk of possible self-incrimination?" La Duca declined to answer each of these questions, at times suppressing the urge to respond on the advice of his attorney.[22]

The committee cited ten witnesses for contempt of Congress for invoking "the Fifth Amendment frivolously." According to a statement issued by the committee, these ten men had abused the amendment by "failing to answer questions pertinent to the Committee's inquiry on which they could not possibly be incriminated"—questions concerning their place of birth and citizenship status. These questions, like those about marriage, were crucial to the committee's efforts to prove to the public the existence of an underworld organization run entirely by people of foreign birth. Italian birth, as the attorneys for these witnesses and the witnesses themselves surely realized, was itself incriminating. As for the constitutional right to "take the Fifth," the committee encouraged members of the media to present this too as proof of guilt. Recalling the rhetoric of McCarthyism, the senators declared: "As might be expected, most of the hoodlum witnesses invoked the Fifth Amendment to all pertinent questions. The hearings convinced the Members of the Committee that underworld infiltration of business and labor is a grave national problem and that the grip of hoodlums and racketeers on the American economy continues to grow."[23]

Eventually, many Teamster officials would also claim the constitutional protection against self-incrimination, allowing the McClellan Committee explicitly to liken the heads of Teamster locals and other union officials to notorious gangsters. In the end, 343 out of 1,526 witnesses (about 20 percent) pleaded the Fifth. As in the case of the Mafia's *omertà*, or code of silence, remaining silent seemed to prove the committee's charge that the underworld controlled labor unions and would soon control the entire U.S. economy.[24] McClellan clearly saw the Fifth Amendment as an obstacle to justice. In a speech before the Economic Club of New York, he said that "in trying to develop the truth and get the facts, we have met with many hindrances and efforts at obstruction. We are repeatedly faced with perjurers, Fifth Amendment artists and 'forgetfulness experts.' " Although Kennedy may have agreed, he did not advocate making any constitutional changes.[25] Virgil Peterson, however, the influential head of the Chicago Crime Commission, suggested limiting the "latitude given the criminal classes in invoking the Fifth Amendment's provision against self-incrimination" as it perverted the intent of the framers of the Bill of Rights. Perhaps the most damning rejection came from within the labor movement itself. In 1956 an AFL-CIO policy stated that union officials and members who took the Fifth would be barred from holding office. Dave Beck, then president of the Teamsters, voted against this policy, but AFL-CIO president George Meany, Walter Reuther of the United Auto Workers, and other prominent labor leaders voted in support.[26]

The common use of the Fifth Amendment enabled the McClellan Committee, successfully if only symbolically, to link organized crime figures to the Teamsters. The "snare" that Robert Kennedy set was constructed in part from the meaning he lent to the silence of these witnesses. Of course, Kennedy exposed much more than silence. But he captured the imagination of the viewing public and their elected representatives through the drama of a monotonous incantation by union officials and organized crime figures alike.

What Is a Truck?

The McClellan Committee followed through on its investigative mandate by uncovering extensive corruption within the Teamsters Union. The charges against Jimmy Hoffa and his associates in the union centered on his associations with organized crime. By questioning his relationships with Johnny Dioguardi (a.k.a. Johnny Dio), Frank Costello, and Meyer Lansky, and recalling the ghosts of Al Capone and Bugsy Siegel, the McClellan Committee intensified public fears that a small cabal of evil conspirators had overtaken virtually every aspect of modern American life. The Teamsters were not just a union, then; they were, according to Robert F. Kennedy, "the most powerful institution in this country—aside from the United States Government itself." To emphasize this point, Kennedy argued that any decision made by a Teamster official could drastically change the day-to-day life of every American:

It is a Teamster who drives the mother to the hospital at birth. It is the Teamster who drives the hearse at death. And between birth and burial, the Teamsters drive the trucks that clothe and feed us and provide the vital necessities of life. They control the pickup and deliveries of milk, frozen meat, fresh fruit, department store merchandise, newspapers, railroad express, air freight, and of cargo to and from the sea docks. Quite literally your life—and the life of every person in the United States— is in the hands of Hoffa and his Teamsters. But, though the great majority of Teamster officers and Teamster members are honest, the Teamsters union under Hoffa is often not run as a bona fide union. As Mr. Hoffa operates it, this is a conspiracy of evil.[27]

Within this framework, negotiation was impossible. Total defeat was imperative. Whoever could eliminate the Teamsters would be a hero. Recalling the paranoid fantasies of an earlier era—such as fears that Catholic priests wielded special control over people through the confessional or that the Masons subverted the political process through secret loyalties—the McClellan Committee envisioned Teamster control of transportation as part of a sinister plot.[28]

Several states, inspired by the committee's findings, passed right-to-work laws in an attempt to eliminate closed-shop contracts.[29] Furthermore, additional sanctions against strategies such as wildcat strikes, sympathy strikes, and secondary boycotts, which had already been criminalized under the 1947 Taft-Hartley Act, weakened several of the Teamsters' most powerful organizing strategies and negotiating techniques. The McClellan Committee members felt it necessary to strengthen these provisions because the trucking industry was particularly adept at the secondary boycott, a strategy whereby a union strikes one target in order to get its management to place pressure on another company that is the actual target. As Hoffa colorfully described it, "You push a button in Kansas City and Omaha jumps."[30] A related tactic—hot cargo clauses—which allowed union members to refuse to handle merchandise made by (or going to), a non-union enterprise, or one where the workers were currently on strike, also came under committee scrutiny.

Three Republican members of the committee who were among the most antilabor senators of the era—Carl Curtis, Karl Mundt and Barry Goldwater—marshaled evidence of Teamster corruption in their attempts to extend the negative publicity to other unions. Goldwater once labeled United Auto Workers president Walter Reuther "a more dangerous menace than the Sputnik or anything Soviet Russia might do to America." These senators used the McClellan Committee as a platform for blaming unions for the economic recession of 1957–58. Reuther, a favorite Goldwater target, singled out the Arizona senator in his eloquent speech before the committee: "I plead to you, gentlemen, fight your political battles, stand up in the market place of free ideas in America, and fight for what you believe in. But fight for what you believe in and try to sell it on its merits, and not by trying to characterize the other fellow as disloyal, dangerous, un-American."[31] Reuther successfully distanced himself from the corrupt leadership of the Teamsters, but he recognized that the investigation of Hoffa represented an ideological indictment of labor unions in general at a moment of vulnerability.

In an attempt to divert attention away from the Teamsters and himself, Hoffa capitalized on the hostility toward Reuther among the anti-labor right.[32] According to Victor Reuther, Walter's brother, Hoffa convinced the Republican members of the McClellan Committee that the UAW would organize former Teamsters if their own union were eliminated. Anti-labor Senator Clare Hoffman of Michigan inserted into the *Congressional Record* a letter praising the Soviet system, written by Walter and Victor Reuther in 1934 when they were working in the Gorky auto plant. This letter was hardly news: it had been trotted out many times since the Hoover administration to red-bait Reuther. This time, however, Goldwater, Mundt, and Curtis used it to pressure McClellan and Kennedy to investigate Reuther and the United Auto Workers, even though the National Labor Relations Board had just completed an investigation of the UAW strike at Wisconsin's Kohler Company. Kohler, the bathroom fixtures manufacturer, was a throwback to an earlier paternalistic corporate era; in 1954 it refused to negotiate a contract with the UAW, the bargaining unit of the Kohler workers since 1952. The Republican and Democratic senators split along partisan lines in their views of the company, though both were willing to find fault with the UAW.[33]

In contrast to the Republican members, who saw their work on the committee as facilitating the destruction of the labor movement, Kennedy made clear that there was no turning back to pre–labor union industrial conditions. He believed that multinational corporations and the labor movement could work as partners rather than adversaries. In this Kennedy reflected the position of postwar liberals, who saw peaceful labor-management relations as necessary to a strong capitalist system. He reminded his audiences of the extraordinary exploitation that had given rise to labor unions in an industrializing America, and he showed a willingness to cast blame on dishonest corporations that cooperated with crooked unions or hired unscrupulous labor consultants. But while businesspeople were guilty of "succumbing to temptation," the onus remained on those within the labor movement who offered the apple.[34]

In particular, Kennedy lamented the growing power of unions, which organized an increasingly significant sector of the economy. Although unions had been an important corrective to brutal conditions during the nation's industrial past, their place within the growing service sector seemed dangerous. The Teamsters had aggressively organized, this sector, among the last to be unionized.[35] But even while Kennedy acknowledged the larger changes occurring within the nation's economy, he blamed the potential for economic disaster on the excesses of the labor movement. Like the anti-labor members of the committee, Kennedy relied on anticommunist rhetoric in order to make his case. Capitalism, according to the Democratic racket buster, was just; it could withstand the threat of external communism. The enemy within posed a more immediate danger. "Neither the labor movement nor our economic system can stand this paralyzing corruption," Kennedy warned. "Premier Krushchev has said that we are a dying house, a decadent society. That he says it does not make it true. But that corruption, dishonesty and softness, physical and moral, have become widespread in this country there can be no doubt."[36]

Although liberals like Kennedy accepted the place of unions within the consensus culture of the 1950s, conservatives like Curtis, Mundt, and Goldwater did not. The contrasting views of right-wing and liberal members of the McClellan Committee revealed the diverse motivations driving the government investigators. But the Teamsters and their defenders pointed to other crucial issues affecting the shifting meanings of working-class identity during the postwar period. In their conspiratorial vision, two factors explained the government's extraordinary efforts to uncover corruption within their ranks. First, the Teamsters argued that the work of the McClellan Committee had been strategized from the beginning, probably within the Hyannisport compound of the Kennedy family, in order to put John F. Kennedy in the White House. Their second explanation that the labor movement had made powerful enemies by improving the quality of life for working people—gained them allies within sectors of a labor force that was otherwise unsympathetic to Hoffa and his union. Together, these two arguments allowed the Teamsters to formulate a defense that ignored the facts supporting many of the committee's charges of criminality. A later remark of Hoffa's condenses these and other explanations in a single paragraph: "The smell of conspiracy was in the air all right but whom did it involve? Was it leading segments of the AFL-CIO playing 'footsie' with the McClellan Committee on the condition that they not be called to answer questions under oath? Was it the union-hating segments of Congress deciding that half-a-loaf is better than none and agreeing to make book with those in organized labor and management who have learned to fear the Teamster powers? Or was it opportunists within the Teamsters' union itself?" Hoffa's contempt for the AFL-CIO was reflected in his sexualization of its support for the committee's work. Ultimately, he claimed that the innocent Teamsters were under attack by self-interested forces hoping to destroy the gains of the movement. Clearly, the combatants were more equally matched than that. The conspiratorial rhetoric of the McClellan Committee was being met with similar rhetoric from a labor union with considerable power and an existing framework for portraying attacks on its leadership. Nevertheless, through its control of the media and its ability to televise the hearings nationally, argued Hoffa and his sympathizers, the committee shaped public opinion and controlled the outcome.[37]

By the late 1950s, business interests had successfully limited the meaning of "Americanism" to exclude the interests of the vast majority of laborers. Many unions had purged leftist members and even capitulated to the bizarre belief that the United States was a classless society.[38] Attempts to organize southern and western workers were worse than failures: by 1995, business had seized on the opportunity to pass fourteen right-to-work statutes that outlawed closed shops in twenty states.[39] Business leaders used evidence of high-level corruption to undermine the power of labor unions more broadly. They disseminated their interpretations of McClellan's findings and suggested correctives to protect what they called the "individual rights" of workers. The National Association of Manufacturers (NAM), for example, produced a film, *Trouble, U.S.A.*, that used the committee's findings to encourage viewers to "restore law and order in your own community and the nation" through right-to-work laws.[40]

The entire labor movement, not just corrupt Teamsters, had much to fear from the uses to which these findings would be put. At the outset of the investigations, the AFL-CIO had denounced the invocation of the Fifth Amendment by labor officials. When this did not successfully distance them from union corruption, they expelled the Teamsters along with the bakers' and laundry workers' unions, also under investigation. When these efforts failed to reverse the declining public support for unions, the AFL-CIO began a broader public relations campaign that emphasized public service through blood drives and lobbying in favor of school construction and housing. Then, in the late 1950s, the AFL-CIO began a $1.2 million publicity effort that included television and radio shows on the major networks. During the McClellan hearings, the AFL-CIO aired the radio show *Labor Answers Your Questions* for thirteen weeks.[41]

Fighting the image of unions as corrupt fiefdoms that achieved power by threatening management and their own membership, the unions presented themselves as the benevolent protectors of American values. The Teamsters and Hoffa had a particularly strong investment in counteracting the McClellan Committee's accusations and the criminal convictions and legislation that resulted. One way they did so was by arguing that the AFL-CIO and the McClellan Committee assaulted the U.S. Constitution when they questioned the rights of individuals to take the Fifth. In March 1957 the union's monthly magazine, *International Teamster*, assured union members that "any officers or member of our organization shall have the same right as any other American citizen to invoke the privileges of the Bill of Rights without, by such action alone, subjecting himself automatically to trial or disciplinary action by our union." With typical aplomb, the next issue featured a cover story on George Mason, a framer of the Bill of Rights, with a sidebar story on the Fifth Amendment.[42] By taking a civil libertarian position, the Teamsters were able to argue that the refusal to answer questions placed union officials in the tradition of the founding fathers.

This cover story was consistent with the union's broader explanations for the McClellan Committee's charges. In particular, *International Teamster* provided its readership with a frame of reference that countered the one the senators and crime fighters were disseminating through major media outlets. Hoffa did not rely solely on *International Teamster* to get out his view of the hearings. He also appeared on *Meet the Press* and *Face the Nation*, and was a popular interviewee on national radio networks.[43] These forums, however, did not offer him the level of control that the in-house magazine provided. In addition to heralding Teamster gains in contract negotiations and printing photographs of pension fund recipients, each month the magazine contained at least one article written by Hoffa himself. These "Messages from the General President" supplemented articles about the McClellan Committee, Hoffa's various trials, and what *International Teamster* always called the "Kennedy-Landrum-Griffin Act." The magazine consistently interpreted the McClellan investigation as an assault by "Big Business"—including the corporate mass media—on the labor movement as a whole. The union had been singled out for investigation not because it was corrupt, but because it was an effective negotiator for working-class men and women. The court-appointed monitors overseeing Teamster affairs in the wake of the committee's charges criticized this argument as an example of "the blatant manner in which the union avenues of communication have been used consistently and almost exclusively for the purpose of self-glorification and propaganda."[44]

The popular media, by contrast, portrayed the investigators as crusaders for justice—good, noble, energetic, and visionary, while the union leaders were seen as parasites and financially corrupt predators. The American Trucking Association, an industry trade group, bought seven pages in *Life* magazine in order to present a gentler view of the trucking industry. Seeing the potential danger the attack on the Teamsters posed to the trucking industry in general, the ATA drew on wholesome images to counteract the McClellan Committee's depiction. Readers were asked to imagine "a sweet, cool, healthful, glass of milk—what happens before you get it?" The predictable answer: "100% of the milk for major U.S. markets is hauled by trucks." The ad mirrored the values of *Life*'s America; like the editors, photographers, and reporters of *Life*, the ATA proclaimed that American nationalism presented a force for justice throughout the world, engaging ideological and military targets in the name of freedom, democracy, and capitalism. The ad portrayed the trucking industry as a loyal ally rather than a source of danger "in a world which is struggling against political subversion and economic inertia."[45] The Teamsters echoed the ATA in describing their members as beneficent providers. Hoffa's Teamsters may have been portrayed as a "conspiracy of evil" of biblical proportions in *Look* and *Reader's Digest*, but not in *International Teamster*, which published a poem in March 1957 that asked, "What Is a Truck?"

A Truck is a Bible;
A vial of penicillin for a sick child;
A frilly gown for a young girl's first date;
A loaf of bread for a hungry miner;
A steel beam for a skyscraper;
A new car for a country doctor;
A Geiger counter for a uranium miner;
A refrigerator for a cottage;
A package of seeds for a gardener;
A gallon of gas for the family car;
A side of beef for a deep freeze;
Spare manifolds for U.S. jeeps in Korea and Europe;
A bassinet and a high chair;
A ton of flour from Minnesota;
A vial of perfume for a Fifth Avenue window;
A job that sends a boy to medical school;
A new way of life for 170 million people.

The truck delivers a bountiful, progressive, and holy future, and touches every aspect of daily life in a prosperous, safe, modern domestic utopia. Compare a more typical portrayal of the Teamsters in *Reader's Digest*: "Through this union, Hoffa can keep the food from the tables of millions of Americans; he can withhold the fuel that warms their homes and runs their cars; he can keep them from work by shutting off supplies from factories and stores," a power the trucker-poet saw as no more threatening and no less desirable than an idyllic Norman Rockwell vision.[46]

Unlike conceptions of Americanism that ignored economic inequality, however, the poem also included hungry miners and the dream of a "new way of life." Similarly, the Teamsters saw the McClellan investigation in the context of class conflict. The true patriots were the hardworking and charitable men of the Teamsters Union. While Kennedy wondered aloud if the corruption within the labor movement indicated that "dangerous changes are taking place in the moral fiber of American society," Hoffa described the union as filled with "good men. Great men. Real men. Teamsters." When Kennedy supporters saw Hoffa as a "chunky, cocksure little Napoleon of a man," Hoffa hit back, calling Kennedy a "panty waist." These sexually charged insults embraced certain assumptions about class difference: if manual labor connoted masculinity, then Kennedy—described by Hoffa as a "young millionaire who doesn't know what it is to work in a warehouse"—was effeminate.[47] When the Teamsters called Kennedy a "hatchet-man" who "thinks his father's millions lift him above the common herd," they implied that a man of privilege could not be a real American.[48]

Gentle visions of truckers hauling milk and penicillin interspersed with episodes of name-calling tended to obscure the real evidence of corruption within the union. Teamster leaders attempted to use this obfuscation to their benefit, asking members and those sympathetic to their goals to interpret the images and stories of union corruption through an oppositional consciousness. The *Guild Reporter*, the house organ of the American Newspaper Guild, deconstructed the language and images of a May 12, 1958, *Newsweek* cover story:

> Its cover photo is of "Tough Guy" Jimmy Hoffa, Teamster union president. In 30-point Gothic caps the cover declares "Hoodlums Ride High in Labor." The cover story, a "Special National Report," also rides high, to the extent of more than four pages, in text and pictures in the forefront of the magazine. . . . The lead paragraphs say flatly: "Hoodlums and other unsavory elements still ride high . . . are still feeding at the same troughs . . . have soured the reputation of the entire labor movement." The factual qualifiers which a careful reader can find in the ensuing text are well hidden and the total impact on the casual reader is calculatedly bad.[49]

International Teamster reprinted this analysis as a demonstration of resistant reading strategies.

Hoffa intensified his calls for skepticism toward media accounts when the efforts of the McClellan Committee and the AFL-CIO to weaken his base of support began to succeed. After denying Teamster requests for readmission to the federation in 1961, the AFL-CIO started a rival transportation workers' union to lure members away from the Teamsters. The Teamsters Union itself contained a growing faction of reformers, including large locals in New York, Cincinnati, Chicago, and San Francisco, which were threatening to oust the beleaguered president. Despite the best efforts of *International Teamster* and Hoffa's own public pronouncements, the evidence of wrongdoing created a small but increasing group of disillusioned members. Perhaps in response to the charges of corruption, the magazine printed an open letter from Peter J. Hoban, president of the Milk Wagon Drivers' Union (Local 753 of the International Brotherhood of Teamsters) to Robert Kennedy which "challenged the truth" of Kennedy's anti-Hoffa crusade. Hoban, an Irish immigrant, compared the Teamsters to the Irish Republican Army and the McClellan Committee to British imperialism:

> The propaganda mill of Imperialistic England, swung into action, "press control" was used extensively, the young leaders of the Irish republican Army, were termed "assassins," "gangsters," hoodlums, "murderers," but the seed was sown by the death blood of Ireland's young leaders, on the "scaffold" or before "firing squads" of England. The seed fructified and it blossomed! It won the day for an Irish Republic. A mighty enemy was beaten, England! Mightier than the Rackets Committee, because

truth, honor, and an ideal was on the side of the Irish patriots! Indeed, sir, the Teamsters Movement can not be destroyed by "propaganda" by a "hostile" press, by "televised programs," by "loosely worded televised statements" or a "divided Teamster Movement."

In a final barb, Hoban addressed his fellow ethnic: "I was horrified that a name so honourable as 'Kennedy' could be associated with a type of propaganda which has Hitler like technique."[50] Clearly, according to Hoban, the committee was using the media in its goal to divide and crush the labor movement.

Hoban's Milk Wagon Drivers' Union was a large Chicago local that had achieved some national exposure for fending off takeover attempts by Capone-era criminals. Hoban himself served as the campaign manager for Thomas Haggerty, one of Hoffa's opponents for the Teamster presidency. In spite of his partisan distance from Hoffa, Hoban's position as a full-time paid employee of the union might have made some members suspicious of his histrionics. The same issue of *International Teamster* also featured the reflections of Matt Gelernter, who assured his readers that "I am a rank and filer, having no paid office in our organization and I will continue to be a rank and filer, working for what I believe to be the best interest of our organization . . . believe me." Like Hoban and the *Guild Reporter*, Gelernter focused on the construction of the hearings in the mass media. Gelernter, a member of the Los Angeles local, used the language of the film industry to critique the hearings. According to his eyewitness account: "With the lights going strongly and the television men getting tense, I felt I was back in Hollywood again waiting to hear 'Quiet on the Set! Quiet on the Set! Roll them!' " Gelernter warned how camera operators could influence viewers' perceptions by using "good angles" for committee members and "hard angles" for Hoffa and his attorney. Gelernter asked his readers to consider the hearings a staged event—a fiction constructed by the mass media and the U.S. government to serve their anti-union agenda.[51]

Many in the labor movement feared that this "Hollywood" production would have grave consequences for their ability to bargain effectively. John L. Lewis, president of the United Mine Workers of America and architect of the CIO, made this point when he appeared before the House Labor Subcommittee in 1959. Surveying the history of European criminal justice for the members of Congress, Lewis argued that "the McClellan Committee for my part is a re-establishment of the principle of the star chamber of the Stuart and Tudor Kings, with a slight touch of the Spanish Inquisition. That performance is put on for the edification of the country with movies and cameras and paraphernalia and circus fanfare. It is almost a Roman amphitheater." Some advocated civil disobedience as a form of resisting the abuse of power. A writer for the Catholic Council on Working Life's *Work* magazine argued that because television reporters had an obligation to entertain, a witness's words, intentions, and reputation would be sacrificed in order to "guarantee a good show for TV viewers." Thus, *Work* advised witnesses to refuse to testify before the television cameras. (Of course, those who decided on this strategy, such as Ernest Mark High, publisher of the *AFL Spotlight*, had their names forwarded to the full Senate for contempt citations.)[52]

These accounts asked readers to see the "truth" behind the news stories that were so critical of Hoffa and the Teamster leadership. More often, rather than simply refuting the McClellan Committee's damning revelations, the Teamsters recontextualized the inquiry into an attack on the labor movement more broadly. As Hoffa asserted in one of his monthly columns, "The McClellan Committee, big business, and its political stooges in the Federal government have gone all out to destroy us."[53] By focusing on style and context rather than the specific charges, and then recontextualing the hearings as another attack on the labor movement and other "minorities," Hoffa and his supporters cast the hearings not merely as a personal vendetta but as evidence of class conflict. Hoffa made this point in repeatedly describing the hearings as a battle between a "straight-talking rank-and-filer" with his "heart still where it was when he walked his first picket line" and "arrogant little Bobby Kennedy," the committee counsel with a "millionaire complex." Matt Gelernter, the "rank-and-filer" from L.A., affirmed this view when he agreed that Kennedy had targeted the union because "Jimmy Hoffa has done too good a job for our membership in the labor movement to suit his enemies and that's why they are going to such lengths to try and get rid of him."[54]

Still, the Teamsters could not deny that ex-convicts and well-known organized crime figures were members—even leaders—of their union. Hoffa turned these facts to his advantage, however, by claiming that although there was some corruption within the union, the McClellan Committee's entire case involved only "about a handful of people." Some union spokesmen went so far as to argue that the presence of ex-convicts within the Teamsters was a sign of inclusiveness, not corruption, as Kennedy and McClellan insisted. James A. Romanoff, a self-described "rank-and-filer from Teamster Warehouse Local 860 which is militant, aggressive, and progressive," wrote that he had "met a lot of good men in prison, just a chain of circumstances behind each case."[55]

This mirrored Hoffa's position that prison terms should not exclude people from holding union office, since members of the working class often end up in jail for behavior not considered criminal when committed by members of the middle and upper classes. Hoffa's own arrests served as a case in point: During a 1935 Detroit strike, Hoffa was taken to jail, without being charged, eighteen times in twenty-four hours. "I should have realized then that I would be jailed many times without specific complaint, and that I would be charged in higher courts many times without a shred of evidence to back up the charge." Making the connection to the McClellan Committee explicit, Hoffa claimed that "later in life, when more powerful enemies with more serious intent were joined by powerful politicians and labor leaders who wanted me out of the picture, the trumped-up-charge device was used against me more often. In Detroit, in 1935, I was undergoing a toughening experience. I was learning what it's like to be treated like a criminal though no charge has been brought or, if brought, has been unproved." Rather than a liability, Hoffa's police record thus served as a sign of his lifelong commitment to the labor movement. A criminal background was simply "the price a union member pays for fighting for what he believes in." In fact, Hoffa viewed with suspicion those who had never been arrested: a clean record was a sure sign that a labor organizer "was either buying [the police] off or he wasn't doing his job."[56]

The polarized views of class conflict, "Americanism," and crime served to broaden and solidify the cult of Jimmy Hoffa within the union. Even after the committee released its initial findings, the Teamsters revised their constitution in 1961 to increase Hoffa's salary and power. Among other changes, Hoffa would now have control over state, multistate, and regional conferences, previously semi-autonomous fiefdoms, as well as power to control the elections of local officers. But within the broader society, Teamster efforts to undermine the committee's charges had little effect.

This failure to shape public opinion rested partly with Kennedy's stronger connections to media outlets. Clark Mollenhoff, the reporter for *Look* and the Cowles chain of newpapers who had initially proposed the idea of investigating the Teamsters, was only the most prominent of the journalists with close ties to Kennedy. Ed Guthman, a reporter for the *Seattle Times*, worked for the committee, as did John Siegenthaler of the *Nashville Tennessean*. Siegenthaler would later co-write *The Enemy Within* and serve as Kennedy's administrative assistant at the Justice Department. These connections helped the committee achieve its investigative goals in cities with major Teamster locals, but they also ensured that the larger threat Kennedy saw in Teamster corruption would achieve currency. On the national level, Kennedy made frequent appearances on television programs from *Meet the Press* to *The Jack Paar Show*.[57] In 1959, *Armstrong Circle Theatre* ran an hour-long program, "Sound of Violence," which dramatically tied the union to "racketeers" in the jukebox industry who engaged in organizational picketing and secondary boycotts, two of the most controversial aspects of the committee's investigations and subsequent labor legislation.[58] These efforts worked: from the beginning of the hearings in February 1957 until May 1961, the percentage of people who approved of labor unions dropped from 76 percent to 63 percent, while the disapproval rate jumped from 14 percent to 22 percent.[59] When the Gallup organization asked people what legislation they would most like to see passed, the desire to "clean up corruption and racketeering in unions" ranked second only to a resolution of the Supreme Court's recent school desegregation decision. By January 1959, almost two years into the investigation, half of those polled believed that labor laws were not strict enough.[60] Thus, while the Teamsters did attempt to shape events by offering reporters access to Teamster headquarters and leaders, coverage beneficial to the committee's goals dominated the airwaves and print media.

Ultimately, the resulting competition between interpretive possibilities favored those offered by Kennedy and McClellan. In one month alone, August 1959, legislators reported receiving 1 million letters, most in favor of strict labor legislation. These appeals from the public were often the direct result of Kennedy's public relations efforts. On the day after Kennedy appealed to the public on *The Jack Paar Show*, Senator Everett Dirksen of Illinois received two thousand letters in favor of labor legislation. Immediately following this appearance, President Eisenhower decided to make a radio and television appeal in favor of the Landrum-Griffin Bill, which he described as a preventive measure against "racketeering, corruption and abuses of power," the first public appeal for any legislation by the popular president. Eisenhower posed "the great question [that] is always with us In the basic sense, the issue is: shall the people govern? If they do not, crooks and racketeers could prevail." His efforts were complemented by the appearance of Representative Phillip Landrum and Senator Robert Griffin on the *Today Show* and numerous newspaper advertisements.[61]

An Unholy Coalition

In September 1959, Congress passed the Landrum-Griffin Act. Some of its provisions received support within the labor movement, including the Teamsters. Most notably, Title I, known as the "laborers' bill of rights," guaranteed workers the rights of free speech and free assembly in union affairs. It prohibited raising union dues and levying assessments except by secret ballot or proper action of executive boards. In addition, it protected a member's right to sue the union. Most other provisions did not enjoy the same support. Title II specifically confronted the issues of economic manipulation that were the basis of Teamster corruption. It demanded that unions file annual reports with the secretary of labor. Other sections of the bill stipulated that local trusteeships be filed with the Labor Department within thirty days. Although the Teamsters supported "the principle of reporting and disclosure procedures, a ban on conflicts of interest, fair election procedures," and other reforms, they decried the bill's omission of due process provisions when violations did occur.[62]

Titles V and VI were the act's most controversial sections. Title V prohibited communists and felons from holding office within five years of party membership or incarceration, respectively. The law was limited to certain felonies: robbery, bribery, extortion, embezzlement, fraud, larceny, burglary, arson, violations of the narcotics laws, assault with intent to kill or resulting in grievous bodily injury, or violations of Titles I and II of the act. Title VI authorized the secretary of labor to conduct investigations and prohibited picketing "for personal profit or enrichment of any individual," also known as "professional picketing." Title VII imposed new restrictions on trade union activities, for example, prohibiting picketing to gain union recognition when the employer had already recognized another union. It also banned extortionate picketing, which had already been banned by the Hobbs Act and Taft-Hartley Act, as well as Title VI of Landrum-Griffin.

The passage of this act was made possible by the complementary agendas of anti-labor and anti–civil rights forces in Congress. Northern conservatives and southern Democrats created a coalition that reversed many New Deal reforms and slowed civil rights legislation. In addition, this coalition blocked efforts by more liberal legislators to broaden unemployment benefits and extend medical care for retirees. Though it hardly qualified as the greatest scoop of his career, Joseph Alsop, the Washington columnist for the *New York Herald-Tribune*, disclosed that Representative Charles Halleck, an Indiana Republican, helped Howard Smith, a Virginia Democrat, block civil rights legislation in return for Smith's support for the labor bill. This quid pro quo represented more than the individual votes of two congressmen: Halleck, as minority leader of the House, and Smith, who chaired the powerful Rules Committee, were the leaders of sizable voting blocs in the House of Representatives. The confluence of backroom deals, presidential politics, and AFL-CIO acquiescence drove Teamster conspiracy theorists wild: "Senator John Kennedy's presidential aspirations, an unholy coalition of Southern Democrats and Republicans to block civil rights legislation, the AFL-CIO's bankrupt leadership, and just pure hatred for organized labor were the major contributors last month in the enactment of the vicious, anti-labor Landrum-Griffin Bill by the House of Representatives. . . . It is also a certainty that the American Negro is going to continue to struggle along without being accorded his full rights under the constitution."[63]

After passage of the bill, Teamster frustration and anger intensified over the fruit of Kennedy and McClellan's efforts. Attempts to improve public perception of the trucking industry and the labor movement were not working. True, *International Teamster* magazine and the Teamsters News Service did reach approximately 1.5 million union members, succeeding in creating the image of innocent victims of a destructive campaign brought by the government, business, and the media. They went far in promoting Hoffa—and by extension his union—as a martyr to an all-out attack against the labor movement. Readers of *International Teamster* were assured that while George Meany was selling out the members of the AFL-CIO, Hoffa would sacrifice himself for the movement. These portrayals of the McClellan Committee and the Landrum-Griffin Act rarely penetrated the mainstream media. In fact, Teamster efforts backfired when lobbyist Sidney Zagri threatened representatives from districts with powerful labor voting blocs that they would not survive reelection.[64] By the end of the 1950s, it was clear that the strategy of battling images with more images had failed. Even Hoffa's court victories were being used against him as proof not of his innocence but of the length of his reach.

In response to their near-powerlessness to affect the terms of the debate, the Teamsters opened a second front in May 1959. The new strategy was initiated when William E. Bufalino, president of Detroit's Local 985, petitioned the Senate Judiciary Committee for redress of grievances. Bufalino charged that the McClellan Committee had violated his civil rights as a witness and asked Congress to "expel members who have violated their oaths." Furthermore, he sought to "expunge from the record . . . allegations of his membership in the mythical Mafia." The Senate ignored Bufalino's request, but *Life* and *Newsweek* settled libel cases for $25,000 and $10,000, respectively, for describing Bufalino as being "connected to organized crime."[65]

These settlements provided a model for Hoffa's own final strategy. Kennedy's 1959 and 1960 appearances on *The Jack Paar Show* prompted Hoffa to sue him for libel, also naming Paar and the National Broadcasting Company. Although Kennedy had been protected from libel while working on a Senate investigation, his book and public interviews did not guarantee such protections. Kennedy's comments on Paar's show were no more slanderous then anything he had said during the hearings. He described the Teamsters as "controlled and dominated at the top by racketeers and gangsters, and people who are not interested in unions, or interested in bettering the lives of their fellow man—which union officials should be and which the vast majority are—but only interested in stealing or extorting money, or betraying the union membership." Paar's response brought laughter from the audience: "You know the laws of libel. . . . We may be in court together, you and I." Hoffa threatened to sue after this appearance and followed through after Kennedy appeared again on the show in 1960.[66]

In suing Kennedy, NBC, and Paar, Hoffa once again inverted the former chief counsel's charge that the Teamsters, the International Longshoremen's Association, and the Longshoremen's and Warehousemen's Union were an "unholy alliance" of "the worst elements of the American labor movement." On the contrary, Hoffa argued, he was a victim, not a member, of a conspiracy. His suit charged that, "as a result of the plot, scheme, and unholy alliance engaged in between Kennedy, Paar, NBC, and others, there has been an endless flow of press releases damaging to Hoffa, . . . who has been the target of a series of vicious attacks engineered by the defendant, Kennedy, and others." Paar's humor, according to Hoffa's suit, was not innocuous. Rather, his "unfinished sentences, with overtones of impropriety," created "laughter and thereby degrading, defaming, and humiliating the plaintiff." In 1961 the Teamsters filed yet another libel suit, this time against George Meany, after news outlets widely reported his assertion at the AFL-CIO executive council meeting that "the Teamsters Union is more than ever now under the influence of criminal and corrupt elements."[67] These suits, the union leadership's final acts of desperation, were an extension of their consistent policy of focusing on the rhetorical strategies of the McClellan Committee rather than on the charges themselves.

Although Hoffa's lawsuit failed, his Teamster defenders remained focused on "unholy alliances" of corporate lobbies, the mass media, and government regulators. Hoffa would eventually serve almost five years of an eight-year federal prison sentence for jury tampering, conspiracy, and mail and wire fraud. After his brother was elected president, Robert Kennedy got the opportunity to expand the Organized Crime Section of the Justice Department, tripling the number of lawyers to fifty in his first two years. Along with the sought-after conviction of Hoffa, the Justice Department could boast that its convictions had risen from 385 in 1960 to 645 in 1963, including many for tax-related gambling charges brought by IRS investigators.[68] Kennedy's successes demonstrated that a significant shift had been completed. Corrupt officials within the labor movement had served as a symbol used to discredit the unions. Conversely, the movement had used that same symbol to indicate opposition to larger changes taking place in working-class identity and in the relationships among workers, unions, management, and the federal government. That symbol would shape perceptions of the labor movement that survived in later corruption scandals that would rock the Teamsters.

Larry Brennan's comments with which this chapter opened make clear that the Teamsters have yet to recover from the legacy of the Kennedy-Hoffa battles of the late 1950s. After an independent review board overturned the reelection of Teamster president Ron Carey in 1998 and expelled him from the union he had vowed to clean up, James P. Hoffa won a close race against the reform-minded Tom Leedham.[69] The irony that the candidate who unseated Carey and beat Leedham was the son and namesake of Jimmy Hoffa has not been lost on observers. Carey did learn one lesson from the elder Hoffa: he consistently used the strategy of "not recalling" discussions about the questionable donations and possible funneling of union money to his campaign. There is, however, a larger lesson from the McClellan Committee concerning the meaning assigned to corruption and its use in popular debates over the role of labor unions in the U.S. economy. Corruption and association with criminals consistently compromised the unions' ability to serve the interests of their members. When Brennan reacted to new reports of official misconduct by blaming government investigators, he revealed how corruption and its investigation shape public perceptions—and thus the effectiveness—of the labor movement in general. Economic advancement for American workers is often achieved only through strong advocacy by labor unions, whether during times of economic recession like the late 1950s or great corporate profit like the late 1990s. Many union members, whether voting for Jimmy Hoffa in the 1950s or James Hoffa in the 1990s, truly "don't care about that other stuff." But reformers within the union know that, whether or not corruption results in less lucrative contracts, it most certainly serves as a weapon for anti-labor forces on the lookout for unholy alliances.

FROM *THE UNTOUCHABLES* TO "LA COSA NOSTRA":

Italian American Perceptions of the Mafia

By 1957, the year Eliot Ness wrote *The Untouchables: The Real Story*, it had been over twenty-five years since Al Capone was jailed on tax evasion charges. *The Untouchables* was set in 1929 and 1930, but the new incarnation quickly took its place in 1950s debates over ethnicity, crime, and political clout. The book and the TV series that followed implicitly debated shifts in economic and cultural identities. The meanings of ethnic difference had changed since the 1920s and 1930s, as many white ethnics moved into middle-class jobs or were enjoying higher incomes within the working class. In its reinforcement of an older ethnic hierarchy that placed WASP elites above southern Italian Catholics, *The Untouchables* asked readers and viewers to think about the changes that had taken place over the previous thirty years. Readers and viewers ultimately did more than think; the television version provoked a vigorous reaction from Italian American civic organizations, particularly the Order Sons of Italy in America (OSIA), that catered to a growing white ethnic middle class. Their reaction, no less than the show itself, reveals how the shifting meanings of white ethnic identities were grounded in a changing class hierarchy that intersected ethnic lines. Protests from the largest Italian American civic organization, with "lodges" throughout the United States, Canada, and Bermuda, made explicit the relationship of underlying assumptions about criminality to the reinforcement of ethnic and class identities. The speedy reaction to OSIA's anti-Mafia campaign by the television networks also indicates the growing clout of white ethnic activists in general and Italian Americans in particular during the late 1950s. OSIA's vigorous campaign against the word "Mafia" and the use of Italian names for criminals in American popular culture showed that images exist in a larger process of negotiated meanings. The Mafia itself took on various meanings in the context of contemporary struggles over Italian American identity and the ongoing political debate over immigration reform, crime, and public policy.

Italian Americans would prove essential in both critiquing and reinforcing popular understandings of organized crime. Some Italian Americans vigorously protested both fictional depictions and actual investigations of the Mafia. Others, including former gangsters, would themselves play a central role in revealing the inner workings of what came to be known as "La Cosa Nostra." Just as current, alleged, and former communists served as symbolic foils in anticommunist campaigns of the late 1940s and early 1950s, Italian Americans served as foils in the symbolic and real campaigns over organized crime. *American Legion Magazine* claimed in 1948, "Most cities today contain a nucleus of former F.B.I. men, Army or Navy intelligence officers, former [Communist Party] members who have come over to our side and other trained or experienced men." This coalition, according to the American Legion, was necessary to create an effective bulwark against clever, secretive communists. But the border between the two sides was permeable, with traitors from the "other side" representing the vanguard of anti-subversion. In the same way, the most effective and sensational testimony against organized crime came from ex-gangsters.[1]

In the case of Lucky Luciano, the simultaneous denunciation and fetishization of white ethnic gangsters revealed the ambivalence Americans felt over the increasing corporatization of their lives. Al Capone's image underwent an even greater change during the postwar period, coming to symbolize a cultural discomfort with urban diversity, patterns of consumption and fashion, and sexual liberalism.[2] This shift in the cultural understanding of organized crime occurred amid a debate over the very existence of the Mafia. OSIA's view that the Mafia was a figment of overactive imaginations contradicted the conclusions of many government agencies and virtually all non–Italian American media outlets that an Italian or Italian American organized underworld controlled multiple sectors of the service economy, particularly trucking, garbage hauling, and entertainment. In the year immediately preceding *The Untouchables'* greatest popularity, the U.S. Senate's McClellan Committee hearings, which would eventually center on corruption in the International Brotherhood of Teamsters, displayed to television viewers convicted and suspected mobsters, including Joe Profaci, Vito Genovese, and Thomas Lucchese.[3] The "Apalachin conclave" of November 14, 1957, allegedly proved the existence of an underworld conspiracy of Italian Americans who controlled illegal activity throughout the nation.[4] Earlier in the decade, Senator Estes Kefauver's city-by-city probe of organized crime in interstate commerce incidentally demonstrated to future investigators the power of television in promoting political and social agendas.

These political revelations of organized crime in labor, business, and illicit markets did concern many Italian Americans. But Italian American criminality was only one piece of a larger problem. As Joseph Errigo, the Sons of Italy's recording secretary, wrote: "It is not [OSIA's] duty to suppress crime. Crime is the problem of the nation."[5] The most intense efforts of OSIA and other advocacy groups centered on the fictionalized portrayals of Italian Americans that permeated mass culture. A growing body of work suggests that the cultural distinctiveness of various European origin groups ceased to be a salient force beginning in the postwar period.[6] The sociologist Richard Alba compellingly argues that the post–World War II generation of Italian Americans, in particular, began a process of "muting" their ethnic distinctiveness in relation to a dominant white Protestant culture.[7] This would imply that OSIA's campaign to distance its members from the negative connotations of Italian American cultural associations is evidence of this withdrawal into WASP culture. But was this campaign against negative images evidence that the last vestiges of ethnic cultures were mere symbols that could be put on and taken off like a tam-o'-shanter?[8]

This is a question about class mobility as much as it is about the changing meaning of ethnicity, which, like cultural pluralism more generally, has to do with systemic inequality in the United States.[9] For Italian Americans in the 1950s, the desire to control the meaning of ethnicity depended on their ability to enter the middle class. As their temporal distance from the immigrant generation increased and the conditions that had kept them in positions of relative poverty waned— including a decrease in the stigmatization of southern European ethnicity and an increase in educational accomplishment—Italian Americans lost some of their cultural distinctiveness. Many could still identify with and take pride in their ethnic ancestry, though only in the most general way. By the 1980s, when pressed to explain what their Italian American heritage meant, many answered "that their particular group placed a high premium on family, education, hard work, religiosity, and patriotism."[10] While these were traits they shared with their parents and grandparents, they also shared them with many other Americans.[11]

In some ways, the initiatives of OSIA and other Italian American individuals and organizations in fighting Mafia stereotypes indicate that they were operating within some of the same assumptions as turn-of-the-century Italian immigrants. The first generation entered the American social hierarchy at a position of both privilege and disadvantage within the nexus of race, class, and ethnicity.[12] Yet the system of racial meanings into which they first migrated had experienced a shift by the 1950s. After a period of racial "inbetweenness," most nineteenth- and twentieth-century European immigrants came to be seen (and seemed to see themselves) as "white." Much of this transformation occurred because economic rewards and full citizenship were available only to those accepted as "white."[13] Italian Americans accordingly defined, debated, and reinvented identities within these historically specific contexts.[14] This process, however, does not have a clear beginning, middle, or end. During the postwar period, second- and third-generation Italian Americans continued to struggle with the promise of full inclusion and the negative valuation of their ethnic heritage. This did not interfere with their ability as "white" ethnics to shape U.S. culture or politics. They merely responded to pressures for assimilation and embraced the possibility that their ethnic descent could be compatible with economic and social advances, rather than something one had to discard to gain acceptance.

During the 1950s, assimilation took on a new urgency as ethnicity raised suspicions of potentially dangerous dual loyalties. From the Alien and Sedition Act of 1790 to the red scare of 1919 and the Internal Security Act of 1950, xenophobia and ideological repression often went hand-in-hand. In the anticommunist fervor of the 1950s, accusers would bolster their charges of radical politics by pointing out that a target was of foreign origin. While this tactic was aimed at many ethnic and racial groups, the exposure of Italian American criminality created a unique problem for middle-class Italian Americans: virtually the only Italian Americans who appeared on television in the 1950s were criminals, and this created an impression in the minds of many viewers that criminality and Italian American ethnicity were interconnected—even interchangeable—categories. As Italian Americans sought to eliminate this association by downplaying criminality, denying the existence of the Mafia, and lobbying the television networks, they sought to assign a new meaning to their identity along the lines of race and class.

In light of the shifting meanings of ethnicity and class, the battle over *The Untouchables*—both the book and the television series—serves as a potent symbol of how Italian Americans sought respectability. In returning to his Prohibition-era exploits, Eliot Ness revived a past that Italian Americans thought they had left behind in the economic gains and cultural changes for which they had struggled.[15] Throughout the early chapters of his book, Ness emphasized the differences between cops and robbers by contrasting what he saw as the physical and moral superiority of white, native-born investigators with the physically and morally deficient Italian American criminals: "Cigar smoke hung in a heavy blue haze over the long polished table. Ash trays piled high betrayed the inner emotions of the little group as it listened to a tall spare man with a thin, square-jawed face," later revealed to be "the handsome, light-haired" brother-in-law of Eliot Ness. This was "Chicago in 1929, a city ruled by a knife, pistol, shotgun, tommygun and 'pineapple' of the underworld, a jungle of steel and concrete clutched fast in the fat, diamond-studded hand of a scar-faced killer named Al Capone."[16] The square jaw and fair complexion evoke what an earlier era would simply have labeled the genetic superiority of the "Anglo-Teutonic race." Ness draws an even sharper contrast between his own appearance and that of the stocky, flamboyant, "scar-faced killer" Al Capone: "Eliot Ness, twenty-six years old, six feet tall, 180 pounds, single, blue eyes, brown hair, no scars. Top third of class in both high school and the University of Chicago. Co-operative, neat and modest according to instructors. Played tennis, Ness dresses quietly, lives modestly and soberly and has $410 in the bank." He quickly details his exemplary physical appearance, social grace, and economic habits, drawing a formal division between normal and abnormal bodies and behavior. Capone's executive-sized income seemed particularly suspect in comparison to Ness's modest lifestyle. Despite the blood and booze that filled the pages of *The Untouchables*, the reader could rest assured that Ness and the values he represented would restore order to Chicago. In fact, the end of *The Untouchables* was well known to readers in the 1950s: on October 24, 1931, Al Capone was sentenced to an eleven-year prison term and assessed a $50,000 fine for tax evasion.[17]

Like the ideal fifties man described by Norman Podhoretz, Ness was "poised, sober, judicious, and prudent" in his pursuit both of bad boys and of Betty Anderson, the heterosexual partner necessary to complete the picture. Betty strengthens his confidence and serves as an innocent victim for the hero to protect. One night outside the Evanston home of the Andersons, Ness confronts a Capone henchman who has followed him:

> Grabbing him by the lapels of his coat, I slammed him viciously against the side of the house. As he made a motion to reach for his gun, I gave him a judo chop across the side of the neck with the flat edge of my hand. His legs buckled. I straightened him up savagely and frisked him. "Listen, you ape," I said, "and get this straight. Tell whoever sent you that if I ever catch any more gorillas around here I'll put a hole in them. Not only that, but from now on there's going to be a police guard on this place. Now get out of here—and you'd better keep going."

Then Ness kicks the intruder fifteen feet, straightens his necktie, and takes Betty out for a snack without mentioning the altercation.[18] Significantly, it was not the restoring of order that drove the narrative. In Ness's text, the magnetic attraction of the disorder was *more* powerful than the appeal of a quiet life with Betty: "As I walked away [from Betty], I felt that I could take the whole Capone mob single-handed. But even that memory and my constant desire to be with her couldn't lure me away from the magnetic attraction of the job at hand."[19]

The urban disorder the "gorilla" represents transgressed the physical boundaries of Evanston and the social boundaries of the courtship, but Ness violently re-moved the "beast" from the perceived sanctuary of Evanston. In this sense, Ness became a synecdoche for the political culture that doled out rewards to conform-ists while excluding those who did not conform. Such distinctions had conse-quences. The rhetoric here recalls the nativist furor that dominated the discussion of Italian Americans in the 1920s. The explicit ethnic hierarchy that informed immigration policy earlier in the century had recently been revisited in the debates leading up to the passage of the 1952 McCarran-Walter Act. Despite the opposition of President Truman and other political leaders, the law enforced quotas that favored northern and western Europeans over immigrants from the rest of the world.[20] Foreign-born people were discussed in the same animalistic metaphors Ness used whenever the subject turned to immigration and crime. But, as the *Untouchables* phenomenon would indicate, opinions were changing.

A two-part treatment of Ness's exploits on ABC's *Desilu Playhouse* led to an hour-long series that ran for four seasons, from October 1959 to September 1963. The television show was a sensation during its run, rising to become the eighth most popular program in its second season.[21] The first episode began with a date, a place, and the image of the book on which the show was based: "Chicago, May 5, 1932," the date Al Capone went to prison for tax evasion. Much of the episode hinged on a murder in a barber shop, clearly a reference to the recent killing in New York of Albert Anastasia rather than to any crime that occurred in Prohibition-era Chicago. As columnist and radio personality Walter Winchell nar-rates, the beleaguered barber, Mr. Rossi, begs the famous agent in heavily accented English, "Mr. Ness, help me to do something about these butchers."[22] This scene marked a significant transformation in the conventional portrayal of Italian Amer-icans in U.S. popular culture. No longer the foreign menace invoked to explain the failures of Prohibition, they now represented the kind of hardworking, law-abiding immigrants who were welcome in America. And, like Mr. Rossi, they were necessary informants in the fight against organized crime.

The members of the Untouchables had also been transformed to reflect the shifting perception of ethnicity in postwar America. The television program and the entertainment coverage in the press highlighted the multiethnic character of the agents. Just as Eliot Ness stood in for the archetypal native-born hero, his team served as evidence of the willingness of the United States to absorb and champion difference. It was still true that Ness and other Anglo-Americans gave the orders. But the Untouchables to whom they gave their orders included Enrico Rossi, an Italian American; William Youngblood, "a full-blooded Cherokee"; and Martin Flaherty, an Irish American. In addition, early episodes featured not only the expected Italian American and Jewish villains—"Scarface" Al Capone, Frank "The Enforcer" Nitti, and Jake "Greasy Thumb" Guzik—but also their innocent victims, some of whom were members of the same ethnic groups. These changes emphasized the supposedly meritocratic terms of acceptance operating within postwar mainstream culture.[23]

The show was an instant hit and earned a loyal following. Articles filled the entertainment sections of newspapers, and the show attracted many advertisers.[24] In addition, *The Untouchables* also attracted the attention, if not the admiration, of the Order Sons of Italy in America. Contrary to its name, OSIA did include women as members, though not yet in leadership roles. While the television series revealed the shifting perceptions of ethnic differences in the postwar United States, the protests against the series by Italian Americans indicate that they were struggling with the meaning of their own upward mobility. Despite OSIA's roots in union politics (primarily the garment workers' union), by the 1950s, the organization's national leaders were predominantly professionals, including business executives, lawyers, politicians, a number of judges, and journalists.[25] OSIA's campaign to influence or eliminate *The Untouchables* grew out of its larger argument that the Mafia was nothing more than the stereotypical invention of the anti-Italian American media and an incompetent criminal justice system. In 1954 the Order formed its Public Relations Committee. The initial agenda called for identifying and combating anti-Italian activities, including presentation of stereotypes in the mass media; discrimination in employment, education, and immigration policy; and anti-immigrant movements.[26] It is important to note that these were interrelated issues. Activism against negative images was explicitly tied to the material concerns of this group, since negative representations were seen as having an adverse effect on employment opportunities, upward mobility, and citizenship rights.

The efforts of prior generations of European ethnic advocacy groups illustrate how class position strongly influenced ethnic politics. At the turn of the century, the Ancient Order of Hibernians, an upwardly mobile Irish American voluntary association, launched a campaign against "the stage Irishman," perceiving such stock characters as anti-Irish. During the Prohibition era, ethnic crime became grist for the mill of Hollywood and of politics, and the ethnic press reacted strongly to the stereotyping of immigrants as criminals. But there were important differences. From the turn of the century until the end of Prohibition, working-class European immigrant communities were more likely to question the law, especially Prohibition law, rather than point to the negative impact of stereotypes. As Gary Mormino points out, the Italian American community of St. Louis showed its unwillingness to give up imported social customs by breaking the ban on alcohol that had been imposed by "rural-oriented, middle class . . . waspish America on urban, lower-class European Catholics." Thus, violators of the Eighteenth Amendment were not isolated criminals but members of a large socioeconomic community.[27] The native-born white community demonized "men of alien names" and denied citizenship to Italian-born people on grounds of "bad moral character," but the days of anti-defamation activism were still ahead for Italian American civic organizations. Instead, Italian American daily papers pointed to the hypocrisy of judges, politicians, and journalists who decried the alien menace while casually breaking those same Prohibition laws themselves.[28]

By the 1930s, the activities of American Jews foreshadowed the ethnic activism of Italian Americans in the 1950s.[29] They followed the sensationalized trials of the Jewish American gangsters Longy Zwillman and Irving "Waxey Gordon" Wexler out of concern for the more general reputation of Jews within the host society. Newly middle-class white ethnic groups, including Irish Americans and Jewish Americans, often perceived images of criminality as having damaging consequences for the respect they felt they had earned. For Jewish Americans, this battle had virtually ended by the 1950s. The television version of *The Untouchables* did feature some anti-Semitic stereotypes, but Italian American gangsters were the staple of organized crime shows. Since many Americans associated criminal behavior with ethnic and racial markers of difference, middle-class Italian Americans saw a need to challenge the assumptions of the mainstream media and the criminal justice system.

Tellingly, OSIA did not come to the defense of Italian Americans who were accused of breaking the law. Their interest was, in the words of one president of the organization, in "protecting the good name of Italian Americans." And the interests of the Order's members revolved around the effects of stereotyped images on their dealings in a business world dominated by Americans of northern European descent. OSIA's anti-Mafia campaign expressed no sympathy for criminals but only concern for the tarnished reputation of law-abiding Italian Americans.[30] The Sons of Italy supported the efforts of crime busters such as Estes Kefauver, John McClellan, J. Edgar Hoover, and Robert F. Kennedy. In 1959 Joseph A. L. Errigo, the Supreme Recording Secretary of the Sons of Italy, wrote confidentially to A. Alfred Marcello, the editor of *OSIA News* and head of the anti-Mafia campaign: "As soon as all Americans awaken to the fact that the certainty of punishment is the only way to combat crime the present situation will not only continue but become aggravated as time goes on. Our judicial system is far too lenient on handling criminals. It might be advisable at our next convention at Boston to appoint a committee consisting of judges and lawyers and ask this committee to submit recommendations relative to law enforcement, referring, of course, to crime generally and not to any particular criminals." In addition, U.S. Congressman Alfred E. Santangelo compiled statistics from the Bureau of Prisons which revealed that only 2.5 percent of the federal prison population was of Italian ancestry. For Marcello, this disproportionately low number confirmed his belief that Italian criminals were a creation of the media. (This statistic might also indicate the failure of law enforcement to prosecute Italian American criminals, though that would not have helped OSIA's efforts to disassociate Italian American ethnicity from criminality).[31]

In its boldest move, the Sons of Italy attempted to disprove the existence of the Mafia. In an open letter to President Eisenhower, OSIA asked him to "order an investigation to determine whether an Italian Secret Society known as the Mafia actually exists in the United States." Both the Kefauver Committee and the McClellan Committee, as well as major media outlets, assumed that the Mafia did exist, and this assumption, the Sons of Italy argued, wrongly forced "12 million decent American men, women and children of Italian origin . . . to pay the price for the misdeeds of a slovenly hundred fold of cheap racketeers."[32] In arguing that the Mafia was at most a wild exaggeration, the Sons of Italy sought to break the hold such an organization had on the popular imagination. At the same time that OSIA attempted to disprove the existence of the Mafia, they showed a willingness to hold Italian American criminals up to the same contempt displayed by TV programs, magazine stories, and Senate investigators.

President Eisenhower did not respond. In his stead, Attorney General William P. Rogers assured the organization that "to my knowledge there is no national crime syndicate consisting solely of criminals of any particular national origin. There are, however, operating in this country syndicates of organized criminals who have achieved a large measure of influence in underworld circles." Rogers expressed the hope that his statement would "assist in silencing any slander of our twelve million able and honorable Americans of Italian origin." In addition, FBI chief J. Edgar Hoover promised Marcello that his agency would never substantiate rumors of the Mafia's existence, as it did "not comment upon the origin or ancestry of persons involved in any matter within our jurisdiction." Senator John F. Kennedy expressed his concern about the irresponsible use of the word "Mafia" and asked Marcello to share this concern with the membership at the 1959 OSIA convention.[33] Similar expressions came from the conservative ideologue Barry Goldwater and Edmund G. Brown, recently elected governor of California.

In marshaling the support of these politicians, OSIA was careful to frame its campaign solely in terms of slander. Its leaders assured senators, district attorneys, and presidents that they would never come to the defense of actual criminals: "The Order did not intend to defend those who had put themselves outside the law because of their criminal actions, just because they were Italians. . . . [N]o protection is made or offered to criminal or lawless elements. Rather the Order intended to protect the millions of Italian-Americans who were unjustly slandered and branded with the mark of crime."[34] OSIA wanted to distance itself from the "lawless elements," and it wanted better press.

Even before *The Untouchables* hit the airwaves, George Spatuzza, Supreme Venerable, or president, of OSIA, reported to the 1955 convention that "one of the purposes of the order is to defend and uphold the prestige of the people of Italian birth or extraction in America." This concern with prestige was not wholly symbolic. In the same speech, Spatuzza referred to the strong link between defamatory images and unfair bias when he mentioned the National Origins Act and the firing of Edward Corsi. Corsi, Italian-born commissioner of immigration and sometime Republican candidate for mayor of New York, was dismissed by President Eisenhower just as Congress was debating the National Origins Act of 1924, reaffirmed as the McCarran-Walter Act, which set specific quotas for immigrants. The original proposal allowed for a total of 154,657, of which 125,165 places were reserved for people from western and northern Europe but only 24,502 for southern and eastern Europe and 4,990 for all of Asia and Africa. Congressman Walter's response to Italian American outrage, "I am not afraid of dagoes," proved OSIA correct that the act was at least in part a product of prejudice.[35]

The Public Relations Committee and OSIA's newsletter resisted demeaning images of Italian Americans while promoting more positive conceptions of Italian contributions to American culture: they sponsored a museum devoted to Italian American inventors and encouraged members to "wear purple on Columbus day." OSIA reacted to the Mafia stereotype out of this complex mixture of political goals and desires for class mobility rather then simply out of a wish to control public portrayals of Italian Americans. The Sons of Italy criticized television and the movies, in particular their tendency "to use Italian names almost exclusively in portraying the gangster or the racketeer." The Mafia label was seen by OSIA as a convenient distraction: "Unsolved crimes were perpetrated by the Mafia. Groups of gangsters who gave the police a headache drew their power from this mysterious organization called Mafia. Mafia became the obsession of the moment and the magic word which began and concluded the lurid and fantastic accounts of these mediocre and sensationalist journalists."[36] OSIA interpreted the use of the word "Mafia" as nothing less than a scapegoating of Italian Americans for the inability of the criminal justice system and the media industry to control rising crime rates during the postwar period.

"It All Boils Down to Semantics"

Headed by A. Alfred Marcello, who edited a mainstream Worcester, Massachusetts, daily, as well as the monthly *OSIA News*, the anti-Mafia campaign quickly eclipsed all other initiatives of the Public Relations Committee. Throughout the 1950s, OSIA used several approaches in battling the Mafia stereotype. Letter-writing campaigns, product boycotts, and promotion of positive images were all employed to counteract what the group considered a negative message that soiled the good name of Italian Americans. When the Wilmington, Delaware, *Journal* ran a news article titled "Little Italy Hoodlums, G.I.'s Battle Brings on Near Riot," the local chapter of the Sons of Italy mobilized their membership and others sympathetic to their views in a massive letter-writing campaign. Within twenty-four hours the *Journal*'s editorial offices were flooded with strongly worded condemnations, prompting an apology later in the week: "There is no place in our language for labels which are felt by loyal and devoted Americans as terms of derision and reproach because they seem to mark them as a group apart. Since that is what stereotypes like 'Little Italy' do, let us give them the permanent burial they deserve."[37] This example clearly shows the impact the Sons of Italy had, particularly on the local level. The editor of the *Journal*, echoing the strategy of the OSIA campaign, acknowledged that Italian Americans' desire to assimilate into the American white middle class was being thwarted by stereotypes that "mark them as a group apart." The paper was wrong, he agreed, to treat Italian Americans as distinct from the "G.I.'s" (who, one assumes, lost their ethnicity once they donned their uniforms) they were fighting. In fact, any marker of difference, such as the designation "Little Italy," could be perceived as a negative stereotype and thus became a target of concern for ethnic advocates during the 1950s.

Boycotts, or the threat of boycotts, proved to be a more effective tool for battling the images OSIA found objectionable. It was the organization's preferred method for pressuring television producers. By working directly with advertisers, the Sons of Italy made rapid and effective inroads at the top levels of the national networks. In December 1959, H. P. Hood and Sons, a milk distributor, had agreed to sponsor an episode of *This Man Dawson* featuring Italian American criminals. When Marcello got wind of this, he wrote to Hood: "Frankly, it all boils down to semantics. If we allow the use of the word or the Mafia theme to go by unchallenged, then there will never be an end to this business." Hood backed down. A letter-writing campaign to the Ford Motor Company resulted in NBC's assuring OSIA that "if any crime show is done in the Ford series the show will not reflect on any national or racial group."[38]

Although the Hood and Ford initiatives were successful, other media outlets resisted letter-writing campaigns. Because they often occurred behind the scenes, the wider public rarely became aware of OSIA's grievances. In addition, some producers and sponsors insisted on autonomy and faulted OSIA for blowing things out of proportion. Beginning in 1959, OSIA followed through on threats to boycott advertisers that funded offensive programs. This strategy succeeded owing to the role *OSIA News* played in publicizing it. Alfred Marcello, in his October 1959 editorial, paved the way:

> Lawful boycott! That will be our most potent weapon in combating those forces who persist in picturing Americans of Italian origin as throat-slitting gangsters and hoodlums. For months now we have tried to make Hollywood and television producers understand our position. We have made every reasonable overture. But this has failed so now we have no recourse but to show that we have teeth that bite, we

will hit back where it will hurt the most—the POCKETBOOK. . . . We know that we can enlist the support of every American with Italian blood flowing in his veins. . . . This is an alert. If the current trend in entertainment continues there will be a call to arms.

Beginning in the following month's edition of *OSIA News,* Marcello published the "Sons of Italy Index," listing "entertainment or reading material of an objectionable nature." In addition, he began naming sponsors of objectionable television programs, advising members to "boycott their products and when you do make sure you tell the storekeeper why you are crossing Tums, Luden's Cough Drops, Dial Soap, and products of Johnson & Johnson from your shopping list." Some storekeepers who were members of OSIA pulled these products off their shelves in response to Marcello's call to arms. No longer satisfied with boycotting individual products, in February 1960, *OSIA News* proclaimed, "ABC Should Be 'Off Limits' to All Members," after the network ignored requests to "cancel out the odious program called 'The Noise of Death.' "[39] The pressure brought a swift response from the top levels of ABC.

During the summer of 1959, Marcello spread word of OSIA's boycott to many powerful people in the media, including the producers and sponsors of *The Untouchables,* the president of ABC, and gossip columnist Walter Winchell. He targeted the news services in order to publicize the boycott to a wider audience. ABC and Desilu were at first reluctant to make changes. Bert Granet, a Desilu producer, dismissed Marcello's comments, claiming only that the inclusion of Italian American detectives and police showed their commitment to battling stereotypes.[40] Granet implied that adding culturally valued images of Italian Americans to the gangsters would provide balance and mute OSIA's critique. Winchell, who did voice-overs for *The Untouchables,* sought to discredit OSIA, comparing the Sons of Italy to the political fixes of the "Mobfia," a Winchellism for organized crime. This comparison led many readers to the conclusion that the Sons of Italy was itself a Mafia front organization. But ABC neither mocked nor dismissed the Sons of Italy. Advertisers during this period sought to avoid controversial television shows, regardless of their popularity. Perhaps the most notorious example is the failure of *The Nat King Cole Show* to find a sponsor despite good ratings because of advertisers' fear that association with an interracial variety show hosted by an African American man would hurt sales to southern whites. Not wanting sponsors to flee because of threatened boycotts by Italian Americans, ABC called a landmark series of meetings in the late 1950s and early 1960s, instituting an ongoing relationship with the Sons of Italy.[41]

The first meeting, attended by OSIA officials, representatives from the network, and Desilu executives, as well as Benjamin Epstein, president of the Anti-Defamation League of B'nai B'rith, mirrored earlier agreements reached by representatives of the National Association for the Advancement of Colored People with various media outlets.⁴² The discussion centered on the distinction between fact and fiction, reality and myth. The producers and the network argued that if the Mafia really existed and the show focused on historical figures such as Al Capone, Frank Nitti, and Eliot Ness, then there could be no possible basis for criticism. OSIA argued the even if true, the intertwining of Italian American ethnicity and criminality placed an unfair burden on law-abiding Italian Americans. The two sides eventually reached a compromise. The OSIA delegation agreed not to protest if the show depicted real people in real situations. Marcello himself had earlier warned OSIA members that their protests would be futile if they tried to erase Al Capone from popular culture: "If the program chronicles straight away facts concerning Al Capone and his gangsters during the Prohibition era then we have NO CASE. This is unfortunate, but facts are facts. Al Capone is now a part of American history and what he and his henchmen did is something we must live with." For their part, the network and producers agreed to create new roles for Italian Americans as law-abiding citizens and to cease creating fictional gangsters with Italian surnames. To enforce the agreement, the producers would send scripts to members of the Public Relations Committee for input. In response, OSIA agreed to call off the boycott.⁴³

There were some immediate results. Previously a minor role, the Nick Rossi character (played by Greek American Nicholas Georgiade) gained prominence. Desi Arnaz of Desilu Productions agreed to feature characters with Italian names in roles as "judges, prosecutors, mayors, governors, legislators, and other public officers."⁴⁴ The season's remaining episodes included far fewer Italian American villains, though Frank Nitti, a Prohibition-era gangster and Capone's reputed heir, was a frequent nemesis for the good guys. Episodes broadcast after the fateful meeting also featured an increasingly multiethnic cast of criminals. One episode, "The Snowball," even depicted Frank Nitti and Eliot Ness joining forces to defeat a youthful WASP criminal (played by a boyish Robert Redford) who employs out-of-work "family men" to sell "organization" booze to fraternity boys. Unbeknownst to Nitti or his couriers, the bootlegger substitutes wood alcohol for the whisky in a cost-saving measure that results in poisoning several customers. In a fit of moral outrage, Nitti kills the double-crosser and dumps his body at Ness's feet. Ness does not condemn this act of violence and is satisfied with the outcome.

Desilu's use of Italian American criminals seemed to rebound to earlier levels after the *Saturday Evening Post*, then one of the most popular publications in the country, survived a vigorous campaign mounted by OSIA. In July 1960 the *Post* published a two-part series, "How We Bagged the Mafia," by Milton Wessel, a former special assistant to the attorney general for organized crime. Wessel drew heavily on information provided by three Federal Bureau of Narcotics agents, agreeing without the knowledge of *Post* editors to Commissioner of Narcotics

Harry Anslinger's requirement that the Bureau edit the piece. Not surprisingly, the focus on the Mafia drew immediate and scathing attack from the Sons of Italy. Rather than apologize or alter its policy on the coverage of the Mafia, the *Post* privately dismissed Marcello's requests, but Wessel felt compelled to write a response in his defense, though it was never published.[45]

When backsliding did occur, the meeting with top ABC executives provided the context for additional criticism. Marcello wrote to the network in regard to another episode of *The Untouchables*, "This is the sort of entertainment trash that gets our dander up."[46] The anger that characterized much of the OSIA campaign now included a strong sense of betrayal. The meeting in New York had resulted in an agreement that fictional characters would not be used, but this episode featured a "Lucky Ciano," head of "the Black Hand," in a story about an opera singer. Clearly, ABC was blurring the line between fiction and reality and thus betraying the spirit of the agreement with OSIA. By using "the Black Hand," a common synonym for the Mafia, ABC could avoid the objectionable term "Mafia" without sacrificing the verisimilitude its audience expected.

In a change so subtle that most viewers probably did not notice, some episodes of *The Untouchables* cast Italian American actors as characters with names not necessarily of Italian derivation. For example, Vincent Gardenia was "Jake Petri," head of the Chicago "Syndicate," in a 1961 episode. In this way, ABC continued to portray a conspiratorial nexus of gangsters who looked and sounded Italian American even if their names were not, thus keeping to the letter of the agreement. Names could be changed to satisfy protests from the Sons of Italy, but physical and linguistic codes continued to satisfy the narrative goals of portraying organized crime. Scripts were dutifully sent by ABC to OSIA members, who read them and provided pointed critiques. In response to an Adrian Spies teleplay intended for *The Untouchables*, Marcello made clear that the strategy of including "good" Italians as a counterpoint to the gangsters did not go far enough: "We recognize the fact that the Spies script brings out the good and the bad in Italians. But we ask why make Italians the scapegoat? Must it always be so?"[47] Neither did regional lodges ease their vigilance. The Public Relations Committee provided them with direct access to the networks throughout the 1950s. Their members were told exactly what to look out for when watching television, and as a result, a steady audience of viewers engaged in organized protest against the shows beamed into their living rooms.

Criticism persisted, but by March 1961, Thomas Moore, vice president of ABC, could write to Marcello, "We are making progress toward our mutual aim." The network was happy because its shows were drawing a large audience. OSIA was happy with its access to the highest level of network management. This influence, however, had its own critics among Italian Americans who were frustrated with the sometimes imperceptible pace of change OSIA achieved. Just months before an optimistic Thomas Moore wrote to Marcello, Alfred Santangelo founded the Federation of Italian-American Democratic Organizations (FIADO). In addition to Santangelo, a former New York congressman who had cooperated with the Sons of Italy in the past, three other Italian American members of Congress publicly criticized *The Untouchables*. In contrast to OSIA's gradual approach of beginning with a letter-writing campaign and only later progressing to boycotts, FIADO immediately announced that it would picket ABC's New York headquarters on March 9, 1961, Amerigo Vespucci Day, unless the president of the network agreed to a meeting with its board.[48]

As he had with OSIA, Leonard Goldenson, the president of ABC, agreed to meet with Santangelo. Goldenson told Santangelo about the ABC-Desilu agreement with OSIA, but Santangelo found this unsatisfactory. As threatened, approximately 250 people picketed the network's headquarters carrying signs and banners reading "A.B.C. Is Un-American" and "Italians Are Not Gangsters." Later that evening, they picketed a meeting of broadcast executives at the Waldorf-Astoria Hotel. A third group, the Italian-American League to Combat Defamation (IALCD), represented by two prominent Italian American judges, was founded in 1961 to push for cancellation of *The Untouchables*. One New Yorker voiced what was surely the frustration of many Italian Americans when he sided with FIADO and IALCD over OSIA: "These groups are not interested in concessions. They will be content only when 'The Untouchables' goes off the air."[49]

Typical of its tough approach, FIADO enlisted Anthony "Tough Tony" Anastasio, the head of the fifteen thousand–member Local 1814 of the International Longshoremen's Association. Anastasio was featured in many newspapers carrying a picket sign in front of ABC's New York headquarters. A veteran of Kefauver's inquiry into organized crime with a police record dating back to 1925 which included murder charges, Anastasio was a frequent example for Robert F. Kennedy's contention that the ILA was controlled by mobsters. In the early 1950s, Walter Cronkite paraded him in front of viewers of his TV news magazine, *The Twentieth Century*. With his heavily accented English, Anastasio made a dramatic guest. Many confused him with his brother, Albert Anastasia, a reputed hit man for Louis "Lepke" Buchalter and Jacob "Gurrah" Shapiro's murder-for-hire enterprise, Murder, Inc., of the 1920s and 1930s, though Albert had been shot and killed while getting a shave at the Park Sheraton Hotel's barber shop in 1957, an event that served as the theme for the inaugural episode of *The Untouchables*.[50]

OSIA feared that "Tough Tony" would make a mockery of their efforts. Persistent rumors that the anti-Mafia campaign of the late 1950s and early 1960s was wholly a ruse of mobsters stemmed from Anastasio's involvement. His contribution was not what the Sons of Italy had had in mind when they declared a desire to make "known the many contributions of Italians to the progress of America." Marcello was livid. In a harshly worded letter to OSIA president Joseph Gorrassi, he asked, "Imagine how untenable our position would be at this point if we, at one time or another, agreed to go along with Congressman Santangelo and his crowd in the current dispute with the American Broadcasting Co." With sinister overtones revealing an awareness that Italian American criminals were more than figments of overactive imaginations, Marcello told Gorrassi that he had "been warned by certain sources in New York to steer clear of Santangelo and his thinking. One source said that 'he did not like the company Santangelo keeps.'" In contrast to the mockery OSIA's cautious letter-writing campaign and boycott had received in the mainstream press, "Tough Tony" got immediate results. As the *New York World Telegram* reported, "Tough Tony's Threat Hits TV Untouchables." FIADO made the program too controversial for the Liggett and Myers tobacco company. It dropped its sponsorship of three ABC series, representing a loss to the network of $10 million in revenue.[51]

Prior to the agreements with OSIA and the other organizations, *The Untouchables* was one of the most popular television programs in the country, and ABC quickly found new sponsors. Now, however, ABC was so rattled that all Italian American characters were dropped from the show, including Frank Nitti. *The Untouchables* continued for two more seasons, turning to villains who, like the Russian "Joe Vodka," were less controversial to Cold War sensibilities. But in the absence of Italian American gangsters from Prohibition-era Chicago, the show could not hold its audience. The protests by the Sons of Italy and other Italian American groups certainly contributed to the loss in popularity, but it was neither OSIA nor Tough Tony that put the final bullet in *The Untouchables*. Instead, NBC scheduled *Sing Along with Mitch* opposite Eliot Ness and his squad during the 1961–62 season. Competition from the musical variety hour dropped Eliot Ness from number eight to number forty-one that year. Viewers, it seemed, preferred to "sing along" while Mitch Miller flashed the lyrics of upbeat songs on their screens rather than watch a toned-down *Untouchables*. The show was finally canceled in 1963.[52]

"This Thing of Ours"

The defeat of *The Untouchables* did not stop OSIA from fighting the Mafia stereotype. Robert F. Kennedy's Justice Department vigorously prosecuted Italian Americans while publicizing Mafia stories in local and national media outlets. From a low of 19 in 1960, organized crime indictments rose to 687 by 1964, a trend that continued after Kennedy left the Justice Department.[53] After 1963, OSIA's strategy of denying the existence of the Mafia faced a new obstacle. That year OSIA protested narcotics violator Joseph Valachi's appearance before the Senate Permanent Subcommittee on Investigations, chaired by Senator John McClellan. OSIA feared that Valachi, "a high ranking member of the Anthony Strollo, Vincent

Mauro, and Frank Caruso Group," according to the Federal Bureau of Narcotics, would lead viewers to believe that Italian Americans had a particular proclivity for criminal activity. According to Valachi's own testimony, he was a soldier in the crew of Anthony Strollo (also known as Tony Bender), a lieutenant in the Genovese crime organization, formerly the Luciano crime organization.[54]

Because of the concerted, publicity-driven campaign by groups such as OSIA, the Justice Department felt the need to find conclusive proof that the Mafia existed. Pressure brought by Italian American ethnic advocacy organizations had thrown the basic assumptions of the gangbusters into question. By promoting Valachi's revelations, the Justice Department and the FBN seemed to confirm OSIA's suspicion that Italian Americans were receiving greater scrutiny than other organized criminals.

For his part, Valachi joined OSIA in its critique of *The Untouchables*. The grounds for his criticism, however, show that not all Italian Americans denied the existence of the Mafia. While in federal prisons in Atlanta and Washington, D.C., Valachi had watched *The Untouchables* in disgust. As he complained to an interviewer, "It's all wrong. How can they put on something like that?"[55] Valachi was not upset with the show for creating the "myth" of the Mafia. In fact, he was the most important former mobster to provide an insider's testimony about the size, scope, rituals, and criminal activities of an Italian American criminal organization. Valachi was upset because the fictionalized depictions of underworld operations did not reflect his experience.

The Federal Bureau of Narcotics and the FBI had promised that Valachi's testimony would prove the existence of the Mafia and "counteract public indifference." What looked and sounded like conclusive proof, however, was carefully scripted and edited. This is not to say that Valachi lied, merely that Valachi and others shaped his story to fit specific organizational needs in the government's efforts to fight organized crime. First Valachi and later Peter Maas, author of *The Valachi Papers*, based on twenty-two interviews with Valachi, charged that they had been asked to eliminate "material the Justice Department deemed injurious to law enforcement."[56] The material included Valachi's charges of corruption against the Bureau of Prisons and the Federal Bureau of Narcotics. In addition, Valachi claimed that Senator McClellan had asked him to eliminate from his testimony any mention of Hot Springs—in McClellan's home state of Arkansas—which he agreed to do. Hot Springs had long been a place where laws against gambling were openly violated with police protection. The presence of organized criminals had been widely reported since Lucky Luciano hid out there prior to his 1936 conviction on prostitution charges.

Because it ultimately both confirmed and destroyed OSIA's critique, the story of Joe Valachi marks a crucial endpoint for the Mafia obsession of 1950s America. The concerted campaign of crime fighters to seek out and script a key informant's testimony smacks of the discovery and promotion of former communists such as Elizabeth Bentley, Whittaker Chambers, and Louis Budenz as anticommunist witnesses in the late 1940s and early 1950s.[57] McCarthyist tactics had been at least partially discredited by the early 1960s, but their use in fighting organized crime, as we have seen, seemed an appropriate means of informing and outraging the public about another alien menace. In 1961, Charles Siragusa, the FBN's liasion to the attorney general's Organized Crime and Racketeering Section, enlisted narcotics agents across the country to recommend prisoners "who have knowledge of the activities of major narcotic racketeers and who you believe could contribute to the development of a case against those individuals if granted immunity by the Government." The agents quickly generated a list of people they thought would make excellent witnesses if promised immunity. Although the list contained names of Chinese, Mexican, and African Americans, as well as others of northern and western European descent, it was the discovery of Joseph Valachi by the FBN's district supervisor in New York that piqued Siragusa's interest. Siragusa and Robert Kennedy hoped that Valachi's testimony would finally silence the Italian American naysayers. As one of the Organized Crime Section's prosecutors put it, "Valachi's testimony would provide the opportunity once and for all to explain the Mafia . . . to the American public and dispel the cynical view that it was a figment of our overly imaginative gangbuster minds."[58]

Joseph Valachi hadn't the celebrity or wealth of Vito Genovese, Lucky Luciano, or Frank Costello. The East Harlem–born son of immigrants from Naples, Valachi described his family as "the poorest family on earth." Valachi, his parents, and five siblings survived on the small income Dominick Valachi earned first as a vegetable peddler and later working at the city garbage dumps. In 1919, after a short stint at the New York Catholic Protectory, an orphanage and reform school where Valachi was sent after hitting a teacher with a rock, he dropped out of school and went to work with his father at the dump. He was fifteen and had only completed the seventh grade.[59]

Joe Valachi did not last long at the dump. He joined a small gang of Harlem residents who, he estimated, committed hundreds of thefts between 1919 and 1923. Valachi was finally convicted of burglary in 1923 and served nine months in Sing Sing. Over the next decade, Valachi worked with a multiethnic gang that included descendants of Irish, Jewish, and Italian immigrants living in East Harlem. He served several more stints in various New York prisons on other burglary and theft charges.[60] In 1930, in between the murders of two "Mustache Petes," Giuseppe Masseria and Salvatore Maranzano, Valachi was initiated into a criminal organization he knew as "La Cosa Nostra," or "This Thing of Ours." In a large room in a colonial-style house outside New York City, Maranzano grasped Valachi's hands, motioned to a gun and knife lying on a table in the center of the room, and said, "This represents that you live by the gun and the knife, and you die by the gun and the knife." After holding up his right forefinger—his trigger finger—Valachi cupped his hands. Maranzano ignited a piece of paper he had placed in Valachi's hands and asked him to repeat, "This is the way I will burn if I betray the secret of this Cosa Nostra." Maranzano then assigned Valachi to Joseph Bonanno, who concluded the ceremony by pricking the end of Valachi's trigger finger and squeezing out blood. This detailed description of a blood oath provided his most sensational testimony.[61]

To Valachi, his initiation meant a sudden escalation in the severity of his crimes. No longer a thief who specialized in breaking windows and grabbing furs, now he frequently carried out murders on the orders of his superiors. During the post–World War II period, he became a heroin dealer. Mafia membership did not mean that Valachi could no longer work with non–Italian American gangsters. In fact, the arrest that brought him to the attention of the Senate and Justice Department investigators resulted from a deal with John Freeman, a successful African American dealer prior to his conviction. Valachi claimed that he had come forward as a witness for fear that his former cellmate and boss, Vito Genovese, had marked him for death. His fear was so great that Valachi murdered fellow inmate Joseph Saupp in 1962, mistaking him for Joseph DiPalermo, the man he suspected Genovese had ordered to kill him. (Federal Bureau of Narcotics records indicate, however, that Freeman provided Valachi's name as a potential witness against the Mafia in 1961, a full year before the gangster "mistakenly" murdered Saupp in Atlanta Federal Penitentiary.)[62]

After he began cooperating with federal investigators and prosecutors, Valachi was moved to Fort Monmouth in New Jersey, a short distance from Genovese's former estate in Atlantic Highlands. Valachi's televised testimony and subsequent book went beyond even the sensational Apalachin revelations of 1957. In addition to his detailed description of his ritual-laced initiation, Valachi can be credited with initiating the contemporary understanding of the Mafia by providing the name "La Cosa Nostra," still used by federal investigators as the official name for Italian American organized crime. He also described his involvement in theft, drug dealing, and murder, and explained the secrecy oath of omertà. Perhaps most important, he outlined the bureaucratic structure of New York's five crime families.[63]

Virtually every point in Valachi's testimony and book, from the name of his first arresting officer in the 1920s to the confirmation of illegal government wiretaps, was verified by subsequent police work, journalistic investigation, and witness testimony. Despite this verification, OSIA was not convinced.[64] Along with Representative Peter Rodino, Il Progresso, and the Italian American League to Combat Defamation, OSIA held up publication of The Valachi Papers, the Peter Maas book based on a manuscript by Valachi, even lobbying President Lyndon Johnson. It took Maas until 1968 to get a court to reverse on appeal the Department of Justice's injunction against the book. Maas remained angered by Italian American protests for at least twenty years, though officials in the Justice Department told him "protests like this occurred every time [we] prosecuted a criminal who happened to have an Italian name."[65] Indeed, in a 1961 letter to Robert Kennedy, OSIA challenged an assumption on which the attorney general had been operating since his days as chief counsel for the McClellan Committee: "We . . . maintain that there is no such organization as the Mafia in the United States. Crime syndicates yes, but not the Mafia."[66]

OSIA's critique of false images was more than a debate over semantics. The organization insisted that popular images and law enforcement practices reinforced social inequalities. By protesting, OSIA sought to control the damage these links could do to Italian Americans' chances for economic advancement and acceptance in American society. The outrage had not cooled in close to a decade of fighting the Mafia stereotype. That decade, though, had not taught OSIA that established fact was a small and often irrelevant part of the Mafia's appeal.

In distancing Italian Americans from connotations of criminality, OSIA's anti-*Untouchables* campaign transformed the meaning of white ethnic identities even while it revealed the persistence of widely accepted assumptions over which Italian Americans had little control.[67] OSIA did not eliminate the Mafia from the airwaves and best-seller lists, just as the Justice Department did not eliminate Italian American organized crime from the underground economy. But its critique of *The Untouchables* illuminates the role ethnic advocacy groups play in reshaping what ethnic images we see and how we perceive the groups in question. These popular images of Italian American criminals appeared at a time of high-visibility inquiries into organized crime, which included the sensational Apalachin revelations and investigations of La Cosa Nostra. Middle-class Italian Americans campaigned against these images on the premise that they called into question an entire ethnic group's collective devotion to the law. They feared that viewers would be unable to distinguish drug dealers like Joe Valachi, bootleggers like Al Capone, Frank Nitti, and Lucky Luciano, gambling "kingpins" like Frank Costello, and corrupt union officials like Anthony Provenzano and "Tough Tony" Anastasio from Italian American lawyers, judges, professors, journalists, barbers, and grocers. Their insistence that the Mafia did not exist pushed the limits of credibility as investigative agencies continued to uncover evidence of Italian American organized crime. Nevertheless, while some Italian Americans critiqued the popular representation of Italian American criminality, others provided living proof of it.

CONCLUSION

"Inside Truth About Crime!! Police Facts!"

In 1970 two aging gangsters were being held in the federal prison in La Tuna, Texas. Joseph Valachi—physically ill after years of confinement and mentally exhausted from decades of fearing he was about to be killed by the gangsters he'd betrayed—sat down and wrote a later to Blanche Teresa, wife of the second gangster, informant Vincent Teresa. "Dear Mommie," he began:

> To make raw tomatoes sauce just put some oil in a pot or frying pan, a little powder garlic. This recipe is for two, then you judge it for 4. Say about 6 tomatoes—squeeze them with your hand and put them in the pot. Then you put say, 3, cups of water— let them boil with cover for half hour to get the substance out of the tomatoes. Then take cover off and simmer it down to become sauce. By the way, I forgot, after you put tomatoes in the pot, put a large spoon of black pepper in the sauce also a pinch of oregano. Let cover off until sauce is made, of course, you taste sauce to your liking. Good luck to you, all my mob, a good mob. Joe.[1]

By the early 1970s, the transition from the Castellammarese War to what Valachi referred to as the "modern Cosa Nostra" was complete. Valachi's death in the spring of 1971 and subsequent burial in an unmarked grave in Buffalo, New York, occurred during a new transition personified by the gangster whose wife was the recipient of Valachi's famous marinara recipe. Vincent "The Fat Man" Teresa would be an even more important government witness than Valachi. The Boston-based Teresa had joined financier and real estate speculator George Kattar and his brother Peter in establishing several companies designed to finance aggressive loan-sharking enterprises, the most famous under the name "Piranha, Inc." Teresa testified against reputed gangsters such as Henry Tamaleo and Gennaro Angiulo. But he was not like the gangsters of the Luciano era. The crimes Teresa shed light on included a wide range of stock swindles and securities scams occurring within seemingly legitimate business operations. He hinted at a future rife with stock manipulation and securities fraud—a forecast confirmed by the FBI's "Uptick" undercover operation, which resulted in indictments against twenty-one defendants in the late spring of 2000, according to the *Wall Street Journal*, "the largest number of defendants ever arrested at one time on securities-fraud-related charges." Included among the defendants were members of the Bonanno and Columbo crime families suspected of manipulating the prices of nineteen publicly traded companies and bilking unsuspecting investors of $50 million. Of course, such practices—pumping up the value of little-known stocks then dumping shares before the value plummets—are not uncommon. In fact, in the year before this case broke, investigators alleged that the brokerage houses of Sterling Foster and A. R. Baron had each earned $75 million through financial fraud. Many investors probably took little comfort in white-collar crime lawyer Jerry D. Bernstein's assertion that "the notion that markets would be influenced by the threat of violence rather than the threat of a margin call, if true, is disturbing."[2]

Perhaps this recent criminal enterprise proves Vincent Teresa's classic assertion, "I can tell you to stop buying cheap cigarettes or cars that have ridiculous price tags, but you probably won't because everybody looks for a bargain, everybody has some larceny in his soul."[3] But the transformation in criminal practices from Prohibition-era bootlegging to the stock swindles of the twenty-first century illustrates more than the malleability of criminal organizations or even the essential greed of humanity. Trying to understand changing patterns of crime and policing helps us make sense of changing social, political, and economic relations, even as they reinforce long-held notions of class hierarchy and social difference.

By questioning the very existence of Italian American organized crime, the Sons of Italy showed how battles over criminality can also be battles over political power. Uncovering the truth has always been the chief goal of the criminal justice system, from police investigation through jury deliberation. But if the history of organized crime in postwar America proves anything, it may be that getting at the truth is often impossible. We expect the criminal justice system to reveal whether there is adequate evidence to determine guilt in a particular case. The question "Did he or she do it?" appears impartial, tied to acts rather than ideologies. Yet questions of guilt or innocence depend on frames of reference. Organized crime's putative sources of income in the twentieth century—prostitution, gambling, Prohibition violations, drug smuggling, loan-sharking—are activities that have been tolerated or even legal at some places and times if not at others. Lucky Luciano certainly may have been a drug smuggler. Jimmy Hoffa appears to have been guilty of many of the illegal and unethical practices of which Robert F. Kennedy accused him. Some Italian Americans worked in collusion to smuggle drugs, own gambling enterprises, loan money, and run labor unions to the detriment of the members. FBI surveillance tapes have captured Italian Americans calling their criminal enterprises "La Cosa Nostra" or "the Organization." And the mobs of Cicero certainly committed atrocities against the Clark family. These were not innocent people persecuted by demagogues. Nevertheless, their illegal acts mobilized arguments and resulted in consequences that had little to do with their misdeeds.

Despite the inaccesibility of the truth, the debate is itself instructive. The focus on organized crime in the postwar years helped define and reinforce social and economic hierarchies that were being destabilized by the rising fortunes of the white ethnic middle class and by claims that crime had social and economic roots in the failures of capitalism and racialized class divisions. Assertions of authenticity are themselves narrative acts. This is exemplified by the eager promise of a 1950s comic book, *Real Clue Crime Stories*, which assured its readers that they would get the "Inside Truth About Crime!!" and "Police Facts!" "Within its pages," it promised, "the youth of America will learn to know crime for what it really is: a sad, black, dead-end road of fools or tears."[4]

In the December 1950 issue, several goons in purple and green suits are seen extending an invitation to the Italian American proprietors of a new candy store to join Vic Plassa's "East Side Benevolent Society." For fifty dollars a week the society will make sure that the owners "don't get pushed around." The simple story of extortion is quickly complicated by the revelation that the candy store owners are actually Plassa's hardworking immigrant parents. Plassa is no ordinary gangster: he is the head of "Plassa Enterprises," and the goons are employees of his "collection department" with responsibility for "District F." Rather than ordering a "hit," Plassa authorizes a "muscle slip," or "m.s.," to intimidate the candy store owners. Plassa's disdain for his downtown immigrant origins is further indicated by his uptown headquarters and his seductions of native-born white women. The plot thickens when his "agents" begin to resent Plassa's lifestyle. Fearing for his life, Plassa drives downtown and crawls through the window of his parents' apartment in the hope that no one will think to search for him there. Believing that Vic is one of the hit men coming after him, Plassa's father shoots him. The story closes with the distraught father's words: "Our son—he finally came home. . . . He *came home* at last, mama."

Vic Plassa's move uptown was the beginning of his downfall. Coming home, even in death, signals the return to a well-ordered society. This was not a blanket indictment of all Italian Americans. The story features hardworking barbers and merchants as well as rank-and-file hoodlums, all of whom express outrage at the parasitic Plassa's rejection of the Lower East Side and his failure to work for his riches. Whether in the "inside truth" of this comic book or the "confidentiality" of Jack Lait and Lee Mortimer's books, representations of criminals helped readers negotiate the shifting meanings of class, ethnicity, and race in the 1950s. Vic Plassa's move uptown would have been impossible without concurrent challenges to state legislatures, private clubs, and professional organizations that routinely barred those of foreign origin—along with African Americans and other racial minorities—from occupations and places dominated by native-born whites.[5]

The comic book's denunciation of Vic Plassa's brash crossing of class and ethnic lines complemented the narrative's hope that young people would see crime as a "dead-end road." The readers of these comic books participated in making these messages meaningful. Their attraction to stories about transgression and criminality might indicate a widespread discontent with the criminal justice system, or it might indicate their outrage over criminality itself. Regardless of their motivations and responses, consumers of popular crime stories demonstrated the increasing power of mass culture—and television in particular—in issues of government regulation. If, as Benedict Anderson argues, the work of creating the widespread acceptance of nation-states was largely accomplished during the 1800s via the reading of newspapers, then so did television viewership in the 1950s transform the process of nation building. After all, one of the few magazines actually to gain readership during the decade was *TV Guide.* Virtually all the mass-market magazines catering to middle-class readers (*Life, Saturday Evening Post, Collier's*) saw sharp declines in circulation during the decade, and the growth of television was certainly the primary reason. Anderson explains how widespread literacy among the nineteenth century bourgeoisie helped to popularize and solidify the modern nation-state. During the 1950s, the new medium of television engaged in the conceptual project of transforming and reasserting what Anderson calls "languages-of-power."[6]

This process was firmly situated in the political and social context of the period. "Crime is international," remarked Estes Kefauver; criminals "have no patriotic concept of country." Although this critique of internationalism referred only to communists and organized criminals, Kefauver's warning that "national borders are of no more concern to them than county lines" could have been equally applied to a wide range of corporations seeking foreign markets.[7] Like anticommunist rhetoric, the allegation that organized criminals lacked patriotism served to magnify their threat. Raising the specter of internationalism made their criminality seem particularly intractable. State and local police agencies could not prosecute criminals across state lines and had little jurisdiction across national borders.

Organized crime was thus unlike other forms of criminal activity; it could be construed as a treasonous form of supranationalism. At the same time that this sinister portrait was being displayed, crime shows and government inquiries were discrediting those who argued that crime could be explained by social and economic inequalities, physical addiction, or cultural dislocation.[8]

The fallout from the attacks on organized crime and labor racketeering outlasted the 1950s, albeit in manifestations peculiar to new times, places, and political exigencies. Robert F. Kennedy's assistant attorney general, Ramsey Clark, ascended to Kennedy's post during Lyndon Johnson's presidency. Clark continued to pursue Italian Americans engaged in organized criminal activity, but he refused to make the Mafia the focus of Justice Department investigations and prosecutions. Recognizing its symbolic power, Clark wrote, "Organized crime is something that everyone can hate." Unlike Kennedy and narcotics commissioner Harry Anslinger, however, Clark considered the emphasis on organized crime a self-serving gesture on the part of the criminal justice system. "Arrest a bunch of Sicilians and the latest 'crime wave' is over—and America lives happily ever after," he scoffed. "For many organized crime is the alien conspiracy that absolves us of the responsibility for crime in America." In sharp contrast to earlier crime busters, Clark recognized a wide range of causes for crime, among them: "slums, racism, ignorance and violence, corruption and impotence to fulfill rights, poverty and unemployment and idleness, generations of malnutrition, congenital brain damage and prenatal neglect, sickness and disease, pollution, decrepit, dirty, ugly, unsafe, overcrowded housing, alcoholism and narcotics addiction, avarice, anxiety, fear, hatred, hopelessness and injustice." Clark described and attempted to implement a compassionate vision for solving one of the nation's most difficult and politically sensational problems. A fierce opponent of the death penalty, he sought to limit access to guns, improve housing and education, improve health care, and achieve full employment in order to lower crime rates.[9]

Clark was no more successful than the Sons of Italy in excising the Mafia from public debates over criminality. The most famous example of the continuing power of the Mafia mystique was still a decade away. The *Godfather* films turned that mystique on its head, honoring the Corleones as a close-knit Italian American family while locating the real corruption in a U.S. senator modeled on Nevada's immigrant-baiting Patrick McCarran. To be sure, these films featured simplistic stereotypes of misogynist, violent, and greedy Italian American men and dutiful but ignorant Italian American women. As in the past, these depictions were vigorously protested by the Sons of Italy and other organizations; but they were also firmly situated in the ethnic politics of the 1970s, and their creators were Italian Americans—writer Mario Puzo and director Francis Ford Coppola.[10]

In the famous opening scene of the film, a middle-class undertaker named Amerigo Bonasera, tells Don Vito Corleone, and the audience, "I believe in America." The film provides a clever twist on early 1970s ethnic revivalism. Instead of distancing themselves from criminality, *The Godfather*'s largely Italian American creators celebrated a history of corruption, criminality, violence, and often brutal sexism. But they did so within the context of nostalgia for a community and a family whose members looked out for one another (when they weren't ordering their execution). The film's popularity spoke to broader changes facing third- and fourth-generation Italian Americans, as well as other descendants of the "new immigrants" who transformed America's cities at the turn of the twentieth century. Upward mobility in what many white ethnics perceived as a WASP-dominated culture meant giving up the very institutions and practices that provided a cultural and religious home. The film asked if the children and grandchildren of immigrants could advance economically without compromising their basic cultural values.

The Godfather was a new kind of Mafia film, one that reflected a *Bonnie and Clyde*–influenced return to the "realistic" violence of pre–Hays Code Hollywood, incongruously merged with the identity politics of the 1970s, superimposed on a narrative of postwar America. But perhaps the most unusual aspect of *The Godfather* lies in the paradox that it confirmed the myth of the American Dream of upward mobility by un-ironically making the route to that dream an organized criminal enterprise. Much as *The Untouchables* turned to the 1920s to help viewers sort out the social changes of the late 1950s and early 1960s, *The Godfather* turned to the late 1940s and 1950s to help viewers sort out social changes in 1970s America.

The closing decades of the twentieth century—the period in which the research for and writing of this book took place—would witness another transformation of the themes and issues I have discussed here. Anti-immigrant sentiment once again intersected with crime-fighting ideology at a time when it seemed that the modifier "illegal" always preceded "alien." This sentiment went beyond media hyperbole, with stunning upsurges in criminal deportations at the turn of the twenty-first century. Of the approximately 30,000 people deported in 1989 alone, over 20,000 were, like the targets of the 1954 "Operation Wetback," Caribbean and Central and South American immigrants who had entered the United States illegally or overstayed their visas. From a handful of people deported for crimes in the years after World War II, the numbers had swollen to almost 7,000—over 5,000 of them for drug offenses.[11] As disturbing as the figures from the 1980s are, in 1999 there were 180,000 deportations (now called "removals"), a sixfold increase in one decade. The number of criminal deportations rose even more sharply to almost 70,000—a tenfold increase.[12] This upsurge is largely a result of two pieces of legislation, the Anti-Terrorism and Effective Death Penalty Act of 1996 and the Illegal Immigration Reform and Immigrant Responsibility Act of 1996. Taken together, these two laws created mandatory detention (without bond) for aggravated felons, expanded the definition of aggravated felonies to include all crimes of violence, any drug trafficking offense, any forgery, some fraud, and even some DUI's. Virtually any crime that carries a sentence of one year or more (down from five) results in a mandatory deportation hearing, in which the judge has little discretion. In addition, the Anti-Terrorism Act allows for the use of secret evidence against some non-citizens.[13]

Anticommunism and crime fighting intersected during the later decades of the Cold War, with the war on drugs being fought in the same places as the war against communist ideology, as Christian Parenti argues, providing the rationale for efforts such as funding the Nicaraguan Contras and escalating the militarization of urban and federal police agencies.[14] Several pieces of federal legislation, along with state and local laws too numerous to list in this conclusion, provided the axis around which the war on drugs revolved. The 1984 Comprehensive Crime Control Act extended provisions of the anti-Mafia law of 1970. The Racketeering Influenced Criminal Organization Law allowed for the seizure of assets of those involved in drug use or sale. (Seizures climbed from a 1981 rate of $100 million to over $1 billion in 1987.)[15] And the Anti–Drug Abuse Act of 1986 created mandatory minimum sentences in the wake of a real and media-fanned "crack epidemic." This law did little to curb drug use, but it did greatly expand the prison population, filling state and federal prisons with low-level drug offenders serving sentences far out of proportion to their offenses.[16] It also created a new cabinet position, a "drug czar," with discretion over the Office of National Drug Control Policy, a centralized crime commission that would have pleased Estes Kefauver. Congress passed these acts in the waning years of the Cold War. One final piece of legislation at the center of post–Cold War crime fighting is the Violent Crime Control and Law Enforcement Act of 1994. As the eagerly expected "peace dividend" from the collapse of the Soviet Union was blown like the winnings from an office pool on police grants, the Border Patrol, and prison construction, the Violent Crime Control Act expanded federal capital punishment and lengthened some of the already long sentences mandated by the Anti–Drug Abuse Act.

Mafia images remain vital in American popular culture but no longer affect public policy to the same extent. Contemporary mobsters such as those portrayed on HBO's *The Sopranos* or by Robert DeNiro in many of his film roles in the 1980s and 1990s are humorous or self-reflective types with psychotherapists who ask them questions like, "How many more people have to die for your personal growth?"[17] Most do not embody the positive images sought by groups like the Sons of Italy and others, which continue their vigorous protests in their ongoing desire to see images in popular culture that promote a deeper understanding of Italian American diversity.[18] Under the auspices of its Commission on Social Justice, the Sons of Italy has protested Godfather's Pizza among other companies, and defeated the U.S. Postal Service's plan to create a stamp honoring Francis Ford Coppola's *Godfather* trilogy.[19]

Mafia images have been replaced by a new "greatest menace," best exemplified in those late 1980s and early 1990s films dubbed "the new ghetto aesthetic" by Jacquie Jones. These films are among the most popular Hollywood fare. Not only do they amplify and distort the activities of a small minority of African Americans, but also they often dangerously reaffirm the more transparently racist images of black criminality so prevalent in films made by white directors for the major studios. Although, as Jones concedes, the films by African American directors tend to "be executed with a greater degree of truth and sensibility," they ultimately take a small range of unrepresentative characters and make them stand in for the whole spectrum of African American lives. Mario Van Peebles's 1991 *New Jack City*, which grossed over $40 million in less than four months and was among the first of the genre to break through to a wide audience, depicts a Harlem peopled with African Americans unwilling to make changes in their lives. Most problematic is the standard this film set for future films in this genre. As Jones puts it, "That one 'bitch' is elevated to the status of psychopathic murderer hardly seems an achievement."[20]

The next such film to reach a wide audience was *Boyz N the Hood* (1991), directed by twenty-three-year-old John Singleton. The film, based in part on Singleton's own upbringing, details the difficult personal and communal decisions necessary to avoid the violence of south central Los Angeles. The biographical connections and interpersonal dynamics—including a sensitive depiction of the conflicting factors that lead one character to commit crimes—made this film stand out from other films of the early 1990s. Despite the strides Singleton made in lending depth to material familiar from the evening news broadcasts, the politics of the film, according to some critics, continued the pattern set by Van Peebles in that it came "dangerously close to blaming Black women for the tragedies currently ransacking Black communities."[21] These images responded to and influenced the war on drugs, with the strongest impact felt not by white ethnics and European immigrants but by African Americans and Latinos. According to the Bureau of Justice Statistics, "Black offenders are 50 to 60 percent more likely to be sentenced for larceny than white offenders, and twice as likely as whites to be sentenced for weapons offenses." The disparities for drug offenses are even greater: whereas 65 percent of crack users are white, 92.6 percent of all those convicted for this crime are African American.[22]

Aspects of all these complexities and inversions yet to come were foreshadowed during the 1950s. In the jailings of Jimmy Hoffa and Frank Costello—as well as the deportation of Lucky Luciano—denunciation of Italian American gangsters coexisted with their celebration. During the 1950s, the consequences transcended the fates of these individuals, extending to the McCarran-Walter Act's "national origins" system for determining the desirability of immigrants, the Federal Bureau of Narcotics' insistence that targeting a small cartel of drug smugglers would solve the problem of drug addiction, as well as the McClellan and Kefauver committees' exclusive reliance on conspiracy theories to explain crime and racketeering. In addition, law enforcement officials and politicians constructed a limited notion of normality as it applied to citizenship, even as they presented detailed, titillating accounts of people who transgressed the boundaries of social propriety. In first offering the possibility of release from social conventions but then reasserting the concept of justice as the containment of these acts, crime writers and crime fighters allowed readers and viewers to identify with the status quo while experiencing the pleasure of viewing the bad boys and girls.

NOTES

Prologue

1. *New Larousse Encyclopedia of Mythology* (New York: Prometheus, 1969); s.v. "Vesta"; Ariadne Staples, *From Good Goddess to Vestal Virgins: Sex and Category in Roman Religion* (New York: Routledge, 1999).

2. Edward M. Peters, "Prison before the Prison: The Ancient and Medieval Worlds," in *The Oxford History of the Prison: The Practice of Punishment in Western Society*, ed. Norval Morris and David J. Rothman (New York: Oxford University Press, 1995), 15.

3. New York State Legislature, Joint Legislative Committee on Government Operations, *Interim Report on the Gangland Meeting in Apalachin, New York* (New York: The Committee, 1959); Arthur L. Reuter, Acting Commissioner of Investigation, State of New York, *Report on the Activities and Associations of Persons Identified as Present at the Residence of Joseph Barbara, Sr., at Apalachin, New York, on November 14, 1957, and the Reasons for their Presence*, Submitted to His Excellency Averell Harriman, Governor of the State of New York, 23 April 1958.

4. Reuter, *Report*, app. C.

5. "Edgar Croswell; State Police Veteran" [obituary], *Times Union*, Albany, N.Y., 19 November 1990, B9.

6. "65 Hoodlums Seized in a Raid and Run Out of Upstate Village," *New York Times*, 15 November 1957, A1.

7. Joseph Bonanno with Sergio Lalli, *A Man of Honor: The Autobiography of Joseph Bonanno* (New York: Simon and Schuster, 1983), 211.

8. "65 Hoodlums Seized," 1.

9. Dollar estimates vary. According to the *New York Times* report of the round-up, the smallest amount found was $450 and the largest was $10,000. Ibid.

10. Sam and Chuck Giancana, *Double Cross* (New York: Warner Books, 1992), 352. The New York Commissioner of Investigations was looking into Lanza and the New York Board of Parole at the time of the Apalachin meeting. The board came under close scrutiny after paroling Lanza, who had been convicted of conspiracy and extortion in January 1943. New York State, Joint Legislative Committee on Government Operations, *Special Report of the Joint Legislative Committee on Government Operations on the Parole of Joseph Lanza* (Albany: The Committee, 1958).

11. "65 Hoodlums Seized," 1.

12. Joseph Bonanno later claimed that Gaspar DiGregorio (not named in the police reports) was carrying Bonanno's driver's license and so was misidentified. He claimed that he was in Endicott, New York, arguing with his cousin, Stefano Magaddino (head of the Buffalo crime organization), during the raid. Bonanno, *Man of Honor*, 216. His eldest son, Bill Bonanno, later told author Gay Talese that his father was in fact at the Apalachin meeting. Gay Talese, *Honor Thy Father* (New York: World Publishers, 1971).

13. New York State Legislature, *Interim Report*, 21.

14. "65 Hoodlums Seized," 21.

15. According to famed informant Joseph Valachi, the murder of Albert Anastasia was the work of Vito Genovese and Anastasia associate Carlo Gambino. See Peter Maas, *The Valachi Papers* (New York: G. P. Putnam Son's, 1968), 248; on Lepke, see Albert Fried, *The Rise and Fall of the Jewish Gangster in America*, rev. ed. (New York: Columbia University Press, 1993), 227.

16. Maas, *Valachi Papers*, 252; Larry Elkin, "Defense Reveals Ploy at Racketeering Trial: Attorney Admits Mafia Commission Exists," *Times Union*, Albany, N.Y., 19 September 1986, B6; Richard J. H. Johnston, "Gang Strife Linked to Apalachin Edict against Narcotics," *New York Times*, 28 February 1960, A1.

17. Bonanno, *Man of Honor*, 213; on the 1956 meeting, see also New York State Legislature, *Interim Report*, 14–15.

18. Robert Lacey, *Little Man: Meyer Lansky and the Gangster Life.* (New York: Little, Brown, 1991), 302; Edward Ranzal, "27 Apalachin Men Indicted by U.S. in Drive on Mafia," *New York Times*, 22 May 1959, A1; Glenn Fowler, "Milton R. Wessel, 67, Prosecutor of Crime Meeting at Apalachin" [obituary], *New York Times*, 28 May 1991, D16.

19. "Barbara's Home Sold," *New York Times*, 22 May 1959, 15; "Apalachin Zoning Upheld," *New York Times*, 2 December 1960, 58; "Gang Mansion Sold: Apalachin Convention Scene Nets Reported $125,000," *New York Times*, 7 November 1961, 15.

20. "Fifth Apalachin Man Jailed for Silence," *New York Times*, 16 August 1958, 36; "Luciano Disclaims Link to Apalachin," *New York Times*, 25 July 1958, 20.

21. James Q. Wilson argues that the switch occurred in direct response to the Apalachin arrests. Hoover authorized illegal bugging of criminal organizations shortly after the meeting. James Q. Wilson, *The Investigators: Managing FBI and Narcotics Agents* (New York: Basic Books, 1978), 202–3; see also Richard Gid Powers, *Secrecy and Power: The Life of J. Edgar Hoover* (New York: Free Press, 1987). Hoover quoted in "Hoover Calls Crime 22-Billion Business," *New York Times*, 30 January 1960, 22.

22. Joseph Bonanno, *Man of Honor*, 203.

23. Stephen Fox, *Blood and Power: Organized Crime in Twentieth-Century America* (New York: Penguin, 1989), 328.

24. New York State Legislature, *Interim Report*, 8.

25. Edward Ranzal, "Tactical Switch Marks U.S. Crime," *New York Times*, 16 February 1959, 14.

26. Vincent Teresa with Thomas C. Renner, *My Life in the Mafia* (Greenwich, Conn.: Fawcett Crest, 1973).

27. Maas, *Valachi Papers*, 107.

28. Ibid., 112.

29. Ibid., 211.

30. Ranzal, "Tactical Switch," 14. Rogers served as a prosecutor under New York district attorney Thomas E. Dewey from 1938 to 1942 as part of the team that won the conviction of Lucky Luciano. David Stout, "William P. Rogers, Who Served as Nixon's Secretary of State, Is Dead at 87," *New York Times*, 4 January 2001, B7.

31. Stephen Whitfield, *The Culture of the Cold War*, 2d ed. (Baltimore: Johns Hopkins University Press, 1996), 35; J. Edgar Hoover, "Address before the National Convention of the American Legion," Atlantic City, New Jersey, 19 September 1957; George MacKinnon Papers, MacKinnon Campaign, Speech Material, Crime, 1953–1957, Minnesota Historical Society, St. Paul; Virgil Peterson, *Barbarians in Our Midst* (Boston: Little, Brown, 1952).

32. Adlai Stevenson, "Crime and Politics," *Journal of Criminal Law and Criminology*, 41 (November–December 1950): 397–405. Stevenson recalled Louis Brandeis's defense of civil liberties in his opinion in *Whitney v. California* (1927): "The greatest menace to freedom is an inert people." Eric Foner, *The Story of American Freedom* (New York: Norton, 1998), 185; Vincent Blasi, "The First Amendment and the Ideal of Civic Courage: The Brandeis Opinion in *Whitney v. California*," *William & Mary Law Review*, 29 (Summer 1988), 653–97.

33. Ellen Schrecker, *Many Are the Crimes: McCarthyism in America* (Princeton: Princeton University Press, 1998), 120.

34. Ibid., 144.

35. Nan Alamilla Boyd, *Wide Open Town: A Queer History of San Francisco, 1933–1963* (Berkeley: University of California Press, forthcoming).

36. Whitfield, *Culture of the Cold War*, 163.

37. John Higham, *Strangers in the Land: Patterns of American Nativism, 1860–1925* (1995; reprint, New York: Atheneum, 1970), 4, 161.

38. Schrecker, *Many Are the Crimes*, 370.

39. Arthur A. Sloane *Hoffa* (Cambridge, Mass.: MIT Press, 1991), 80, 89; James R. Hoffa, "Hoffa Reports on Year of Problems and Achievements," *International Teamster* 56 (February 1959): 5.

40. For discussion of the relationship between politics, social structure, and representation, see Stuart Hall, "Encoding/Decoding," in *Culture, Media, Language*, ed. Stuart Hall et al. (London: Hutchison, 1980), 128–38; idem, "Notes on Deconstructing 'The Popular,' " in *People's History and Socialist Theory*, ed. Raphael Samuel (London: Routledge and Kegan Paul, 1981), 227–40; Louis Althusser, "Ideology and Ideological State Apparatuses (Notes towards an Investigation)," in *Lenin and Philosophy* (New York: Monthly Review Press, 1971), 127–86; Ellen Seiter et al., eds., *Remote Control: Television, Audiences, and Cultural Power* (New York: Routledge, 1989); Frederic Jameson, "Reification and Utopia in Mass Culture," *Social Text*, 1 (Winter 1979): 130–48; idem, *The Political Unconscious: Narrative as a Socially Symbolic Act* (Ithaca: Cornell University Press, 1981); Darrell Y. Hamamoto, *Monitored Peril: Asian Americans and the Politics of TV Representation* (Minneapolis: University of Minnesota Press, 1994); Sut Jhally and Justin Lewis, *Enlightened Racism: The Cosby*

Show, Audiences, and the Myth of the American Dream (Boulder, Colo.: Westview Press, 1992).

41. Whitfield, *Culture of the Cold War*, 153.

42. Christopher P. Wilson, *Cop Knowledge: Police Power and Cultural Narrative in Twentieth-Century America* (Chicago: University of Chicago Press, 2000).

43. M. H. Abrams, *A Glossary of Literary Terms*, 4th ed. (New York: Holt, Rinehart, and Winston, 1981), 111. For the etymology of the word *myth*, see Raymond Williams, *Keywords: A Vocabulary of Culture and Society*, rev. ed. (New York: Oxford University Press, 1983), 210–12.

44. Roland Barthes, *Mythologies*, trans. Annette Lavers (New York: Hill and Wang, 1972), reprinted as "Myth Today," in *A Barthes Reader*, ed. Susan Sontag (New York: Hill and Wang, 1982), 131.

1. Organized Crime as an American Way of Life

1. Sid Feder and Joachim Joesten, *The Luciano Story* (New York: David McKay, 1954); Paul Sann, *Kill the Dutchman! The Story of Dutch Schultz* (New Rochelle, N.Y.: Arlington House, 1971).

2. Christopher P. Wilson, *Cop Knowledge: Police Power and Cultural Narrative in Twentieth-Century America* (Chicago: University of Chicago Press, 2000); David R. Papke, *Framing the Criminal: Crime, Cultural Work, and the Loss of Critical Perspective, 1830–1900* (New York: Archon Books, 1987); David Ruth, *Inventing the Public Enemy* (Chicago: University of Chicago Press, 1996).

3. Papke, *Framing the Criminal*, xiv.

4. Robert Rockaway, "The Rise of Jewish Gangster in America," *Journal of Ethnic Studies*, 8 (Summer 1980): 39.

5. Francis Ianni and Elizabeth Reuss-Ianni, *A Family Business: Kinship and Social Control in Organized Crime* (New York: Russell Sage Foundation, 1972), 52.

6. Frederick Jackson Turner, "The Significance of the Frontier in American History," from *Proceedings of the Forty-first Annual Meeting of the State Historical Society of Wisconsin* (Madison: State Historical Society of Wisconsin, 1894).

7. Nicholas Gage, *The Mafia Is Not an Equal Opportunity Employer* (New York: McGraw-Hill, 1971), 49.

8. Ibid., 47.

9. Jacob Riis, *How the Other Half Lives* (New York: Scribners, 1890), 38.

10. Robert W. Snyder, "Glimpses of Gotham," *Media Studies Journal*, 6 (Winter 1992): 195.

11. Jenna Weissman Joselit, *Our Gang: Jewish Crime and the New York Jewish Community, 1900–1940* (Bloomington: University of Indiana Press, 1983), 36.

12. Lincoln Steffens, *The Autobiography of Lincoln Steffens* (New York: Harcourt, Brace, and Company, 1931), 224.

13. Alan Block, "Aw! Your Mother's in the Mafia: Women Criminals in Progressive New York," *Contemporary Crisis*, 1 (1977): 8.

14. Joselit, *Our Gang*, 13.

15. Daniel Bell, "Crime as an American Way of Life," *Antioch Review*, 8 (September 1953): 133.

16. Ibid., 147.

17. James O'Kane, *The Crooked Ladder: Gangsters, Ethnicity, and the American Dream* (New Brunswick, N.J.: Rutgers University Press, 1992); Humbert Nelli, "The Ethnic Factor in American Urban Civil Disorders," *Ethnicity*, 2 (Fall 1979): 230–43.

18. Ellen Andrews Knodt, "The American Criminal: The Quintessential Self-Made Man?" *Journal of American Culture*, 2 (1979): 32.

19. Joselit, *Our Gang*, 34.

20. Ibid., 40.

21. Ianni and Reuss-Ianni, *Family Business*, 9.

22. Robert Lacey, *Little Man: Meyer Lansky and the Gangster Life* (Boston: Little, Brown, 1991), 537.

23. Dwight C. Smith, *The Mafia Mystique* (New York: Basic Books, 1975), 8.

24. Gage, *The Mafia*, 49.

25. Egal Feldman, "Prostitution, the Alien Woman, and the Progressive Imagination, 1910–1915," *American Quarterly*, 22 (1967): 194.

26. Ibid., 196.

27. William Howard Moore, *The Kefauver Committee and the Politics of Crime, 1950–1952* (Columbia: University of Missouri Press, 1974), 9.

28. John R. Brazil, "Murder Trials, Murder, and Twenties America," *American Quarterly*, 33 (1981): 180.

29. Snyder, "Glimpses of Gotham," 197.

30. Elliot G. Gorn, "The Wicked World: The *National Police Gazette* and Gilded Age America," *Media Studies Journal*, 6 (Winter 1992): 3.

31. Snyder, "Glimpses of Gotham," 196.

32. Toni Morrison, *Beloved* (New York: Plume, 1987), 156.

33. See Joseph L. Albini, *The American Mafia: Genesis of a Legend* (New York: Meredith Corporation, 1971); Hannah Arendt, "Lawlessness Is Inherent in the Uprooted," *New York Times Magazine*, 28 April 1968, 24; Albert Fried, *The Rise and Fall of the Jewish Gangster in America* (New York: Holt, Rinehart and Winston, 1980); Kay Ann Holmes, "Reflections by Gaslight: Prostitution in Another Age," *Issues in Criminology*, 7 (1972): 83–101; Ivan Light, "The Ethnic Vice Industry," *American Sociological Review*, 42 (June 1977): 464–79; Erik H. Monkkonen, "A Disorderly People? Urban Order in the Nineteenth and Twentieth Centuries," *Journal of American History*, 68 (1981): 539–59; Humbert Nelli, *The Business of Crime: Italians and Syndicate Crime in America* (New York: Oxford University Press, 1976); Dan Schiller, *Objectivity and the News: The Public and the Rise of Commercial Journalism* (Philadelphia: University of Pennsylvania Press, 1981).

34. Iris Marion Young, *Justice and the Politics of Difference* (Princeton: Princeton University Press, 1990), 171.

35. Mary Louise Pratt, "Daring to Dream: Re-visioning Culture and Citizenship," Working Paper 41, Stanford Center for Chicano Research, Stanford University (April 1993), 9–10.

36. Lee Quinby, *Anti-Apocalypse: Exercises in Genealogical Criticism* (Minneapolis: University of Minnesota Press, 1994), 47. See also Renato Rosaldo, "Social Justice and the Crisis of National Communities," in *Colonial Discourse/Postcolonial Theory*, ed. Francis Barker, Peter Hulme, and Margaret Iversen (New York; St. Martin's Press, 1994) 239–52, Paul Gilroy, *There Ain't No Black in the Union Jack* (Chicago: University of Chicago Press, 1987).

37. Benedict Anderson argues that nations are constructed (or "imagined") out of a variety of historical particulars. The most prominent medium for accomplishing this has been newspapers. Reading the newspaper constituted much more than learning about the

latest events; it helped define membership in the nation. Anderson leaves unasked questions about what effect crime news, which has long been a staple of print and television news, has on this polity. Benedict Anderson, *Imagined Communities: Reflections on the Origin and Spread of Nationalism* (New York: Verso, 1983), 45, 77. See also Snyder, "Glimpses of Gotham," 195. Anderson also sees the "imagined community" both as the beginning of nationalism and the beginning of contestation. Interestingly, according to Anderson, contestation sometimes sounds a lot like the nationalism that precipitated the protest: "The first groups to [pirate a model of the independent nation-state] were the marginalized vernacular-based coalitions of the educated" in the second decade of the nineteenth century (*Imagined Communities*, 81).

38. Richard Hofstadter, *The Paranoid Style in American Politics and Other Essays* (1964; reprint, Cambridge, Mass.: Harvard University Press, 1996); Michael Rogin, *Ronald Reagan, the Movie and Other Episodes in Politician Demonology* (Berkeley: University of California Press, 1987); Virginia Carmichael, *Framing History: The Rosenberg Story and the Cold War* (Minneapolis: University of Minnesota Press, 1993); Elaine Tyler May, *Homeward Bound: American Families in the Cold War Era* (New York: Basic Books, 1988); Alan Nadel, *Containment Culture: American Narratives, Postmodernism, and the Atomic Age* (Durham: Duke University Press, 1995). For a useful critique of the metaphor of containment, see Anna Creadick, "Incredible/Shrinking Men: Masculinity and Atomic Anxiety in American Postwar Science-Fiction Film," in *Fear Itself: Enemies Real and Imagined in American Culture*, ed. Nancy Lusignan Schultz (West Lafayette, Ind.: Purdue University Press, 1999), 285–300.

39. Snyder, "Glimpses of Gatham," 197.

2. Capone's Old Town

1. Laurence Bergreen, *Capone: The Man and the Era* (New York: Simon and Schuster, 1994), 106; David E. Ruth, *Inventing the Public Enemy: The Gangster in American Culture, 1918–1934* (Chicago: University of Chicago Press, 1996); Robert St. John, *This Was My World* (Garden City, N.Y.: Doubleday, 1953), 184.

2. This account of the Cicero riot is based on various sources, including "Convictions in Cicero," *Newsweek*, 16 June 1952, 35; Daniel M. Cantwell, "Postscript on the Cicero Riot," *Commonweal*, 15 September 1951, 543–45; "Ugly Nights in Cicero," *Time*, 23 July 1951, 10–11; National Association for the Advancement of Colored People, "Report of the Secretary to the Board of Directors for the Months of July and August, 1951" (September 1951), in *Papers of the NAACP Executive Office Reports, 1951–1955* (Frederick, Md.: University Publications of America, 1987), 46; Homer A. Jack, "Cicero Nightmare," *Nation*, 28 July 1951, 64–65; *New York Times*, 13 July 1951, 38; "Barbed Wire Bars Rioters in Chicago," *New York Times*, 14 July 1951, 28; Langston Hughes, *Fight for Freedom: The Story of the NAACP* (New York: W. W. Norton, 1962), 120.

3. "Ugly Nights in Cicero," 11.

4. The Clarks first turned down the offer from Norwalk, instead vowing to stay and fight for their rights. Despite their earlier intentions, by August 1951 the Clarks were in Norwalk, and Cicero remained all white. *New York Times*, 11 August 1951, 28; editorial, *Chicago Tribune*, quoted in "Defeat in Cicero," *Christian Century*, 25 July 1951, 862–63.

5. Daniel Cantwell, "Riot Spirit in Chicago," *Commonweal*, 54 (December 1951): 375–76; Walter White, "This Is Cicero," *The Crisis*, 58 (August–September 1951): 437; "Ugly Nights in Cicero."

6. *Chicago Tribune*, quoted in "Defeat in Cicero," 862.

7. Camille De Rose, *The Camille De Rose Story* (Chicago: De Rose Publishing, 1953), 18.

8. Cantwell, "Riot Spirit," 375.

9. The Cook County grand jury did indict Police Chief Konovsky on charges of official misconduct. Also indicted was a man who distributed communist literature in Cicero a month after the trial. "Cicero Officials Indicted," *The Crisis*, 59 (January 1952): 40; "Convictions in Cicero," *Newsweek*, 16 June 1952, 34–35. Konovsky was not the first to meet this fate. In 1943 an earlier chief of police and a subordinate in Cicero were indicted and removed from office by a blue ribbon grand jury. Arthur Buller, "Legal Remedies against Corrupt Law Enforcement Officers," *Journal of Criminal Law, Criminology, and Police Science*, 48 (1957): 429.

10. Cantwell, "Postscript," 544.

11. "Ugly Nights in Cicero," 11.

12. "Vet Defies 6,000 Rioters to Insist on His Right to Live in Cicero Apartment," *The Afro-American*, 21 July 1951, 1; "New Disgrace for Cicero: In Capone's Old Town a Mob Pillages a Negro's Home," *Life*, 23 July 1951, 22. Wendy Kozol describes a 1953 *Life* photo spread in similar terms. Wendy Kozol, *Life's America: Family and Nation in Postwar Photojournalism* (Philadelphia: Temple University Press, 1994), 145.

13. "The Cicero Riots," *New York Times*, 15 July 1951; sec. 4, 8; Virgil Peterson, *Barbarians in Our Midst: A History of Chicago Crime and Politics* (Boston: Atlantic/Little, Brown, 1952), 339.

14. Willie J. Pearson Jr., "Percy Lavon Julian," in *Encyclopedia of African-American Culture and History*, ed. Jack Salzman, David Lionel Smith, and Cornel West (New York: Simon and Schuster, 1996), 1515–16. Hughes, *Fight for Freedom*, 119; *Hansberry v. Lee*, 311 U.S. 32 (1940).

15. White, "This Is Cicero," 437; Cantwell, "Postscript," 543–45; St. John, *This Was My World*, 184.

16. Ronald P. Formisano. *Boston against Busing: Race, Class, and Ethnicity in the 1960s and 1970s* (Chapel Hill: University of North Carolina Press, 1991); Anthony J. Lukas. *Common Ground: A Turbulent Decade in the Lives of Three American Families* (New York: Knopf, 1985); William H. Chafe, *Civilities and Civil Rights: Greensboro, North Carolina, and the Black Struggle for Freedom* (New York: Oxford University Press, 1980).

17. Courtlandt C. Van Vechten, "The Criminality of the Foreign Born," *Journal of Criminal Law and Criminology*, 32 (July–August 1941): 139–47. Furthermore, Van Vechten argued that this rate would drop as the male immigrant population aged because crime rates among older men were lower across all other demographic categories, and the influx of new immigrants had slowed considerably since World War I. During the period of his study, immigrant groups included a disproportionately large number of young men. Donald Taft found that while migration seemed to increase the amount of crime, "immigrants as a whole are, however, much less criminal than natives as a whole." Of course, the incarceration figures could be used to argue that foreign-born criminals were simply better at staying out of jail. Donald Taft, *Criminology* (New York: Macmillan, 1942), 116; Mabel A. Elliot and Francis E. Merrill, *Social Disorganization*, 3d ed. (New York: Harper and Brothers, 1950), 587; Emil Frankel, *Two Thousand State Prisoners in New Jersey: A Statistical Picture*, Research Bulletin no. 118, State of New Jersey Department of Institutions and Agencies, May 1954, 27; Hermann Mannheim, *Group Problems in Crime and Punishment* (London: Routledge and Kegan Paul, 1955), 194–95.

18. On the range of criminological viewpoints during the 1950s, see Clarence Jeffery,

"The Structure of American Criminological Thinking," *Journal of Criminal Law, Criminology, and Police Science*, 46 (1956): 658–72.

19. *Christian Science Monitor*, 6 August 1955, clippings file, George Mackinnon Papers, Minnesota Historical Society, St. Paul.

20. Michael Kimmel, *Manhood in America: A Cultural History* (New York: Free Press, 1996), 232; Ruth, *Inventing the Public Enemy*, 120, 132; Fred Pasley, *Al Capone: The Biography of a Self-Made Man* (New York: Ives, Washburn, 1930).

21. Robert Warshow, "The Gangster as Tragic Hero," *Partisan Review*, 15 (1948): 240; C. Wright Mills, *White Collar* (New York: Oxford University Press, 1953), 109; David Riesman with Nathan Glazer and Reuel Denney, *The Lonely Crowd: A Study of the Changing American Character* (Garden City, N.Y.: Doubleday, 1953), 183; E. Franklin Frazier, *Black Bourgeoisie: The Rise of a New Middle Class in the United States* (1957; reprint, New York: Collier Books, 1962), 112; Edwin Sutherland, *White Collar Crime* (New York: Holt, Rinehart and Winston, 1949); Robert Lindner, *Must You Conform?* (New York: Rinehart Co., 1955), 23, quoted in Barbara Ehrenreich, *The Hearts of Men: American Dreams and the Flight from Commitment* (Garden City, N.Y.: Anchor Press/Doubleday, 1983), 30.

22. They continue: "To be sure, European ethnics had benefited from the postwar economic expansion, and many had been able to enter the middle class. Moreover, the public dimensions of traditional ethnic life had begun to fade as old neighborhoods declined and new generations came of age, conveying the impression that ethnicity itself was fast disappearing as a force in American life. Although blacks still resided at the margins of society and struggled against racism and discrimination, some analysts believed that the early achievements of the civil rights movement held promise for their eventual inclusion in the great American mainstream." David R. Colburn and George E. Pozzetta, "Race, Ethnicity, and the Evolution of Political Legitimacy," in *The Sixties: From Memory to History*, ed. David Farber (Chapel Hill: University of North Carolina Press, 1994), 120.

23. Podhoretz quoted in James Wechsler, *Confessions of an Angry Middle-Aged Editor* (New York: Random House, 1960), 21–22; Daniel Bell, *The End of Ideology: On the Exhaustion of Political Ideas in the Fifties* (Glencoe, Ill.: Free Press, 1960); Edward Shils, "The End of Ideology?" *Encounter*, 5 (November 1955): 52–58; Seymour Martin Lipset, *Political Man* (Garden City, N.Y.: Doubleday, 1959). For a discussion of these and other postwar sociologists, see Wini Breines, *Young, White, and Miserable: Growing Up Female in the Fifties* (Boston: Beacon Press, 1992), 25–46; Terence Ball, "The Politics of Social Science in Postwar America," 76–92, and Lary May, introduction to *Recasting America: Culture and Politics in the Age of Cold War*, ed. Lary May (Chicago: University of Chicago Press, 1989), 1–16.

24. George B. Leonard Jr., "The American Male: Why Is He Afraid to Be Different?" *Look*, 18 February 1958, 95, quoted in Ehrenreich, *Hearts of Men*, 30; on "matriarchy," see Ehrenreich, 37 and in general, chap. 3, "Early Rebels: The Gray Flannel Dissidents." Arguments concerning "matriarchy" found a ready audience in publications such as H. L. Mencken's *American Mercury*, Hugh Hefner's *Playboy*, and, most outrageously, Philip Wylie's *Generation of Vipers* (New York: Rinehart, 1955).

25. "This Is Cicero," 436. In *White Collar*, Mills argued that the middle class would remain docile because it "carr[ied] authority" but was not its source: "But your authority is confined strictly within a prescribed orbit of occupational actions, and such power as you wield is a borrowed thing" (80).

26. Quoted in Dean Jennings, *We Only Kill Each Other: The Life and Bad Times of Bugsy Siegel* (Englewood Cliffs, N.J.: Prentice-Hall, 1968), 223.

27. Quote from Vernon Fox and Joann Volkakis, "The Negro Offender in a Northern

Industrial Area," *Journal of Criminal Law, Criminology, and Police Science*, 46 (1956): 641. Gunnar Myrdal, *American Dilemma* (New York: Harper and Brothers, 1944), 2: 966. Myrdal was joined by many prominent black sociologists, including Alison Davis, St. Clair Drake, E. Franklin Frazier, Charles S. Johnson, and Horace Cayton. See John Bracey, August Meier, and Elliot Rudwick, eds., *The Black Sociologists: The First Half of the Century* (Belmont, Calif.: Wadsworth Publishing, 1971). See also Hans von Hentig, "The Criminality of the Negro," *Journal of Criminal Law and Criminology* 31 (January–February, 1940): 662; Guy B. Johnson, "The Negro and Crime," *The Annals*, 217 (September 1941): 93–104; Minutes of Board of Directors Meeting, December 14, 1959, in *Papers of the NAACP* (Frederick, Md.: University Publications of America, 1987), reel 1. See also *Papers of the NAACP pt. 8, Discrimination in the Criminal Justice System, 1910–1955* (Frederick, Md.: University Publications of America, 1987).

3. "Cruising the Urban Inferno"

1. Croswell Bowen, *They Went Wrong* (New York: McGraw-Hill, 1954), 16. The phrase quoted in the chapter title is from Susan Sontag, *On Photography* (New York: Anchor Books, 1977), 56. The full passage reads: "Gazing on other people's reality with curiosity, with detachment, with professionalism, the ubiquitous photographer operates as if that activity transcends class interests, as if its perspective is universal. In fact, photography first comes into its own as an extension of the eye of the *flâneur*, whose sensibility was so accurately charted by Baudelaire. The photographer is an armed version of the solitary walker reconnoitering, stalking, cruising the urban inferno, the voyeuristic stroller who discovers the city as a landscape of voluptuous extremes. . . . The *flâneur* is not attracted to the city's official realities but to its dark seamy corners, its neglected population—an unofficial reality behind the facade of bourgeois life that the photographer 'apprehends,' as a detective apprehends a criminal."

2. Federal Bureau of Investigation, Uniform Crime Reports, 1948–60; New York crime statistics reported in *New York Post*, 14 August 1952. The Uniform Crime Reports collected information on murder, rape, robbery, aggravated assault, burglary, larceny, and auto theft during the 1950s.

3. William H. Sheldon, *Varieties of Delinquent Youth: An Introduction to Constitutional Psychiatry* (New York: Harpers, 1949); Clarence R. Jeffery, "The Structure of American Criminological Thinking," *Journal of Criminal Law, Criminology, and Police Science*, 46 (1956): 672.

4. Earnest Hooton, *Crime and the Man* (Cambridge, Mass.: Harvard University Press, 1940), 366–67; see also 376, 181, 190, and idem, *The American Criminal* (Cambridge, Mass.: Harvard University Press, 1939); *Why Men Behave Like Apes and Vice Versa* (Princeton: Princeton University Press, 1939); *Up from the Ape* (New York: Macmillan, 1946).

5. Walter Bromberg, M.D, "American Psychiatric Achievements in Criminology (from 1938–1950)," *Proceedings of the Second International Congress of Criminology*, 3 (Paris, 1952): 24. The *Journal of Criminal Psychopathology* began publication in 1940. An important early article compared Nazi Germany to a gang. See Ernst Kris, "The Covenant of the Gangsters," *Journal of Criminal Psychopathology*, 4 (1943): 445–58; David Ruth, *Inventing the Public Enemy* (Chicago: University of Chicago Press, 1996).

6. Leo J. Orenstein, *Report for the Year (1948)* (New York: Psychiatric Clinic Court of General Sessions, 1948); Ralph Banay and L. Davidoff, "Apparent Recovery of a Sex Psy-

chopath after Lobotomy," *Journal of Criminal Psychopathology*, 4 (July 1942): 59–66; Robert M. Lindner, *Rebel Without a Cause: The Hypnoanalysis of a Criminal Psychopath* (New York: Grune and Stratton, 1944); Walter Bromberg, *Crime and the Mind* (Philadelphia: Lippincott, 1948); Melitta Schmideberg, "The Psychiatric Treatment of Offenders as a Method of Preventing Recidivism," *Proceedings of the Second International Congress of Criminology*, 3 (Paris, 1952): 376–79.

7. Edwin Sutherland, review of *The American Criminal* and *Crime and the Man* by Earnest Hooton, *Journal of Criminal Law and Criminology*, 29 (1939): 911–14; idem, review of *Varieties of Delinquent Youth* by William Sheldon, *American Sociological Review*, 18 (1951): 142–48. Other criminologists agreed with Sutherland's strictly legalistic definition of crime. See Thorsten Sellin, "Crime," in *Dictionary of Sociology*, ed. P. Fairchild (New York: Philosophical Library, 1944), 73; Paul W. Tappan, "Who Is the Criminal?" *American Sociological Review* 12 (February 1947): 96. Some adopted a sociological position but broadened the definition of crime beyond strictly legal terms, employing notions of community norms; thus, any behavior harmful to a group could be labeled criminal. See Harry Elmer Barnes and Negley K. Teeters, *New Horizons in Criminology* (New York: Prentice-Hall, 1945), 2; Walter C. Reckless, *The Crime Problem* (New York: Appleton-Century-Crofts, 1950), 20; Alfred Lindesmith and H. Warren Dunham, "Some Principles of Criminal Typology," *Social Forces* 20 (March 1941): 307.

8. Edwin H. Sutherland, *Principles of Criminology*, 4th ed. (New York: Lippincott, 1947), 6. The belief that crime was the product of socialization predated Sutherland. Frederick Thrasher's *The Gang* influenced Sutherland, who had studied and taught at Chicago during the height of the sociology department's influence. Frederick Thrasher, *The Gang* (Chicago: University of Chicago Press, 1927). Others had gone much further than Sutherland, arguing that crime was an indicator of a healthy capitalist society. According to Emile Durkheim, the criminal "plays a definite role in social life. Crime, for its part, must no longer be conceived as an evil that cannot be too much suppressed. There is no occasion for self-congratulation when the crime rate drops noticeably below the average level, for we may be certain that this apparent progress is associated with some social disorder." Emile Durkheim, *The Rules of Sociological Method*, trans. Sarah A. Solovay and John H. Mueller (Glencoe, Ill.: Free Press, 1965), 68–69 (*Les règles de la méthode sociologique*, Paris, 1927). See also Robert K. Merton, "Social Structure and Anomie," *American Sociological Review*, 3 (October 1938): 672–82; Marshall B. Clinard, "Sociologists and American Criminology," *Journal of Criminal Law and Criminology*, 41 (January–February 1951): 549–77; Thorsten Sellin, "The Sociological Study of Criminality," *Journal of Criminal Law and Criminology*, 41 (November–December 1950): 406–22.

9. Edwin H. Sutherland, *Principles of Criminology*, 5th ed., rev. Donald R. Cressey (New York: Lippincott, 1955), 78; idem, *White Collar Crime* (New York: Holt, Rinehart, 1949), 218. Sutherland's thesis of white-collar crime was first presented as the presidential address to the 1939 meeting of the American Sociological Society and later reprinted in *American Sociological Review*, 5 (February 1940): 1–12.

10. Sutherland, *White Collar Crime*, 235, 117.

11. Their academic field rewarded Sutherland and Lindesmith, but Lindesmith faced persistent attempts to discredit his ideas, which were seen as subversive in the Cold War political climate. Alfred Lindesmith, "Organized Crime," *The Annals*, 217 (September 1941), 78–79. Lindesmith, a sociologist at Indiana University, advocated the legalization of drugs and a medical response to the problem of addiction throughout the fifties and sixties. The

Federal Bureau of Narcotics kept a file on Lindesmith from 1940 until 1960, which included reprints of his articles and book reviews of his works. Commissioner Harry Anslinger personally wrote to media outlets that published Lindesmith's works in attempts to discredit him. Papers of the Federal Bureau of Narcotics, Record Group 170, Box 72, National Archives and Records Administration, College Park, Md. For Lindesmith's views on narcotics, see Alfred R. Lindesmith, "Traffic in Dope: Medical Problem," *The Nation*, 21 April 1956, 337–39; idem, "Dope: Congress Encourages the Traffic," *The Nation*, 16 March 1957, 228–231.

12. Frank E. Hartung, "White Collar Crime: Its Significance for Theory and Practice," *Federal Probation*, 17 (June 1953): 32; Edwin H. Sutherland, "Crime and Business," *Annals of the American Academy of Political and Social Science*, 207 (September 1941): 113.

13. Allison Davis and Robert Havighurst, "Social Class and Color Differences in Child-Rearing," *American Sociological Review*, 11 (December 1946): 698–710. It is possible that class distinctions merely stepped into the frames established by the earlier racial positivists. Despite a growing African American middle class, E. Franklin Frazier reported that only one-sixth of southern African Americans and one-fifth of northern African Americans could be characterized as middle class. According to the 1950 census, over half of all African Americans still made less than $1,000 per year, 30 percent less than $500. E. Franklin Frazier, *Black Bourgeoisie: The Rise of a New Middle Class in the United States* (1957; reprint, New York: Colliers, 1967), 45–48; Walter Miller, "Lower Class Culture as a Generating Milieu of Gang Delinquency," *Journal of Social Issues*, 14 (1958): 9.

14. New York Labor Youth League, "A Program to Deal with the Needs of Young People in New York State" (New York: 1955), Leonard Covello Papers, Box 117, Balch Institute for Ethnic Studies, Philadelphia; Albert Cohen, *Delinquent Boys: The Culture of the Gang* (Glencoe, Ill.: Free Press, 1955); "Youth Study Cites Cultural Factor," *New York Times*, 17 March 1956, 21; C. Wright Mills, *White Collar: The American Middle Classes* (New York: Oxford University Press, 1951); Lewis Yablonsky, "The Delinquent Gang as a Near-Group," *Social Problems*, 7 (Fall 1959): 108–17.

15. Julius Bauer, *Constitution and Disease: Applied Constitutional Pathology*, 2d. ed. (New York: Grune and Stratton, 1945); on the history of anthropometry, or the "Bertillon system," see Henry T. F. Rhodes, *Alphonse Bertillon: Father of Scientific Detection* (New York: Abelard-Schuman, 1956).

16. J. Edgar Hoover, "The Twin Enemies of Freedom: Crime and Communism," speech delivered before the twenty-eighth annual convention of the National Council of Catholic Women, Chicago, 9 November 1956, in *Vital Speeches*, 1 December 1956, 105, 107. The Federal Bureau of Narcotics shared this dismissive approach. According to Commissioner Anslinger: "Parents should know that 90 percent of narcotic addiction is directly attributable to the influence of bad associates. This in turn is largely the result of lack of proper parental control over children. Where the church, the school, and the home are well integrated children are reared in a wholesome environment where you do not find addiction." Harry Anslinger, statement taped for broadcast over radio station KCBQ, San Diego, 3 February 1959, Papers of the Federal Bureau of Narcotics, Record Group 170, Box 74, National Archives and Records Administration, College Park, Md.

17. Logan Wilson, "Newspaper Opinion and Crime in Boston," *Journal of Criminal Law and Criminology*, 29 (July–August, 1938): 202–15; Donald R. Taft, *Criminology* (New York: Macmillan, 1942), 206.

18. Taft, *Criminology*, 199.

19. Stephen Whitfield, *The Culture of the Cold War*, 2d ed. (Baltimore: Johns Hopkins University Press, 1996), 68; "Obituary Notes: Lee Mortimer," *Publishers Weekly*, 25 March 1963, 48; circulation figures from *Ayer's Directory* (Philadelphia: Ayer and Sons, 1953).

20. Victor Navasky, *Naming Names* (New York: Viking, 1980); Neal Gabler, *Winchell: Gossip, Power, and the Culture of Celebrity* (New York: Knopf, 1994).

21. "An explanatory narrative that achieves the status of perfecting myth serves to reconcile discrepancies and irrationalities while appearing to obviate public or official scrutiny of actual circumstances. Such a narrative becomes effectively monolithic and saturating, demonizing its opposite and canceling or absorbing all mediatory and intermediate terms and kinds of activity." Virginia Carmichael, *Framing History: The Rosenberg Story and the Cold War* (Minneapolis: University of Minnesota Press, 1993), 7. See also Michael Paul Rogin, *Ronald Reagan, the Movie* (Berkeley: University of California Press, 1987); Elaine Tyler May, *Homeward Bound: American Families in the Cold War Era* (New York: Basic Books, 1988).

22. Jack Lait and Lee Mortimer, *Chicago Confidential* (New York: Crown, 1950), 150, 160, 152.

23. Ibid., 81.

24. Ibid.

25. Gwendolyn Brooks, "The Sundays of Satin-Legs Smith," in *Selected Poems* (New York: Perennial Classics, 1999), 14.

26. Lait and Mortimer, *Chicago Confidential*, 38–39.

27. Jack Lait and Lee Mortimer, *Washington Confidential* (New York: Crown, 1951), 38–39, 94.

28. Guy B. Johnson, "The Negro and Crime," *The Annals*, 217 (September 1941): 93–104.

29. Lait and Mortimer, *Chicago Confidential*, 44. See also idem, *Washington Confidential*, 40 and 39: "It is not uncommon to see white girls with colored men, especially jazz band musicians, who seem to exert a magnetic appeal for Caucasian women all over the country. Many Negro madames and pimps employ white girls for their colored trade."

30. Ed Reid, *Mafia* (New York: Random House, 1952), 58. *Mafia* sold so well that Random House quickly published Reid's second book, *The Shame of New York* (New York: Random House 1953). He had already won a Pulitzer Prize for a series of stories on bookie Harry Gross's payoffs to New York City police officers, judges, and elected officials. Jack Lait and Lee Mortimer, *U.S.A. Confidential: The Lowdown on All of Us* (New York: Crown 1952), 14.

31. *Washington Confidential*, 14. See also *Washington Confidential*: "The Syndicate is an international conspiracy, as potent as that other international conspiracy, Communism, and as dirty and dangerous, with its great wealth and the same policy—to conquer everything and take over everything, with no scruples as to how" (178); J. Edgar Hoover, *Masters of Deceit: The Story of Communism in America and How to Fight It* (New York: Henry Holt and Company, 1958), 89, 228.

32. Jack Lait and Lee Mortimer, *New York Confidential* (New York: Crown, 1951), 226; idem, *U.S.A. Confidential*, 15; George Trow, "Costello Finds Social Level in a Cell; Veneer on His Hoodlum Crown Faded" *New York Post*, 15 August 1952, 3. Costello's trial in January 1952 also received substantial coverage. Robert Williams, "Costello on Trial Completes Cycle of Young Gun-Toter to 'Big Shot,'" *New York Post*, 7 January 1952, 2. See also Robert H. Prall and Norton Mockridge, *This Is Costello: On the Spot* (New York: Gold Medal Books, 1951).

33. Daniel Bell, "Crime as an American Way of Life," *Antioch Review*, 8 (September 1953): 147; "Costello on Trial," 2; Lait and Mortimer, *Washington Confidential*, 179.

34. Lait and Mortimer, *Washington Confidential*, 181; Lee Mortimer, "Frank Sinatra Confidential: Gangsters in the Night Clubs," *American Mercury*, 73 (August 1951): 31; "The Low Down," *Time*, 17 March 1952, 40.

35. Hoover, "The Twin Enemies of Freedom," 107; Lait and Mortimer, *Washington Confidential*, 185, 195–96; idem, *U.S.A. Confidential*, 29; Lee Mortimer, "Maryland Confidential: The Crusading Senator O'Conor," *American Mercury*, 73 (September 1951): 29. *Washington Confidential*, 195–6. This alleged conspiracy extended to all the workings of Washington: "The Syndicate's interests in countless large legitimate businesses and industries give it a responsible, respectable voice in Washington through trade associations, lobbyists, law firms, banks, Congressmen who do a favor for a local businessman but would not be seen dead with a gangster, and a considerable segment of the press, daily and periodical, and the radio." Lait and Mortimer, *Washington Confidential*, 185.

36. Lait and Mortimer, *U.S.A. Confidential*, 238, 241; idem, *Washington Confidential*, 259, 186. "The organized underworld's influence in official Washington is incalculable. Its direct ties, even to the top, are so firm that in many instances even a political revolution will not dislodge them. They succeeded in doing that which the Communists failed to do; they infiltrated and took over the government. They are the true subversives, though that never comes out in Congress" (*Washington Confidential*, 184–85).

37. Harvey Breit, "Talk with Lait and Mortimer," *New York Times Books Review*, 15 April 1951, 23; J. R. Savage, review of *Chicago Confidential*, *Chicago Sunday Tribune*, 5 March 1950, 5; Cabell Phillips, review of *Chicago Confidential*, *New York Times Book Review*, 1 April 1951, 33; John P. Mallan, "*U.S.A. Confidential*: Voyeurism in Politics," *New Republic*, 28 April 1952, 16; Karl Schriftgiesser, "The Low-Down in High Gear," *Saturday Review of Literature*, 7 April 1951, 17. The comparison to anti-Semites and fascists might have particularly irked Mortimer. Himself Jewish, he changed his name from Mortimer Lieberman early in his career. In *New York Confidential* he and Lait called Hitler a "mad megalomaniac" and excoriated younger "emancipated" Jews who harassed older Orthodox Jews (93–100).

38. Lait and Mortimer, *U.S.A. Confidential*: on Smith, 88; Beck, 121–23; Neiman Marcus, 196. The lawsuits are described in "Libel Unconfidential," *New Republic*, 2 June 1952, 8; see also "Died: Lee Mortimer," *Newsweek*, 11 March 1963, 66. In 1955, one year after Lait's death, Mortimer took out an ad in Dallas newspapers stating that "in retrospect and on more careful examination, these statements, we are now convinced, are untrue and were made without proof or credible evidence." "Assassins at the Bar," *Time*, 16 May 1955, 51–52.

39. Benjamin Gayelord Hauser, *Look Younger, Live Longer* (New York: Farrar, Straus and Young, 1951); Breit, 23; "Libel Confidential," *Time*, 19 May 1952, 92; Lee Mortimer, *Around the World Confidential* (New York: Putnam, 1956); Lee Mortimer, *Women Confidential* (New York: J. Messner, 1960); "Obituary Notes: Lee Mortimer," *Publishers Weekly*, 48.

40. George Legman, *Love and Death: A Study in Censorship* (New York: Breaking Point, 1949), quoted in "Libel Unconfidential," 92.

41. Rogin argues that "the Soviet Union replaced the immigrant working class as the source of anxiety, and the combat between workers and capitalists, immigrants and natives, was replaced by one between Moscow's agents (intellectuals, government employees, students and middle-class activists), and a state national-security apparatus" (*Ronald Reagan*, 237). In contrast, I would argue that the demonology of the immigrant working class was changed by the attention to communism, but it did not disappear. Sander Gilman, *Difference and Pathology* (Ithaca: Cornell University Press, 1985), 71, 21.

42. William P. Rogers, "Nothing Comic about Crime: Public Opinion Must Be Aroused," speech delivered at the graduation of the FBI National Academy, 20 November 1953, *Vital*

Speeches, 1 February 1954, 244–45; Marshall McLuhan, "Crime Does Not Pay," in *The Mechanical Bride: Folklore of Industrial Man* (New York: Vanguard Press, 1951), 30. The idea of the "cultural work" of popular texts is Frederic Jameson's from "Reification and Utopia in Mass Culture," *Social Text,* 1 (Winter 1979): 130–48.

43. Gramsci argued similarly: "The bourgeois class poses itself as an organism of continuous movement, capable of absorbing the entire society, assimilating it to its own cultural and economic level. The entire function of the State has been transformed; the State has become an 'educator.' " Antonio Gramsci, *Selections from the Prison Notebooks,* ed. and trans. Quinton Hoare and Geoffrey Nowell Smith (New York: International, 1971), 260.

4. "An All-Star Television Revue"

1. *New York Times,* 14 March 1951, 1; 17 March 1951, 6. The "ceremonial" nature of this trial and execution has been widely commented on, but the phrase is taken from Blanche Wiesen Cook, "The Rosenbergs and the Crimes of a Century," in *Secret Agents: The Rosenberg Case, McCarthyism, and Fifties America,* ed. Marjorie Garber and Rebecca L. Walkowitz (New York: Routledge, 1995), 23–39.

2. Robert Lewis Shayon, "An Open Letter to the Television Industry," *Saturday Review of Literature,* 7 April 1951, 31. Although the Rosenbergs had little support in the mainstream media, their executions were actively protested by many who sympathized with their plight, as their sons have made clear in numerous public appearances and published writings. See, e.g., Robert Meeropol, "Rosenberg Realities," in Garber and Walkowitz, *Secret Agents,* 235–51.

3. The Kefauver Committee was formed by Senate Resolution 202 in January 1950. Eric F. Goldman, *The Crucial Decade—and After: America, 1945–1960* (New York: Vintage, 1960), 195; Gregory Lisby, "Early Television on Public Watch: Kefauver and His Crime Investigation," *Journalism Quarterly,* 62 (Summer 1985): 236–42; Stephen Whitfield, *The Culture of the Cold War,* 2d ed. (Baltimore: Johns Hopkins University Press, 1996), 166.

4. Jack Gould, "The Crime Hearings: Television Provides Both a Lively Show and a Notable Public Service," *New York Times,* 18 March 1951, sec. 2, 13. For more background on the committee, see Joseph Bruce Gorman, *Kefauver: A Political Biography* (New York: Oxford University Press, 1971); Michael Woodiwiss, *Crime, Crusades, and Corruption: Prohibitions in the U.S., 1900–1987* (Totowa, N.J.: Barnes & Noble Books, 1988); William Howard Moore, *The Kefauver Committee and the Politics of Crime, 1950–1952* (Columbia: University of Missouri Press, 1974); Jeanine Derr, "The Biggest Show on Earth: The Kefauver Crime Committee Hearings," *Maryland Historian,* 17 (1986): 19–37.

5. Estes Kefauver, interview, *Editor & Publisher,* 12 May 1951, 50; idem, "Crime in the U.S.: What I Found in the Underworld," *Saturday Evening Post,* 7 April 1951, 24; idem, "Crime in the U.S.: What I Found Out about the Miami Mob," *Saturday Evening Post,* 14 April 1951, 24. These *Post* stories were ghostwritten by Sidney Shalett, who later helped Kefauver write *Crime in America.* Both *The Enforcer* and *Captive City* are discussed in Jay Robert Nash and Stanley Ralph Ross, *The Motion Picture Guide* (Chicago: Cinebooks, 1986), 354, 768; Gorman, Kefauver, 98.

6. As Richard Johnson put it: "More commonly texts are encountered promiscuously; they pour in on us from all directions in diverse, coexisting media, and differently-paced flows. In everyday life, textual materials are complex, multiple, overlapping, coexistent, in

a word, 'inter-textual.' " Richard Johnson, "What Is Cultural Studies Anyway?" *Social Text*, 16 (1986): 38–80.

7. Advertisement, *New York Times*, 16 March 1951, 26; Goldman, *Crucial Decade*, 198–99.

8. White asked for FBN help to locate Julie Bender, who was ducking the committee. He was found in a bookmaking office in Poughkeepsie, New York. Telegram to Mr. Harney for George White from Washington Bureau of Narcotics, 28 June 1950, Papers of the Federal Bureau of Narcotics, Record Group 170, National Archives and Records Administration, College Park, Md. (hereafter FBN Papers); A. E. Myers, District Supervisor, District no. 7 (Tennessee, Kentucky, Mississippi, Louisiana), "List of Names of Allegedly Prominent Underworld Figures," 3 May 1950. This list was supplemented by communication with the committee throughout the hearings.

9. Harry Anslinger, memorandum to E. H. Foley Jr., 5 May 1950, "Kefauver's Crime Conference," FBN Papers.

10. Drew Pearson, "Washington Merry-Go-Round," *Washington Post*, 19 August 1950, 12B.

11. For a brief discussion of Pearson, see Wendy L. Wall, "America's 'Best Propagandists': Italian Americans and the 1948 'Letters to Italy' Campaign," in *Cold War Constructions: The Political Culture of United States Imperialism, 1945–1966*, ed. Christian Appy (Amherst: University of Massachusetts Press, 1999), 90. On other newspaper columnists of the Cold War, see Edwin M. Yoder Jr., *Joe Alsop's Cold War: A Study of Journalistic Influence and Intrigue* (Chapel Hill: University of North Carolina Press, 1995); Neal Gabler, *Winchell: Gossip, Power, and the Culture of Celebrity* (New York: Knopf, 1994).

12. Statement of Commissioner Harry J. Anslinger, U.S. Bureau of Narcotics, to the Kefauver Committee, 28 June 1950, FBN Papers. On the parallels to communist conspiracy theories, see J. Edgar Hoover, *Masters of Deceit: The Story of Communism in America and How to Fight It* (New York: Henry Holt and Company, 1958).

13. Remarks of Commissioner of Narcotics H. J. Anslinger on the Secret Document of the Bureau of Narcotics, dated 19 May 1950, 6 June 1950, FBN Papers. The secret document to which Anslinger refers is not in the available files of the National Archives. Many of the documents relating to the Kefauver Committee, like all files related to criminal investigations, are not available for public viewing at this time. The secret document, however, was reprinted in Jack Lait and Lee Mortimer's true crime book *Washington Confidential* (New York: Crown, 1951), 302–06; see also Estes Kefauver, *Crime in America* (Garden City, N.Y.: Doubleday, 1951), 20.

14. Estes Kefauver, "Crime Is International," *U.N. World* (September 1951): 18; idem, *Crime in America*, 21. Edward Martin, "Happenings in Washington," radio address reprinted as "extension of Remarks of Hon. Estes Kefauver of Tennessee," in *Appendix to the Congressional Record*, 81st Congr., 2d sess. (1950), vol. 96, pt. 16, A4983.

15. Spruille Braden, "Statement at Tuesday, March 20, 1951, Session of the United States Senate Crime Investigating Committee," *Appendix to the Congressional Record*, 82d Cong., 1st sess. (1951), vol. 97, pt. 12, A1690–91.

16. Philip Kastel to Harry Anslinger, 13 September 1950; Harry Anslinger to Philip Kastel, 18 September 1950, FBN Papers. For more information on Kastel, see Albert Fried, *The Rise and Fall of the Jewish Gangster in America*, rev. ed. (New York: Columbia University Press, 1993), 207, 235; Stephen Fox, *Blood and Power: Organized Crime in Twentieth-Century America* (New York: Penguin, 1989), 282. According to Fox, Kastel and Costello co-owned the Beverly Club in Jefferson Parish outside New Orleans. The club closed in 1951 in the wake

of the Kefauver hearings. Kastel would soon become a part owner of the Tropicana in Las Vegas.

17. It is possible that Maryland senator Herbert O'Conor, not Anslinger, was the source of this leak. A later leak to Pearson was tracked to O'Conor. Verbatim quotes from the closed-door testimony of Chicago businessman George May, who owned a bar where illegal gambling occurred, appeared in Drew Pearson's column, "The Washington Merry-Go-Round," *Washington Post*, 7 June 1951, 9C. On the Kefauver Committee's response, see memo from Downy Rice and George Martin (Martin is identified elsewhere as a publicity adviser) to Richard G. Moser, chief counsel, 7 June 1951, FBN Papers.

18. T. J. Walker, Supervisor, District 11 [Kansas City], to Harry Anslinger, 28 September 1950, FBN Papers.

19. Kefauver, *Crime in America*, 21; see also Morris Ploscowe, ed, *Organized Crime and Law Enforcement: The Report by and Research Studies Prepared for the ABA Commission on Organized Crime* (New York: Grosby Press, 1952). Kefauver himself wrote the introduction to the ABA's published findings. This cooperation was reciprocated when the commission chair, Morris Ploscowe, drafted the third (final) interim report of the Kefauver Committee. Rudolph Halley, Chief Counsel, Special Committee on Organized Crime in Interstate Commerce, memorandum to the American Bar Association Commission on Organized Crime, 27 October 1950, Papers of the Special Committee on Organized Crime in Interstate Commerce, National Archives and Records Administration, Washington, D.C.

20. See Albert Fried, *The Rise and Fall of the Jewish Gangster in America*, rev. ed. (New York: Columbia University Press, 1993); Robert Lacey, *Little Man: Meyer Lansky and the Gangster Life* (New York, Little, Brown, 1991); Leo Katcher, *The Big Bankroll: The Life and Times of Arnold Rothstein* (New York: Harper, 1959).

21. Secretary of the Treasury to Senator Herbert H. Lehman, n.d., FBN Papers, Anslinger's reply to Herman Edelsberg, director of the ADL, 19 October 1950, is recorded in Anslinger's notes, FBN Papers.

22. Jack Lait and Lee Mortimer, *Chicago Confidential* (New York: Crown, 1950), 163. In another book in the *Confidential* series, Lait and Mortimer nevertheless noted the danger of applying their sensational frames of reference to legislation: "We write as reporters, not as informers or reformers." Jack Lait and Lee Mortimer, *U.S.A. Confidential: The Lowdown on All of Us* (New York: Crown, 1952), 254. Michael Woodiwiss, "Capone to Kefauver: Organized Crime in America," *History Today* (June 1987): 8–15. Lait and Mortimer were Republicans who often criticized Senator Kefauver and chief committee counsel Rudolph Halley, both Democrats.

23. In fact, this corporate comparison runs through much of the literature on organized crime. Historians speak of criminal "visionaries and innovators" much like Henry Ford and Andrew Carnegie. Francis Ianni and Elizabeth Reuss-Ianni, *A Family Business: Kinship and Social Control in Organized Crime* (New York: Russell Sage Foundation, 1972); Nicholas Gage, *The Mafia Is Not an Equal Opportunity Employer* (New York: McGraw-Hill, 1971); U.S. Congress, Senate, *Second Interim Report of the Special Committee to Investigate Organized Crime in Interstate Commerce* (Washington, D.C.: U.S. Government Printing Office, 1951), 4; U.S. Congress, Senate, *Third Interim Report of the Special Committee to Investigate Organized Crime in Interstate Commerce* (Washington, D.C.: U.S. Government Printing Office, 1952), 2.

24. "Crime—It Pays to Organize," *Time*, 12 March 1951, 22–26.

25. "Quizzing Kefauver: An Interview with Senator Estes Kefauver, Chairman of the Special Senate Committee to Investigate Organized Crime in Interstate Commerce," *U.S.*

News and World Report, 20 April 1951, 26–33; Albert Maisel, "Return of the Numbers Racket," *Colliers*, 15 January 1949, 21; "Crime—It Pays to Organize," 22.

26. David Halberstam, *The Fifties* (New York: Villard, 1993), 144–54, 118.

27. Press release, Special Committee Investigating Organized Crime in Interstate Commerce, 17 May 1950, National Archives and Records Administration, Washington, D.C.

28. Advertisement, *New York Times*, 16 March 1951, 26; "Crime—It Pays to Organize," 22.

29. Jack Anderson and Fred Blumenthal, *The Kefauver Story* (New York: Dial Press, 1956), 4.

30. Frank McNaughton, "Would a TV Congress Improve Democracy?" *Public Utilities Fortnightly*, 4 February 1954, 150–51; Moore, *Kefauver Committee*, 200–201; Gorman, *Kefauver*, 91; G. D. Wiebe, "Responses to the Televised Kefauver Hearings: Some Social Psychological Implications," *Public Opinion Quarterly*, 16 (Summer 1952): 189.

31. Inter-University Consortium for Political and Social Research, *Study 00003: Historical Demographic, Economic, and Social Data: U.S., 1790–1970* (Ann Arbor: ICPSR, 1999).

32. Lester Velie, "Rudolph Halley: How He Nailed America's Racketeers," *Collier's*, 19 May 1951, 24; Irving Gitlin and David Moore, *A Nation's Nightmare*, radio broadcast, Columbia Broadcasting System, 1950; "Splendid Nightmare," *Newsweek*, 13 August 1951, 48. The CBS television network would bring back the dead and deported to appear before a fictional crime committee in its short-lived program *The Witness* in 1960.

33. Gould, "The Crime Hearings," 13.

34. Andy Edmonds, *Bugsy's Baby: The Secret Life of Mob Queen Virginia Hill* (New York: Birch Lane, 1993), 148; Dean Jennings, *We Only Kill Each Other: The Life and Bad Times of Bugsy Siegel* (Englewood Cliffs, N.J.: Prentice-Hall, 1968), 131; Florabel Muir, *Headline Happy* (New York: Holt, Rinehart, and Winston, 1950).

35. Lee Mortimer, "Underworld Confidential: Virginia Hill's Success Secrets," *American Mercury*, 72 (June 1951): 662–69; Lait and Mortimer, *U.S.A. Confidential*, 8, 7, 2; Moore, *Kefauver Committee*, 192.

36. Emanuel Perlmutter, "Slain 'Bugsy' Siegel's 'Girl Friend' Steals Senate Crime Inquiry Show," *New York Times*, 16 March 1951, 24. In fact, Hill originally moved to Hollywood with the intention of acting. In her memoirs, prominent madam Polly Adler described similar treatment during her 1935 trial: "The reporters greeted my return to the spotlight with whoops of joy. I was pleasantly surprised by the tone of much of the publicity. It was more jocular than condemnatory, I was treated more as a 'character' than a public enemy." Adler was convicted despite press "jocularity," but clearly the threat of her crimes was small enough that she could be treated as a character. While not a prostitute, Hill received similar treatment, and some condemned her actions. Polly Adler, *A House Is Not a Home* (New York: Rinehart, 1953), 263.

37. Velie, "Rudolph Halley," 78; "Excerpts of Yesterday's Testimony before the Senate Crime Committee," *New York Times*, 16 March 1951, 24; Edmonds, *Bugsy's Baby*, 216. A second lien for $48,369 (for unpaid taxes in 1946–47) was later filed in Chicago (*Bugsy's Baby*, 204–5). As to the source of her income, Hill told an interviewer toward the end of her life that Joe Epstein, a Chicago gambler with whom she had a sexual relationship when she was seventeen, provided a substantial income for her throughout her life. Jennings, *We Only Kill Each Other*, 138, 214–49, and passim. According to Andy Edmonds, she was murdered by "thugs who worked for [Joe] Adonis," though the fact that Hill attempted suicide at least three times since Siegel's 1947 murder and that she left a suicide note calls into question Edmonds's conclusions. Her earlier attempts at suicide involved Valium or chloral

hydrate. This time she used the sleeping pill Mogadon, a popular prescription in Europe (*Bugsy's Baby*, 253).

38. Fox, *Blood and Power*, 299–304.

39. Gorman, *Kefauver*, 89.

40. Jack Gould, "Costello TV's First Headless Star; Only His Hands Entertain Audience," *New York Times*, 14 March 1951, 1; U.S. Congress, Senate, *Hearings before the Senate Special Committee to Investigate Organized Crime in Interstate Commerce*, pt. 7 (Washington, D.C.: U.S. Government Printing Office, 1951), 877–78; Emanuel Perlmutter, "Costello a 'Flop' in Starring Role," *New York Times*, 14 March 1951, 29.

41. James A. Hagerty, "Costello Defies Senators, Walks Out of Hearing Here; Faces Arrest on Contempt," *New York Times*, 16 March 1951, 1.

42. Jack Gould, "Millions Glued to TV for Hearings; Home Chores Wait, Shopping Sags," *New York Times*, 20 March 1951, 1; "Rutgers Assigns Class to Watch Hearings on TV," *New York Times*, 14 March 1951, 29; "The Crime Hearings," 13.

43. "The Big Show," editorial, *New York Times*, 14 March 1951, 32; "Truth by Television," *The Spectator*, 31 March 1951, 405.

44. Martin, "Happenings in Washington," A4983.

45. Herbert Monte Levy, staff counsel of the ACLU, to the editor of the *New York Herald-Tribune*, 30 March 1950, cited in Gorman, *Kefauver*, 93; Abe Fortas, "Outside the Law," *Atlantic Monthly* (August 1953): 43.

46. Alan Barth, *Government by Investigation* (New York: Viking, 1955), 72. Walter Lippman, "Today and Tomorrow: On the Television Problem," in *Appendix to the Congressional Record*, 82d Cong., 1st sess. (1951), vol. 97, pt. 12, A1724.

47. Telford Taylor, "The Issue Is Not TV, but Fair Play," *New York Times Magazine*, 15 April 1951, 12, 68.

48. Barth, *Government by Investigation*, 78.

49. Allen T. Klots, "Trial by Television," *Harper's*, 203 (October 1951): 91; "The Unanswered Questions," *The Nation*, 31 March 1951, 292–94; McNaughton, "*TV Congress*," 153; "The Biggest Show," *Newsweek*, 26 March 1951, 52; "Millions Witness Crime Probe," *Christian Century*, 4 April 1951, 421; Gorman, *Kefauver*, 93–94; Shayon, "Open Letter," 31–32; Martin, "Happenings in Washington," A4984.

50. Lippman, "Today and Tomorrow," A1724.

51. Anderson and Blumenthal, *Kefauver Story*, 154; Moore, *Kefauver Committee*, 201.

5. "The Proper Act of Citizenship"

1. Virgil Peterson, "Citizens Crime Commissions," *Federal Probation*, 17 (March 1953): 9; G. D. Wiebe, "Responses to the Televised Kefauver Hearings: Some Social Psychological Implications," *Public Opinion Quarterly*, 16 (Summer 1952): 187.

2. A similar crime commission, financed by U.S. Steel president Elbert H. Gary, had been founded in 1925. This organization included future president Franklin Roosevelt, former secretary of war Newton Baker, Charles Evans Hughes, Chief Justice of the Supreme Court, and others. Virgil Peterson, *Crime Commissions in the United States* (Chicago: Chicago Crime Commission, 1945), 5–6. On the National Association of Citizens Crime Commissions, see Charles Grutzner, "New National Unit Will Combat Crime," *New York Times*, 7 November 1952, 24; "Dock Rackets Cost Put at $350,000,000," *New York Times*, 8 November 1952, 29.

3. "Dock Rackets Cost Put at $350,000,000," 29.

4. Kansas City Crime Commission, Constitution and Bylaws, Minutes of the Board of Directors, 20 February 1950, unpublished material in possession of KCCC. J. Edgar Hoover, *Masters of Deceit: The Story of Communism in America and How to Fight It* (New York: Henry Holt and Company, 1958), 310.

5. Vernon Fox, "Citizens' Groups and Penal Progress," *Journal of Criminal Law, Criminology, and Police Science*, 48 (1958): 518; U.S. Congress, Senate, Special Committee to Investigate Organized Crime in Interstate Commerce, *Final Report* (Washington, D.C.: U.S. Government Printing Office, 1952), 1; U.S. Congress, Senate, *Third Interim Report of the Special Committee to Investigate Organized Crime in Interstate Commerce* (Washington, D.C.: U.S. Government Printing Office, 1951), 30.

6. John 3:19–20, quoted in *Report of the Special Citizens Investigating Committee of the Commission Council of New Orleans*, vol. 1, *Conclusions and Recommendations* (April 1954), Metropolitan Crime Commission of New Orleans, Clippings File and Unpublished Reports. The passage was probably quoted in reference to the police department, which shut down the MCC's investigations after corruption in the police force was reported.

7. Special Committee to Investigate Organized Crime in Interstate Commerce, *Final Report*, 1. In 1958 fifteen states included some type of group devoted to the improvement of corrections, most often prisoners' aid organizations, which oversaw the transition to life outside prison. Few groups served as advocates for widespread prison reform. Most notably, the Pennsylvania Prison Society, which dated back to an eighteenth-century Quaker society, the Georgia League of Women Voters, the Prisoners' Aid Society of Maryland, the Osborne Association, and the John Howard Association served as important advocates for prisoners and prison reform. In addition, several religious (South Dakota Council of Churches, Sioux Falls Ministerial Association, Louisville Council of Churches) and university (University of Alabama, Florida State University, University of Michigan, and Wayne State University) groups encouraged politicians to improve correctional systems. See Fox, "Citizens' Groups and Penal Progress"; Leon T. Stern, "Report of the Committee on Citizen Participation," *Proceedings of the American Prison Association* (1954): 37–40.

8. Virgil Peterson, "How to Form a Citizens Crime Commission," *Journal of Criminal Law, Criminology, and Police Science*, 46 (November–December 1955): 490; 492–93.

9. Stuart Hall and David Held "Citizens and Citizenship," *New Times: The Changing Face of Politics*, ed. Stuart Hall and Martin Jacque (New York: Verso, 1991), 174, 177. 174, 177; New York City Anti-Crime Committee, annual report for the Year 1952, New York Public Library.

10. George Fiske, foreman of the Jackson County Grand Jury, called for the formation of the committee in September 1949 after the grand jury expired. Minutes of the opening meeting of the Kansas City Crime Commission, 13 September 1949, Saddle and Sirloin Club, Johnson County, Kansas, in possession of the Kansas City Crime Commission. A predecessor, the Kansas City Law Enforcement Association, existed from 1920 until about 1932. Peterson, *Crime Commissions in the United States*, 3, 17–19; idem, "Citizens Crime Commissions," 9–15.

11. Initiated in 1951, the Citizens Crime Commission of Philadelphia was incorporated as a nonprofit agency in 1955. "History of the Commission," *Annual Report* (Philadelphia: Citizens Crime Commission, 1984); Peterson, "How to Form a Citizens Crime Commission," 486; Tony Radosti, interview with author, 11 October 1996; Peterson, "Citizens Crime Commissions," 11; *Fourth Annual Meeting of the New York City Anti-Crime Committee*, 8 February 1955, oral report presented by Hon. Spruille Braden, chairman, copy in New York

Public Library. Braden had direct access to the *New York Times* via the publisher, General Julius Ochs Adler. Mrs. Adler served on the NYCACC's board of directors. *Third Annual Meeting of the New York City Anti-Crime Committee*, 4 February 1954, transcript of oral report by Hon. Spruille Braden, chairman, copy in New York Public Library; William Howard Moore, *The Kefauver Committee and the Politics of Crime*, 1950–1952, (Columbia: University of Missouri Press, 1974), 38. The Chicago Crime Commission, the Cleveland Crime Commission, and the Baltimore Criminal Justice Association were the only 1950s commissions that dated back to the crime commission movement of the 1920s. All the rest were founded in the years leading up to the Kefauver Committee or immediately after the proceedings concluded. Peterson, "Citizens Crime Commissions," 9.

12. Kansas City Crime Commission, minutes of meeting of 13 February 1953, in possession of Kansas City Crime Commission; *Third Annual Meeting of the NYCACC*.

13. Moore, *Kefauver Committee*, 38; Joseph Bruce Gorman, *Kefauver: A Political Biography* (New York: Oxford University Press, 1991), 81; "Press Conferences of the United States Senate Committee Investigating Organized Crime in the United States," San Francisco, 21 and 22 November 1950, transcript at National Archives and Records Administration, Washington, D.C.

14. Jackson County Grand Jury, report to the Hon. Ray G. Cowan, Judge of the Circuit Court, Division 7, Circuit Court of Jackson County, Kansas City, Missouri (May term, 1950), 3, copy in possession of the Kansas City Crime Commission; Kansas City Crime Commission, minutes, 14 July 1950; "Racketeer Nears Deportation," *New York Times*, 3 January 1954, 52.

15. "Binaggio and Gargotta Slain," *Kansas City Star*, 6 April 1950, 1; Virgil Peterson, *Barbarians in Our Midst* (Boston: Little, Brown, 1952), 258. Clippings from *Kansas City Star*, 29 April 1950; and *St. Louis Post-Dispatch*, 29 April and 10 January 1950, in possession of Kansas City Crime Commission. Moore, *Kefauver Committee*, 98. Tom Pendergast still dominated the Kansas City Democratic scene in the early 1950s. Although Kefauver did not agree, the anti-Pendergast *Star* opined that Binaggio's attempt to influence the appointment of police commissioners who would not pursue his gambling interests drew Pendergast's retaliation. Moore credits the Binnagio slaying for pushing quick Senate authorization of Kefauver's proposed committee (*Kefauver Committee*, 59); On Salvatore Giuliano, see Michael Stern, *No Innocence Abroad* (New York: Random House, 1953). Others blamed the Sicilian Mafia for killing Giuliano; see Herbert L. Matthews, "Mafia Interests Go Beyond Crime," *New York Times*, 13 April 1954, 21. On Luciano, see "Missouri Narrowly Escaped Falling into Control of Gamblers," *Kansas City Star*, 28 February 1951, 1.

16. U.S. Congress, Senate, *Hearings before the Special Committee to Investigate Organized Crime in Interstate Commerce*, pt. 7, *New York–New Jersey* (Washington, D.C.: U.S. Government Printing Office, 1951): 157–58.

17. Adducci quoted in Peterson, *Barbarians in Our Midst*, 311. Vito Marcantonio, longtime representative from New York's East Harlem, never appeared before the committee, but he faced similar accusations in the press, most often from anticommunists. The *New York Mirror*'s coverage of the hearings often mentioned that Frank Costello was born in the same district that produced Fiorello La Guardia and Vito Marcantonio; see "Crime Hunt in Foley Square," *Time*, 26 March 1951, 22.

18. Peterson *Crime Commissions*, 26, 28; idem, *Gambling: Should It Be Legalized?* (Springfield, Ill.: Charles C. Thomas, 1951), 30.

19. Peterson, *Gambling*, 8.

20. Peterson, *Barbarians in Our Midst*, 255, 321.

21. Ibid., 337.

22. Renato Rosaldo, "Social Justice and the Crisis of National Communities," in *Colonial Discourse/Postcolonial Theory*, ed. Francis Barker, Peter Hulme, and Margaret Iversen (New York: St. Martin's Press, 1994), 243; idem, "Cultural Citizenship in San Jose, California," *PoLAR*, 17 (1992), 57–63.

23. Walter Benn Michaels, *Our America: Nativism, Modernism, and Pluralism* (Durham: Duke University Press, 1995), 16.

24. New York City Anti-Crime Committee, *Annual Report for the Year 1952* (New York: NYCACC, 1953), copy in New York Public Library.

25. Charles Grutzner, "New National Unit Will Combat Crime," *New York Times*, 7 November 1952, 24; *Fourth Annual Meeting*. "Mr. X" was quickly exposed in newspapers as Ben Levine, a wealthy New York garment manufacturer. When he found out about the NBC program, Levine compelled the network to remove references to him. As in the case of televising only Frank Costello's hands, the use of "Mr. X," insinuating conspiratorial control of the garment industry, made Levine's power more sinister than it would have seemed had his name been used. *Third Annual Meeting*.

26. *Fourth Annual Meeting*. This method sometimes put the NYCACC outside the law. On December 5, 1952, Robert W. Greene, an investigator for the committee, was indicted by the Hudson County, New Jersey, grand jury for conspiring to defame John V. Kenny, mayor of Jersey City; NYCACC, *Annual Report for the Year 1952*.

27. Aaron Kohn, *The Kohn Report: Crime and Politics in Chicago* (Chicago: Independent Voters of Illinois, 1953), iv, 90, 97, 107; Gibbons was asked to take a leave of absence in 1953.

28. "Crime Report Issued," *New York Times*, 7 December 1954, 49; *Report of the Special Citizens Investigating Committee of the Commission Council of New Orleans*, Dudley C. Foley Jr., Chairman, vol. 3, *The New Orleans Police Department—Police Practices*, April 1954, copy in possession of Metropolitan Crime Commission of New Orleans. Although completed in April, this report was suppressed by the City Commission until December 1954, when city councilman Fred Cassibry made it public.

29. Tony Radosti, interview with author, 11 October 1996.

30. *Report of the Special Citizens Investigating Committee*, 23.

31. Ibid., 67.

32. Douglas Cater, "The Wide-Open Town on the Chattahoochee," *The Reporter*, 24 February 1955, 22–27. Phenix City had approximately 24,000 residents in 1954; Columbus, Georgia, just across the river, had over 80,000. See "Anti-Vice Nominee Slain in Alabama," *New York Times*, 19 April 1954, 32.

33. "Alabama Murder Calls Out Troops," *New York Times*, 20 June 1954, 88; "Troops Tighten Phenix City Martial Rule; Occupation Called Unique in U.S. History," *New York Times*, 24 July 1954, 6; "Alabama Invites Graham," *New York Times*, 27 August 1954, 11; "Phenix City Drive Set," *New York Times*, 26 November 1954, 23. During the civil rights movement, martial law would again be used to deprive local police of their powers in the South, though the governor would be on the other end of the gun.

34. "Behind the Alabama Assassination," *Christian Century*, 7 July 1954, 813; John M. Patterson, as told to Furman Bisher, "I'll Get the Gangs That Killed My Father!" *Saturday Evening Post*, 27 November 1954, 20–21. The Reading, Pennsylvania, Citizens' Committee for Good Government was credited with restoring citizens' faith in that city in the wake of Senator Kefauver's investigation of political corruption. Reading, too, was declared an "All American City" in 1955. "1955's All American Cities," *American City* (February 1956):

127; "All American Cities," *Look*, 10 January 1956, 36; "'Sin City' Sizzles Again, but on Film," *Life*, 26 September 1955, 123–28.

35. Grutzner, "New National Unit," 24. Walter W. Ruch, "Crime War Urged by Unity of Cities," *New York Times*, 3 December 1949, 3; "War on Syndicated Crime Urged of A.M.A.," *American City* (January 1950): 86–87.

36. Grutzner, "New National Unit," 24; Virgil Peterson, "Barbarians in Our Cities," *Criminal Justice*, 77 (January 1950): 20–23; Adlai Stevenson, "Crime and Politics," *Journal of Criminal Law and Criminology*, 41 (November–December 1950): 401; Alfred R. Lindesmith, "Organized Crime," *The Annals*, 217 (September 1941): 76–83. In 1948 Stevenson had won election on an anti-crime platform after a murder in Peoria, Illinois, resulted in criticism by a grand jury of the state's Republican establishment. A similar movement in Minneapolis resulted in Hubert H. Humphrey's unexpected mayoralty in 1945. See Peterson, *Barbarians in Our Midst*, 244.

37. Peterson, *Gambling*; Edwin Sutherland, *White Collar Crime* (New York: Holt, Rinehart and Winston, 1949).

38. Benedict Anderson, *Imagined Communities: Reflections on the Origin and Spread of Nationalism* (New York: Verso, 1983), 12, quoted in Jeanine Derr, "The Biggest Show on Earth": The Kefauver Crime Committee Hearings," *Maryland Historian*, 17 (1986): 24.

39. Estes Kefauver, *Crime in America* (Garden City, N.Y.: Doubleday, 1951), 333.

40. Eugene Kinkead, *In Every War But One* (New York: W. W. Norton, 1959), 15. Philip Wylie, *Tomorrow!* (New York: Rinehart & Company, 1954), 34.

41. Wylie, *Tomorrow!*, 80–81.

42. George MacKinnon, speech before the Minneapolis Rotary Club, [1956], MacKinnon Papers, Racketeering Files, 1953–58, Minnesota Historical Society, St. Paul. MacKinnon had been a popular U.S. attorney in Minneapolis and had served in the U.S. House of Representatives. Minnesota Legislature, Commission to Study Juvenile Delinquency, Crime, and Corrections, *Anti-Social Behavior and Its Control in Minnesota* (St. Paul: State of Minnesota, 1957).

43. Minnesota Legislature, *Anti-Social Behavior*, 24; press conferences of the United States Senate Committee Investigating Organized Crime in the United States, San Francisco, 21 and 22 November 1950, transcript, Papers of the Committee Investigating Organized Crime in Interstate Commerce, National Archives and Records Administration; see also Moore, *Kefauver Committee*, 37; United States Department of Justice, "Advance Release for Morning Papers of Sunday, 8 January 1956," Mackinnon Papers.

44. J. Edgar Hoover, "Address before the National Convention of the American Legion," Atlantic City, N.J., 19 September 1957, MacKinnon Papers. Although Hoover did not directly cooperate with the private committees, many FBI agents went on to work as investigators for citizens' crime committees after retiring.

45. Lester Velie, "The Capone Gang Muscles into Big-Time Politics," *Collier's*, 30 September 1950, 18.

46. The Bureau of Immigration filed a petition to summarily denaturalize Costello in 1954 for his refusal to answer questions at a pretrial denaturalization hearing. Costello pleaded the Fifth. See "Costello Victor in Alien Dispute," *New York Times*, 2 December 1954, 36; U.S. Congress, Senate, *Third Interim Report of the Special Committee to Investigate Organized Crime in Interstate Commerce* (Washington, D.C.: U.S. Government Printing Office, 1952), 15; Estes Kefauver, *Crime in America* (Garden City, N.Y.: Doubleday, 1951), 292. This policy was not limited to Italian Americans. Hans Hauser, the Austrian-born husband of Virginia Hill, left the United States after the INS threatened to deport him. He

had been detained for three years during World War II as an enemy alien. Andy Edmonds, *Bugsy's Baby: The Secret Life of Mob Queen Virginia Hill* (New York: Birch Lane, 1993), 216.

47. Juan Ramon Garcia, *Operation Wetback: The Mass Deportation of Mexican Undocumented Workers in 1954* (Westport, Conn.: Greenwood Press, 1980), 193; 876,000 of the 1 million deported were Chicanos. Along with Mexican Americans, Jewish and Japanese American groups were among the most vocal opponents, perhaps in reaction to the use of "security facilities" in Los Angeles and Nogales, Arizona, that bore a frightening similarity to the concentration camps and internment camps of World War II. For a leftist critique of "Operation Wetback," see Patricia Morgan, *Shame of a Nation: Police-State Terror against Mexican-Americans in the U.S.A.* (Los Angeles: Los Angeles Committee for the Protection of the Foreign Born, 1954). This pamphlet—along with all other LACPFB and American Committee for the Protection of the Foreign Born materials cited—is available at the Labor Archives and Research Center at San Francisco State University.

48. Willard Carpenter, "Punishment by Exile: Can Native-Born Americans Be Deported?" *Frontier* (November 1955): 10–11. This article discusses the case of Bernardo Diaz, an American of Mexican descent who went AWOL during World War II. After serving his eighteen-month sentence at Fort Leavenworth, Kansas, Diaz was stripped of his citizenship, a punishment that was applied to all foreign-born personnel who went AWOL. Diaz was later declared an "inadmissable Alien" at a Border Patrol checkpoint after a brief trip to Tijuana, Mexico.

49. Edith Lowenstein, *The Alien and the Immigration Law: A Study of 1446 Cases Arising under the Immigration and Naturalization Laws of the United States* (New York: Common Council for American Unity and Oceana Publications, 1958), 165.

50. Benjamin J. Davis, *Ben Davis on the McCarran Act at the Harvard Law Forum* (New York: Gus Hall–Benjamin J. Davis Defense Committee, 1962). Available at the Labor Archives and Research Center, San Francisco State University.

51. Judge Learned Hand disagreed: "Deportation means exile, a medieval form of punishment abandoned by the common consent of civilized nations." Los Angeles Committee for the Protection of the Foreign Born, *Pride of a Nation: A History of the Los Angeles Committee for the Protection of the Foreign Born* (Los Angeles, LACPFB, 1988), 5.

52. Stephen H. Legomsky, *Immigration Law and Policy* (Westbury, N.Y.: Foundation Press, 1992), 411.

53. Constantine M. Panunzio, *The Deportation Cases of 1919–1920* (New York: Commission on the Church and Social Service, 1921), 15.

54. The 1917 law provided a five-year statute of limitations, which was removed for illegal entry in 1924 and then for other offenses in 1952.

55. Sidney Kansas, *U.S. Immigration, Exclusion, and Deportation and Citizenship of the United States of America*, 3d ed. (New York: Matthew Bender Company, 1948), 228.

56. Lowenstein, *The Alien*, 213.

57. *U.S. ex rel. Iorio v. Day*, 34 F.2d (1929), 920, 921; Lowenstein, *The Alien*, 213; Gerald Gunther, *Learned Hand: The Man and the Judge* (New York: Knopf, 1994). The key Supreme Court decision is *Fong Haw Tan v. Phelan* 333 U.S. 6, 68 S.Ct. 374, 92 L.Ed. 433 (1948). The federal law stated that "an alien who is sentenced more than once to imprisonment for a term of one year or more because of conviction in this country of a crime involving moral turpitude committed after his entry shall, with exceptions not material here, be deported." Fong Haw Tan was convicted of committing two murders (on the same day) and received two life sentences. Later granted parole, he was immediately taken into custody by the Immigration Service. The Supreme Court decision hinged on whether the sentences were

to run consecutively (thus amounting to two sentences under the law) or concurrently. The Court (Justice William O. Douglas writing for the majority) found for the defendant, deciding that the law was meant to deport those who "commit a crime and are sentenced, and then commit another and are sentenced again." Legomsky, *Immigration Law*, 415.

58. Lowenstein, *The Alien*, 264. A final deportation order could be stayed by the attorney general in specific cases in which "an alien would be subject to physical persecution in the country to which he would be deported" (280).

59. Lewis Wood, "M'Granery Starts a Drive to Deport Alien Racketeers," *New York Times*, 3 October 1952, 1; "High Court Stays Deporting Order," *New York Times*, 16 March 1954, 20. Adonis's deportation case didn't end with the order. He claimed he'd been born in Passaic, New Jersey. As a U.S. citizen by birth, Adonis could not be denaturalized. The government first needed to prove that he had lied about his birthplace, which it did in 1954, clearing the way for his deportation. William R. Conklin, "Adonis Convicted by Jersey Judge," *New York Times*, 19 January 1954, 21; "Albert Anastasia Loses Citizenship," *New York Times*, 15 April 1954, 1. According to U.S. District Court judge William F. Smith, "Anastasia perpetrated fraud on the Government in two proceedings leading to his naturalization by failing to disclose a police record that included three charges of homicide." Albert Anastasia never left the United States. He was murdered in 1957.

60. Jeanine Derr, "The Biggest Show on Earth," *Maryland History*, 17 (1986): 24.

61. Roger Daniels, *Coming to America: A History of Immigration and Ethnicity in American Life* (New York: Harper Perennial, 1991), 332. Protests came from numerous sources. The American Committee for the Foreign Born, the NAACP, the American Jewish Committee, the Sons of Italy, Representative Emanuel Celler and Senator Herbert Lehman of New York, and many others collectively and individually worked to defeat this bill. Senator Patrick McCarran also lent his name to the Internal Security Act of 1950 (often called the McCarran Act), which contained deportation provisions for foreign-born people with political views deemed a threat to the United States. See Bernard Lemelin, "Emanuel Celler of Brooklyn: Leading Advocate of Liberal Immigration Policy, 1945–1952," *Canadian Review of American Studies*, 24 (Winter 1994): 88–103. According to Dean Jennings, McCarran, a Republican from Nevada, had helped Bugsy Siegel get building materials for the Flamingo Hotel during the shortages of World War II. Dean Jennings, *We Only Kill Each Other: The Life and Bad Times of Bugsy Siegel* (Englewood Cliffs, N.J.: Prentice-Hall, 1968), 152.

62. U.S. Congress, Senate, *Third Interim Report*, 7–20.

63. Robert F. Kennedy, *The Enemy Within* (New York: Harper & Row, 1960); see also chapter 6; Braden quoted in Clark Mollenhoff, *Tentacles of Power* (Cleveland: World Publishing Company, 1965), 99.

6. The Man in the Pin-Striped Suit

1. Sloan Wilson, *The Man in the Gray Flannel Suit* (New York: Simon and Schuster, 1955). The film was released in 1956.

2. Thorstein Veblen, *Theory of the Leisure Class* (New York: Macmillan, 1899), 237; Edwin Sutherland, *White Collar Crime* (New York: Holt, Rinehart and Winston, 1949), 217–33, 3.

3. Joseph McCarthy, "Speech at Wheeling, West Virginia, February 9, 1950," *Congressional Record*, Senate, 81st Cong., 2d sess., 20 February 1950, 1954, 1956–57. Irving Kaufman, "Sentencing of Julius and Ethel Rosenberg" (5 April 1951), reprinted in Ellen Schrecker, *The Age of McCarthyism: A Brief History with Documents* (New York: Bedford Books, 1994), 145.

4. Charles Siragusa as told to Robert Wiedrich, *The Trail of the Poppy: Behind the Mask of the Mafia* (Englewood Cliffs, N.J.: Prentice-Hall, 1966).

5. On the relationship of the "Letters to Italy" campaign to Italian American ethnic identity, see Wendy L. Wall, "America's 'Best Propagandists': Italian Americans and the 1948 'Letters to Italy' Campaign," in *Cold War Constructions: The Political Culture of United States Imperialism, 1945–1966*, ed. Christian Appy (Amherst: University of Massachusetts Press, 1999), 89–109.

6. Toni Howard, "Dope Is His Business," *Saturday Evening Post*, 27 April 1957, 39, 148; Sid Feder and Joachim Joesten, *The Luciano Story* (New York: David McKay, 1954), 43; Martin A. Gosch and Richard Hammer, *The Last Testament of Lucky Luciano* (Boston: Little, Brown, 1974), 16, 20.

7. Michel Foucault, *Discipline and Punish: The Birth of the Prison* (New York: Vintage, 1979), 184; Howard, "Dope Is His Business," 147.

8. Gosch and Hammer, *Last Testament*, 3. Luciano's posthumous autobiography—of questionable authenticity—*The Last Testament of Lucky Luciano*, originally formed the basis of a script for a never-made Hollywood film and was turned into a book to recover losses. There is no evidence beyond claims made by the ghostwriters of actual interviews between Luciano and Martin Gosch. See Peter Maas, "The White House, the Mob, and the Book Biz: Footnotes to 'The Valachi Papers,'" *New York Times Book Review*, 12 October 1986, 3; Richard Hammer, letter to the editor, *New York Times Book Review*, 2 November 1986, 16.

9. Siragusa, *Trail of the Poppy*, 34–35.

10. Ibid., 37.

11. Ibid., x–xi.

12. Gosch and Hammer, *Last Testament*, 73–74.

13. Mary M. Stolberg, *Fighting Organized Crime: Politics, Justice, and the Legacy of Thomas E. Dewey* (Boston: Northeastern University Press, 1995), 152. Though largely beyond the scope of this chapter, the history and politics of the Dewey-Luciano trial are the subject of Stolberg's book. Stolberg shares my belief that the prosecution of Luciano (and organized crime figures more generally) was intentionally overstated to further Dewey's political ambitions. In 1937 several key witnesses, including the only witnesses to link Luciano to prostitution—Nancy Presser and Flo Brown—claimed that Dewey's assistants had threatened them with jail sentences if they did not testify, then paid them $200 afterwards (158). See also Gosch and Hammer, *Last Testament*, 188.

14. Tibor Koeves, "Lucky Luciano vs. The United Nations," *U.N. World*, 3 (August 1949): 38; "Eight of Luciano's Pals under Probe in Havana," *New York Daily Mirror*, 27 February 1947, 6.

15. "Operation Underworld" is detailed in Rodney Campbell, *The Luciano Project: The Secret Wartime Collaboration of the Mafia and U.S. Navy* (New York: McGraw-Hill, 1977); see 15, 18. In addition, Luciano was also credited in the press with helping to strategize the Allied landing on Sicily. Many Italian Americans provided "photographs, postcards, letters, and documents about their hometowns," but Luciano seems to have been involved in only one wacky scenario: Haffenden requested that Luciano be released from prison and sent to Italy to gather intelligence for the navy. His proposal was rejected. Campbell, *Luciano Project*, 146.

16. Ibid., 125, 193–212.

17. John Lardner, "How Lucky Won the War," *Newsweek*, 31 January 1955, 66; Max Lerner, "Payoff Blues," *New York Post*, 18 October 1950, 48; "Luciano Seized in Cuba, Will Be Shipped to Italy," *New York Daily Mirror*, 23 February 1947, 3.

18. During the Kefauver crime hearings several years later, George White wrote to Narcotics Commissioner Harry Anslinger: " 'Gene' told me yesterday the parole fix on Luciano was arranged by Costello thru James Bruno, Republican ex Deputy Com. of NY State Athletic Com, now believed to be a clerk in NY Supreme court. The Haffenden stuff was only 'window-dressing' because they had to have something on which to hang their hat.— GAW." "GAW" [George White] to Harry Anslinger, 1 November 1950, Record Group 170, Papers of the Federal Bureau of Narcotics, National Archives and Records Administration, College Park, Md. See also Gosch and Hammer, *Last Testament*, 255–56, 268. It is probable that the FBN was directly responsible for the rumor that Luciano had bribed public officials in order to obtain his commutation. Some historians have seen evidence of conspiratorial wrongdoing in the FBN's strategy. According to one study, the outcry over Luciano's deportation was part of a concerted effort by agents of the Federal Bureau of Narcotics to discredit Dewey's presidential aspirations. In fact, during the buildup to the 1952 presidential race, Luciano insinuated that the FBN's anti-Luciano campaign was part of the anti-Dewey forces' strategy. John C. McWilliams and Alan A. Block, "All the Commissioner's Men: The Federal Bureau of Narcotics and the Dewey-Luciano Affair, 1947–54," *Intelligence and National Security*, 5 (1990): 171–92. This was accomplished by feeding false information to several media sources, most notably Michael Stern of *True* magazine, and by giving false or purely speculative testimony to the Kefauver Committee. See Michael Stern, *No Innocence Abroad* (New York: Random House, 1953). McWilliams and Block are correct, but this was also part of a general strategy of Anslinger's rather than proof of a personal vendetta against Dewey. "Luciano Says He'll Talk," *New York Times*, 5 August 1951, 53.

19. Walter Winchell, *New York Mirror*, 11 February 1947; *New York Times*, 22 February 1947, 1; "People: Unlucky Lucky," *Newsweek*, March 3, 1947, 20–21; "Cuba: Hoodlum on the Wing," *Time*, 3 March 1947, 36–37; Stern, *No Innocence Abroad*; Feder and Joesten, *Luciano Story*.

20. "Luciano Seized in Cuba, Will be Shipped to Italy," *New York Daily Mirror*, 23 February 1947, 3; "Unlucky Lucky," 20–21; Dean Jennings, *We Only Kill Each Other: The Life and Bad Times of Bugsy Siegel* (Englewood Cliffs, N.J.: Prentice-Hall, 1968), 170.

21. John C. McWilliams, *The Protectors: Harry J. Anslinger and the Federal Bureau of Narcotics, 1930–1962* (Newark: University of Delaware Press, 1990), 140; Stern, *No Innocence Abroad*, 33. Stern was one of the primary outlets for the FBN's misinformation campaign. See text for discussion of other conduits of FBN information. McWilliams and Block, "All the Commissioner's Men," 171–92.

22. "$640,000 Heroin Is Seized on Liner; 6 Vulcania Stewards Queried about Narcotics—Luciano Linked to Shipment," *New York Times*, 2 October 1948, 30; "Opium, Heroin Worth $1,000,000 Found Hidden in French Ship Here," *New York Times*, 8 January 1949, 1; McWilliams and Block, "All the Commissioner's Men," 140; Camille M. Cianfarra, "Luciano Detained by Italian Police; Deported Vice King Is Held for Questioning on Any Link to Smuggling of Cocaine," *New York Times*, 9 July 1949, 28.

23. Narcotics and marijuana arrests totaled 2,855 in 1947, 3,180 in 1948, 5,851 in 1950, 4,874 in 1951. U.S. Treasury Department Information Service, press release, 15 August 1948, FBN Papers. Narcotics were primarily opiates. The figures on seizures are, for opium and various forms: 7,894 ounces in 1947, 4,990 ounces in 1948; cocaine: 36 ounces in 1947, 175 ounces in 1948; marijuana: 27,314 in 1947, 48,822 ounces in 1948. U.S. Treasury Department press release, 5 March 1949, FBN Papers. The *New York Times* reported slightly different opiate figures for 1948 and 1949 (3,895 and 5,273, respectively). "Narcotics Arrests Show Sharp Rise;

New York Leads All Districts in U.S.," *New York Times*, 5 March 1950, 17; "Narcotics Unit Cites Lure to Teen-Agers," *New York Times*, 2 March 1951, 19.

24. "U.S. Reports 'Lead' in Narcotics Haul," *New York Times*, 9 January 1949, 56; "Five in Ring Convicted," *New York Times*, 3 March 1951, 28; "Narcotics Air Courier Ring Broken; 5 in New York–Canada Cartel Held," *New York Times*, 5 August 1951, 1.

25. "2 Get Long Terms in 400G Dope Raid; Heroin Peddler, Aide Off to Prison Today," *New York Post*, 11 May 1956, 1; McWilliams, *Protectors*, 152.

26. Howard, "Dope Is His Business," 38, 147.

27. Harry J. Anslinger with J. Dennis Gregory, *The Protectors: The Heroic Story of the Narcotics Agents, Citizens, and Officials in Their Unending, Unsung Battles against Organized Crime in America and Abroad* (New York: Farrar, Straus, 1964), 108–9.

28. "Luciano Cries 'Frame-Up,' " *New York Times*, 9 January 1949, 56; "Luciano Says He'll Talk," *New York Times*, 5 August 1951, 53.

29. Anslinger was appointed commissioner of narcotics by Herbert Hoover in 1930, when the Federal Bureau of Narcotics was formed out of the old Prohibition Bureau. Many hoped that his policies would be discontinued after he retired in 1962, but their ongoing effects can hardly be overstated. As recently as May 2001, the U.S. Supreme Court unanimously found that medical use of marijuana violated federal law. The "drug war," as U.S. policy is commonly called, clearly owes much to the criminalization of narcotics by Anslinger's FBN. See, for example, David E. Rosenbaum, "I.R.S. Bans Deducting Medical Cost of Marijuana," *New York Times*, 23 February 1997, 19.

30. Harry J. Anslinger, Memorandum to All District Supervisors, 10 March 1950, FBN Papers, Box 43; A. B. Crisler, District Supervisor for District 15 [Seattle], to Harry Anslinger, 21 March 1950; Terry A. Talent, District Supervisor for District 13 [Denver], to Harry Anslinger, 31 March 1950, FBN Papers.

31. Stanley Meisler, "Federal Narcotics Czar," *The Nation*, 20 February 1960, 160. Tompkins coauthored Anslinger's *The Traffic in Narcotics*; "Confidential Investigation of Abe S. Berliner," FBN Papers, Box 46. Internal documents describing the group state: "Mr. Abe S. Berliner conducts a vest pocket organization known as the New Jersey Narcotic Defense League for self-glorification and to aid him in the sale of insurance and real estate. Recently he has begun soliciting funds for his organization. Federal and State officials regard his organization as a collection racket." Secretary of the Treasury, Memorandum to Mr. Matthew J. Connelly, Secretary to the President, 9 October 1951, FBN Papers. Although Anslinger clearly relayed this information to the secretary of the treasury (his immediate superior), the report submitted by the New Jersey State Police never called the NJNDL a "collection racket." It is possible that a bureau agent conducted a separate investigation that either was never included or was later removed from the file.

32. Harry J. Anslinger to Mr. Herbert D. Sullivan, Chairman, Sub-Committee on Education and Research, Mayor's Committee for the Rehabilitation of Narcotic Addicts, City of Detroit, Michigan, 4 June 1951, FBN Papers, Box 50; M. L. Harney, Assistant to the Commissioner of Narcotics, Memorandum to the Commissioner, 28 May 1951, FBN Papers. Missouri prosecutors found that few juries convicted minor narcotics offenders in the face of harsh penalties. Meisler, "Federal Narcotics Czar," 161.

33. Roland H. Berg "The Dope Addict: Criminal or Patient," *Look*, 15 October 1957, 40; George H. White, District Supervisor for California, to Harry Anslinger, 1 October 1957, FBN Papers, Box 72.

34. The FBN's relationship with Mortimer was particular strong. Lee Mortimer revealed

that Charles Siragusa served as a source for *Around the World Confidential,* though he did not want to be quoted. Mortimer pushed Anslinger's theory that the drug trade originated in China and Cuba, both in the book and in his "New York Confidential" column in the *New York Mirror.* See Charles Siragusa to Harry Anslinger, 28 March 1956, FBN Papers, Box 10. See also Lee Mortimer to Harry Anslinger, 10 June 1960, FBN Papers, Box 10: "I want you to know how much your help and assistance meant to me and how fine your boys were in Beirut, Istanbul, Rome and Paris. Incidentally, I suppose Sirgusa told you I saw him in Geneva. Since my return I have been with Sam Pryor a couple of times and hope to come down to see you in the near future. I ran across some amazing and startling situations and as soon as I finish coordinating my notes I'll let you know what I found." Anslinger wrote the foreword to Frederic Sondern, *Brotherhood of Evil: The Mafia* (New York: Farrar, Straus and Cudahy, 1959). Letters, rough drafts, and recommended changes to *Life* articles in the National Archives' FBN Papers document the long-standing relationship between *Life* and the FBN. *Life,* however, ran at least one story that Anslinger hated: William Sparks's "For a Sensible Narcotics Law" (April 1956). In response to Anslinger's objections, the editor offered to run a rebuttal, including Anslinger's objections, alongside it. Donald M. Wilson, editor of *Life,* to George W. Cunningham, Deputy Commissioner of Narcotics, 19 April 1956, FBN Papers, Box 10.

35. Anslinger to District Supervisors, 20 October 1950, FBN Papers, Box 10. The FBN kept a file on Krieg. She wrote to Anslinger at one point, saying, "It seems to me that your attempt to suppress information on the nature and extent of the drug traffic only served to delay help." Margaret Krieg to Harry Anslinger, 27 July 1951, FBN Papers, Box 10. In addition, *San Francisco Examiner* and *Chronicle* columnist Herb Caen often published confidential FBN information, although it is clear that he got it from sources outside the bureau. Apparently Caen had his own sources in Chinatown and refused to cooperate in naming them to the FBN. For example, Caen wrote a column about FBN agent Gon Sam Mue (discussed later in this chapter) in December 1949, while Gon was still performing undercover work. Caen also wrote about agent Earl Teets and his "detective dog," at the time a little-known method of discovering narcotics. See George H. White, District Supervisor for California, to Harry Anslinger, 20 January 1950, FBN Papers. The bureau objected to another Caen article in the *Examiner* on 28 March 1951.

36. Samuel F. Pryor, Executive Vice President, Pan American Airways, to Harry Anslinger, 26 September 1961, FBN Papers, Box 10. Pryor later attended the Narcotic Agents' School and carried an FBN badge. When a jealous Lee Mortimer found out about the badge, he asked for his own, but he didn't get one. Samuel F. Pryor, "Should the Government's Narcotic Control Program Be Changed?" *St. Joseph Magazine* (September 1960), n.p.

37. Joseph I. Breen, vice president of the MPAA in the early fifties, was suspicious of all those who claimed that they hoped to educate viewers by depicting drug use. See Breen to Anslinger, 4 July 1951, FBN Papers, Box 10; Harry Anslinger, memorandum of telephone conversation with Samuel Goldwyn, 14 October 1954, FBN Papers, Box 10. According to Anslinger, Goldwyn "stated he wanted to make a picture showing addiction occurring in a nice respectable family with all of the tragic consequences. He would then show the addict having the courage to pull through and again become a member of a happy family. He wanted to show the courage of a battle against drug addiction." Anslinger refused. "Sam Goldwyn Says—Movies Best Years Ahead: Television No Threat," *U.S. News and World Report,* 5 March 1954, 38–43.

38. Harry Carson, narcotics agent, to Elizabeth Bass, district supervisor for Illinois, Wis-

consin, and Indiana, 29 September 1937, FBN Papers, Box 4; K. C. Rudd, Narcotics agent, to T. W. McGeever, district supervisor, Atlanta, 12 May 1952, FBN Papers, Box 4.

39. Richard Clendenen and Herbert Beaser, "The Shame of America," *Saturday Evening Post*, 8, 15, 22, 29 January and 5 February 1955; Harry Anslinger, memorandum to Charles Siragusa, 7 February 1957, FBN Papers, Box 10.

40. Shortly after Pope leveled these charges, a story in the *New York Times* tied him to Kefauver Committee witness Frank Costello. Anslinger leaked a statement on Jewish bank-rollers to columnist Drew Pearson in October 1950. The Concord, New Hampshire, ADL contacted Senator Charles Tobey, a member of the Kefauver Committee, who wrote in outrage to Anslinger, and Senator Lehman complained to the secretary of the treasury. Anslinger discussed the matter with Herman Edelsberg, director of the ADL, on 19 October 1950, denying that any reference had been made to people of the Jewish faith. See Secretary of the Treasury to Senator Herbert H. Lehman, n.d., FBN Papers.

41. Meisler, "Federal Narcotics Czar," 162; Federal Bureau of Narcotics, "Bureau Organization, History, 1960," FBN Papers, Box 49.

42. David Riesman with Nathan Glazer and Reuel Denney, *The Lonely Crowd: A Study of the Changing American Character* (Garden City, N.Y.: Doubleday, 1953), 50; C. Wright Mills, *White Collar: The American Middle Classes* (New York: Oxford University Press, 1951); Feder and Joesten, *Luciano Story*, 7, 234.

43. Mills, *White Collar*, 109; Riesman, *Lonely Crowd*, 349.

44. Morris Ploscowe, *Sex and the Law* (New York: Prentice Hall, 1951), 248, 168; *People v. Luciano*, 277 N.Y. 348, 14 N.E. 2d 433 (1936). For discussions of sexuality in Cold War America, see Elaine Tyler May, *Homeward Bound: American Families in the Cold War Era* (New York: Basic Books, 1988); Wini Breines, *Young, White, and Miserable: Growing Up Female in the Fifties* (Boston: Beacon Press, 1992); Donna Penn, "The Sexualized Woman: The Lesbian, the Prostitute, and the Containment of Female Sexuality in Postwar America," in *Not June Cleaver*, ed. Joanne Meyerowitz (Philadelphia: Temple University Press, 1994) 358–81; Joanne Meyerowitz, "Beyond the Feminine Mystique: A Reassessment of Postwar Mass Culture, 1946–1958," *Journal of American History*, 79 (March 1993): 1455–82.

45. Koeves, "Lucky Luciano," 35; Siragusa, *Trail of the Poppy*, 205–6; Jack Lait and Lee Mortimer, *Washington Confidential* (New York: Crown, 1952); "Opium, Heroin Worth $1,000,000 Found Hidden in French Ship Here," *New York Times*, 8 January 1949, 1. Similarly, according to Donna Penn, postwar cultural media as well as some psychologists associated prostitution with lesbianism in order to contain female sexuality within monogamous heterosexual relationships. She argues that "these two examples of deviant female sexual behavior were constructed to define, bind, and contain the so-called norm. Prescriptions for the 'normal' were defined in strict inverse relationship to that which was deviant." Penn, "Sexualized Woman," 360.

46. Koeves, "Lucky Luciano," 38.

47. Malcolm Anderson, *Policing the World: Interpol and Politics of International Police Co-operation* (Oxford: Clarendon Press, 1989), 44. See Michael Fooner, *Interpol: Issues in World Crime and International Criminal Justice* (New York: Plenum Press, 1989); "The International Criminal Police Commission," Interpol, 1953, FBN Papers, Box 47.

48. Lieutenant Commander David C. Reid of the U.S. Navy was the "observer" for the Treasury Department delegation. Reid was the supervisor of the American Naval Criminal Investigation Division for Europe. Siragusa sent reports of Interpol activities to Anslinger. George W. Cunningham, acting U.S. commissioner of narcotics, to M. Sicot, secretary

general of Interpol, 7 September 1954, FBN Papers, Box 47; "National and International Black List—Confidential List," FBN Papers, Box 47, a document sent to "police services of the interested countries" in western Europe and North America.

49. "Luciano Dies at 65; Was Facing Arrest," *New York Times*, 26 January 1962, 1; "Unlucky at Last," *Newsweek*, 5 February 1962, 28; "Charles Siragusa, Ex-Agent; Took Action against Luciano," *New York Times*, 19 April 1982, sec. 2, 6.

50. "Cuba Said to Push Opium Sales in U.S.," *New York Times*, 15 March 1962, 9; Arnold H. Lubasch, "Cuba Is Accused of Cocaine Plot," *New York Times*, 14 April 1962, 3.

51. "Alfred McCoy, *The Politics of Heroin in Southeast Asia* (New York: Harper and Row, 1972), 8.

52. Feder and Joesten *Luciano Story*, 8.

7. Unholy Alliances

1. Jeffrey Goldberg, "Jimmy Hoffa's Revenge," *New York Times Magazine*, 8 February 1998, 68.

2. Clark R. Mollenhoff, *Tentacles of Power: The Story of Jimmy Hoffa* (Cleveland: World Publishing 1965) 126; Arthur A. Sloane, *Hoffa* (Cambridge, Mass.: MIT Press, 1991), 4.

3. Eric Hobsbawm, *Bandits* (New York: Pantheon, 1981).

4. R. Alton Lee, *Eisenhower and Landrum-Griffin: A Study in Labor-Management Politics* (Lexington: University Press of Kentucky, 1990), 4; Gary Gerstle, *Working-Class Americanism: The Politics of Labor in a Textile City, 1914–1960* (Cambridge: Cambridge University Press, 1989), 304–5.

5. Thomas Sugrue, *The Origins of the Urban Crisis: Race and Inequality in Postwar Detroit* (Princeton: Princeton University Press, 1996), 7; Elizabeth Fones-Wolf, *Selling Free Enterprise: The Business Assault on Labor and Liberalism, 1945–1960* (Urbana: University of Illinois Press, 1994).

6. Mike Davis, *Prisoners of the American Dream: Politics and Economy in the History of the U.S. Working Class* (London: Verso, 1986), 89.

7. George Lipsitz, *Rainbow at Midnight: Labor and Culture in the 1940s* (Urbana: University of Illinois Press, 1994), 191, 264.

8. Gerstle, *Working-Class Americanism*, 264, 288. Nelson Lichtenstein discusses the "chilling effect" of the Cold War on efforts to organize southern workers and the attempt to build a progressive third party in "From Corporatism to Collective Bargaining: Organized Labor and the Eclipse of Social Democracy in the Postwar Era," in *The Rise and Fall of the New Deal Order, 1930–1980*, ed. Steve Fraser and Gary Gerstle (Princeton: Princeton University Press, 1989), 122–52. Ronald Schatz documents the rise of anticommunism and the decline of left-wing influence with electrical unions during the 1950s in *The Electrical Workers: A History of Labor at General Electric and Westinghouse, 1923–1960* (Urbana: University of Illinois Press, 1983).

9. The United Office & Professional Workers of America and the United Public Workers of America together numbered fewer than fifty thousand members at the time they were expelled from the CIO. Steve Rosswurm notes that one of the tragedies of this expulsion was the negative effect it had on the influence of labor unions over this growing sector of the economy. He also points out the masculinist underpinnings of this failure to organize office workers, many of whom were women. Steve Rosswurm, "An Overview and Prelim-

inary Assessment of the CIO's Expelled Unions," in *The CIO's Left-Led Unions*, ed. Steve Rosswurm (New Brunswick, N.J.: Rutgers University Press, 1992), 3.

10. Kefauver also looked into Detroit Local 985 of the Teamsters Union. Detroit Teamster and Hoffa supporter William E. Bufalino was a major target of the Rackets Committee. See U.S. Senate, Special Committee to Investigate Organized Crime in Interstate Commerce, *Investigation of Organized Crime in Interstate Commerce*, 82d Cong., 1st sess, p. 9 (1951), and Robert Leiter, *The Teamsters Union: A Study of Its Economic Impact* (New York: Bookman Associates, 1957), 229; Sloane, *Hoffa* 42; John Hutchinson, *The Imperfect Union: A History of Corruption in American Trade Unions* (New York: Dutton, 1970), 142–47; Malcolm Johnson, *Crime on the Labor Front* (New York: McGraw-Hill, 1950). The McClellan Committee had its origins in the waterfront investigation in New York City, headed by Kefauver Committee veteran Senator Charles Tobey of New Hampshire. The inquiry was sparked by a popular nonfiction book, Malcolm Johnson's *Crime on the Labor Front*, and by exposés by the New York City Anti-Crime Committee and the New York State Crime Commission. Tobey's investigation further increased public awareness of the harsh working conditions on the New York–New Jersey waterfront and led to the withering away of the outdated and corrupt practice of the "shape up," long eliminated in most industries, which was the twice-daily practice of putting together a crew to load or unload cargo. On the New York City Anti-Crime Committee, see Lee Bernstein, "The Greatest Menace: Organized Crime in U.S. Culture and Politics, 1946–1961" (Ph.D. diss, University of Minnesota, 1997). On the New York State Crime Commission, see Hutchinson, *Imperfect Union*, 101, 343.

11. Robert F. Kennedy, *The Enemy Within: The McClellan Committee's Crusade against Jimmy Hoffa and Corrupt Labor Unions* (New York: Harper and Row, 1960), 40; Sloane, *Hoffa*, 72.

12. Mollenhoff, *Tentacles of Power*, 214–19; Kennedy, *Enemy Within*, 57. Kennedy did not express similar outrage that the government's team of lawyers included Harry Alexander, also African American. See Ronald Goldfarb, *Perfect Villains, Imperfect Heroes: Robert F. Kennedy's War against Organized Crime* (New York: Random House, 1996), 182. The Teamsters ran an editorial advertisement in the *Baltimore Afro-American* that featured a photograph of Martha Jefferson. The ad, captioned "The Facts behind the Hoffa Trial," focused on Judge Burnita Matthews, a native Mississippian, and McClellan's ties to southern businesses while heralding the integrated Teamsters. There was also a column that supported Hoffa and attacked the prosecution. Judge Matthews promptly sequestered the jury. The histrionics surrounding the trial clearly made for interesting press coverage, but race hardly needed to be "inserted," as Mollenhoff charged. Instead, racial and ethnic politics had been factors all along. Both sides exploited the connections between race, ethnicity, class, and crime.

13. Kennedy, *Enemy Within*, 59–61; Walter Sheridan, *The Fall and Rise of Jimmy Hoffa*, (New York: Saturday Review Press, 1972), 34. On organized crime in professional boxing, see David Remnick, *King of the World: Muhammad Ali and the Rise of an American Hero* (New York: Random House, 1998), 10, 28, 46, 61; Michael "Mickey" Cohen as told to John Peer Nugent, *In My Own Words: The Underworld Autobiography of Michael Mickey Cohen* (Englewood Cliffs, N.J.: Prentice-Hall, 1975). During the McClellan hearings, Kefauver ran a Senate investigation of boxing, including among the witnesses Frank Carbo, then serving a twenty-five-year sentence for undercover control of fighters and illegal matchmaking. See Remnick, *King of the World*, 62–68.

14. In 1953 Senator Clare Hoffman conducted a short-lived investigation of Detroit's

jukebox and vending machine businesses, including ties to the Teamsters Union. This was an attempt to capitalize on aspects of the Kefauver investigation that had not been fully explored.

15. Many of these provisions were first gained in the 1950 "Treaty of Detroit" between General Motors and the United Auto Workers, but Hoffa deserved credit for making improvements in the trucking industry. Sloane, *Hoffa*, 80, 89. On "the Treaty of Detroit," see Nelson Lichtenstein, *The Most Dangerous Man in Detroit: Walter Reuther and the Fate of American Labor* (New York: Basic Books, 1995), 271–98; Daniel Bell, "The Treaty of Detroit," *Fortune* (July 1950): 53; "Why the Teamsters Are Under Attack," *International Teamster*, 56 (December 1959): 14–16. For a firsthand discussion of how the Teamsters capitalized on changes during the postwar period, see Joseph Franco with Richard Hammer, *Hoffa's Man: The Rise and Fall of Jimmy Hoffa as Witnessed by His Strongest Arm* (New York: Prentice Hall, 1987), 205.

16. John Bartlow Martin, "The Struggle to Get Hoffa, Part One: Kennedy Sets a Snare," *Saturday Evening Post*, 27 June 1959, 21. This series was later published as a mass-market paperback, John Bartlow Martin, *Jimmy Hoffa's Hot* (Greenwich Conn.: Fawcett, 1959); idem, "The Struggle to Get Hoffa, Part Two: The Making of a Labor Boss," *Saturday Evening Post*, 4 July 1959, 27; Clark Mollenhoff and David Zingg, "Jimmy Hoffa: The Man Who Outsmarted Himself," *Look*, 13 May 1958, 37.

17. Kennedy, *Enemy Within*, 320, 303, 304. Robert F. Kennedy, "Hoffa's Unholy Alliance," *Look*, 2 September 1958, 31.

18. Kennedy, *Enemy Within*, 75.

19. There was talk of pressing conspiracy charges after the Federal Bureau of Narcotics' Charles Siragusa gained information that the meeting had involved "the directorate of organized crime." Siragusa believed that the meeting had been called to abandon drug trafficking as "too risky." Richard J. H. Johnston, "Gang Strife Linked to Apalachin Edict against Narcotics," *New York Times*, 28 February 1960, 1.

20. U.S. Congress, Senate, Select Committee on Improper Activities in the Labor or Management Field, *Hearings*, pt. 32, 30 June and 1–3 July 1958 (Washington, D.C.: Government Printing Office, 1958), 12228–29.

21. Ibid., 12364.

22. Ibid., 12355, 12363, 12280.

23. U.S. Congress, Senate, Select Committee on Improper Activities in the Labor or Management Field, press release, 8 August 1958, National Archives and Records Administration, Washington, D.C. The ten men were Joseph Aiuppa, Anthony Accardo, Dan Lardino, Joe DiVarco, Sam "Teets" Battaglia, Marshall Caifano, John Lardino, Ross Prio, Jack Cerone, and Abraham Teitelbaum. U.S. Senate, Select Committee, press release, "For Release on Filing of Part III of the Final Report," 23 March 1960.

24. The figures were released on the occasion of the fourth and final report. U.S. Congress, Senate, Select Committee on Improper Activities in the Labor or Management Field, press release, 31 March 1960, National Archives and Records Administration, Washington, D.C.

25. When he became attorney general, Kennedy fought for and received increased powers to grant immunity from a wide variety of charges. Witnesses granted immunity from prosecution could be jailed on contempt charges if they failed to testify. By 1961, witnesses could testify and implicate themselves without fearing jail time. Goldfarb, *Perfect Villains*, 46, 58, 73; John L. McClellan, "A Challenge to All of Us," speech delivered before the Economic Club of New York, 9 March 1959, *Vital Speeches of the Day*, 15 April 1959, 386–

89; John L. McClellan, *Crime without Punishment* (New York: Duell, Sloan, and Pearce, 1962).

26. Virgil Peterson, "Fighting Nationally Organized Crime: Metropolitan Areas Should Cooperate," speech before the Economic Club of Detroit, 29 September 1958, *Vital Speeches of the Day*, 15 December 1958, 148–50; Leiter, *Teamsters Union*, 241.

27. Kennedy, *Enemy Within*, 162. Senator McClellan would later parrot this choice of words in his own *Reader's Digest* article: John L. McClellan, "These Labor Abuses Must Be Curbed," *Reader's Digest*, 81 (December 1962): 98. See also Lester Velie, "The Riddle in the Middle of America's Most Powerful Union," *Reader's Digest*, 67 (December 1955): 91.

28. Organized crime has also been compared to the Masons: "The hierarchy of the Unione Siciliano is organized and complicated, like degrees in Masonry." Jack Lait and Lee Mortimer, *U.S.A. Confidential* (New York: Crown, 1952), 15. See also Richard Hofstadter, "The Paranoid Style in American Politics," in *The Paranoid Style in American Politics, and Other Essays* (Cambridge, Mass.: Harvard University Press, 1996), 3–40, for an extended discussion of how paranoid rhetoric shaped Cold War political speech.

29. These efforts predated the committee. Between 1947 and 1955, seventeen states passed right-to-work statutes that limited or prevented closed-shop contracts. Florida was the first state to do so, using amorphous charges of "racketeering" to garner support for an amendment to the state constitution. Fierce fights in other states brought narrow defeats of right-to-work laws and amendments. Gilbert J. Gall, *The Politics of Right-to-Work: The Labor Federations as Special Interests, 1943–1979* (New York: Greenwood Press, 1988).

30. Sloane, *Hoffa*, 22.

31. Lichtenstein, *Most Dangerous Man*, 347–48; Arthur Schlesinger, *Robert Kennedy and His Times* (Boston: Houghton Mifflin, 1978), 175.

32. Reuther also faced criticism from within the UAW. However, extensive layoffs in Detroit and Flint during the recession of 1957–58 showed that cost-of-living adjustments and annual improvement factors decreased job security. This confirmed Reuther's initial skepticism of Hoffa's COLAs.

33. Victor C. Reuther, *The Brothers Reuther* (Boston: Houghton Mifflin, 1976); Lee, *Eisenhower and Landrum-Griffin*, 65; Lichtenstein, *Most Dangerous Man*, 167, 347; Walter H. Uphoff, *Kohler on Strike: Thirty Years of Conflict* (Boston: Beacon Press, 1966); Kennedy, *Enemy Within*, 279; U.S. Congress, Senate, *Hearings*, 10250.

34. "The labor leaders who became thieves, who cheated those whose trust they had accepted, brought dishonor on a vital and largely honest labor movement. The businessmen who succumbed to the temptation to make a deal in order to gain an advantage over their competitors perverted the moral concepts of a free American economic system." Kennedy, *Enemy Within*, 324.

35. In a *Nation's Business* interview, Kennedy warned that "gangsters have taken complete control of a number of industries to obtain a monopoly, often with the help of dishonest union officials." Specifically, said the chief counsel, "the so-called service industries have been particular targets; the providing of linen to hotels and restaurants; the paper towels that are provided to restaurants; even the silverware; the providing of laundry; the handling of cartage." Robert F. Kennedy, "Gangster Invasion of Business Grows: An Interview with Robert F. Kennedy," *Nation's Business* (May 1959): 41.

36. Kennedy, *Enemy Within*, 324.

37. James R. Hoffa as told to Donald I. Rogers, *The Trials of Jimmy Hoffa: An Autobiography* (Chicago: Henry Regnery Company, 1970), 193. "Hoffa Not Guilty," *International*

Teamster, 54 (August 1957): 3; Sidney Zagri, *Free Press, Fair Trial* (Chicago: Chas. Halberg, 1966). Zagri, a labor lawyer, mounts a partisan, though carefully documented, case for the evil machinations of Kennedy and the "Get Hoffa" forces. Again, though the actions Zagri documents did occur, his citing them as evidence supports my description of this argument as paranoid.

38. George Lipsitz quotes CIO president Philip Murray's argument that "we have no classes in this country; that's why the Marxist theory of the class struggle has gained so few adherents. We're all workers here. And in the final analysis the interests of farmers, factory hands, business and professional people, and white collar toilers prove to be the same." Lipsitz, *Rainbow at Midnight*, 192.

39. Several were repealed under intense pressure from state labor movements; five others were defeated. Fones-Wolf, *Selling Free Enterprise*, 261; Gall, *Politics of Right-to-Work*. 54.

40. Fones-Wolf, *Selling Free Enterprise*, 268.

41. Gerald Pomper, "The Public Relations of Organized Labor," *Public Opinion Quarterly*, 23 (Winter 1959): 483–94.

42. "The Teamster Position," *International Teamster*, 54 (March 1957), 6; *International Teamster*, 54 (April 1957).

43. Jimmy Hoffa, "An Interview with Hoffa," *International Teamster*, 57 (May 1960): 30–34. Hoffa's outlaw image would later make him an attractive subject for two *Playboy* interviews. G. Barry Colson, ed., *The Playboy Interview* (New York: Playboy Press, 1981); see also "Another Kind of Public Enemy," *Life*, 9 September 1957, 34; "Labor's Hoodlums Rule On; Adding Up the Results of the Senate's Probe," *Newsweek*, 12 May 1958, 28–30.

44. *Initial Report of the Board of Monitors*, 1, Supplemental Report, 27 May 1958, 189 (unpublished report located in Select Committee on Improper Activities in the Labor or Management Field, Publicity Files, National Archives and Records Administration, Washington, D.C.). Prior to 1957, *International Teamster* was edited personally by the general president of the Teamsters. In 1957 the union established the Teamsters News Bureau, which directed public relations and served as the magazine's editorial offices. See *International Teamster* 54 (May 1957): 21. During the 1950s the magazine boasted a circulation of 1.312 million and an estimated readership of 3.510 million. Sam Romer, *The International Brotherhood of Teamsters: Its Government and Structure* (New York: John Wiley, 1962), 74.

45. American Trucking Association advertisement, *Life*, 15 April 1957, 25–33. On the ideological power of postwar photojournalism in *Life* magazine, see Wendy Kozol, *Life's America* (Philadelphia: Temple University Press, 1994).

46. Walter Belson, "What Is a Truck?" *International Teamster*, 54 (March 1957): 7, Velie, "Riddle," 91.

47. Kennedy, *Enemy Within*, 324–25; James R. Hoffa, "Hoffa Reports on Year of Problems and Achievements," *International Teamster*, 56 (February 1959): 5.

48. Hoffa, *The Trials of Jimmy Hoffa*, 118; Matt Gelernter, "Rank-and-Filer's View of Hearings," *International Teamster* (September 1958): 17; "British Writer Hits Kennedy Technique," *International Teamster* (April 1959): 16. Although Hoffa did occasionally draw attention to the many women within the Teamsters Union, the battle with Kennedy most often described the union in masculine terms.

49. American Newspaper Guild, *Guild Reporter*, reprinted in "Newsweek Story 'Smear,' " *International Teamster*, 55 (July 1958): 12.

50. Sloane, *Hoffa*, 126–27, 150. In 1961 the AFL-CIO refused a request by the Teamsters for readmission. George Meany, AFL-CIO president, was authorized to issue charters to locals wishing to leave the Teamsters. Among others, a group of over-the-road drivers from

a Philadelphia local spearheaded a campaign to defect to the AFL-CIO in 1963. Hoffa was successful in thwarting this attempt (269–70); Peter J. Hoban, "Letter to Robert F. Kennedy," *International Teamster*, 55 (September 1958): 13.

51. Gelernter, "Rank-and-Filer's View," 17, ellipsis in original; "Racketeering Inquiry," *New York Times Magazine*, 11 August 1957, 10.

52. John L. Lewis, "Statement before the House Labor Subcommittee," *International Teamster*, 56 (May 1959): 10; Ed Marciniak, "Protests Probe TV," *International Teamster*, 55 (December 1958): 29; U.S. Senate, Select Committee on Improper Activities in the Labor or Management Field, press release, 8 August 1958, National Archives and Records Administration, Washington, D.C.

53. James R. Hoffa, "A Message from the General President," *International Teamster*, 55 (October 1958): 2.

54. *International Teamster*, 55 (April 1958): 4; "Now, Now, Mr. Kennedy," *International Teamster*, 55 (December 1958): 12; "British Writer Hits Kennedy Technique," 16; Gelernter, "Rank-and-Filer's View," 17.

55. Hoffa, "Message," 3; James A. Romanoff, "From the Field," *International Teamster*, 56 (March 1959): 2.

56. Hoffa, *The Trials of Jimmy Hoffa*, 79; James R. Hoffa, "Time to Step Up Our Pace: Message from the General President," *International Teamster*, 55 (July 1958): 2; Sloane, *Hoffa*, 17.

57. Kennedy, *Enemy Within*, 256; Goldfarb, *Perfect Villains*, 24; *The Jack Paar Show*, NBC, 22 July 1959; Zagri, *Free Press*, 105–10.

58. Alan K. McAdams, *Power and Politics in Labor Legislation* (New York: Columbia University Press, 1964), 175–76; Lee, *Eisenhower and Landrum-Griffin*, 120; Fones-Wolf, *Selling Free Enterprise*, 277.

59. "In general, do you approve or disapprove of labor unions?"

	Approve	Disapprove	No Opinion
Feb. 1957	76%	14%	10%
Sept. 1957	64	18	18
Feb. 1959	68	19	13
Feb. 1961	70	18	12
May 1961	63	22	15

Source: Hazel Gaudet Erskine, "The Quarter's Polls," *Public Opinion Quarterly*, 25 (Winter 1961): 660–61.

60. George H. Gallup, *The Gallup Poll* (New York: Random House, 1972), 1591; Lee, *Eisenhower and Landrum-Griffin*, 97.

61. Fones-Wolf, *Selling Free Enterprise*, 277; Dwight D. Eisenhower, "Shall the People Govern," address broadcast 6 August 1959, *Vital Speeches of the Day*, 1 September 1959, 674–75; McAdams, *Power and Politics*, 177.

62. Two Teamster officials, Sidney Zagri and David Previant, appeared before the House Labor Subcommittee on labor legislation in May 1959. "House Hears Union's Views," *International Teamster*, 56 (June 1959): 5. The AFL-CIO initially helped draft the predecessor of Landrum-Griffin, the so-called Kennedy Bill, but withdrew support after early successes by Zagri in killing the bill. Lee, *Eisenhower and Landrum-Griffin*, 127.

63. "A Black Day for Labor," *International Teamster*, 56 (September 1959): 4. Hoffa's

charge that the AFL-CIO backed Landrum-Griffin was nonsense. The union mounted a vigorous lobbying effort against the bill's passage. See Lichtenstein, *Most Dangerous Man*, 353.

64. Lee, *Eisenhower and Landrum-Griffin*, 127.

65. Bufalino, a Detroit lawyer with long-standing ties to the Teamsters, had been characterized by the committee as "kingpin of the juke box union." (Local 985 authorized the region's jukebox distributorships). The committee argued that Bufalino provided Hoffa with access to the Mafia. Bufalino did not face imprisonment because of these allegations, but he did face disbarment. "Teamster Petitions Congress for Redress of Grievances," *International Teamster*, 56 (May 1959): 21; Steven Brill, *The Teamsters* (New York: Simon and Schuster, 1978), 41.

66. *The Jack Paar Show*, 22 July 1959 and 8 March 1960.

67. Robert F. Kennedy, "Hoffa's Unholy Alliance," *Look*, 2 September 1958, 31; "Hoffa Sues Kennedy for Libel and Slander," *International Teamster*, 57 (June 1960): 6–7; "Teamster Ask $1 Million for Meany's Slanderous Statements," *International Teamster*, 58 (November 1961): 18.

68. The charges against Hoffa resulted from the financing of a Florida retirement community the union had created for members. Goldfarb, *Perfect Villains*, 196, 245–46.

69. David Corn, "The Prosecution and Persecution of Ron Carey," *The Nation*, 6 April 1998, 11–16; Jim Larkin, "Teamsters: The Next Chapter," *The Nation*, 4 January 1999, 17–20.

8. From *The Untouchables* to "La Cosa Nostra"

1. James F. O'Neil, "How You Can Fight Communism," *American Legion Magazine* (August 1948): 16–17, 42–44, reprinted in Ellen Schrecker, *The Age of McCarthyism: A Brief History with Documents* (Boston: Bedford Books, 1994), 109–12.

2. Michael Kimmel, *Manhood in America: A Cultural History* (New York: Free Press, 1996), 232; David Ruth, *Inventing the Public Enemy: The Gangster in American Culture, 1918–1934* (Chicago: University of Chicago Press, 1996), 120, 132; Fred Pasley, *Al Capone: The Biography of a Self-Made Man* (New York: Ives, Washburn, 1930). See my discussion in chapter 1.

3. U.S. Congress, Senate, Select Committee on Improper Activities in the Labor or Management Field, *Hearings* (Washington, D.C.: Government Printing Office, 1958), 12228–29.

4. Richard J. H. Johnston, "Gang Strife Linked to Apalachin Edict against Narcotics," *New York Times*, 28 February 1960, 1.

5. Order Sons of Italy in America Papers, Box 9, folder 26, Immigration History Research Center, University of Minnesota, Minneapolis.

6. Peter Kivisto, "Does Ethnicity Matter for European Americans? Interpreting Ethnic Identity in the Post–Civil Rights Era," *Migration* (April 1994): 3–11.

7. Richard D. Alba, *Italian Americans: Into the Twilight of Ethnicity* (Englewood Cliffs, N.J.: Prentice-Hall, 1985), 160. On the importance of muting ethnic distinctions in order to achieve upward mobility, see Micaela di Leonardo, *The Varieties of Ethnic Experience: Kinship, Class, and Gender among California Italian-Americans* (Ithaca: Cornell University Press, 1984), esp. chap. 5.

8. Herbert Gans, ed. *On the Making of Americans* (Philadelphia: University of Pennsylvania Press, 1979). See also Herbert Gans, "Ethnic Invention and Acculturation, A Bumpy-Line Approach," *Journal of American Ethnic History*, 12 (Fall 1992): 42–52: "For third and

later generations, ethnicity is often *symbolic*, free from affiliation with ethnic groups and ethnic cultures, and instead dominated by the consumption of symbols, for example at ethnic restaurants, festivals, in stores that sell ethnic foods and ancestral collectibles, and through vacation trips to the Old Country" (44).

9. Stephen Steinberg, *The Ethnic Myth: Race, Ethnicity, and Class in America* (Boston: Beacon Press, 1981), 261. Steinberg, however, takes this point too far, blaming class cleavages on those who seek to maintain ethnic distinctiveness. On the inability of some groups to control the meaning of their ethnicity, see Nazli Kibria, "Migration and Vietnamese American Women: Remaking Ethnicity," in *Women of Color in U.S. Society*, ed. Maxine Baca Zinn and Bonnie Thornton Dill (Philadelphia: Temple University Press, 1994), 258.

10. Alba, *Italian Americans*, 117–29. See also Mary Waters, *Ethnic Options: Choosing Identities in America* (Berkeley: University of California Press, 1990).

11. These arguments about ethnic change resemble those applied to prior generations. Sociologists at the University of Chicago in the 1920s would have recognized them. Often basing their theories of assimilation on studies of southern and eastern Europeans undergoing cultural and economic change, they observed that these groups moved from one fixed state ("ethnicity") to another fixed state ("American"). The Chicago sociologists posited that after a period of confusion that often resulted in pathological behavior, immigrants inevitably adjusted to the communal norms of the United States as their Old World ways proved ineffectual in the new environment. Robert Park, Herbert Miller, and W. I. Thomas, *Old World Traits Transplanted* (Chicago: University of Chicago Society for Social Research, 1921); Peter Kivisto. "The Transplanted Then and Now: The Reorientation of Immigration Studies from the Chicago School to the New Social History," *Ethnic and Racial Studies*, 13 (October 1990): 459–60.

12. The litany of immigration reforms (including the Dillingham Plan, the Cable Act, and the Immigration Act of 1924) gives evidence of the anti-Italian sentiment of the opening decades of the twentieth century. Roger Daniels, *Coming to America*, (New York: HarperCollins, 1990), 280–94. David Roediger writes: "The success of the Irish in being recognized as white resulted largely from the political power of Irish and other immigrant voters. The imperative to define themselves as white came but from the particular 'public and psychological wages' whiteness offered to a desperate rural and often preindustrial Irish population coming to labor in industrializing American cities." David Roediger, *The Wages of Whiteness: Race and the Making of the American Working Class* (New York: Verso, 1991), 11. Tomas Almaguer, *Racial Fault Lines: The Historical Origins of White Supremacy in California* (Berkeley: University of California Press, 1994), particularly chap. 2, "The True Significance of the Word 'White,' " explores the intertwining of race, ethnicity, and class among the ranchero elites of California during the early years of statehood, who were deemed white while poor Mexicans were not. The distinction was clearly tied to political and economic power rather than national origin.

13. James R. Barrett and David Roediger, "Inbetween Peoples: Race, Nationality, and the 'New Immigrant' Working Class," *Journal of American Ethnic History*, 16 (Spring 1997): 3–44.

14. Werner Sollors, introduction to *The Invention of Ethnicity* (New York: Oxford University Press, 1981), xi.

15. Eliot Ness and Oscar Fraley, *The Untouchables: The Real Story* (1957; reprint, New York: Pocket Books, 1987); Laurence Bergreen, *Capone: The Man and the Era* (New York: Simon and Schuster, 1994).

16. Ness, *Untouchables*, 11. "Pineapple" was slang for a hand grenade.

17. Ibid., 22. Ernest Mandel argues similarly for detective fiction in general: "The detective story is the realm of the happy ending. The criminal is always caught. Justice is always done. Crime never pays. Bourgeois values, bourgeois society, always triumph in the end. It is soothing, socially integrating literature, despite its concerns with crime, violence and murder." Ernest Mandel, *Delightful Murder* (Minneapolis: University of Minnesota, 1984), 48.

18. Ness, *Untouchables*, 157. As Elaine Tyler May has written, figures like Betty and Eliot were central to the culture of containment that characterized U.S. culture at the time. "More than merely a metaphor for the Cold War on the homefront, containment aptly describes the way in which public policy, personal behavior, and even political values were focused on the home." Elaine Tyler May, *Homeward Bound* (New York: Basic Books, 1988), 14. Podhoretz quoted in James Wechsler, *Confessions of an Angry Middle-Aged Editor* (New York: Random House: 1953), 109.

19. Ness, *Untouchables*, 87. Ness's use of his relationship with Betty was wholly symbolic. Although Ness depicts a youthful courtship, Betty Anderson was Eliot Ness's third wife. They met and married in 1946—long after Al Capone was imprisoned. Bergreen, *Capone*, 602. Bergreen also argues that Ness was an alcoholic who had difficulty keeping a job throughout his life.

20. Roger Daniels, *Coming to America: A History of Immigration and Ethnicity in American Life* (New York: Harper Perennial, 1991), 332.

21. This rating represented 27 percent of all households with television sets during the 1960–61 season. Cobbett Steinberg, *TV Facts* (New York: Facts on File, 1985), 106; Tim Brooks and Earle Marsh, *The Complete Directory to Prime Time Network TV Shows, 1946–Present*, rev. ed. (New York: Ballantine Books, 1981), 791–92. The *Desilu Playhouse* version aired in two parts on April 20 and 27, 1959; Alex McNeil, *Total Television*, 3d ed. (New York: Penguin, 1991), 802.

22. This episode of *The Untouchables*, "The Empty Chair," first aired on October 15, 1959.

23. Bob Lardine, "The Unnoticeables: Robert Stack's Good Guys," [New York] *Sunday News*, 23 October 1960, 8.

24. The advertisers included Armour, Warner-Lambert Pharmaceuticals, Ludens, E. I. duPont de Nemours, Lewis Howe (makers of Tums), Liggett & Myers Tobacco (makers of Chesterfield, L&M, and Lark cigarettes), Carnation, Procter and Gamble, and Bulova.

25. The membership of many local branches, or lodges, nevertheless remained largely working class. The upward mobility embodied by the leadership reflected a fracturing along class lines rather than universal advancement. See David R. Colburn and George E. Pozzetta. "Race, Ethnicity, and Evolution of Political Legitimacy," in *The Sixties: From Memory to History*, ed. David Farber (Chapel Hill: University of North Carolina Press, 1994), 119–46.

26. The committee was founded in 1954 as the National Committee on Racial Prejudice, but was quickly renamed the National Anti-Defamation Committee. It was later renamed the National Committee for Public Relations and finally the Public Relations Committee. For the purposes of clarity, I refer to it as the Public Relations Committee except in the notes. OSIA Papers, Box 2, folder 9.

27. Michael F. Funchion, ed., *Irish American Voluntary Associations* (Westport, Conn.: Greenwood Press, 1983); Gary Mormino, "A Still on the Hill: Prohibition and Cottage Industry," *Gateway Heritage*, 7 (1986): 2–13.

28. Rudolph J. Vecoli, "The Italian Immigrant Press and the Construction of Social Reality, 1850–1920," in *Print Culture in a Diverse America*, ed. James P. Danky and Wayne

A. Wiegand (Urbana: University of Illinois Press, 1998), 17–33; George E. Pozzetta, "The Italian Immigrant Press of New York City: The Early Years, 1880–1915," *Journal of Ethnic Studies,* 1 (Fall 1973): 32–46.

29. Rather than protesting images, middle-class Jewish organizations of the World War I era such as Kehillah and the Jewish Uplift Society joined forces with Protestant and government anti-vice efforts. During Prohibition, as Jenna Weissman Joselit discusses, the wide array of reactions to Prohibition within the New York Jewish community reflected the fracturing along class and ideological lines taking place among Jewish Americans in general. Some opposed the constitutional amendment on the grounds that it was a reactionary and prescriptive measure aimed at immigrants and the working class. Some community leaders and rabbis were in favor of Prohibition as a strong moral stance against alcohol abuse. Jewish newspapers responded strongly to Prohibition agents such as Lincoln Andrews and Chester Mills who specifically targeted Jews. Congressman and future mayor Fiorello La Guardia, who represented a multiethnic district in New York City and whose mother was Jewish, accused Andrews of trying to "reorganize the ancient Jewish religion." Aware that the Volstead Act was being selectively enforced, New York's Jews reacted to sensationalized stories with suspicion and outrage. Arthur A. Goren, *New York Jews and the Quest for Community: The Kehillah Experiment, 1908–1922* (New York: Columbia University Press, 1970); Edward J. Bristow, *Prostitution and Prejudice: The Jewish Fight against White Slavery, 1870–1939* (New York: Schocken Books, 1983); Jenna Weissman Joselit, *Our Gang: Jewish Crime and the New York Jewish Community, 1900–1940* (Bloomington: Indiana University Press, 1983); David J. Langum, *Crossing over the Line: Legislating Morality and the Mann Act* (Chicago: University of Chicago Press, 1994); Jenna Weissman Joselit, "Dark Shadows: New York Jews and Crime, 1900–1940" (Ph.D. diss., Columbia University, 1981), 170, 184, 202.

30. The roots of this strategy can be seen in the basic aims of the Order: [1] "to unite in a single organization persons of Italian origin who are living in the United States; 2) to increase the prestige of the Italian people by spreading Italian culture and making known the many contributions of Italians to progress of America; 3) to promote the advancement of its members and to help charitable associations; 4) to promote Americanism and absolute loyalty to the Constitution." Ernest L. Biagi, *The Purple Aster: A History of the Sons of Italy* (New York: Veritas, 1961), 26. Similarly, in its campaign against D. W. Griffith's *Birth of a Nation,* the NAACP advocated for African Americans on the level of image, taking potential resources away from programs that might have directly helped poor African Americans. Thomas Cripps, *Slow Fade to Black* (New York: Oxford University Press, 1977).

31. OSIA Papers, Box 9, folder 26; Alfred E. Santagelo, M.C., to A. Alfred Marcello, 23 March 1961, OSIA Papers, Box 9, folder 23.

32. Associated Press, 10 June 1959, clippings from OSIA Papers, Box 1, folder 15.

33. William P. Rogers to A. Alfred Marcello, 29 July 1959, FBN Papers; J. Edgar Hoover to A. Alfred Marcello, 10 July 1959, FBN Papers; John F. Kennedy to A. Alfred Marcello, 12 August 1959, FBN Papers.

34. Biagi, *Purple Aster,* 103.

35. George Spatuzza, "Supreme Venerable's Report to 1955 Convention," reprinted in *OSIA News* (January 1956): 4. For a sharp criticism of the National Origins Act, see Edward Corsi, *Paths to the New World: American Immigration—Yesterday, Today, and Tomorrow* (New York: Anti-Defamation League of B'nai B'rith, 1953), 27–41.

36. Jannette Dates and William Barlow, *Split Images: African Americans and the Mass*

Media (Washington, D.C.: Howard University Press, 1991), 3, 5; National Anti-Defamation Committee, Second Annual Report, 10 December 1954, OSIA Papers, Box 2, folder 9; Biagi, *Purple Aster*, 101.

37. National Anti-Defamation Committee, Fourth Annual Report, 20 August 1957, OSIA Papers, Box 2, folder 9.

38. *This Man Dawson* aired only during 1959. It was a half-hour crime show about a U.S. Marine in charge of an urban police department. McNeil, *Total Television*, 759; In August 1959 Ford agreed to sponsor thirty-nine episodes of NBC programming beginning in October of that year. Some of them were to focus on the Mafia. John R. Bowers, manager, Car Advertising Department of the Ford Motor Company, to A. Alfred Marcello, 13 August 1959; Robert Sarnoff, chairman of the board of the National Broadcasting Company, to A. Alfred Marcello, 18 August 1959, FBN Papers, Box 10.

39. A. Alfred Marcello, "We'll Hit Where It'll Hurt Most," *OSIA News* (October 1959): 3, ellipses in original; idem, "We Take Inventory: The Case of the 'Mafia U.S.A.' " *OSIA News* (February 1960): 1; "Supreme Treasurer Cernuto Hits Back at TV Show Sponsor," *OSIA News* (February 1960): 1.

40. "In line with what you say about the Mafia, we too are trying to correct this situation in a coming project entitled, 'MEETING AT APALACHIN.' Our leading character in this story will be an Italian detective who rebels at the aspersions cast on his people because of the misbehavior of some. I think this a sound approach and one particularly fair to people of Italian extraction." Bert Granet, executive producer, Desilu Productions, to A. Alfred Marcello, 27 July 1959, Joseph Gorrasi Papers, Immigration History Research Center, University of Minnesota, Minneapolis.

41. Examples and outcomes of more recent meetings are discussed in Linda Lichter and S. Robert Lichter, *Italian-American Characters in Television Entertainment*, prepared for the Commission on Social Justice, Organization Sons of Italy in America (May 1992); Commission for Social Justice, New York Lodge, Order Sons of Italy in America, *Guidelines for Responsible Television Programming* (n.d.). A meeting between CBS and a delegation of Italian Americans was arranged by the Commission on Social Justice, 6 January 1982. All these materials and a transcript of the 1982 meeting are available at the Center for Migration Studies, Staten Island, New York. This meeting was called in reaction to a *60 Minutes* segment, "Welcome to Palermo," 13 December 1981. The Grand Lodge of California got NBC to read an apology over the air after "Mafia" was used as an answer on a 1979 episode of *Password Plus*. Gerard B. Petry, director of Broadcast Standards, National Broadcasting Company, to Peter Tubiolo, Grand Venerable of the Order Sons of Italy in America, Grand Lodge of California, reprinted in Vincent Licata, *The Golden Lion: A History of the OSIA Grand Lodge of California (1961–1983)* (San Francisco: OSIA Grand Lodge of California, 1984), appendix.

42. For example, NAACP executive secretary Walter White attempted to get *Amos 'n' Andy* taken off the air. White wrote a letter to the show's sponsor, the Blatz Brewing Company, protesting the show and alluding to the "twelve billion dollars" African Americans spent annually. Walter White, Report of the Secretary to the Board of Directors for the Months of July and August 1951, *Papers of the NAACP*, supplement to part 1, 1951–1955, ed. August Meier (Frederick, Md.: University Publications of America, 1987).

43. Special Advisory Bulletin to lodges from National Committee on Public Relations, October 1, 1959, Joseph Gorrassi Papers. This meeting is discussed in an advisory bulletin from the National Committee on Public Relations, Joseph Gorrasi Papers, Box 1, folder 17;

on a later meeting, see Richard F. Shepard, "TV Show Agrees on Italian Names," *New York Times*, 18 March 1961, 47.

44. Reported nationally by UPI and AP, 18 March 1961. See, e.g., "Untouchables Will Limit Italian Names," *Boston Globe*, 18 March 1961.

45. Milton Wessel, "How We Bagged the Mafia," *Saturday Evening Post*, 16 and 23 July 1960. George Gaffney, Tom Dugan, and Martin Pera were the three agents. All of Wessel's correspondence with the *Post*'s editors are in the FBN files at the National Archives and Records Administration. In his letters to Anlslinger, he makes clear that the FBN was more than simply a source. In fact, the bureau never cooperated with journalists beyond providing basic information without final editorial approval. The editor of the *Saturday Evening Post* wrote to Wessel: "As you will see, you and we have been assailed by the 'Sons of Italy.' I am enclosing copies of my correspondence with their Chairman—as well as the file of material that they sent me." Robert Fuoss, executive editor of the *Saturday Evening Post*, to Milton Wessel, 29 July 1960, FBN Papers, Box 10.

46. A. Alfred Marcello to Thomas W. Moore, 11 November 1960, OSIA Papers, in reference to the teleplay "The Great Scarpi."

47. "Nate Selko" (Peter Falk) was the other villain in the Vincent Gardenia episode. Both of these characters had names ending in vowels, though not Italian. Falk would of course go on to play the Italian American detective Columbo, beginning in the 1970s. A. Alfred Marcello to Thomas W. Moore, vice president, ABC, 16 November 1960, OSIA Papers, in reference to the teleplay "Augie 'The Banker' Cimino."

48. The three members of Congress were Joseph Addabbo and Victor Anfuso of New York and Peter Rodino of New Jersey. Richard F. Shepard, "Italians to Picket," *New York Times*, 18 January 1961, 67; Thomas Moore to A. Alfred Marcello, 16 March 1961, OSIA Papers.

49. The judges were Samuel DiFalco and Ferdinand Pecora. "TV Show Agrees on Italian Names"; Eugene J. Castellano to the Radio-Television Editor, *New York Times*, 9 April 1961, sec. 2, 15.

50. Val Adams, " 'Untouchables' Protested," *New York Times*, 10 March 1961, 55. The brothers (who spelled their surname differently) were born in Tropea, Italy, and came to the United States as young adults. "Anthony Anastasio, Labor Boss, Dies in Brooklyn at Age of 57," *New York Times*, 2 March 1963, 7.

51. Marcello to Gorrassi, 13 March 1961, OSIA Papers; Paul Meskil, "Tough Tony's Threat Hits TV Untouchables," *New York World Telegram*, 10 March 1961; "NY Group to Picket ABC-TV Mar. 9," *Il Popolo Italiano*, 2 March 1961; clippings in OSIA Papers. Liggett and Myers claimed that it dropped sponsorship because ABC had rescheduled *The Untouchables* to 10 P.M. from 9:30. Both the AP and Italian-American newspapers, however, made reference to OSIA's campaign in their news coverage of this decision. Associated Press, "Sponsors to Drop Untouchables," 14 March 1961, *Il Popolo Italiano*, 16 March 1961, 1; Richard Shepard, "Sponsor Drops Untouchables," *New York Times*, 15 March 1961, 79.

52. Jack Gould, "Disturbing Pact," *New York Times*, 26 March 1961, sec. 2, 17; Brooks and Marsh, *Complete Directory to Prime Time TV*, 792, 682–83. Mitch Miller's popular series of "sing along" albums led to a four-year series on NBC, from 1961 to 1965. Les Brown, *Les Brown's Encyclopedia of Television*, 3d ed. (Detroit: Visible Ink Press, 1992), 509.

53. Ramsey Clark, *Crime in America* (New York: Simon and Schuster, 1970), 65.

54. Peter Maas, *The Valachi Papers* (New York, G. P. Putnam's Sons, 1968), 113.

55. Ibid., 51.

56. Ibid., 13.

57. Ellen Schrecker, *Many Are the Crimes: McCarthyism in America* (Princeton: Princeton University Press, 1998), 172, 174, 125; Alger Hiss and Whittaker Chambers, testimony, House Committee on Un-American Activities, *Hearing Regarding Communist Espionage in the United States Government*, 80th Cong., 2d sess. (Washington, D.C.: U.S. Government Printing Office, August 1948), portions reprinted in Ellen Schrecker, *The Age of McCarthyism*, 121–34.

58. Charles Siragusa, Memorandum to District Supervisors, 18 April 1961, FBN Papers, Box 51; George H. Gaffney, district supervisor of New York, to Harry Anslinger, 25 May 1961; Gaffney to Anslinger, 31 May 1961, both FBN Papers; Ronald Goldfarb, *Perfect Villains, Imperfect Heroes: Robert F. Kennedy's War against Organized Crime* (New York: Random House, 1996), 149.

59. Maas, *Valachi Papers*, 64–65, 49.

60. Valachi's arrest record is reprinted ibid.

61. Ibid., 95–97.

62. George Gaffney, "List of Federal and State Prisoners with Knowledge of Major Narcotic Racketeering," 29 May 1961, FBN Papers, Box 51.

63. Jon Blackwell, "The Turncoat and the Boss," *Asbury Park (New Jersey) Press*, 17 July 2000, B1.

64. Mass, *Valachi Papers*, 49, 11. See, for example, Vincent Teresa with Thomas C. Renner, *My Life in the Mafia* (Greenwich, Conn.: Fawcett Crest, 1973); Joseph Bonanno with Sergio Lalli, *A Man of Honor: The Autobiography of Joseph Bonanno* (New York: Simon and Schuster, 1983).

65. Maas, *Valachi Papers*, 15; Peter Maas, "The White House, the Mob, and the Book Biz: Footnotes to *The Valachi Papers*," *New York Times Book Review*, 12 October 1986, 3. One FBI agent recalled, "I used to kid Kennedy about his pizza squad." Victor S. Navasky, *Kennedy Justice* (New York: Atheneum, 1971), 51; William V. Shannon, *The Heir Apparent: Robert Kennedy and the Struggle for Power* (New York: Macmillan, 1967).

66. A. Alfred Marcello to Robert F. Kennedy, 17 July 1961, Joseph Gorrassi Papers, Box 1, folder 17.

67. On this dual-focus construction of ethnic identities, see Nazli Kabria and Joane Nagel, "Constructing Ethnicity: Creating and Recreating Ethnic Identity and Culture," *Social Problems*, 41 (February 1994): 152–74.

Conclusion

1. Vincent Teresa with Thomas C. Renner, *My Life in the Mafia* (Greenwich, Conn.: Fawcett Crest, 1973), 318.

2. Randall Smith and Michael Schroeder, "Stock-Fraud Case Alleges Organized-Crime Tie," *Wall Street Journal*, 15 June 2000, C1.

3. Teresa, *My Life*, 341.

4. Edward Cronin, ed., "Plassa Comes Downtown," in *Real Clue Crime Stories* (Chicago: Hillman Publications, December 1950).

5. Only ten years earlier, the U.S. Supreme Court had overturned an Illinois decision allowing whites to deny housing to African Americans and other minorities. *Hansberry v. Lee*, 311 U.S. 32 (1940); Langston Hughes, *Fight for Freedom: The Story of the NAACP* (New York: W. W. Norton, 1962), 119.

6. Benedict Anderson, *Imagined Communities: Reflections on the Origin and Spread of Nationalism* (New York: Verso, 1983).

7. Estes Kefauver, "Crime Is International," *U.N. World* (September 1951): 18.

8. See, e.g., Marshall B. Clinard, "Sociologists and American Criminology," *Journal of Criminal Law and Criminology* 40 (January–February 1951): 551; Thorsten Sellin, "The Sociological Study of Criminality," *Journal of Criminal Law and Criminology* 40 (November–December 1950): 408; see also *Proceedings of the Second International Congress on Criminology*, 6 vols. (Paris: Presses Universitaires de France, 1952).

9. Ramsey Clark, *Crime in America* (New York: Simon and Schuster, 1970), 5, 66, 324.

10. Mario Puzo, *The Godfather* (New York: Putnam, 1969). The first film in the *Godfather* trilogy was released in 1972, the second in 1974, and the third in 1990.

11. Stephen H. Legomsky, *Immigration Law and Policy* (Westbury, N.Y.: Foundation Press, 1992), 414.

12. http://www.ins.gov/graphics/aboutins/statistics/msraugoo/removal.html.

13. John Gibeaut, "Alien Criminals Sent Packing," *ABA Journal*, 83 (April 1997): 107; idem, "Alien Criminals Get the Boot," *ABA Journal*, 85 (April 1999): 24.

14. Christian Parenti, *Lockdown America: Police and Prisons in the Age of Crisis* (New York: Verso, 1999), 55.

15. Ibid.; Eric Blumeson and Eva Nilsen, "Policing for Profit: The Drug War's Hidden Economic Agenda," *University of Chicago Law Review*, 65 (Winter 1998): 36–112.

16. Jennifer Gonnerman, "Roaming Rikers," *Village Voice*, 19 December 2000, 44–72.

17. From *The Sopranos*, 14 October 2001, HBO.

18. For a contemporary effort to champion representations that reflect Italian Americans' diverse achievements and contributions, see A. Kenneth Ciongoli and Jay Parini, eds., *Beyond the Godfather: Italian American Writers on the Real Italian American Experience* (Hanover, N.H.: University Press of New England, 1997).

19. Bill McAllister, " 'Godfather' Takes a Licking," *Denver Post*, 29 November 1998, 14H; OSIA Papers, Box 2, folder 9, Immigration History Research Center, University of Minnesota, Minneapolis. On the ethnic context for this continued activism in the 1980s and 1990s, see Micaela di Leonardo, "White Ethnicities, Identity Politics, and Baby Bear's Chair," *Social Text*, 41 (Winter 1994): 165–91.

20. Jacquie Jones, "The New Ghetto Aesthetic," *Wide Angle*, 13, nos. 3–4 (July–October 1991): 34; see also Ed Guerrero, *Framing Blackness: The African American Image in Film* (Philadelphia: Temple University Press, 1993), esp. chap. 5, "Black Film in the 1990s: The New Black Movie Boom and Its Portents"; and Lee Bernstein, "Screens and Bars: Confronting Cinema Representations of Race and Crime," in *Reversing the Lens: Crossing Cultures through Film*, ed. Lane Hirabayashi and Jun Xing (Boulder: University Press of Colorado, forthcoming).

21. Jones, "Ghetto Aesthetic," 34.

22. David Cole, *No Equal Justice: Race and Class in the American Criminal Justice System* (New York: New Press, 1999), 149.

INDEX